METRO MOVIES

METRO MOVIES

CINEMATIC URBANISM IN POST-MAO CHINA

■

HARRY H. KUOSHU

Southern Illinois University Press / *Carbondale and Edwardsville*

Copyright © 2011 by the Board of Trustees,
Southern Illinois University
All rights reserved
Printed in the United States of America

14 13 12 11   4 3 2 1

Library of Congress Cataloging-in-Publication Data
Kuoshu, Harry H., [date]
Metro movies : cinematic urbanism in post-Mao
China / Harry H. Kuoshu.
    p. cm.
Includes bibliographical references and index.
Includes filmography.
ISBN-13: 978-0-8093-3018-8 (pbk. : alk. paper)
ISBN-10: 0-8093-3018-0 (pbk. : alk. paper)
ISBN-13: 978-0-8093-8617-8 (ebook)
ISBN-10: 0-8093-8617-8 (ebook)
1. Cities and towns in motion pictures. 2. City and
town life in motion pictures. 3. Motion pictures—
China—History—20th century. I. Title.
PN1995.9.C513K76 2010
791.43'621732—dc22   2010014440

Printed on recycled paper. ♻
The paper used in this publication meets the minimum
requirements of American National Standard for Information Sciences—Permanence of Paper for Printed
Library Materials, ANSI Z39.48-1992. ∞

Melvina, we grow together.

CONTENTS

Preface ix

Introduction 1
    Faustian versus *Apollonian* 2
    The 1990s versus the 1980s 4
    Urbanism, Everydayness, and Common Culture 7
    Youth, Consumerism, and *Xiaozi* Lifestyle 13
    Urban Space, Tian'anmen, and Heterotopia 18

1. *X-Roads*: Old and New City Films 23
    Contrasting Urbanisms 25
    The Doll and Mickey Mouse: *Crossroads* and *X-Roads* 30
    Two Caged Birds: *Street Angel* and *Good Morning, Beijing* 34
    Reclaiming Fame: *Springtime in a Small Town*
        by Fei Mu and Tian Zhuangzhuang 39

2. *Dislocation*: Huang Jianxin's Urban Searching for Roots 45
    Machines and Alienation: The First Trilogy 48
    Communal Politics and Fragmentation: The Second Trilogy 55
    Humor in Disenfranchised Cities: Films
        beyond the Two Trilogies 62

**3. *No One Cheers*: The Later Fifth Generation
and the Urban "Situation Movie"** 70
    Indigenous Conditions and the Situation Movie 71
    Xia Gang: Sentiments of Comedians 78
    Peng Xiaolian: Women in Exile 86
    Li Shaohong: Threats of Materialism 89
    Huo Jianqi: Bridging Past and Present 95
    Ning Ying: Cinema Verité and the City of Beijing 99

4. *Beijing Bastards*: **Century's End Rock Scenes and China's Generation X** 106
    Beijing Bastards: A Rock Scene and Generational Discourses 107
    Beijing Rocks: A Rock Band and Two Cinematic Approaches 118
    My Father and I: Rock Lovers Bowing Out 124

5. *Captives of Love*: **Emotional Styles and the New Urbanites** 134
    A Dionysian Turn, Lifestyles, and the McWorld 135
    Pirated Copy: Transplanted Emotions and Possessed Lives 139
    The Wildness: Love and Revenge in Performing the Play 143
    Dazzling: To Daydream Varied Fashions of Love 146
    Suzhou River: To Question Romance 150

6. *Lunar Eclipse*: **Elusive Urban Realities** 158
    The Orphan of Anyang: Does Reality Sting? 159
    Beijing Bicycle: Retrieving Western Cinematic Counterparts 163
    Mother: Zhang Yuan and Documentary Lyricism 171
    Go for Broke: A Stroke of Luck for Documentary Realism 174
    East Palace, West Palace: To Understand Queer Lives 178
    Lunar Eclipse: The Moonstruck Reality 182

7. *City Paradise*: **Urbanization Looms over an Old Land** 188
    The Missing Gun: An Allegory of Urban Mobility and Otherness 189
    A Country Boy in Shanghai: Glass Walls and Urban Newcomers 192
    In Expectation: Zhang Ming, Jia Zhangke, and Provincial Backwaters 200

Conclusion 211

Notes 223

Selected Bibliography 247

Selected Filmography, by Director 253

Index 261

PREFACE

This book is not a theoretical thesis on urbanism. Rather, it is a survey of an episode of Chinese filmmaking informed by an exploration of cinematic urbanism in post-Mao China. My focus is the last decade of the twentieth century, but I necessarily have to cover films produced in the 1980s and in the first few years of the current century as well. For the title of the book, I chose the loud and eye-catching term *metro movies* to invoke my subject, which is equally eye-catching on the Chinese cultural scenes, especially at the turn of the twentieth and twenty-first centuries. Throughout the book, however, I respect readers' expectations and stick to the more commonly used term *city film*.

Cinematic urbanism in contemporary China fascinates me because it has turned from a genre indicator, referring to a group of films, to an era indicator, suggesting that urbanism has become the most dominant feature of today's Chinese cultural reconstruction. To understand the general orientation of contemporary Chinese cinema, one must explore the cultural significance of the emergence of this historically specific cinematic urbanism—the general issues it leads us to see, the cultural changes it ushers in (such as new subjects, themes, and aesthetics), and the new China it reinvents on the silver screen. A discussion of this cinematic urbanism helps identify a field of investigation and the related themes that a survey needs to explore.

The survey itself is done primarily through discussions of directors and films in relation to an overall mapping of structures of feelings in the new cinematic landscape. To understand the scope and diversity of the emerging cinematic urbanism, I include many directors and their representative films. This broad range may keep me from getting deep into the issues they raise. In discussing the films, I also have to leave out aspects that are not directly related to the concerns of each chapter. Nonetheless, I have woven a net of films that are related by certain topics of urban cinema and that intertextually refer to each other. To let some films stand out and correspond to my topics of this survey, I use film titles metaphorically in many of my chapter titles and section headings. I am satisfied that with this overview of the new cinematic urbanism, my readers will get the chance to know quite an array of newer directors and films.

My ideas for this book grew with the emergence of post-Mao urban cinema in China. Ever since some of the early Fifth Generation films captured international attention in the late 1980s—films such as Zhang Yimou's *Red Sorghum* and Huang Jianxin's *Black Cannon Incident*—I have been a faithful viewer of the burgeoning new cinema from across the ocean. Every time I travel to China, I search all kinds of video dealers (the state-run and the obscure) not only for my general film collection but also with the hope that I may come across some rare films not readily available elsewhere but useful for my research. These searches are often interesting and educational. They teach me the context of a diversified visual culture from which the new Chinese cinema emerged.

During the past decade, nobody could ignore the stunning physical impact of the outside world on China—the change of cityscape, lifestyles, fashions, ways of living, and the enrichment of material consumption. Yet a less visible but more stunning impact is accompanying all this. The Chinese of today, old and young, have turned into what cultural scholar Zhang Yiwu has dubbed a "disk-watching generation." Their DVD and VCR players, in a myriad of darkened private spaces, were provided with a booming video production industry, both legitimate and bootleg. Video shops and street-corner vendors mushroomed across the land, selling all kinds of films, which were predominantly foreign. In this greatly enriched, diversified cultural consumption of visual artifacts, the world came to China and touched the lives of its people. *Pirated Copy*, an independent film by young director He Jianjun, which I discuss in this book, offers an impressive glimpse into this market and into the lives of individuals involved in it. In the 1930s leftist filmmakers in Shanghai had to challenge Hollywood's dominance in producing their own films. Films then, however, were only shown in cinemas, and their consumption was confined primarily to middle-class urbanites. In today's China, although the official import of Hollywood films is controlled by the central government with a yearly quota, the unofficial presence of foreign films knows no controls. The Chinese-produced video and DVD market is known not only for the quantity of the products it distributes but also for its scope—people urban as well as rural, and people of all walks of life, as well as different ages, are drawn to it.

I am also drawn to this market and have become accustomed to the puzzled looks of dealers when I tell them that I primarily want to look at their

Chinese titles. The foreign film collection maintained by my younger brother, who lives in Beijing and freelances in film production fine arts, easily dwarfs my collection of Chinese films. My personal experience with this market advised me to heed this cultural context in my study and not to overlook its impact on the emergence of urbanism in post-Mao cinema.

I often confess to friends about having an ambivalent personality. I grew up in China but have lived as an immigrant in the States for more than two decades. Initially trained as a literary scholar of Western studies in China and then transformed to engage in Chinese studies in the United States, I congratulate myself that I am nourished by both cultures—I am resourceful with two cultures and they each contribute to my personality. Yet there are sunny and cloudy days in one's life. Bathed in bright sunshine, I tend to feel more resourceful—I can taste the cream of both cultures and avoid their pitfalls. Under a gloomy sky, I tend to feel sad and believe that I don't belong to either culture—living in the States, I miss China and romanticize my vision of a Chinese life; traveling to China, I am surprised that I don't fit in that well anymore. I am feeling more and more at home in a land where I obviously look different, and I often feel like a foreigner in the land where I was born. Much to my dismay, I can often relate my sense of detachment from my roots to the themes and characters of the films that I discuss in this book. Post-Mao urbanization has caused the biggest demographic migration in China. The anxiety of being removed from one's roots is a preeminent topic of contemporary urban cinema.

Harvard University has been an important place for keeping me in touch with films and film directors. Here I met with Zhang Yuan, presented him an earlier article I wrote on his *Beijing Bastards*, and had the chance to ask him some questions during a discussion of his films chaired by Professor Leo Ou-fan Lee. Here I had a nice walk and talk with director Jiang Xiaozhen after a screening of her *X-Roads*. Here I watched many films discussed in this book and heard several directors (Ah Nian, Wang Quan'an, and Guo Xiaolu) talking about them. Here, in 2001, I was among the faithful audience of the film series The Urban Generation: Chinese Cinema and Society in Transformation, which greatly inspired me and germinated into the initial ideas for this book. One of the organizers of the event, Zhang Zhen, has since edited an anthology of critical essays (*The Urban Generation: Chinese Cinema and Society at the Turn of the Twenty-first Century*, Durham, NC: Duke University Press, 2007) to absorb the impact of the film series. My book complements the anthology by presenting a broader range of studies and by including more film directors. In the academic year 2004–5, I was appointed a research associate at Harvard University's Fairbank Center for East Asian Studies and devoted most of my time of affiliation to writing this book. The stimulating intellectual atmosphere and the abundance of ideas circulating in workshops and seminars at Harvard nourished my writing.

Ideas and some discussion in chapter 5, "*Beijing Bastards*: Century's End Rock Scenes and China's Generation X," are derived from an earlier article published in *Asian Cinema* titled "*Beijing Bastards*, the Sixth Generation Directors, and 'Generation-X' in China" (*Asian Cinema* 10 [1999]: 18–28). An earlier version of the introduction of this book, "Urbanism and Post-Mao Cinema," appeared in *Southeast Review of Asian Studies* 28 (2006): 29–50. I thank Christian Gilmartin, Cui Junyan, Xu Hailin, and Hong Wu for arranging my interviews with film directors Huang Jianxin, Xia Gang, and Zhang Yang and for arranging my access to certain films. When I was conducting research in preparation for writing this book, a faculty research fund at Northeastern University financed a trip to China to collect data, visit film studios, and interview film directors. A faculty research grant, as well as grants from the Curry donation to promote Chinese studies at Furman University, supported my final work on the manuscript. Five anonymous readers of the Southern Illinois University Press and my editors there, Bridget Brown and Wayne Larsen, made many helpful comments for revision. I remain indebted to them for their suggestions and endorsement. Friends and colleagues offered valued feedback. They are Harlow Robinson, Jan Kiely, and Richard Letteri. Jill Kelly and Ann Barrington helped edit my language. They also sharpened my ideas. Gratitude also goes to my students at Reed College in Portland, Oregon, at Northeastern University in Boston, and at Furman University in Greenville, South Carolina, for the stimulating discussions we had on various Chinese films in my film seminars and other courses.

METRO MOVIES

Introduction

The growth of urbanism in Chinese cinema gained full momentum during the concluding decade of the twentieth century. The time was important, since it lent a birthmark to this particular kind of cinematic trend. It dictated the meanings of being urban on-screen in China then.

City films in post-Mao cinema were first identified as an emerging tendency in the mid-1980s. They were hailed as a deviation from the preeminent roots-searching films that had marked the onset of Fifth Generation filmmaking only a few years earlier.[1] As such, they were seen as a departure from the grand narrative of national culture discourse, shifting from an allegorical redemption of the nation and its people to a down-to-earth attention to the

Tian'anmen Square, the political space of a bygone era, was turned into a mental space that accompanied the new zeal and leisure of consumerism. *After Separation* (dir. Xia Gang, 1992). Courtesy of China Film Archive, Beijing.

fragmented situations of individuals. In immediate post-Mao China, the concept of the city film became a test balloon for the general direction of the culture.[2]

Faustian versus Apollonian

German sociologist Oswald Spengler's contrast of city and countryside offered some Chinese film critics an early terminology for pinpointing the cultural significance of this emerging cinematic trend. Using Western culture as a model but believing that his urbanism was applicable to non-Western cultures as well, Spengler proposed the idea of a cyclical development of a city: First, the agrarian phases of a culture will develop a particular identity or "folk spirit." Second, this cultural identity will be fragmented by the development of the city, which encourages individuality and separateness in its members. Third, the inevitable corruption of the city—through over-institutionalizing the process of human interchange and a "routinism" that reduces warm personal contact between individuals—will lead the culture to revert to another agricultural phase and another round of growth and decline. While one may not agree with Spengler's idea of cycles, what is fascinating in his thinking on urbanism is how urbanization may obliterate a particular cultural identity and how dismal the prospect of urbanization can be. Applying Spengler's insight to contemporary postcolonial globalization, we are also forced to see that urbanization in developing countries has often used routinized Western life to erase various national cultures.

Spengler's thoughts on city culture connect him to other prominent sociologists of the German School, such as Max Weber and Georg Simmel. Their critical thinking about city culture in the first half of the twentieth century identified the cold, impersonal aspects of city development such as bureaucracies, fragmentation, and isolation.[3] For Chinese film criticism, the German School's warnings about urbanization were almost inaudible. Political bureaucracies were already highly developed in Chinese socialist totalitarianism. The Chinese "folk spirit" at the threshold of the new push for urbanization was a blend of ancient Confucianism based on closely knit communities with the Communist ideology of collective social action. The culprit behind the dismal urban future, individualism, had become an inspiration rather than something to fear ever since it was introduced into Chinese culture during the New Cultural Movement at the beginning of the twentieth century. Urbanization was also a cultural change with political implications. The tendency was not to look down the road for the problems of urbanization but to focus on how individualism and heterogeneity of urbanization challenged monolithic cultural and political totalitarianism. An emerging cultural discourse in post-Mao China was speaking of the separation of *individual beings* (geti ren) from *collective beings* (qunti ren), and of *economic beings* (jingji ren) from *political beings* (zhengzhi ren). In light of this discourse, individuality took an affirmative tone that was a far cry from how the German School used it in relation to its discussion of urban culture.

Urbanization, with all its modernist implications, was playing a different cultural role in post-Mao China. Prior to and contemporary with the emergence of the new city films, in Fourth Generation filmmaking, as Chinese film scholar Dai Jinhua observed, the city had already been provoking an underlying contrast between itself and the countryside (even when the films involved did not have an urban subject).[4] The *city* represented constant reformation, openness, science, education, and civilization; the *countryside* stood for the inertia of history, closure, ignorance, an antihuman attitude, and decay. In the Fourth Generation's film language and in their idealistic "missionary" sense of cultural redemption, the countryside became the synonym for the post-Mao Chinese cultural status quo. This countryside could refer to the vast rural areas, and it could also refer to, as one film title suggested, "villages in the metropolis," that is, urbanites who possessed a rural mentality. So that China might leave behind the disappointment caused by the revolution, many hopes for cultural change were read into the symbiosis of the city. This was indeed a willful misreading. "If the Fourth Generation film texts represented old China, the ancient countryside, and the national homeland as doomed," Dai Jinhua commented sharply, "what they provided as a rescue—science, progress, and humanism—was also a shattered dream in the West.... In the majority of Fourth Generation texts, the existence of the first world—be it political and economic infiltration or a cultural perspective—was not a social reality but an imaginary *other*."[5]

It was in this context that film critics borrowed, through the writing of a Chinese sociologist, Spengler's adjectives of *Apollonian* and *Faustian* to contrast countryside and city.[6] In this interpretation, *Apollonian* stands for a monolithic social order and the human acceptance of it and *Faustian* speaks to the spirit of conquering and the prospect of endless changes that the future has in store for human beings. What Chinese film critics read into the Faustian spirit was their general fascination with the novelties of urbanization. One critic wrote, "[The Faustian spirit] is in a constant search for change. It never ceases generating passionate drives for overcoming obstacles. It is an exploration, groping for the unknown and challenging the order of the status quo."[7]

Although thoroughly fascinated, the Chinese film critics were not superficially optimistic; they pinpointed all kinds of discomfort in the representation of the city: marginal characters, suspicious values, offensive styles, social ills, anger, loss, loneliness, and alienation.[8] Chen Xiaoyun, for example, related urbanization to the isolation of individuals and their modern feeling of lonely anxiety, a common topic in Western writing about the city. Concluding his exploration, however, Chen called for an effort to appreciate the unavoidable progress of urbanization: "Faced with the contrast of city and countryside, artists can't help but love and praise the countryside and put down the noise and chaos of the city. The Chinese countryside films are always relatively more emotive.... As China moves toward the twenty-first century, however, the progress of civilization and urbanization has become irresistible. A big job faced by film artists now is how to experience, dig, discover, and express the unique beauty of the contemporary city."[9] Obviously, Chen didn't need to see urbanization as an unavoidable "natural" development but rather saw it as a collective desire to see what the city had in store for the post-Mao Chinese who were so fed up with Apollonian totalitarianism. She began her article by stating that "the city, as a sign of freedom and symbol of civilization, has endless attractions for people," and her article ended with a short but meaningful one-sentence paragraph: "We are hopeful."[10]

The 1990s versus the 1980s

More changes came along with the emergence of the new city films, and many differences can be found between the first two post-Mao decades: the 1980s and the 1990s. For the sake of contrast, Dai Jinhua offered in her lyrical writing style the following intellectual index to the two decades. The 1980s, during which various discourses supported an optimistic goal of China reaching for the outside world, brought a sense of crisis, discontinuity of history, allegories of death and rebirth, China opening to the outside world, and China's fight to earn the right to knock on the gates of the twenty-first century. The 1990s, with the loss of a clear goal and the coexistence of heterogeneous motives and wishes, brought cultural dissent, the fall of the arts, a reformulated postmodernism, post–Cold War ideology, and postcolonialism.[11]

With the 1980s as a time for deliberation and experiments, the state-engineered, market-driven transformation started to show its most visible impact on Chinese cities. The decade saw drastic demolition of the old cityscape for the rebuilding of the new, witnessed a large volume of rural migrants pouring into the cities for employment, and testified to the state-monitored growth of a state capitalism that shattered the older ways of urban life. With the Tian'anmen Square massacre of 1989 serving as a tragic watershed between the two decades, and with "national stability" as a justification, the 1990s were a politically reticent era when dissident voices were curbed. The decade was marked with a tension between economical loosening and political tightening, both for the sake of ushering in the market. A cynicism marked by keeping one's mouth shut to get rich was the goal of the day.[12] Zhang Zhen observed this tension in filmmaking in China: "If, above all, *zhuanxing* [transformation] means the dissolution of a planned economy—or the giving way of state control to privatization and capitalist modes of management, which affects the national economy and social experience on a large scale—the state is reluctant to completely let loose of the film system while 'unleashing' it, albeit with many strings attached; into the market."[13] Here, the tearing down of the state monopoly to make the industry market-driven (shown in the emergence of private and semiprivate film production companies) and the new effort to insert state oversight (shown in the persistence of censorship and the establishment of a more specified government agency, the Ministry of Broadcasting, Television, and Film, in the mid 1990s) occurred simultaneously.

In the transition between decades, a group of diversified film artists stepped onto the scene. Their filmmaking was outside or on the margins of the state monopoly of production, drawing funds from the emerging venture capitalism in China and seeking the support of overseas funding. It further illustrated the heterogeneity and globalization of cultural production in the new decade. Since the films they produced were clearly different,[14] these film artists were interchangeably described as "self-centered," "marginal," "alienated," "embittered," "decadent," "nihilistic," "carnal," "vulgar," and so on. The diverse descriptions of the group corresponded to the multiple names these artists have received both as a collective and as smaller groups. In China they were associated with such trends and terms as *independent filmmaking* (duli zhipian yundong), *auteurism* (geren dianying), *new-image movement* (xin yingxiang yundong), *situation movie* (zhuangtai dianying), and *new city films* (xin dushi dianying). Overseas, they were known as Chinese underground filmmakers, independent filmmakers, or dissident filmmakers. The two umbrella names for them everywhere have been the *Sixth Generation* and the *Newborn Generation* (xinsheng dai).

Some film critics cautioned against the continued use of generation names because they held that generation labels had become increasingly irrelevant to the emerging group of film artists. The post–Fifth Generation Chinese filmmaking, as these critics suggested, had entered a nongenerational, individualistic, diversified, and urban-oriented era.[15] The emerging film artists themselves also resisted being labeled as an identical filmmaking generation, declaring that they did not want to bear the burden of being a new generation.[16] Indeed, the strong feelings for the irrelevance of generational labels in the 1990s suggested an era with no commanding social concerns and reflected an artistic resistance to the tendency of using a certain hegemonic discourse of the time to mark a group identity.

The resistance of the new artists to generation labels illustrated their changed cultural status. My explanation for this change is the companion transition of Chinese cultural discourse from modernity to postmodernity and the changing role of intellectuals in this transition.[17] The modernist discourse on culture, either in the May Fourth era or in the post-Mao decade of the 1980s, featured such grand narratives of cultural resurrection as enlightenment, Nationalism, individualism, and democracy. The intellectuals of modernist discourse assumed the role of, in Michel Foucault's term, *universal* intellectuals: "speaking in the capacity of a master of truth and justice . . . the spokesman of the universal."[18] Postmodernist discourse emerged on the Chinese intellectual scene in the 1990s, when China started to engage itself in developmental urbanization and integrated itself into the global market economy at full speed. Rising consumerism cold-shouldered the modernist narrative of the elite culture (jingying wenhua) and encouraged the expansion of popular culture through the mass media. The grand narratives of modernism were also fragmented, with the intellectuals themselves humbled not only economically but also by their lost access to those narratives. In a way, the Chinese intellectuals in this situation moved very close to what Foucault called *specific* intellectuals, those dealing more with questions of "real, material, everyday struggles" and the confrontation with "multinational corporations."[19]

The Foucaultian contrast of *universal* and *specific* intellectuals coincided with the changing horizons of Chinese intellectuals from the 1980s to the 1990s. Chinese cinema's corresponding transition from the era of grand narratives (e.g., historical, allegorical, and cultural roots searching) in the 1980s to the urban-focused, artistic heterogeneity of the 1990s further illustrates how the changed roles of artists may have significantly affected a particular aspect of cultural production.

With the transition between decades and the emergence of new film artists, and with more artists—old and new, serious and playful, conventional and avant-garde, commercial and highly artistic—turning their cameras on the city, the perception of post-Mao city films changed in the 1990s. The city film was no longer considered just a cinematic trend within trends; all of Chinese cinema appeared to have stepped into an urban-focused era. Indeed, the city film turned into the predominant symbol of cultural production in Chinese filmmaking. It became not just a window to the contemporary urbanization of China but also itself part of its genesis. It dramatized varied aspects of everyday life in urbanization by producing a spectrum of feelings, lifestyles, fashions, and values.

Urbanism, Everydayness, and Common Culture

The importance drawn by the city film in the first two post-Mao decades reflected a profound change in urbanism in China. What contemporary Chinese filmmaking projected on the screen was China's change from a utopian urbanization to a developmental urbanization. As scholars commonly attest, the urbanism of Maoist China was a blend of utopianism and a peculiar model of antiurban development.[20] Utopianism not only kept revolutionary myths alive but also curbed urbanization by forcing a limited set of standards on everyone through political campaigns and central control. This model had institutional features such as strict migration controls, a penetrating residential work-unit organizational system, a highly developed bureaucratic allocation system, an emphasis on production rather than consumption, a relatively egalitarian distribution system, and so on. Putting aside the painful price of political enforcement that its members had to sustain, the social consequences of this urbanization model, as Whyte and Parish have observed, were impressive and capable even of invoking nostalgia in today's China for what was seen as "high stability in jobs and residences, involvement and familiarity with neighbors and workmates, minimal differentiation of consumption patterns and lifestyles, low divorce, high female work participation, and rapid changes in fertility, religious customs, and other realms of behavior."[21]

There were historical reasons for China's antiurban development. Modern Chinese history is characterized by a century of foreign incursion, from the Opium Wars of the mid-nineteenth century to U. S. intervention against the Communist takeover of China in the mid-twentieth century, all of which had taught the Chinese about the alien corruption and social ills of the modern city. The impact of a century of urbanism had erased China's own ancient, mainstream, favorable images of cities as administrative centers, seats for garrisoned troops, and a home for commerce and the cultural industries encouraged by the court and the troops; of cities as epitomes of power, order, stability, and prosperity.[22] The Chinese leftist filmmaking based primarily in the treaty-port city of Shanghai illustrated this changed perception: *city*, in most leftist films produced there, connoted colonialism, capitalism, individualism, exploitation, corruption, and alienation. The implied solution for shattering this alien entity of city was the Communist revolution, a collective social action whose roots lay in the countryside. This cinematic tradition, in turn, influenced the antiurban (*urban* read as capitalist corruption) development of Maoist cinema. After all, the tenet for success of the Chinese Communist revolution was the revolutionary countryside "gulping down" reactionary cities. Antiurban development was a logical follow-up to this tenet.

The deep-rooted ideological reason for this antiurban development was, thus, an equation between the city and the social ills of modern capitalism. Theoretically, there were ample supplies of this train of thought from the West. Marxism, as the ideological fountainhead for the Chinese Communist revolution, emphasized the increasing inequality of social classes and the alienation of human beings that accompany capitalist urbanization. Spengler and other German sociologists stressed the urban growth of overdeveloped bureaucracies, isolated individuals, and impersonal rationality. "The predominant tone of most Western social commentary on the modern city," Whyte and Parish noted, "has been negative":

> [M]odern cities tend to be characterized by increased bureaucratization and unresponsiveness of the authorities; stark inequalities, class and ethnic group conflicts, and the existence of an unemployed underclass; slums, neighborhood decay, and other symptoms of the inability to provide needed services for all; impersonality, anonymity, and alienation; the primacy of cash transactions and segmental role relationships over relationships between individuals as whole human beings; the fragmenting of kinship, family, and other primary ties and with them a shared sense of moral values; and rising rates of crime and other forms of deviant behavior.[23]

Today many of the descriptions here ring true of Chinese cities. The large number of unemployed state workers share the city with the big population of rural migrant laborers. Many new city films tell the touching stories, often with much misery, of these people.²⁴ In these stories the people are simultaneously drawn to and discarded by the fast-growing market economy, and they become living indicators for a changed China. These films leave the viewer with no doubt that the city has become a hotbed of new forms of class, gender, and ethnic conflicts. Urban unrest has become an inexhaustible source of inspiration for the post-Mao city film. The utopian urbanism in China had indeed become fragmented and had given way to the developmental urbanization distinguished by market distribution systems. In this transition, such tradeoffs as centralized political sovereignty and decentralized consumer sovereignty, direct state allocation and private market distribution, as well as regulated social equality and economic efficiency, pushed China into the same situation faced by many other formerly socialist countries. Indeed, in China and in other formerly socialist countries, the transition from socialism to postsocialism has always been the context and subtext for any discussion of modernity and postmodernity. This political and social dimension should inform, if it has not done so already, the ways scholars choose to describe modernity and postmodernity in these countries in relation to their use of Western sources in discussing the topic. The features of these approaches can well be seen in the adjectives, such as *contra-*, *trans-*, *alternative*, and *hybrid*, assigned to the topic.²⁵

In a study of city films, one particular aspect of this transition from utopian to developmental urbanization, the representation of everyday life, becomes especially meaningful. The emergence of the new city film, I suggest, represents a transition from Maoist *sacred* everyday life to the post-Mao *secularized* everyday life. *Sacred* and *secular*, terms borrowed from Western intellectual history, imply how China's post-Mao reconception of everydayness resembles strikingly a social and cultural process in Western intellectual history. *Depoliticization*, *privatization*, and *pluralism* were key words for Western secularization. Pluralism was the legendary ancient wisdom, as Edward Gibbon described: "The various modes of worship which prevailed in the Roman world were all considered by the people as equally true; by the philosophers as equally false; and by the magistrates as equally useful. And thus toleration produced not only mutual indulgence, but even religious concord."²⁶ The separation of state and religion during the sixteenth-century Reformation was to undermine the spirit of obedience to any clerical authority so that pluralism might flourish again. Secularization involved a decentered privatization of faiths or the individual access to beliefs. The post-Mao secularization of everyday life was also a process of depoliticization. It was a transition from an abstract ideological monopoly to an opening up to the richness of diversified, individual situations. It aimed at dismantling the state monopoly of upholding the sacred status of the everyday and opening up to a privatized, decentered re-creation of the everyday.

Maoist cultural production of the everyday, in its representational blend of "realism plus romanticism," refuted trivial deviations from the glorious revolutionary goals, curbed distracting heterogeneity in favor of collective actions, and ignored uninteresting profanity for the benefit of inspiring ideals. "A collective desire to resist the inertia of everyday life," as Xiaobing Tang observed, "was an integral part of the grand socialist movement in modern China."[27] Examining peasant painting, Tang noticed such utopian features as completeness and transcendence, aesthetics of scale but not detail, panoramic perspective, stylization of socialist ideals, and homogeneity. This Maoist effort to overcome the anxiety of everyday life, Tang commented, was "often at the cost of impoverishing it."[28] The case of peasant painting is relevant here because Maoist China, with its antiurban development, was a sum of villages, rural and urban. The urban spirit associated with diversity, individuality, and impersonality was greatly discouraged. In Maoist cinema, films of urban spirit were hard to find. Films on urban subjects usually featured not individuality, alienation, or diversity but such efforts as curtailing "bourgeois" lifestyles, promoting equality of all walks of urban life (e.g., people in the service sector were not seen as lower in social status), and praising altruism for urban public benefit.

We may gain a better understanding of the changing concept of the everyday by referring to Raymond Williams's proposal of common culture, or culture as ordinary. Williams proposed this concept against the backdrop of a particular nineteenth-century British distinction between *culture* as the realm of noble, elegant, and ideal standards and *nonculture*, which was associated with a modern, industrial, dehumanized society featuring a semiliterate populace catered to by vulgar, popular forms of entertainment. What this British distinction implies, in reference to the situation in China, is a sacred, nostalgic, and narrow concept of culture that excludes various emerging modes of everyday life. In *Culture and Society* and *The Long Revolution*, Williams refuted the concept of using culture to oppose the historical development of a society and suggested that culture was always "ordinary." Turning its back on closed traditions and embracing the possibilities of openness, Williams's common culture ("lived experience"; "a whole way of life") calls for a cultural revolution that pushes for new modes of communication, the growth of public education, and a more participatory democracy.[29] This British lesson for post-Mao China was not so much that of a public education, which the utopian urbanization of China had achieved, but one of broadening the meaning of culture to recognize the importance of the ordinary, to reveal underrepresented realms, and to make room for diversity. The post-Mao Chinese redefinition of the everyday calls for the removal of tightly centralized control. The loosening of centralized control will lead to a more participatory democracy that will allow the public (people of different gender, age, ethnicity, religion, social status, economic standing, etc.) more access to the meaningful production of everyday life. It is a change from the monolithic to the plural, from closure to openness, and from regulation to negotiation.

On this point, Zhang Yuan's filmmaking comes to mind. In his independent or semi-independent filmmaking since 1990, Zhang has focused on such underrepresented subjects as single mothers, developmentally delayed children, alcoholism, mental illness, homosexuality, reformed prisoners, and the emotional turbulence of the young. His filmmaking has forced people not to overlook the shaded, less-than-ideal, and marginal realms of Chinese everyday life. Zhang leads us to see a contemporary or consequence trend of the documentary-like movie: Sun Zhou's *Breaking the Silence* (Piaoliang mama, 1999) featured a developmentally delayed child along with the professional actors; Wang Guangli's *Go for Broke* (Heng shu heng, 2001) used a group of unemployed state workers playing themselves; Zhang Yang's *Quitting* (Zuotian, 2001) had a drug-addicted film actor playing his own story, with his real-life family members, about his difficult mental journey of quitting. Stylistically, there was a return to the "documentary aesthetics" (jishi meixue) that had been advocated by the Fourth Generation directors nearly a decade before. The style then, in the hands of such directors as Zheng Dongtian and Zhang Nuanxin, served to deviate from the dominant ideological discourse and a melodramatic representation. Now, in the hands of a younger group, this style helped draw attention to the ignored margins of a gradually decentralized culture. In mapping these areas of everyday life, the candid camera became that of exploration, using what is real (what is underrepresented) to challenge what is artificial (what is overrepresented).

A further implication of Williams's common culture, the issue of cultural hierarchy, has a wider association than broadening the scope of everyday life. In China, long before Maoist utopianism, elite literary genres (poetry, prose, and narratives of history) had kept despised genres (storytelling, fiction, and theater) on the margins and had thus kept the masses from the center of cultural production. The reigning Confucian tenet had been *wen yi zaidao*, or writing as the vehicle of the *Tao* (the dominant ideology and the cultural mainstream). The Tao, through such institutions as the civil service examination, decided the cultural status of various forms of communication. Even in the Chinese modernist movements of the May Fourth and early post-Mao eras, the commitment to the Tao (the grand narrative, the sense of totality, or cultural resurrection) remained intact. "Carrying the Tao in a modern context," as Tonglin Lu observed, "often means to spread the discourse of modernity in order to contribute to the modernization process in China. In its ambiguity, this discourse can be articulated from different or even opposite perspectives, from communism to liberal humanism."[30] The Tao, connoted differently, still functioned to keep out the ordinary and the profane. When the post–Fifth Generation younger directors emerged in Chinese cinema, their initial breakthrough was to attack the Tao of the by then elite Fifth Generation with their allegorical representation of China related to the national cultural discourses of roots searching, national resurrection, and cultural redemption. Ironically, the initial criticism of these younger directors was also their lack of Tao or reason for making films.[31] Today, with the initial shocking effects of new films dissipated, it is time to investigate how these films opened a window to the common culture in the act of creating a new round of Chinese urbanization.

One Chinese critic's changing perception of post–Fifth Generation filmmaking illustrates my point here. In 1996 Li Yiming proclaimed the end of Fifth-Generation filmmaking in his landmark two-part article "Century's End: Ethnic Crisis and the Funeral for the Fifth Generation Filmmaking."[32] Li offered sharp comments on the "dictatorship of consumerism" in China in the 1990s and on the spiritual, ethical, and social crisis it was causing: loss of belief; corruption; distanced, cold human relations; drugs; prostitution; the flooding of profanity; bad taste. With these comments, he criticized the Fifth Generation's allegorical filmmaking, claiming that these directors had indulged in "faking history," had ignored the cultural status quo of the 1990s, and had betrayed their roles as humanist intellectuals. To the emerging younger directors, Li was also unsympathetic; he believed their filmmaking showed more interest in film technique than in cultural values. For these directors' narcissism, interest in novelty, and focus on urbanites living on the cultural margins, Li observed that they were "faking reality." With the Fifth Generation faking history and the post–Fifth Generation faking reality, the prospect of Chinese cinema looked, to him, really dismal. Two years later, Li published another article on these younger directors with a more affirmative stance.³³ He emphasized that the post–Fifth Generation directors had never learned *wen yi zaidao* (writing as the vehicle of the *Tao*) and thus would be unable to represent the cultural mainstream. Emerging as *other* and existing on the cultural margins, Li asserted, the post–Fifth Generation knew only how to express themselves ("things in their bones," as the post–Fifth Generation directors suggested) or how to express the marginal. Nevertheless, he stopped asserting that these younger directors were "faking reality." Instead he cautioned that "there must be multiple channels between the cultural margin and the cultural center" and affirmed that the cultural margin will enrich the understanding of the culture as a whole. Behind Li's affirmation of the post–Fifth Generation was his "pan-cultural theory," as I call it: "The multi-cultural and multi-ethnic heterogeneity constituted by reform and the opening up [of China] has also cracked open the traditional, closed ideological fortress of China beyond repair. In the mid-1990s . . . this cracking fell into the tracks of the commodity market, circling around '*cultural-ized* capitals' and 'capitalized cultures.' One product of this circling was the rise of mass and popular cultures, which forced avant-garde arts to discard their pride and move closer to each other, albeit reluctantly."³⁴ Obviously, a broadened concept of culture, admitting the center and the margin, high and low, heterogeneity and capitalization, led to Li's changed concept of the post–Fifth Generation. Li was himself moving closer to a particular vision of common culture in China.

Youth, Consumerism, and *Xiaozi* Lifestyle

Considering the youth of the post–Fifth Generation film artists themselves and youth as the dominant subject of the new cinema since the 1990s, Paul Willis's study of urban youth in light of Raymond Williams's concept of common culture resonates with the Chinese situation of new city films. With the British urban youth of the 1980s as the subject of study, Willis argued for broadening the scope of the arts and becoming attentive to the symbolic work at play in the everyday culture of the young: "'Official culture' has hardly recognized informal everyday culture, still less has it provided usable materials for its dialectical development. Worse, the "holiness" of "art" has made the rest of life profane."³⁵ Further, he noted, "Commerce and consumerism have helped to release a profane explosion of everyday symbolic life and activity. The genie of common culture is out of the bottle—let out by commercial carelessness. Not stuffing it back in, but seeing which wishes may be granted, should be the stuff of our imagination."[36] The same open-minded orientation should also be part of the study of post-Mao city film. In today's China, one obviously might doubt if it is possible for art to survive the invasion of consumerism into everyday life. One might also be uncertain about the forms of new arts. A recent Chinese film offered an interesting response to this uncertainty. *Chicken Poets* (Xiang jimao yiyang fei, 2002), the first feature by celebrated experimental theater director Meng Jinghui, illustrates a new product of common culture, or artwork, emerging out of the profanity of commercialized everyday life. As experimental as his earlier theatrical works, *Chicken Poets* is a dreamlike meditation on the role of poetry (or art) in everyday life in a rapidly changing China that has given way to consumerism. The hero, an established poet who has lost the ability to continue writing poetry, joins his entrepreneurial former classmate to market black chicken eggs from his experimental farm. His usual muse, a girl who has fallen for him and who is always confident that he will write again, does not inspire him. Instead, he is tempted by a black market CD-ROM that plays with various schools of poetry and writes poems for you with the parameters you enter into the program. As a result, he becomes a publishing and marketing star. The success of this chicken poet is the same as the success of Meng's film. Definitely avant-garde, the film is fun to watch even for an audience that is not particularly interested in art films. Although there are underlying meanings in many nonnarrative excursions of the film, the playful multimedia mixture of animation, video, computer graphics, electronic games, music videos, and advertisements is hard to miss. With *Chicken Poets*, hybrid elements of mass media, popular entertainment, and consumerist literature compete with traditional poetry writing for the status of art, and they all end as art exactly because they find a way to coexist.

In post-Mao cinema's re-creation of everyday life, one can detect a strong interest in the emotional life and an unmistakable yearning for intimacy. So many films bear testimony to this interest and yearning.[37] The complexity of human sentiments, of course, had been an underrepresented subject in Maoist China, and now it was opening up for exploration. More interestingly, the search for intimacy involves a redefinition of human relations and society in post-Mao urbanization. Richard Sennett concluded his lengthy book *The Fall of Public Man* with a brief chapter on intimacy. He first drew a contrast between two kinds of tyrannies in the forms of intimacy. In capitalist society, a person is obligated by the domestic routine of everyday life. In a police state (although Sennett had a Stalinist state and Fascism in mind, Mao's

China suited his description as well), "one's activities, friends, and beliefs pass through the net of governmental surveillance."[38] Both tyrannies of coercion, however, only lead to a more subtle tyranny of intimacy: the seduction of security in the flux of ordinary life or one's need for a single authority, be it a person, an institution, or a belief. In other words, the personal realm of private life reinforces the glorious sense of a human being who can allay his troubles in the impersonal public life. Confronting drastic urbanization in post-Mao China, film artists were retaining humanist ideals. Just as the humanist logic of ambiguity, complexity, psychological uncertainty, or emotional subtlety had served to replace the oversimplified, social class concept of human beings in immediate post-Mao cinema, humanism was now challenging a new enemy: the modern city. Post-Mao urbanization was the instrument of impersonality, chance encounters, formality, distance, coldness, insincerity, and so on. The film artists who searched for intimacy hoped to hold on to humanism, while their films braved the flux of new everyday life in modern Chinese cities.

A corresponding cultural trend to this cinematic interest in emotional life and the yearning for intimacy is the contemporary rise of *xiaozi* (petty-bourgeois) and their claim to representation. According to a two-volume critical anthology of ten female *xiaozi* writers, all born since the 1970s, *xiaozi* has almost become a synonym for today's urban lifestyle of the young. "*Xiaozi*," as one critic elaborates, "is not created by God, nor produced by Nüwa. *Xiaozi*'s mother is the metropolis." "*Xiaozi*," this critic continues to explain, "is not a social stratum. It is a lifestyle, a cultural taste, a manner, and a standard."[39] How should we visualize this lifestyle in concrete terms, that is, what should we look for in contemporary city films that reflect the *xiaozi* lifestyle? Another critic in this anthology offers us help in this respect. This critic writes an interesting checklist of *xiaozi* culture, which offers us such details as where do *xiaozi* people like to go, what movies they watch, what music they listen to, what books they read and talk about, what literary styles they adopt for their self-expression, what characterizes their sensibility, and what distinguishes their lifestyle.[40] Obviously, *xiaozi* cares about styles, follows fashions, is particular about brand names, emphasizes aesthetic taste, nourishes sentiments, searches romance, loves the aura of the metropolis, travels in cyberspace . . . *Xiaozi* is absolutely urban.

The checklist, while offering us details for understanding *xiaozi* culture, is also unmistakably sarcastic. According to the editor, all the critics writing in the anthology are about the same age as the *xiaozi* writers and have an insider's knowledge of this lifestyle. Their criticism itself is an elaboration of *xiaozi* culture. Reading these critics, we detect a shared disgust of *xiaozi*'s bad taste, their submission to the market demands, their materialism, narcissism, vanity, and hybridism in cultural orientation (postcolonial influences of the West, Hong Kong, and Taiwan). If these critics are part of the *xiaozi* culture, what they exemplify is exactly the self-consciousness of the *xiaozi* writers. This self-consciousness reminds me of a contemporary *xiaozi* novelist Wei Hui, who would censure postcolonialism in today's Shanghai in her *Shanghai Baby*, while in the meantime making her foreign-inspired sensual life in the city (she cites foreign writers constantly to guide her navigation in sensibilities) and her love affair with a foreigner an integral part of a postcolonial spectacle.[41]

While *xiaozi* writers are often self-consciously critical of themselves, the editor of the anthology, Ge Hongbing, clearly subscribed to the discourse that I identified earlier while discussing the rise of the post-Mao city films.[42] The discourse features a deviation from the grand narrative of the Maoist revolutionary ideology and a rekindled interest in the everyday. Informed by this same discourse, Ge relates *xiaozi* with the collapse of revolutionary ideology. He assigns some light colors—pink (suggesting warmth and gentility), light green (symbolizing love for nature and human beings), and light blue (implying such qualities as quiet, elegant and tasteful)—as the symbolic colors of *xiaozi*, letting them contrast the revolutionary, violent red of the Maoist ideology. In this light, Ge believes that the light-colored *xiaozi* taste of life has contributed to the social stability of the most recent Chinese history. Using this contrast, Ge has actually elevated *xiaozi* from a subculture limited to educated, white-collar urban youth to the prevailing feature of today's urban life—materialistic, everyday, and profane. "The spiritual essence of our era," Ge writes, "is becoming more and more *xiaozi*. The materialist glory of *xiaozi* culture presents concretely a spiritual void that is close to 'nothingness' (wu) and that has a façade of everyday-ness."[43] Ge's description of the market dominance of *xiaozi* culture—how market has deprived the individuality, uniqueness, and depth of the culture—may have reflected some of his not-so-optimistic view of this culture. This view, which may even remind us of the German School's warning of the cold aspect of urbanization that I wrote about earlier, is only fleeting. The contemporary Chinese mind, as Ge's writing indicates, does not want to think much about the negative social effects of *xiaozi* culture but wants to live it first. "In the new century," Ge writes, "*xiaozi* is no longer just confined to the literary interests of intellectuals with bourgeois tastes. *Xiaozi* is no longer found just in words flowing in fashionable *xiaozi* journals but is found everywhere alive on city streets. *Xiaozi* sings in the hearts of the young. It has become a popular tendency of life, a mass movement of life."⁴⁴ Clearly, the same social and ideological factors in today's China are setting the critical perception of *xiaozi* culture and urbanism of post-Mao cinema into the same trajectory.

That Ge described *xiaozi* subculture as a mass movement becomes more interesting when it is contrasted with another urban subculture, *pizi* (hooligans and hooliganism), which I discuss in chapter 4. To contrast them briefly, while *xiaozi* subculture is derived from the full advance of the globalized market in China, *pizi* subculture claims earlier origins—it is related both to China's Maoist political past (*pizi* make it their object of jeering) and to the post-Mao elite cultural discourses of humanism, enlightenment, and the reconstruction of the national identity (*pizi* also make fun of these). While *xiaozi* are accustomed to live regulated lives of a commercial culture, *pizi* needed the chaos of the market initiation in a former totalitarian state to locate their playgrounds and to display their mischief. In the concluding decade of the twentieth century, as Sheldon Lu observes, "both elite culture and official ideology were in retreat."⁴⁵ Instead, the popular culture of daily life started to reign. "'Cultural fast food' (wenhua kuaican) became the order of the day."⁴⁶ With this cultural backdrop, it is no big surprise that while *xiaozi* subculture started to push more for its representation, *pizi* started to bow out of the historical stage at the turn of the century, as I discuss in the case of Xu Jinglei's film *My Father and I* (Wo he baba, 2003) in chapter 4.

In addition to "cultural fast food," *xiaozi* film has started to emerge. Take *Shanghai Panic* (Women haipa, 2002), a film shown at the 2002 Vancouver International Film Festival, as an example. Written and performed by the Internet *xiaozi* writer Mian Mian, this film documents the emotional and sensual life of a group of young people—their indulgence in drugs and alcohol, their sexual drives (homosexual and heterosexual), their fear of AIDS, their roaming of the city streets, their riding of cyberspace, and their anxiety about their lives.⁴⁷ Set in contemporary Shanghai, this film echoes Zhang Yuan's earlier films about young people living in Beijing, *Beijing Bastards* (Beijing zazhong, 1992) and *Sons* (Erzi, 1995). If these films are still rare examples of independent or underground filmmaking, in a broader sense, *xiaozi* tastes and lifestyles have also started to prevail in state-issued films. In Xia Gang's *Love at First Sight* (Yijian zhongqing, 2002), a comedy of war between sexes, the characters are all stylish, young professionals who are independent (no family ties at all), well educated, tasteful in life, and diversified in personalities. Compared with the youth of the Maoist and immediate post-Mao China, they are depoliticized, down to earth, and profane. They don't bother to be heroes, they don't talk about missions and goals of life, and they don't care about personal sacrifice for the sake of the state. Chinese youth today are finally distant enough from the country's revolutionary past to allow *xiaozi* tastes and lifestyles to win out.

The ascendancy of *xiaozi* tastes is related to what David Chaney described as a change from "ways of life" to "lifestyles," which brings the distance between West and East closer.[48] *A way of life* is typically associated with premodern, Apollonian society at a particular geographical locale. Its social significance ties more to ownership and organization of means of production. It is displayed in features such as shared norms, rituals, and patterns of social orders. It is based on the production and reproduction of stable institutions. A way of life describes the Maoist China of antiurban development. *Lifestyles*, in contrast, can prevail only in an era of modernity or even late modernity. They are forms of social status derived from mass access to consumption and leisure. They are often as widespread as the global market and the distribution networks of communication and entertainment. Whereas lifestyles have long prevailed in developing countries, post-Mao China has recently opened up to the flow of not only material commodities but also lifestyles. In this sense, the winning through of *xiaozi* tastes is part and parcel of China's exposure to market-distributed international lifestyles. Here, let's take a couple of films distributed on Valentine's Day 2004 for examples. First of all, the holiday itself is a recent import catering to the rising *xiaozi* culture. The casts of these films are also international so as to better appeal to the Mainland audience. Ye Weixin's *Leaving Me, Loving You* (Dacheng xiaoshi, 2004), set in contemporary Shanghai, mixes Hong Kong and Mainland stars. *Last Love* (Zuihou de ai, zuichu de ai, 2004), also set in Shanghai, is a coproduction of China and Japan. Hong Kong and Japan are among the places of fashions that the Mainland *xiaozi* care about.

Urban Space, Tian'anmen, and Heterotopia

A study of urbanism and cinema necessarily involves the issues of urban space and its representation. If the most enduring spatial symbol of the roots-searching films of the 1980s was the vast span of yellow earth (its grandeur, depth of history, and status as a reminder of social structure, mode of production, hardship of life, endurance of the people, and limitation of the culture), what would be the corresponding spatial symbol for post-Mao city films? First of all, the heterogeneous and ever-changing nature of urban space challenges the very idea. Urban space is exactly what Michel Foucault calls a "heterotopia," that is, heterogeneous spaces of sites and relations. Any attempt made to capture the city's essence, I must emphasize, is going to be partial and reductive.

Once this argument is made, it does not keep us from finding some interestingly allegorical uses of space. For the allegorical function of the space, Foucault also assures us that "the heterotopia is capable of juxtaposing in a single real place several spaces, several sites that are in themselves incompatible."[49] In the emergence of post-Mao city films, especially in the initial phases when filmmaking had to break with a politically controlled past, there was an excellent and telling example of a "single real place" that might function as a spatial symbol, partial and reductive as it was, for the diversified drives of city films: the well-known Tian'anmen Square.

To delineate this role of Tian'anmen Square, I rely on Henri Lefebvre's threefold approach to construing space as a historic and social product. In *The Production of Space* (1974), Lefebvre proposes three related perspectives for understanding a space: the actual *production of space* (practices of building or creating a space), *representations of space* (how through theories and figures people identify what is lived and what is perceived with what is conceived), and *representational spaces* (historical experiences, images, and symbols that are crucial for one's recognition of these spaces). Tian'anmen Square, at the center of the city of Beijing, undoubtedly is a typical representational space; its unmistakable images have been woven into the memories of modern Chinese history. A representational space as such, plus the perspectives of its space production and representation, has allowed Tian'anmen Square to move closer, in its symbolic suggestiveness, to the role that yellow earth played in the roots-searching films.

First constructed as a functional and ritual place to display the power of emperors, Tian'anmen Square was reconstructed time and again throughout modern Chinese history to be a public and political place remembered for various student demonstrations or government-sponsored mass gatherings and parades. In 1989, when the student occupation of this representational space led to a massacre and to the consequent politically reticent consumerism of the 1990s, the specter of this political space was even linguistically transferred into the new culture milieu; *square* (guangchang) became a fashionable name for many new shopping plazas.[50] The political space of the bygone eras of revolution was turned into a mental space that accompanied the new zeal and leisure of consumerism. Here this particular reference to Tian'anmen Square involved both a new historical process of space production and, interestingly enough, several mental transfers.

The mental transfers, albeit exciting to see as space production, are triggered by a representation of the space. Tian'anmen Square has played the gamut of representational roles in city films. Some films have used the Square as a setting to contrast certain unconventional behaviors, such as in Mi Jiashan's *Trouble Shooters* (Wan zhu, 1988), in Huang Jianxin's *Samsara* (Lunhui, 1988), and in Mabel Cheung's *Beijing Rocks* (Beijing yue yu lu, 2001). Some used the Square to contrast confusions both in personal lives and in the country's public history, as in Guan Hu's *Dirt* (Toufa luanle, 1994). Some let the Square indicate the lures for the country folk to be in Beijing, as in Sheng Zhimin's *Two Hearts* (Xin xin, 2002), or Jia Zhangke's *The World* (Shijie, 2004). Yet a profound representation of Tian'anmen Square—covering the long historical process from the last emperor until today, contrasting the drastic changes of the past and present, and reflecting the globalized nature of today's consumerism in China—is found in Feng Xiaogang's *Big Shot's Funeral* (Dawan, 2001). The film is not exactly set in Tian'anmen Square, and for purposes of this discussion, I have broadened the concept of the Square to include the adjacent buildings and open spaces in the Forbidden City. In this case, after all, both Tian'anmen Square and the Forbidden City are the political symbols that are reprocessed by the market. In the film, the refigured square (a representational building and space accommodating mass gatherings) has spatially represented the mental transfer of Tian'anmen Square, or any square in this sense, in the consumerism of today.

Big Shot's Funeral tells the story of Taylor, a big-shot Western film director (played by Donald Sutherland) who comes to China to shoot another film about the last emperor. Before falling into a (first real, then feigned) coma, he entrusts Yoyo, a Chinese photographer, with planning and running his funeral. What Yoyo does, on the movie set where Taylor plans to shoot his last-emperor film, is an advertising-driven and -funded funeral that surpasses by ten times the crowning of the last emperor in the grandeur of its spectacle. Shocked by the inspiration of how the massive gathering of advertisements has transformed the square, Taylor decides that his own funeral run by Yoyo is actually what he wants to shoot about China.

In a way, this is also advice to a Western audience as to what kind of China they should now expect. If cinematic perceptions about China were still dominated by Bertolucci's *The Last Emperor*, it was high time to discard them. *The Big Shot's Funeral*, by transforming Tian'amen Square, showcases a China transformed from that of the last emperor through that of Maoist totalitarianism to that of today's rule of consumerism. Since the 1980s, as Deborah Davis observed in an earlier study of Chinese post-Mao urbanization, Chinese cities best illustrated the nation's "material and ideological dislocation," they became "a critical meeting ground" for new urbanites freed from "the reduced scope of political controls," and they "provided the physical and social space where previously suppressed economic, political, and cultural activities emerged into public view."[51] By transforming the square, *The Big Shot's Funeral* provides us with such a public view, which, when compared with the implications of the yellow earth in the roots-searching film, is not as holistic in denotation. Indeed, the view reflects a collective drive toward market modernization. It, however, makes one more aware of the multiple levels of reality constituting it—to think of the funeral as a showcase, one has to think of the many kinds of people it involves (entrepreneurs, opportunists, gangsters, performers, and rural migrants); all the images, fads, and styles it has to invoke and manipulate; and all the ideas it brings into collision (China and the world, revolution and commodities, brand names and piracies, and so on).

To understand the implications of this kind of public view, we have to return to the concept of heterotopia that we emphasized before looking into the allegorical use of Tian'anmen Square. In discussing Chinese urban cinema of the 1990s, Linda Chiu-han Lai elaborates the implication of this concept: "The new cities of China are best approached as *heterotopia*—that is, each city is a single space with multiple orderings, encounters, cores, and planes; they are many places in one, of different levels of realities, and allude to many sites here and elsewhere; and they are the juxtaposition of incommensurate things, independent and yet collective, disrupting and at the same time layering upon one another."[52] Heterotopia is the spatial expression of developmental urbanization taking root in China. The social fragmentation it renders has uprooted millions of Chinese from their traditional ways of life, thrusting them into the flux of a new urban way of living. Cinematic urbanism, which is the subject of my book, responds to the spatial restructuring of social relations, ideas, and feelings in today's China. This urbanism is what Linda Chiu-han Lai calls "an action-concept" or "a speech act" of heterotopia: "such usage to make sense of a place at once effectuates a critic's determination and concrete action to deconstruct established knowledge about the place in question, via (re-)reading and (re-)writing, and by begging multiplicity and heterogeneity."⁵³ Urbanism in post-Mao China discursively reconstructs China on the silver screen, and it lets this reconstruction cut into the episteme, feelings, and viewing horizon of its audience. As I am concluding this book, the momentum of urbanization has not yet shown signs of slowing down in China. On a daily basis, urbanization is still drastically changing the Chinese landscape and everyday life. Along with these changes, urbanism of post-Mao cinema keeps reinventing both China and itself.

1

X-Roads: Old and New City Films

X-Roads (Xin shizi jietou, 2001) is a co-memoir. Director Jiang Xiaozhen and the male lead Zhao Jin are the daughter of Bai Yang and the son of Zhao Dan, two Chinese superstars who played lovers in *Crossroads* (Shizi jietou, 1937) over six decades before. *Crossroads* portrayed the trials and tribulations of the young people of the 1930s in the hostile urban jungle of Shanghai. *X-Roads* updates their love story.

Bai Yang and Zhao Dan, supported by footage of their various film roles since *Crossroads*, have become fictional characters who were once in love (in *Crossroads*), who lost touch later as they were drawn into their revolutionary careers (in later films), and both married someone else. Yet they missed each other and kept each other's favorite doll. Bai Yang remained in Shanghai,

Good Morning, Beijing (dir. Zhang Nuanxin, 1990) reverses logic and indicates a changing perception about material well-being.
Courtesy of China Film Archive, Beijing.

while Zhao Dan settled in a provincial town.[1] Not knowing much of their parents' romance in colonial Shanghai, Bai Yang's daughter and Zhao Dan's son happened to meet in post-Mao Shanghai and were destined to continue the unfinished romance of their parents.

In the film, Yang Shao, Bai Yang's cinematic daughter, and Zhao Ming, Zhao Dan's cinematic son, not only have had different upbringings (in the metropolis versus a provincial town) but have also lived in different parts of the world. In another allegorical situation suggesting the need to decide which way to go, their lives cross paths for the first time when Shao returns to Shanghai for her mother's funeral after living in New York for over a decade. Suffering from culture shock and frustrated by the difficulties of handling her mother's estate, Shao stays longer than planned and becomes acquainted with Ming, her mother's handyman. Striving to make it in Shanghai, Ming befriends Shao with the hope of turning the house left by Shao's mother into a nightclub. Juxtaposed with footage of their parents' on-screen romance, the two begin to realize their feelings for each other despite the fact they each have significant others and their relationship is marred by many misunderstandings.

In *X-Roads*, the glamorous smile of the youthful Bai Yang from *Crossroads* flashes repeatedly, beckoning the daughter to move on. Here we detect not only a daughter's private memory but also the audience's collective remembrance of the youthful spirit that Bai Yang's beauty represented. Ming's preparation for his date with Shao is similarly accompanied by footage showing his father's high spirits in doing the same; nostalgia for the romantic innocence of an earlier era is equally private and collective. The nostalgia, nevertheless, is clearly misplaced. In *Crossroads*, the "youthful spirit" and the "romantic innocence" were both weapons for denouncing a rotten, materialist society. In *X-Roads*, they have been appropriated to promote a renewed pursuit of materialism.

As a parody of its antecedent, *X-Roads* brings together in the same city two different eras, two generations of urbanites, and two film cultures. In this chapter, *X-Roads* serves as a symbolic locale for juxtaposing three pairs of films that relate the post-Mao city film to pre-PRC (People's Republic of China) leftist filmmaking: Jiang Xiaozhen's *X-Roads* as a parody of Shen Xiling's *Crossroads*, Zhang Nuanxin's *Good Morning, Beijing* (Beijing ni zao, 1990) as a retrieval of Yuan Muzhi's *Street Angel* (Malu tianshi, 1937), and Tian Zhuangzhuang's *Springtime in a Small Town* (Xiaocheng zhi chun, 2002) as an update of Fei Mu's 1948 film of the same title. These pairs of films offer an interesting array of comparisons that also lead to some generalized considerations of how cinematic urbanisms across Maoist China play different historical roles. Comparing the first two pairs demonstrates more of the contemporary city film's deviation from the alleged tradition, while comparison of the third pair involves contemporary filmmaking's search for an alternative tradition in a neglected film among the limited pre-PRC films that are still available.

Contrasting Urbanisms

A flowering of studies of colonial Shanghai has greatly enriched our understanding of this enigmatic city.[2] The varied perspectives reveal a rich spectrum of love-and-hate representations. "Cosmopolitan Shanghai," an English-language travel guide of 1935, describes a "city of amazing paradoxes and fantastic contrasts; Shanghai the beautiful, bawdy, and gaudy; contradiction of manners and morals; a vast brilliantly-hued cycloramic, panoramic mural of the best and the worst of Orient and Occident. . . . [I]t's a great old town, and how we hate it and love it."[3]

The two 1937 films studied in this chapter both correspond to this travel guide narrative and offer us glimpses of the different faces of the city. The credit sequence of *Street Angel*, with its multiple cuts, creates a collage of city scenes that resembles the paradoxes described in the 1935 travel guide: glaring neon lights of commercial prosperity, well-dressed middle-class people taking leisurely walks in the parks, rush-hour flows of people going to or leaving work, ballroom dancing in the foreign concessions, chaotic street markets that are unmistakably Chinese, and varieties of Western buildings. *Street Angel*, nevertheless, argues against the lure of the city. In this nearly three-minute sequence, with a lighthearted tune as its score, the low-angle camera will tilt, climbing various Western-style buildings until it is stopped by a harsh boom in the music and followed by close-ups of a statue of a threatening lion. Then a new round of climbing will start again. Along with its musical score, the camera movement symbolizes the soaring, romantic spirit encouraged by the city, which time and again is pulled down to the ground. Most interestingly, a similar symbolism is also present in the credit sequence of *Crossroads*. In a set of tilt shots, the amorous camera climbs all kinds of modern high-rise buildings, but this climbing is persistently interrupted by a high-angle shot of a busy crossroads—the reality of life at the crossroads checks the soaring romanticism encouraged by the modern city. Considering the stories of both films, we realize that this pattern indicates the film artists' disappointment with the city, which has a tendency in both films to crush the youthful idealism of the characters. For leftist filmmakers, the city is antiromantic and filled with sin.

Here lies a highly politicized, antiurban urbanism. The social ills of colonialism and capitalism weighed heavily on the minds of the leftist filmmakers in Shanghai. They had no leisure to appreciate the aura of the city but were urged to use city stories as social critique. Xia Yan's two films, *Shanghai 24 Hours* (Shanghai ershisi xiaoshi, 1933) and *The New Year's Gift* (Ya sui qian, 1937), illustrate in the extreme the tendency to expose the colonialist/capitalist culprit in contemporary urban life. *Shanghai 24 Hours* contrasts a day's life in the family of a manager of a foreign textile factory with that of a family and the concerned neighbors of an injured worker from the same factory. The film starts at four in the afternoon when the worker is injured and dismissed while the manager's family is getting ready for the excitement of the city's nightlife. The film ends at four P.M. the following day as the injured worker dies and the manager's family gets ready for another round of excitement. With constant crosscuts showing the misery of the urban poor, the luxury of the leisure class in the city—restaurants, gaming tables, racetracks, ballroom floors, and neon lights—all appear to stink with the worker's blood. This luxury is also shown to be colonial in nature. The manager has gotten rich by working for the foreigners, and he puts Chinese labels on foreign products to defraud the Chinese citizens who are boycotting foreign products.

The New Year's Gift is an early example of a "Chinese New Year film"[4]; it opened in Shanghai in 1937 on the eve of the holiday. This gift, nonetheless, is a lesson in urban ills. A grandfather gives two silver dollars to his granddaughter as a New Year's gift. The money is spent right away, and the film follows the quick changing of hands of the money, thus presenting different people dealing with the silver dollars within a panorama of contemporary urban crisis in Shanghai: unemployment, bankruptcy, monetary crisis, and social unrest. Money, in its colonial and capitalist status in Shanghai, is shown as the culprit of all these social ills.

The leftist filmmakers would not take this city of sin as the future of China. In their filmic critique of Shanghai, there was an implied endorsement of the countryside. Fei Mu's *City Night* (Chengshi zhi ye, 1933) depicts how a young woman from a poor family resists the seduction of the urban rich by leaving the city, with several other poverty-stricken people, for the countryside. Yuan Muzhi's *City Scenery* (Dushi fengguang, 1935) lets a few country people get into a series of urban caricatures to illustrate how far the urban ways of life have become alienated from the down-to-earth virtue of rural culture. Yang Hansheng and Shen Fu's *Myriads of Lights* (Wan jia denghuo, 1948) portrays urban middle-class life as uncertain, cold, and alienating. As an antidote, it points to the countryside as the roots of warmth, understanding, and reconciliation. The abundance of such films leads us to see that the film artists themselves also felt alienated by foreign influences in Shanghai.

In an interview in *Shen bao* (*Shanghai Daily*), film director Cheng Bugao talked about his feelings when location shooting for *To the Northwest* (Dao xibei qu, 1934) took him away from Shanghai: "The further I was away from Shanghai, the further I took leave of material civilization. I felt like I was finally able to go to the real China. What I saw was real Chinese people, and I seemed to become a foreigner."[5] Here the city/country contrast has gained a national implication, that is, what is real for China.

For leftist filmmakers, colonialism in Shanghai was the worst scenario for China as a nation. Their dark depiction of Shanghai may appear identical to their Western contemporaries' perception of Shanghai as "a city of sin," a "paradise of adventurers," a "capitalists' paradise," and a city where everything was "for sale."[6] Nevertheless, they would not have believed, as Western scholarship then suggested, that the colonization of Shanghai was a "necessary evil" that China had to bear before it modernized. The leftist filmmakers were inspired by Western intellectual imports, ranging from Marxism to literary romanticism, but they despised the colonial import of materialist culture. Rather, their implied city/country contrast contained both the traditional Chinese elite culture's disdain for materialism and the Communist social revolution ideology. The city was a symbol of the modern social ills of corruption, decadence, alienation, and fragmentation, which the social revolution wanted to denounce. The countryside, on the other hand, was believed to have rich soil for sowing the seeds of community-based collective actions, for conquering the city, and for building the new China.

X-Roads brings us to today's Shanghai, where the belief in the "necessary evil" of economic modernization and the city as a "paradise of adventures" has returned. Earlier on, as *X-Roads* indicates, Yang Shao had traveled all the way to the United States to look for adventure and to find her prince. Returning to a changed China for her mother's funeral, she realizes that her real romance resides with the youthful energy of early capitalism that is here at home, and she falls in love. The most spectacular scene in the film is a romantic one of Shao sitting on a swing gently pushed by Ming. Its power lies in the fact that it is cross-cut and choreographed with old footage of the scene in *Crossroads* that it is modeled after. The aura of the old Shanghai is brought back by this crosscut, and the viewer is dazed by the elegance of the scene. The young woman and young man are fashionably dressed in Western-style clothing as the princess and prince, while soft lighting, lyrical music, and dreamy facial expressions of indulgence all lend to the romance of the scene. The glamorous use of this old footage reflects a general nostalgia for old Shanghai.

The old footage, as emphasized before, is a misplaced object of desire. The elegance of the swing sequence in *Crossroads* is Yang's daydream, and it is designed to be sarcastic: at the height of the romantic buildup, a big label reading "unemployed" is printed on the face of Zhao, which brings Yang back to reality. Here the elegance is a style that *Crossroads* ridicules. *X-Roads*, however, does not want to reproduce the mockery scene. It wants to maintain a romantic vision of Shanghai's glamour. Similarly, the young characters in the film show a great curiosity about discovering their parents' generation's private lives instead of their politicized screen personas. They press a bosom friend of Shao's mother, an amiable old man of style, to reveal more. They want to dig out a Shanghai hidden from the leftist films.

This desire could be found in a variety of cultural texts published at the time when *X-Roads* was produced. *The Aura of Shanghai*, a Chinese collection of essays and memoirs about the colonial city, bears testimony to this. The collection was published in the midst of a contemporary trend in China to search for a renewed and enriched understanding of everyday life, at different locales and times.[7] The postscript to a five-volume book on everyday China (one for each decade from the 1950s through the 1990s) explains this desire well:

> In the latter half of the twentieth century, everyday life has been the constant object of reform; everyday life has been made to suit the grand goal of modernizing and strengthening the nation. However, the profane, trivial, and irreverent qualities that are innate with everyday life make it hard to serve the goal. . . .
>
> We have experienced the failure of modernization, the bankrupting of grand narrative, and the loss of elitism. Today, when poetic visions are turned into profane groping, will our everyday life be able to deviate from the grand goals for the future and be on its own?[8]

The time frame for this reformation of everyday life surely needed to be extended. Leftist filmmaking in the two decades prior to the founding of the PRC had already started to subjugate everyday life to the goal of saving China. In accordance with this widespread desire of rediscovery, *The Aura of Shanghai* offers various perspectives of everyday life in the colonial city—street scenes, anecdotes, novelties, lifestyles, fashions, hobbies, trends, cuisine, and so on. With a touch of nostalgia, it wants to break the monopoly of a politicized and oversimplified representation of Shanghai.

The anecdotal writing by novelist Cheng Naishan in *The Aura of Shanghai* also offers a clue to understanding two characters in *X-Roads*: Zhao Ming as an *Ah Fei* (an extraordinary guy) and the old friend of Yang Shao's mother as *Lao Kele* (an old colorful guy).[9] Both phrases are phonetic adaptations of English into Shanghai dialect. *Ah Fei* actually means "a figure," referring to a fashionable, foreign appearance and personage. *Ah Fei*, as Cheng delineates, was brought into everyday language by American soldiers in post–World War II Shanghai, where bubble gum, Coca Cola, and Collin milk powder also became fashionable. The phrase was neutral at first coinage and described those young people influenced by foreign fashions—they were eye-catching *figures* standing out from the ordinary. Corresponding to middle-class or high-society playboys (huahua gongzi), the term *Ah Fei* was the grassroots product of popular culture. Later on, especially in the PRC era when perceptions about foreign influences changed, *Ah Fei* gradually turned derogatory, referring to hooligans who were the culprits of decadence in everyday life.[10]

Zhao Ming is an *Ah Fei*, both in its original sense and with a touch of its later implications. He is an unconventional *figure*: a provincial man becoming fashionable in the big metropolis, a sleek, sociable person capable of finding his way around all sorts of people, and a self-made man without a state job but some business ideas of his own. He has taught himself English and has made foreign friends, people of his sort, a few young Americans who have no money but who want to make it in Shanghai. According to conventional values, Ming is a suspicious person. He can be easily seen as profane, greedy, untrustworthy, and insincere. Family friends use these exact words when warning Shao about Ming, who befriends her around the nightclub dream. Ming has been the handyman in the last few years of her mother's life. In turn, the mother has, without Ming's knowledge, left him half of her property in her will.

The mysterious fondness of Shao's mother for Ming is a great puzzle to her relatives and family friends. Enter her pal from the old days, Uncle Tang, now considered a *Lao Kele* (*lao* = old; *kele* = color), what folks of new Shanghai call those who have retained the style of old Shanghai. The literary and artistic youth of Shanghai were well known for their romantic (Western) lifestyle. The renowned left-wing writer Ding Ling, for example, was known for living with two of her beloved young men, who were also left-wing writers.

In *X-Roads*, this *Lao Kele* and Ming's father are thought to have been intimate with Shao's mother, an intimacy the three of them all had to keep hidden while living in Red China. In *X-Roads*, Uncle Tang is vague about this past when questioned by the young, creating a gap between the older generation's private Western-style selves and their public, revolutionary persona (politicized screen characters). With this gap, it is natural to imagine that the old-timers' familiarity with the Western-style living of old Shanghai allow them not to reject, as others do, Ming's style of living. Later in the film, this *Lao Kele* is found enjoying gatherings at Ming's Western-style nightclub, a lifestyle he appears to already be familiar with. From the *Lao Kele's* fondness for Ming, one can imagine why Shao's mother also loved this young man in addition to the fact that he is the son of her former lover.

The subtle communication between *Ah Fei* and *Lao Kele* in *X-Roads* suggests a changed understanding of and renewed hope for a Western presence in China. Partially as a critique of the leftist filmmakers' urban portrayal of Shanghai, the new urbanism here functions as an implicit advocate for economic modernization and the Western influences that come with globalization. It relates today's Shanghai to the future of China. It shows a profound interest in material pursuits, it encourages adventures, and it tolerates necessary evils.

The Doll and Mickey Mouse: *Crossroads* and *X-Roads*

To further understand the changes in ideology that *X-Roads* represents, we need to return to its antecedent, *Crossroads*. This movie classic is a love story between Zhao and Yang, who have both graduated from school and come to Shanghai to work. They have also unknowingly lived next door to each other. Zhao works for a newspaper at night, and Yang works as a technician at a textile factory during the day. Their rooms are separated by a section of wall that does not reach the ceiling.

While the two are romantically attracted and fall in love when they meet outside their apartment, back inside, they engage in constant mischievous "battles." Because of their mutual intrusion into each other's space through the opening of the wall that does not reach the ceiling, they throw nasty worded notes, or even trash, into the other's room. This comic misconduct is the foil to the real societal battle that they have to fight: their high-spirited, youthful dreams can hardly survive the cruelty of a city troubled by colonialism, economic crisis, and Japanese invasion. In the film, while their misunderstanding is easily overcome, the harsh realities such as unemployment and these young people's disappointment with the city remain.In this romantic comedy, the clash between their dreams and the harsh reality of urban Shanghai reflects the ideology of leftist filmmaking in the 1930s. In this clash, both dreams and disappointments can be traced to the May Fourth New Cultural Movement, wherein Chinese youth identified with such Western bourgeois ideals as individualism and social equality to contrast what they believed to be the decay of Confucianism and China's semicolonial culture and society. May Fourth was the outcome of a cultural crisis. The dreams it inspired were supposed to shed light on a dark society, but they might not always be triumphant in this society. "The dreamers versus the guns" has been an oversimplified but forceful depiction of the modern Chinese journey of ideals.[11] Given the harsh political situation in post-emperor China, it was not coincidental that May Fourth ideals would eventually merge into the Sino-Marxist ideology of grassroots social revolution, which would later became an ideological harbinger of leftist filmmaking.[12]

In *Crossroads*, three toys—a doll, a college graduate in Western academic attire, and Mickey Mouse—become part of the identities of Zhao and Yang, as well as the ideological focus of the film. The film educates Zhao, whose modern Western education and comedic style associate him with both Hollywood romantic comedies and Disney's Mickey Mouse. The film wants this kind of comedy to first reflect such grim subjects as unemployment, housing shortages, sexual harassment in the workplace, suicide, and foreign invasion to prove that the Western-oriented high spirits of Zhao and Yang impractical. It then revises the reason for their high spirit at the end of the film: the four young friends, all unemployed, lock arms while marching down the city streets in defiance; they have decided to leave the city to join the war against the Japanese invasion; their decision implies that the city is no place for the young—or for the nation.[13] Yang's doll relates to femininity, to the post–May Fourth culture of "wandering at a loss," and to the Western romantic influence shown by Yang's reading of *The Lady of the Camellias* by Dumas *fils*. The leftist filmmaking has produced enough films to show that a bourgeois New Woman will never make it on her own and that she must join a collective course of social revolution before she can reach her feminist goal. *Crossroads* situates Yang in a textile factory, juxtaposing her with the female proletarian. The sexual harassment she encounters in the workplace is a social ill that all workingwomen cope with. Zhao's interviews of Yang and his writing on Yang produce a critical subtext designed to divert their romance from a petty-bourgeois ideal to a pro-proletarian one.

These toys, which have all passed down from *Crossroads* to *X-Roads*, are shown to be valued highly by the younger generation. If the toys in *Crossroads* are used to address, revise, and adapt romanticism, individualism, and idealism by contrasting these Western ideologies with the harsh social conditions of colonial Shanghai, how has *X-Roads* dealt with them?

In post-Mao China, the social revolutionary ideology was defunct. Romanticism and individualism have become liberating agents pitted against the remnants of any central social control, be it institutional, ideological, ethical, or cultural. Zhao Ming's *Ah Fei* character, which bears clear traits of Western imports, is set against the routine living of everyday folks in Shanghai. Whereas in *Crossroads* young characters embrace ideals and distain materialism, *X-Roads* materializes youthful dreams from the very beginning. Adventures in the new territory of the market economy carry these dreams, and they are depicted as agents for modernizing China. As for the similar social problem of unemployment that *Crossroads* emphasized, *X-Roads* treats it as a challenge for starting anew and for finding unusual business opportunities. In a way, *X-Roads* represents a new sort of romanticism, one with a market economy and personal adventures. This romanticism does not need to be sensitive to the severe social problems caused by the onset of the market and the fragmenting of socialism, resulting in unemployment, polarization of the rich and the poor, and social unrest. It only needs to focus on the general prosperity and inspiration that the market has brought.

The toys in *X-Roads* suggest a new round of love affairs with the West, one of body and soul. When the colonial anxiety of leftist filmmakers is removed and an interest in materialism is kindled, these toys also lead the film into a romantic courting of Hollywood. While leftist filmmaking in the old Shanghai was suspicious and critical of Hollywood, *X-Roads* marches toward it. Post-Mao China's ten-foreign-film-per-year quota of imports allowed the Chinese audience to see only the best of Hollywood, and the general reception of American films has been overwhelmingly positive.[14] Reflecting this admiration, Jiang Xiaozhen, the director of *X-Roads*, was not shy in talking about her film's affinity to Hollywood. At a Harvard screening of *X-Roads*, she spoke of how several Hollywood directors first suggested that she update her mother's film, and they supported the film project once it began. She wrote the script, assembled an international production team, and secured a multinational cast led by Taiwanese box-office star Rene Liu and supported by American sitcom star Alan Thicke. To make things easier for all on the set, she even asked everyone in the film to speak English throughout to make an all-English overseas edition of the film.[15]

With all these efforts, one can't even be sure if the film is by a Chinese director or just another Hollywood film about China. However, the eagerness of this film to assimilate into the Hollywood mainstream and to be accepted by an international market has only backfired. Seeing the two protagonists deprived of their linguistic intimacy and falling in love in poor English has annoyed audiences overseas.[16] A Web site, *OffOffOff*, ridiculed the film for the "Chinese actors speaking bad English."

A sharp contrast to this insensitivity to language is a Hong Kong film that also updates the Shanghai of the 1930s. Directed by Stanley Kwan, *Center Stage* (Ruan Lingyu, 1991) demonstrates a sophisticated understanding of past and present. It uses a Pirandellian approach (revealing a performance as a performance) to remind the audience of the relationship between past and present, between a touching story and good acting, and between Ruan Lingyu as a superstar of the 1930s and Zhang Manyu (Maggie Cheung), who plays Ruan Lingyu in this film, as a superstar today. A combination of past and present filmmaking, *Center Stage* pays meticulous attention to the linguistic reality, making sure that each actor speaks the right dialect.

X-roads' march toward Hollywood resonated with a profound cultural desire of the Chinese to make it in the world. In her study of the popular reception of literature of the Chinese diaspora, Dai Jinhua relates the fad to a "new trauma" in popular consciousness. This trauma involves a torn imaginary map: China has lost its centrality in this map supported by the discourses of world revolution, and it has rediscovered itself as a developing country miserably lagging behind. In this sense, the yearning to "go global," the "desire for the West," and the "American complex" (the Chinese fascination with the American dream and the love/hate American experiences of Chinese overseas) may all be seen as an unconscious effort to mend this imaginary map. In the new ideology emphasizing everyday life, the success stories of Chinese overseas boost a popular hope for a renewed centrality of China in that map.[17]

X-Roads not only transfers the "American complex" to the city of Shanghai but it also touches on a sensitive issue in the Chinese diaspora—the marriage of Chinese women to foreigners. Today's Shanghai has offered small-town person Zhao Ming ample opportunities to pursue his dreams. He is even capable of winning Yang Shao back from her American fiancé and from the diaspora. Ming's story in Shanghai is comparable to the many Chinese success stories in America. The guarantee of this comparison, which results in winning the Chinese back from America and renewing a sense of national pride, as *X-Roads* implies, is the success of Shanghai. For Ming to achieve his goals, Shanghai has to become continually more American. To this end, Ming's story is the American dream come true in Shanghai. The new urbanism implied here is a romantic rendezvous with materialism.

Two Caged Birds: *Street Angel* and *Good Morning, Beijing*

To continue our comparison of urbanisms across Maoist China, I would like to turn to another pair of films not only to highlight the different allegorical roles played by women in these urbanisms but also to contrast the current urbanism we are investigating in this book with a slightly earlier fashion of the immediate post-Mao urbanism, the allegorical one held by the Fourth Generation directors.

Other than her undoubted familiarity with *Street Angel*, Fourth Generation director Zhang Nuanxin never mentioned this 1937 classic as her source of inspiration for directing *Good Morning, Beijing* in 1990. At first glance, the two films appear a far cry from each other. *Street Angel* is set in the colonial treaty port of Shanghai of the 1930s. The forced cohabitation of Western dominance and Chinese misery is effectively portrayed by the film's opening sequence. In a wedding procession, Western and Chinese bands walk into each other (edited as if in violation of the commonsense rule that the directions of motions in a particular film sequence should be consistent) to create a clashing and chaotic sense of this particular "marriage" of the foreign and the Chinese. Xiao Hong, a teahouse singer, befriends a group of young men in her neighborhood: a trumpeter in a Western-style band, a newspaper vendor, a barber, and some unemployed factory workers. When Xiao Hong is to be sold by her abusive, adoptive parents to a rich local gangster, this group of young men, though besieged by their own problems of urban poverty, comes to her rescue. Xiao Hong elopes and marries the trumpeter, whom she has always loved.

The half century between the films covers the time span when direct foreign presence in China ended. Ai Hong (Ma Xiaoqing) in *Good Morning, Beijing* is a ticket seller on a state bus. She first befriends a fellow ticket seller but soon moves on to date Zou (Wang Quan'an), a bus driver, whose profession is of higher social status than that of a ticket seller. Not able to persuade

Zou to leave their state bus company for uncertain but lucrative private ventures, Ai Hong becomes the girlfriend of Keke (Jia Hongsheng), a foreign student who is not as he first appears.[18] As we come to learn, he is neither a foreigner nor a college student but a college dropout and con man who seeks to change his life through the private venues made possible by the newly open Chinese market. At the end of the film, with their misunderstandings removed, Ai Hong marries Keke and they go into private business together.

The two films, nonetheless, use strikingly similar cinematic tropes and share comparable cultural concerns that, in part makes Zhang's film a parody of *Street Angel*. Both films show concerns about the lower social stratum and how the foreign presence in these cities, usually felt most in the high-rise, foreign buildings, influences even the life of the "lower depths."[19] Both films use almost identical crane shots to move down such tall buildings to indicate this descent, and both films have similar sequences of everyday working people experiencing dazed visits to the top floors of such buildings. Both films use a woman's life to represent this social change, and the men around the central women forge brotherhoods in both films. Even the names of the central women, Xiao Hong and Ai Hong, are similar. Both films also feature a caged bird to indicate the need for these women's liberation.

The comparable allegorical representation of women in both films implies that the woman's pursuit of happiness, shown in their selection of mates, has gained a social and cultural importance; that is, their personal selection of men reflects the cultural systems each woman values. While Xiao Hong of *Street Angel* selects an idealist man, Ai Hong selects a materialist. A historical change has taken place. Conventionally, as observed by Chinese film critic Zhang Wei, the logic for this kind of allegory is that the central woman will be happy if she sticks to the "nonmaterialist" good guy and will be lost if she goes with the "materialist" bad guy,[20] but *Good Morning, Beijing* reverses the logic and indicates a changing perception about material well-being. This change reiterates the romantic rendezvous of the new urbanism with materialism.

As a layer of the allegory, implications of the brotherhood forged around the central women also change. In *Street Angel*, it is not just the love of the trumpeter but also the friendship of the brotherhood that wins Xiao Hong. The collective entity of brotherhood goes well with the discourse of social revolution that the film subscribed to. In *Good Morning, Beijing*, it is interesting to note, the two losers in the competition for Ai Hong strike up an unusual friendship in staying with their older jobs with the state bus company. Zou, the driver, does not get to follow his dream of getting on a motorcycle to hit the road, as indicated by the poster in his living space and the songs he learned to play. He can hardly leave behind the demands of his parents and other elders—as portrayed in his habit of taking care of their hot-water basin for foot washing, nor can he ignore the demands of the state, which has trained him for the job. In the sadness that wraps up the film, the brotherhood of the morally good guys are not necessarily the heroes the ideology of economic reform endorses. The bad guy, Keke, embarks on a journey that will inscribe the new urbanism.

The birdcages, as important tropes in both films, have also changed implications. In *Street Angel*, the birdcage stands for the decaying old China that is imprisoning Xiao Hong. The national dimension of the allegory, which attempts to identify Xiao Hong with China's national crisis, is achieved through many channels: the opening wedding sequence depicting a symbolic cohabitation of the Chinese misery and the foreign power may well be Xiao Hong's own, the Japanese invasion that Xiao Hong's singing alludes to endangers her life, the Western-style lawyer is apathetic to Xiao Hong's fate, and the gangsters (decayed Chinese social forces in colonialism) desire to possess her.[21] To break the cage involves a social revolution that aims at overthrowing, as a Chinese Communist tenet lists, imperialism, capitalism (the lawyer), and feudalism (the abusive parents and the gangsters). The group of young men that Xiao Hong befriends, through many subtle and entertaining frames of the film, conveys this message clearly. One frame, for example, shows all the brothers posing as soldiers with unlikely weapons, such as the barber's razor; another frame presents a shadow performance in which the brothers enact a scene of militant uprising. In sum, the birdcage in *Street Angel* is associated with the discourses of a social revolution.

In *Good Morning, Beijing*, the implications of the birdcage are not conveyed through a melodrama for social revolution but are rather invested with the idea of human bondage. The market economy with materialist lure is dawning in Beijing. It beckons the young people to get involved. Ai Hong and her bus-driver friend, however, are "caged" by many concerns: how to repay the state's investment in them, how to disavow the ideal of serving the people, and how to talk to their elders (who are absolutely loyal to the state) about the fact that they are deserting their state jobs. They also must come to grips with discovering whether they are determined enough to give up the moderate state guarantee of salary to deal with the uncertainty of the market. They need to change their mode of thinking. Mobility and loyalty, for example, are contrasted in Zou and Keke, the two men who attract Ai

Hong. Mobility undoubtedly is an urban feature emerging out of the rural loyalty to land (or mode of production), family, and community (read as "state" in the film). Both Zou and Keke love mobility. Zou has posters of a motorcycle and the rebel rock star Cui Jian in his living quarters, but in real life he is caged by his loyalty to his family and the state. On the other hand, Keke sings Cui Jian's music aloud and turns the lyrics into his own searching for a new way of life:

> I want to go from north to south.
> I also want to go from morning till night.
> I want folks to all see me
> but not know who I am.
> . . .
> I have two feet and two legs.
> I have all the mountains and rivers.
> . . .
> I don't want to stay just in one place
> and I don't want anyone to follow me.[22]

Keke uses this song by Cui Jian to serenade Ai Hong, and he wins her over. Considering the allegorical implication of the film and this victory, I am tempted to ask if Ai Hong's allegorical role contains a national significance. On the one hand, my answer is yes. It is not only because Fredric Jameson has noted the possibility that any private Third-World story can be read as a national allegory.[23] Ai Hong's story is indeed typical, and it touches on the difficulties faced by a whole nation that is saying good morning to a new urbanism featuring individuality, mobility, and uncertainty. Yet, on the other hand, such analytical renderings were what director Zhang Nuanxin and many of her contemporaries were beginning to turn their backs on in the early 1990s. When the new urbanism was dawning in China, an urban-realist cinema was beginning to develop. The minute, matter-of-fact, and slice-of-life depiction of the fragmented urban lives was preeminent, which kept national-allegory films, particularly those alluding to a cultural totality, from reappearing.

On this point, I must also consider the concept of urbanism in Fourth Generation filmmaking, of which Zhang Nuanxin was a leading director, to indicate how the newer cinematic urbanism is leaving this behind. In a brief period of the 1980s and the early 1990s, city had a shifting significance in an implied, allegorical contrast with the countryside. The concept of city in this contrast is not based on any real Chinese cities—their images, historical roles, and aura—but on the Western literary representation of the city that became available to China's perpetual search for modernity. It is no surprise then to find that Raymond Williams's summary of the country/city contrast in English-language literature matches perfectly with Dai Jinhua's observation of the same contrast in Fourth Generation filmmaking.[24] The contrast of country and city, as Williams observed, has attracted powerful, generalized feelings, although the actual settlements in country and city in history have been varied. "On the country has gathered the idea of a natural way of life: of peace, innocence, and simple virtue. On the city has gathered the idea of an achieved center: of learning, communication, light. Powerful hostile associations have also developed: on the city as a place of noise, worldliness, and ambition; on the country as a place of backwardness, ignorance, limitation."[25] Although the general contrast between country and city in Fourth Generation filmmaking, as Dai Jinhua attests, often translates into one between the inertia of history, closure, ignorance, antihumanism, and decay on the one side and reformation, openness, science, education, and civilization on the other, in actual films, the emotional appeals move unevenly among the four categories of positive and hostile associations of country/city contrast as summed up by Williams.

The Fourth Generation directors showed a certain wavering in their implied contrast of country and city. Their humanist ideology made these directors emotionally attached to the human values given to the countryside: innocence, life close to nature, tenacity, warm-heartedness, and down-to-earth virtue. This ideology also drew them intellectually to the enlightenment values given to the city: science, progress, reformation, and light. In this wavering within the representative spectrum of country and city, the tone in which the city is portrayed is often decided by how close this allegorical city is to real Chinese cities and whether this city is real enough to affect peoples' everyday life. The train (with its powerful locomotive and whistling) in Hu Bingliu's *Country People* (Xiangmin, 1986), for example, is associated with the city and is the most inspiring element in the narrative of the film. The powerful locomotive and the whistling only suggest what the city represents, or a concept of the city, and introduce nothing specifically about urban life, let alone to allow it to be intrusive of the rural life represented in the film. In Teng Wenji's *On the Beach* (Haitan, 1985), as a contrast, the factory buildings in an adjacent city serve as the narrative backdrop that allows the stories of a fishing village to unfold. Since these urban facilities have actually lured the fishing villagers away, they are represented as cold and threatening. Teng Wenji's factory buildings, in contrast to Hu Bingliu's trains, have moved from an allegorical city that contrasts rural life to a real city that threatens rural life.

Since the 1990s, the advance of urbanization and the rise of new urbanism in cinema have pushed the representation of real Chinese cities to the foreground and have drawn a conclusion to a brief episode of the Fourth Generation allegorical urbanism. These real cities, represented in various modernist/postmodernist hues, have shattered the Fourth Generation contrast based on humanist and enlightenment values. Some Fourth Generation directors themselves were among those who helped to end this allegorical urbanism. Zhang Nuanxin's *Good Morning, Beijing*, along with such other Fourth Generation urban-subject films as Xie Fei's *Black Snow* (Benming nian, 1989), were among the early city films that had abandoned the allegorical urbanism of the Fourth Generation.

Reclaiming Fame: *Springtime in a Small Town* by Fei Mu and Tian Zhuangzhuang

When Tian Zhuangzhuang updated Fei Mu's *Springtime in a Small Town* (1948) in 2002, he provided an interesting case of not only how two "neglected" directors reclaimed their fame but also how the contemporary film culture has searched for an alternative tradition. The two Chinese film classics studied earlier in this chapter, *Crossroads* and *Street Angel*, are both artistically sophisticated and innovative. But they also share a striking similarity, that is, melodrama. This identical style shows how these films ideologically subscribed to the class-struggle tenet of social revolution. *Springtime in a Small Town*, by contrast, has a modernist appeal, and it depicts dilemmas faced by individuals in isolation. Moving away from melodrama, it features fragmentation, uncertainty, ambiguity, and emotional nuances. Although the film is set in an abandoned postwar town that appears almost rural, its cultural concerns remind one of the existential anxieties in contemporary Chinese urban growth. The different artistic style that contemporary Chinese urban cinema started to retrieve also testifies to China's contemporary change from utopian urbanization to a developmental urbanization as discussed in the introduction to this book.

Fei Mu (1906–1951) had been forgotten for over three decades before his *Springtime in a Small Town* was screened at an old-film festival in Beijing in 1983. The film is a chamber piece, purposefully enclosing a few characters in a very limited physical space so that their psychological nuances surface. In the post–World War II springtime in a small country town, Zhichen, a doctor seeking a break from work, pays an unexpected visit to Liyan, a sickly landed gentleman who was once his schoolmate. Upon his arrival, Zhichen is shocked to discover his first love, Yuwen, now Liyan's wife. As former passions rekindle in the two under their polite, repressed demeanors and as modern romance threatens to break the traditional bonds of loyalty, Zhichen and Yuwen are dragged into an emotional dilemma that becomes an allegory of the emotional state of the contemporary Chinese middle class. These people bemoan the harsh political and social reality of postwar China but lack the courage for a breakthrough.

Fei Mu took great care and a long time (three months) in shooting this small-scale, low-budget film. "To convey the grayish moods of an ancient China," Fei Mu indicated, "I've made an ambitious, bold experiment by using long takes and slow tracking of my camera to shoot my [nonartificial] drama."[26] In this, his last film, he continued his career-long experiment of making his film frames look like Chinese ink paintings.[27]

The artistic achievement of this film stunned audiences. One critic's comment summed up much of the praise: he noticed the film's "uniqueness in using film language to create poetic ambience," marveled at the film's "delicately built structure, minutely depicted psyche, harmoniously merged moods of mises-en-scènes and characters," and praised the film as "an amazing peak" (qifeng) in Chinese filmmaking history.[28] Since then, many studies have been published in Mainland China, Hong Kong, and Taiwan that praise *Springtime in a Small Town* as an undisputable gem among film classics and Fei Mu as one of the most accomplished directors.[29] In this revival of the film and the rekindled respect for Fei Mu, regret was expressed that *Springtime in a Small Town* had been ignored in the wartime year (1948) of its release, and that it had been degraded by the narrow teleological standard of China's only book of film history in the PRC's early decades. In fact, the concluding remark in the *History of Chinese Film Development* that sent *Springtime in a Small Town* to a vault for decades reads,

> *Springtime in a Small Town* was screened in September of 1948, at the height of the national liberation war and all kinds of people's campaigns. The negative effect of the film on its time was hard to ignore. The film, in actuality, was opium poisoning people's morale to struggle.
>
> The artistic maneuvers in *Springtime in a Small Town* displayed unmistakably the style of Fei Mu. But their impact, in such a gray-toned and pessimistic

film, would achieve nothing other than deepening the decadent feelings of the decaying social classes and amplify these feelings' social effects.[30]

A self-made genius known for his resourcefulness in reading and watching films, plays, and real life, Fei Mu started his film career with the politically moderate Lianhua Studio.[31] At age twenty-seven, he made his directorial debut in *City Night* (1933), which was praised by critics for breaking the convention of making films as if they were staged performances. Between this debut and his last film, *Springtime in a Small Town*, he directed eight films. His first three films during the silent era (*Chengshi zhi ye, Rensheng,* and *Xiang xue hai*),[32] all starring the legendary Ruan Lingyu, were often considered his trilogy on women. His last silent film, in response to the New Life Movement of the Nationalist government, was the highly praised *Tian lun* (Song of China, aka Filial piety, 1935). It became one of the few early Chinese films to be taken to the United States for a limited release. His subjects were diverse, ranging from the life of the working poor (*Chengshi zhi ye*, 1933) to an anti-Japanese invasion allegory (*Langshan diexue ji*, 1936) to the biography of the ancient sage Confucius (*Kong fuzi*, 1937).[33] Among the remarks made about his films, one topic is persistent: Fei Mu explored the richness of the film medium and enriched the (Western) film language by using it to create a Chinese poetic spirit.

This topic also became the focus for the revival of Fei Mu, which has twofold historical implications. In Mainland China, this revival happened simultaneously with the Fifth Generation film movement and became the alternative tradition this generation would discover. In Fei Mu, the post-Mao film revolt invested its own wishes of being apolitical, nonmelodramatic, humanly complex, and psychologically subtle. Since then, this Fei Mu revival has also been transmitted to Hong Kong and Taiwan. It has been expanded to include the wishes of transnational Chinese filmmaking that the Chinese national culture makes a unique contribution to the legacy of world filmmaking. The emphasis of this expanded revival of Fei Mu has been his filmic accomplishment in creating *yijing*, a meaning-loaded ambience with poetic touches. When Tian Zhuangzhuang updated *Springtime in a Small Town* in 2002, Fifth Generation filmmaking was already spent as a cultural movement. Since the 1990s, more youthful energies devoted to gritty realism and other urban-oriented experiments have been commanding critical attention. In this sense, Tian's choice to update *Springtime in a Small Town* reflected less the Fifth Generation era's endorsement of Fei Mu and more transnational Chinese filmmaking's wish for artistic accomplishment. The selection became not only indicative of his personal artistic orientation but also suggestive of similar mentalities among his Fifth Generation colleagues.

Tian was the central figure of the Fifth Generation film movement. He caught the Chinese general audience off guard with his avant-garde *On the Hunting Grounds* (Liechang zhasa, 1985) and *Horse Thief* (Daoma zei, 1986). He also enriched Chinese film history with his memorable remark that he was making his films for the audience of the twenty-first century. Like his colleagues, such as Chen Kaige and his turn from the experimental *King of Children* and *Life on a String* to the more popular Hollywood-like *Farewell My Concubine*, Tian also was forced to give up overt formal experimentation. After a few less impressive films in more or less conventional styles, he directed *The Blue Kite* (Lan fengzheng, 1993). A semiautobiographical family saga exposing the brutalities and follies of totalitarian rule in China, *The Blue Kite* became an international hit and aroused the fury of the Chinese authorities. It was banned in China, and Tian himself was prohibited from directing films until 1996.[34] Even after the official prohibition was lifted, Tian imposed a self-ban on film directing until, with a lapse of ten years, he decided to update Fei Mu's *Springtime in a Small Town*.

Fifth Generation filmmaking demonstrated the trajectory of a vigorous, difficult breakthrough at home and the prolonged glory of international adoption before it was spent as a cultural movement. The international fame of the Fifth Generation directors, I would suggest, has given them a burden that forced them to consider how to continue producing worthy films for the international audience while maintaining attractive Chinese cultural characteristics. Their response to this "international burden" and their search for artistic niches occurred as the rise of the Sixth or New Generation directors were changing the cultural map of Chinese filmmaking. The Fifth Generation directors were no longer leading the tide; they were no longer the young rebels but now represented the artistic establishment and the cultural elite. As established individuals, they had to subscribe to, in Raymond Williams's term, a changed "structure of feelings" dominated by emerging young talents. This lent more weight to their international burden. Compared with the subjective, raw feelings of some films by China's new directors, many recent accomplishments of the Fifth Generation directors, such as Zhang Yimou's *Hero* (Yingxiong, 2003) and Chen Kaige's *Together* (He ni zai yiqi, 2002), distinguished themselves more with a kind of artistic classicism. Tian Zhuangzhuang's update of *Springtime in a Small Town* further accentuated this pursuit of classicism.

Many may have wondered why Tian should bother to update a classic that was readily available in China's video market, and his version has an initially disarming similarity to the original. Inspired by Fei Mu and aided by his cinematographer Mark Lee, who had previously worked on Wong Kar-wai's *In the Mood for Love* (Hua yang nianhua, 2000), Tian's update was meticulously shot in an elegant flow of long takes and drifting tracking shots. Following Hou Hsiao-hsien's *Flowers of Shanghai* (Hai shang hua, 1998) from Taiwan and *In the Mood for Love* from Hong Kong, Tian has finally offered the international film community a Mainland version of the culturally specific, artistically mature, and psychologically subtle "mood film." In doing so, he also introduced the Chinese film community's rekindled respect for Fei Mu to the global film community. At international film festivals, such as in Venice and Toronto in 2002, his *Springtime in a Small Town* was received warmly.

A closer look at Tian's update vis-à-vis Fei Mu's original reveals a drastic change. Tian has removed the first-person narrative voice-over by Yuwen and woven his third-person narrative with haunting camera work. This change reflects his artistic classicism; he has used a balanced, conventional, and mature style to replace the most innovative feature of Fei Mu's version. Yuwen's mischievous stream of consciousness in an often whispering, occasionally intoxicated voice is the soul of Fei Mu's original. This voice contrasts the cultivated restraint of the two men and of Yuwen herself. It also conducts the rhythm of the camera takes and movements. Tian has surely replaced some of the virtues of this voice with his sophisticated camera work. Yet, as some reviewers have observed, Tian's more mature style has disappointed some lovers of the original Fifth Generation films. Tian's update, one critic writes, is "measured in its pacing, paying close attention to every detail" but "is an exercise in style with no relevant substance."[35] While supporting my point of the lost vigor in Tian's classicism, this reviewer is perhaps a little too harsh on Tian, who had a cultural as well as personal reason for selecting *Springtime in a Small Town* to update. As Shelly Kraicer accurately noted, Tian's update "takes on the project of reattaching the present to the past by bridging chasms, healing wounds. Ruptures of several kinds mark the film: the gulf in the original story between pre- and post-war China; the vast emotional space between the characters' pre- and post-war selves; the ruined city wall, shown as permeable only by the film's end."[36]

Much contemporary cultural significance can be read into these suggestive, haunting ruptures: pre- and post-Mao, pre- and postsocialism, pre– and post–cultural totality, and so on. Tian's selection indicates transcendence—he has decided to transcend direct political confrontation into a more artistically suggestive, soul-searching consideration of today's China. Political confrontation caused such a rupture in his career as a film director. His self-prohibition from film directing following a brief period of official prohibition contained a protest—if there is much political interference and censorship to keep me from doing the films I want to do, I'd rather not do them at all. Tian lifted his self-imposed ban not by producing another critique of revolution but by conducting a psychological study of the pain of emotional paralysis. He has turned his personal anxiety about the Chinese cultural status quo into a portrayal of confinement, disintegration, and frustration. Tian's transcendence has also led him to come full circle. He has returned to his formal-oriented experiment in filmmaking. The two phases of Tian's formal experiment, nevertheless, have subscribed to different cultural contexts, while his own status has changed from a young rebel to a mature elitist.

X-Roads, as a symbolic locale, suggested that post-Mao city films had moved away from the pre-PRC, leftist urban cinema. Gone was the dominant art form of melodrama, the antiurban critique of cities, the appeal of nonmaterialist ideals, and the inspiring collectivism in the name of a social revolution. Instead, a rich spectrum of artistic styles, a renewed fascination with cities, a justification for materialist pursuits, and an interest in diverse individuals occupied the engineering of a new urban cinema. This new cinema emerged in an era marked by China's opening up to and marching toward the outside world. With the return of a foreign presence in China, after a Maoist respite, the colonial consciousness of today's film artists, interestingly enough, was not as keen. The real and postcolonial conditions, no doubt, are different and have produced different cinematic responses. Leftist film artists of colonial Shanghai were engaged in exposing the ills of colonialism and were drawn by the ideology of social revolution that promised to terminate the colonial condition. In post-Mao China, film artists have been drawn to the myth of marching toward the world, being recognized by the world, and succeeding in the world.

2

Dislocation: Huang Jianxin's Urban Searching for Roots

Urban subjects were not prominent at the onset of the Fifth Generation filmmaking of the 1980s, when various national-culture discourses dominated the scene. These discourses contemplated China's weakness and strength, crisis and hope, roots of the past and routes to the future, and they sought alternative means for national resurrection from the Maoist class-struggle ideology. They brought attention to such films as *Yellow Earth* and *Red Sorghum*, which showcased a rural, often legendary China and were considered cinematic responses to the contemporary "roots searching," a reexamination of Chinese cultural traditions in various fields of the arts and humanities. Clearly, national-culture discourses required an allegorical representation

Dislocation (dir. Huang Jianxin, 1986) serves as an index to the underlying themes in Huang Jianxin's oeuvre. Courtesy of China Film Archive, Beijing.

that could allude to a cultural whole. The landscape and social structures of the countryside met this requirement more easily. The allegorical countryside was also a representational displacement. Although the national-culture discourses were produced in the cities through contemporary political reformers seeking socialist modernization via a commodity economy, the discourses projected cultural anxiety onto obscure, remote times and places.

In expressing this cultural anxiety, film director Huang Jianxin stood out from his contemporaries by insisting on directing films of urban subjects. For those strict about the narrow meaning of the Fifth Generation (i.e., the first post-Mao graduating class from Beijing Film Academy), Huang was not in this generation's inner circle. His résumé showed six years of army service, one year as a cameraman for the medical education bureau at Xi'an, and one year of college training in journalism before he became a script editor at Xi'an Film Studio in 1978. From 1981 to 1983, he apprenticed in film directing by assisting various directors at the studio and quickly got his talent recognized. The studio then sent him to Beijing Film Academy, the Fifth Generation's "cradle," for two years of training as a special student. In 1985 Huang returned to Xi'an Film Studio and, at age thirty-one, was appointed the youngest director there.

By 1985 Fifth Generation directors had already started their cinematic new wave from several other provincial studios, and Xi'an Studio's head, Wu Tianming, would soon invite some of them to Xi'an to continue that wave. Xi'an Studio was promoting the Chinese Western, a new genre that would soon make the studio famous. Huang, however, was not interested in banking on this genre. He set off on a different route and pioneered a wave of city films in the post-Mao cinema.

A self-conscious cultivation of urbanism characterizes Huang Jianxin's cinematic career. His films situate an array of antiheroic characters in various cultural microcosms. The urban settings help highlight allegorical undertones of these characters who, in turn, help define their cosmos with their behaviors. *Black Cannon Incident* (Heipao shijian, 1985), *Dislocation* (Cuowei, 1986), and *Samsara* (Lunhui, 1988) constitute his first trilogy. Here, with a formalist emphasis, the cultural roots are rendered political and represented primarily through unique machine imagery—the bureaucratic "machine" of the Party facing the imported Western "machine" or, in other words, China's political reality facing all kinds of Western influences. Machines mirror and comment on the behaviors of urbanites who were caught in this symbolic confrontation. In his later films, a focus on mannerism replaces machine allegory. *Stand Up, Don't Grovel* (Zhan zhi le, bie pa xia, 1992), *Back to Back, Face to Face* (Bei kao bei, lian dui lian, 1994), and *Signal Left, Turn Right* (Da zuodeng, xiang you zhuan, 1995) became the second trilogy, named by Huang as that of "hundreds of manners in daily life" (rensheng baitai). This trilogy marks Huang's self-proclaimed return from foreign-feeling cities to genuine Chinese cities and from emphasizing alienation to focusing on relationships and communal politics. Starting from this point, Huang started to become more like what a critic observed him as an urban "walker" (*flâneur*): "a figure of perception," "an epic camera" and "the precursor of a particular form of inquiry that seeks to read the history of culture from its public spaces."[1] In a renewed effort to understand China's political culture by focusing on urban communities, Huang also depicted how China's provincial cities were caught in the post-Mao social and cultural metamorphosis and how they were regenerating themselves. Huang's films, in a way, are part and parcel of this regenerating process. They are Huang and his characters walking through the cities to map out a self-perception. The city in these films, in a *flânerie*-production, "is what it is only when it is being walked through."[2] The city testifies to and personifies changes found in everyday life then. After producing the two trilogies, Huang kept engaging with various aspects of urban life and added to his oeuvre such diversified films as *Surveillance* (Maifu, 1996), *Mr. Wu: A Police Story* (Shui bu zhao, 1997), *Something about Secret* (Shuochu nide mimi, 1999), *Marriage Certificate* (Shei shuo wo bu zaihu, 2001), and *Gimme Kudos* (Qiuqiu ni, biaoyang wo, 2005).

In retrospect, however, Huang had to justify his urbanism in light of roots searching. "Cultural roots," he argued, "are found in the present time, and with every one of us.... Everyone's behavior and psyche spell out a culture."[3] His observation indicates how roots searching dominated the scene when the post-Mao new cinema started to emerge during the mid-1980s. Indeed, Huang's earlier films share the same cultural spirit with the roots-searching films set in remote and imaginative rural landscapes. As I will discuss later concerning Huang's use of machine imagery, enclosure and inertia emerge as two important underlying themes. The cultural and political implication of these themes, how tradition can overpower individuals, is easily detectable in many of his contemporary rural roots-searching films. Zhang Yimou's *Raise the Red Lantern*, for example, is an allegorical denouncement of patriarchy, illustrating how women are victimized in a polygamous culture. Here, the theme of enclosure is shown by the interlocking courtyards, the circularity of the seasons, and the repeated performance of the same ritual of getting the women ready for their almost "faceless" master (we never see a close-up or get a clear view of him). The theme of inertia, a customary force that drives individuals, is illustrated by how the master's wives are helplessly engaged in dehumanized competition for the favors of the master. Huang shared the rural roots searchers' concerns. It was only that he did not take their detour of projecting the ideas onto a cultural landscape and life that was different from his own immediate urban reality. The exception was *The Wooden Man's Bride* (Wu Kui, 1993); he directed the film as if to show that he could be as spectacular as any other director of the roots-searching genre in dealing with a legendary landscape.[4]

Huang's case proves that it is possible to talk about roots searching in the cities. If one were to insist that displacement is an indispensable feature of roots searching, the urban roots searchers showcased this feature as well—their use of displacement is achieved through formalism. In the mid-1980s, along with rural roots searching, PRC film critics applauded a group of "grotesque and absurd" films set in the cities. Besides Huang's *Black Cannon Incident* and *Dislocation*, they included such titles as *Masquerade in the City* (Chengshi jiamian wuhui, 1985), *Masks* (Jialian, 1985), *The Visit of the Dead to the Living* (Yige sizhe dui shengzhe de fangwen, 1986). These films illustrated how post-Mao new cinema was responding to such contemporary artistic trends as the theater of the absurd, "murky poetry," experimental fiction, and cubist painting. Formalism allowed these arts what displacement allowed roots searching; it opened a route to break away from the convention, it created room for exploration, and it lent depth for the cultural critique.

Machines and Alienation: The First Trilogy

Promoted to the top managerial position of a company, an engineer is thrown into the unceasing mechanical motion of the bureaucratic machine, which renders him no more than a machine part. Just like that perpetual-motion toy he displays on his desk, he is caught in an endless swing. To break this alienating force, he builds a robot, his exact replica, hoping that it will release him by attending to all his routine duties and meetings. The robot, however, is soon corrupted by bureaucratic power and turns from a replica-functionary into an enthusiastic participant in the bureaucratic system. The engineer now has to destroy his replica with the weird feeling that he is destroying himself. This fear awakens him, and the whole thing turns out to be just a nightmare, yet his perpetual-motion toy swings on as he watches in dismay.

So ends Huang Jianxin's futurist *Dislocation*. Although this film is generally considered his most artificial and thus a less important title, its very formalistic orientation, I suggest, serves as an index to certain underlying themes in Huang's oeuvre. The focal point of the sequence is the unstoppable bureaucratic force that enslaves human beings. To decipher this force, we must take note of the machine analogy. The force is mechanical; it moves on with its own logic and routines and is slow in adjusting to change. The alienating effect of the machines, how they change from the slave to the master of the human being, is also true here. A political machine, or a certain political culture, will render the people involved into its parts. Mechanical motion produces inertia. This part of the analogy explains why certain behavioral patterns of machine-enslaved characters will linger. The circular motion is the most typical mechanical motion. This explains Huang's fascination with such round shapes in *Dislocation* as windows, door handles, and coffee tables. Couches and sofas are also arranged in circles. During one sequence, the engineer walks in circles before he gets into a car, and then the camera closes in on the fast turning wheels of the car. The engineer's favorite toy also swings in a circular motion, making us feel that the engineer and his robot replica, who appear in the film alternately, also form a circular representation of individuals thrown into a motion of inertia. The failure of the robot indicates that a mechanical force can't simply be stopped by its duplication; the engineer's nightmare calls for another force to break the inertia. Circles and rounds indicate enclosure. Anxieties caused by enclosure harbor Huang's critique of China's repressive political order.

Huang established his unique machine imagery with *Black Cannon Incident*, his first film and the one to which *Dislocation* is the sequel. *Black Cannon Incident* is an investigative story set against the installation process of imported mining equipment from Germany fictionally known as WD. Hans Schmidt, the German supervisor for the installation, has just returned to China to finish the project. As he starts working, he notices the absence of Zhao, his Chinese partner during the earlier stages of the work. When he inquires about him, he is puzzled by all the unlikely excuses the Chinese authorities give him. It turns out that Zhao has gotten into trouble because of a mysterious telegram he sent on a stormy night—"Lost Black Cannon. Look 301. Zhao." Zhao is now under secret investigation as to his possible involvement in espionage. His friendship with Hans during the early stages of installation has further strengthened the Party's suspicions. The investigation eventually determines Zhao to be loyal to the Party; he is just a little eccentric and sent the telegram because he valued a lost chess piece (a black cannon), although to the Party boss, this was not worth the price of a telegram. The damage of the political interference to the installation of the WD equipment, however, is already done: since experts like Zhao are kept away, a serious translation error goes undetected, and all the equipment burns down two days after Hans leaves China.

Black Cannon Incident showcases the rivalry of two kinds of machines: the imported machine symbolizing Western science and technology and a totalitarian political machine that interferes in the installation of the former. This rivalry becomes the commanding sublanguage of the film and helps organize what Huang terms as the "dispersed symbolism" (sandian xiangzheng) of this film, that is, symbolism on various levels of an absurd but real story.[5] The rivalry is also coded in color, shown in the contrast of yellow versus white and red. A striking yellow is found in the heavy trucks, workers' helmets, and other machinery involved with the installation. In Chinese culture, yellow is a very noble color with a certain shade of it reserved for emperors only. Since its use in modern Chinese life has been rather uncommon, in this film, it helps indicate an exotic sense of something not only new and enticing but also noble and stable.

Yellow represents the installation work scenes, which are constructive elements; these work scenes almost beg to be governed by the rules of science and technology. Red and white, the dominant colors of Party meetings (e.g., a white table cloth and meeting participants' white shirts) and offices (e.g., the red desktop and red telephones), are associated with the investigation. They are destructive elements in the film. During one sequence, when the equipment burns not long after its installation, the red sedans carrying Party bosses are shown zigzagging in front of yellow trucks—the annoying red color just won't let the yellow color alone even in a time of emergency.

The German engineer Hans reinforces the yellow aspect of the machine imagery with a spirit of science. He insists on proper translation so that the installation will be successful, and he admits a mistake on his part when Zhao leads him to see it. Since much of what he demands from the Chinese authorities is about accurate translation, Hans leads us to see that translation is actually a very important issue raised by the film—it boils down to the question of whether Western machines can be properly installed if the Chinese political machine keeps running unaltered. By emphasizing translation, Huang reactivates a critique of *zhongxue wei ti, xixue wei yong* (to keep

Chinese ideas as the backbone and to borrow Western technology for practical uses), a utilitarian proposal to Chinese modernization that dates back to the late Qing Dynasty when China was on the threshold of a modernity that was being forced from the outside.

The history of modern China has constantly shown the unfeasibility of this proposal. Now, after decades of Chinese closure to the outside world, in the post-Mao era of opening China up, Huang raises the issue again in his film language, indicating that the Party's political system, shown as part of the machine imagery, is not coordinating with the other part of the machine imagery: these two parts can't translate into each other, and their clash leads to the disheartening breakdown of improperly installed foreign machines.

It is in the red and white aspects of the machine imagery that the theme of inertia and enclosure surfaces. The red investigative mode, as seen in the telephones and desktops, of the Party enforces all kinds of distinctions: them and us, foreign and Chinese, non-Party and Party, proletarian factory workers and petit-bourgeois professionals, and so on. As these lines of distinction are drawn, people falling into these categories are enclosed accordingly. In the film, it is not hard for this investigative mode to decide that the engineer Zhao is not completely us; he is Chinese all right, but he also has a suspicious Christian (read as foreign) family background and he speaks German. Once the investigation spotlights Zhao, it quickly pulls him out of the scene, believing that keeping him from working with the German engineer will keep him from committing a possible betrayal of "us." The white conference scenes (table cloths, walls, and shirts) all have the unlikely huge clock as backdrops. The clock hands click on and on to make sure that things are executed in accordance with the investigation. The conferences, in the same manner, are shown to be making circular motions, wasting a lot of time and not making any breakthroughs. The frustration and boredom of some conference attendees is captured by the camera with a few close-ups of the things left behind after the long meeting: a round ashtray filled with cigarette butts and a wheel shape formed on the table cloth with used matchsticks. These are all Huang's cinematic remarks about the waste caused by enclosure.

Black is the color that mediates the above-mentioned two groups of colors. The missing chess piece that triggers off the investigative machine is a black cannon. Zhao starts to wear black when the black-cannon chess piece is returned to the set and the investigation turns out to be futile and destructive. Black is an appropriate, bitter color for the kind of comedy that the chess piece and the black-clothed Zhao induce: all is caused by nothing. When

Hans opens the tin box that is used by Zhao as a substitute for the missing black cannon, he is amused to find that it contains nothing. Yet, is "nothing" the cause of all that has happened? Huang's critique is rather about the containment itself, that is, how people are confined in their particular mode of thinking and how this confinement produces a black comedy.

Zhao, a black horse caught between the two groups of colors, demonstrates a split personality. On the one hand, he embodies the scientific spirit best shown in his fight with Hans for what he believes to be true, and, on the other hand, for a sharp contrast, he chooses not to fight his dismissal from the translation job. His images are both heroic (e.g., his confident look with head up, face forward, and hair swept back in the wind when he rides on a huge yellow earthmover to the scene of the machine burning down) and docile (e.g., his humble smile and puppet-like walk when he is asked by the Party bosses to put on a borrowed Western suit before meeting Hans). While science empowers him, politics disarm him. After all, Zhao has been trained to be a docile subject of the totalitarian political system. Here, we need to make a distinction concerning Zhao's split personality before we can endorse Paul Pickowicz's observation that Zhao is "a late-twentieth-century version of Lu Xun's infamous Ah Q," that is, a Chinese Everyman both showing the worst characteristics of the culture and possessing no vision for a better future.[6] I suggest that it is only the docile part of Zhao that is Ah Q–like; his fighter side as a scientist indicates a potential point of breakthrough for cultural change.

What relates the split personalities of Zhao is his childlike innocence. There are several moments during the film when Zhao is juxtaposed with images of children: for example, when he is greatly disturbed to find his mail has been opened by the Party boss but then finds comfort in the church by listening to music and returning the gaze of a little girl with a smile. "These images of children," as H. C. Li observes, "present an ideal picture of simplicity and innocence [in contrast] to the adult world of anxiety and distrust."[7] Since this innocence may equally support the two aspects of Zhao's personality, Huang leaves his prospect for China's political future ambiguous. The conclusion of the film shows Zhao watching two little kids playing a fun game of setting up bricks like dominoes, knocking them down, and then beginning to set them up again. Although one may come up with many different interpretations of this scene, its implication is certainly not as simple and optimistic as one journalist then believed it to be: "Although China is running into a lot of problems on the path of reform, we will overcome them one after another. If this generation can't complete the task, the next will."⁸ What will make the next generation different? The very mechanical nature of that dominoes-like game of the two kids reminds us that children may grow up who, just like Zhao, love machines but can't do much to change the political "machine," a bureaucratic mechanism, that has rendered them a docile part of it. What will make the next generation different, however, is the critical thinking about this political "machine," and therein lies the importance of Huang's *Black Cannon Incident*.

Samsara is the last of Huang's first trilogy. It depicts, in Huang's own words, "how one's spiritual life loses its base when one changes his ways of pursuing material welfare."⁹ Shi Ba, the descendent of a couple of deceased Party officials, quits his state job to engage in China's early post-Mao capitalist ventures. These ventures lack regulation but do not lack cheating and violence. He loses money and becomes crippled (a gangster, demanding money, wounded his leg with a power drill) but falls in love with a girl who, for him, stands for innocence and purity—qualities that Shi Ba finds missing in his current life. His marriage with her, however, does not pull him out of his boredom. While his wife is pregnant with his baby, he commits suicide by jumping off a high-rise balcony.

In this film, Huang's recurrent themes of inertia and enclosure concern both Shi Ba's ideals and how these ideals are recycled. Herein also lies the clue to the film's title: samsara is a Buddhist concept that refers to the cyclic process in which one passes, upon death, one's soul into the body of another person: Shi Ba inherits his anxiety from his deceased Party-official parents, and he passes it to his baby boy. Although he is depicted as a rebel to conventional thinking and living, Shi Ba's sentiment is still contained in the idealism instilled in him by his parents' generation—the sound track at the beginning and end of the film plays "Song of the Young Pioneers," a tune that reflects the implementation of socialist faith throughout Chinese schools in the Mao era. This sound track frames the film, of course, in an ironic way; Shi Ba's materialist pursuit is a far cry from the missions of the young pioneers. Shi Ba's ideals, however, are not far removed from those of the young pioneers, since they resemble the Mao era's yearning for a utopia.

Starting with Shi Ba, more ambiguous antiheroes step into Huang's cinematic gallery. Shi Ba is a rebel; his constant self-denial is part of his effort to break with his heritage as a descendant of Party officials. In one sequence, Shi Ba and two female companions linger for a chat at Tian'anmen Square, a symbolic place of power and tradition. The girls tease Shi Ba for being a "true man" (zhenren, which can also mean an enlightened Taoist master), leading an unconstrained life; then the three of them make fun of the guards at the square. Here the guards, shot with the Monument to Revolutionary Heroes and the Mao Mausoleum looming in the background, stand for the very restraint that Shi Ba and his friends are trying to break from. The bizarre and chilling quality of the confrontation between these young people and the guards is brought out by the shot/reverse-shot structure done with a low-angle camera; it is especially so at the end of the sequence when the changing of the guards comes in view. A frontal low-angle shot shows three robot-like guards marching toward the camera with giant strides: the robotic movement and stoic expressions of these guards here serves as a visual reminder of Huang's political critique contained in the machine imagery of his two earlier films. What these robots-like soldiers are guarding is what they represent: a system that perpetuates itself mechanically, becomes more and more bureaucratized, and removes itself further and further from reality. The confrontation in this 1988 film presages the real-life 1989 tragedy of massacre at the same location. What one feels with the concluding shot of the sequence, that the giant strides of the guards will trample down any challenge to the totalitarian regime, did happen!

If one emphasizes the link between the two confrontations at the same location, however, one may also have some difficulty deciding which side Shi Ba stands on. A prominent demand of the 1989 student demonstrators was to stop corruption, especially that of descendants of Party officials abusing the power of their parents for huge economic gains. Here one finds Shi Ba, who is presented both as an early entrepreneur and one who benefited from the Party power through economic gains. With Shi Ba, Huang has chosen a special angle to illustrate what he believes to be a painful transition from collective being (qünti ren) to individual being (geti ren), and from political being (zhengzhi ren) to economic being (jingji ren). The drama here lies in the transition of Shi Ba: a self-mocking and tongue-in-cheek hustler who turns serious with love, and an insider with power connections who decides to abstain from corruption. Toward the end of the film, Shi Ba denounces his Party power connections and chooses to make a living in a harder way, which, he believes, will make him worthy of the purity of the young woman he marries. Yet it is exactly at this time that he falls into the dark and suicidal period of his life (indicated by his painting his rooms black). In a way, one may say that his suicide is a protest against the corrupted easy life he gives up. Deep down, one finds that it is the "Song of the Young Pioneers" that is causing the pain. This pain, as I will discuss in chapter 4, is rarely found in the films of the post–Fifth Generation younger directors, where most of the protagonists grow up not singing this song at all. For Shi Ba, the pain is not caused by someone still wanting to be a young pioneer but what the song suggests: a warm sense of belonging and the inspiration of a utopia.

In *Samsara*, this utopian inspiration is translated into, in Eugene Yuejin Wang's words, "the rhetoric of mirror, shadow, and moon"—the rhetoric of a humanistic anxiety denied by social change in an urban setting.[10] The suicide sequence explains the elements of this rhetoric. Shi Ba is disgusted by his own image in the *mirror*. Seeing his *shadow* on the wall through a tipped lamp, he makes an angry gesture of protest. He looks up at the *moon* and then looks down at the city traffic before he decides to kill himself. The quality of the hard-to-reach moon is just like the Utopia of old; it is the nostalgia for a hypothetically purified human condition that is thought to be lost but which is, in reality, only a projected idealization contrasting the awkward status quo of a changed city life. To emphasize the source of the tension, an enclosure within the idealism of the past, the contrast of moon and city, or ideal and reality, is represented not in a confrontation between the individual and society but, more important, as a contradiction between the individual and himself. Shi Ba's internal tension is seen in his constant acts of self-denial: for example, his disgust about his whole life except when he was a naked baby and his final denial of the self, his suicide. The cinematography conveys the subjective quality of this tension in a general change of the film's dominant colors: from orange to red, and then to black.[11] As Shi Ba's feelings change, the orange gradually intensifies into blood red; then a grayish color sets in to pave the way for the black tone—the film ends in despair.

Communal Politics and Fragmentation: The Second Trilogy

After *Samsara* (1988), there was a four-year hiatus in film directing at the height of Huang's career. Then came his films of a different style, informed by his theory that he was in pursuit of genuine Chinese city films by pulling his characters out of the isolation of a fragmented, individualistic mode of living and putting them back into a complex urban communal politics. In an interview, Huang contrasted the differences between Chinese cities and the cities of the industrialist West: "According to the post-modernist concept, China has no genuine cities. Chinese cities are the more commercialized places within an agricultural culture and they embody mostly an agricultural structure of thinking.... The basic characteristics of a [genuine] city should be based on industrialization, about how those highly developed industries will speed up the rhythm of life, about how people are alienated by such a society. China is not there yet. My *Dislocation* shows a possibility of this kind of city. Yet, since it has no such reality [in China] as its base, it can't appeal to the average Chinese but it is better understood abroad."[12] Throughout this interview, Huang indicates his changed perception of "city" and the progression of his city films: his first trilogy pursues an outward resemblance to Western (individualistic, fragmented, and isolated) cities; his second trilogy becomes genuinely Chinese, focusing more on using the behaviors of urbanites to depict the Chinese (communal, agricultural, and intimate) city.

This stylistic change, indeed, is important to our understanding of Huang's cinematic urbanism as a whole. This change, however, tells only one side of the story. His mise-en-scène and cinematic styles may have changed. His general interest may have turned from how individuals fight their sense of alienation to how they navigate societal forces and relationships. Huang's political concerns about how individuals are the products of a particular political culture, nevertheless, remain unchanged. Although his earlier films remind us of Western cities and related Western urban issues, these films deal with very specific Chinese issues. Let us take *Dislocation* as an example. In a surreal sequence, Zhao leaves behind the futuristic city to confront an ancient Taoist saint sitting in the wilderness. The saint, having seen, on TV, the world Zhao comes from, comments on the human folly of overdevelopment. In a way, this film does create an association, as Huang suggests in the above quotation, between how alienated human beings may feel in a materialist culture and how they are baffled by technology and urban development. Yet this interpretation is only superficial. What gets overdeveloped in *Dislocation* is bureaucracy, a political culture rather than a materialist culture. Zhao's nightmare at the beginning of the film shows him wearing a white suit (the conference color of *Black Cannon Incident*), fainting as Party directives are showered on him, and being beheaded by doctors whose wooden expressions and movements make them robot-like (in other words, Zhao loses his head to the bureaucratic mechanism). In a way, the rivalry of machines shown in *Black Cannon Incident* is extended to one between Zhao's robot and the "bureaucratic machine" in this sequel. Since the robot, one kind of machine, won't be able to break the machine-like bureaucracy, Zhao's anxiety about whether the usual Party politics may accommodate the demands of modernization becomes urgent and alarming to the audience.

Inertia and enclosure, persistent themes in Huang's earlier films, continue to connect his changed cinematic styles and city mise-en-scènes. Protagonists of both trilogies show strong behavioral inertia as the result of their enclosure within a certain political culture. Just as *Dislocation*'s futuristic city focuses our attention on the alienating features of bureaucratic politics, the communal cities in the second trilogy focus on how individuals are captives of political and cultural behaviors and how they clash with the changed world in their behavioral inertia.

Stand Up, Don't Grovel (1992), the first of the second trilogy, revisits Shi Ba's early capitalist ventures. Gone is the lonely sense of isolation, the terror of gangster association (which reflects the general fear of business ventures at that time), and the implied idealism (a contrast to the discomfort caused by the business ventures). Gone also is the tragic ending of the film. *Stand Up, Don't Grovel* is set in the neighborhood of an apartment building. "Author Gao," a fiction writer who is addressed so by everyone who knows him, moves into an apartment here only to find that he is caught between the warring relationships of his neighbors on both sides. On the one side lives Zhang Yunwu, a rascal who steals, bullies his neighbors, and has just become rich by doing business in rare fish trading. On the other side lives "Cadre Liu," a Party official who is amazed that a rascal like Zhang can become so rich; he wants to collect evidence of Zhang's possibly illegal endeavors and wishes to make a case against him. With Zhang's growing wealth, people in the neighborhood, especially Gao and Liu, have to learn to hide their disdain for him.

Author Gao, played by the well-known comedian Feng Gong, is the onscreen narrative character; his experiences in the neighborhood become the angle from which we view the film. He observes things around him with, as he says, "a writer's unstoppable curiosity." He is involved but not judgmental. In general, he adds no emotional complication or melodramatic intensity to the confrontation around him, but he has a comedian's sense of having fun with whatever comes his way.

Author Gao represents a drastic change in Huang's narrative stance from that in *Samsara*. It seems that Huang has been assimilated by Wang Shuo, a Beijing-based bad-boy writer whose novella *Emerging from the Sea* (Fuchu haimian) is the literary basis for *Samsara*. Since the mid-1980s, as I also discuss in chapter 4, the popularity of Wang Shuo's writing has lured Chinese film directors into a so-called "Wang Shuo craze"—four films based on Wang Shuo's novellas came out in a few months from late 1988 through mid-1989. The craze offered a space for high culture and pop culture to meet, to influence each other, and to become more alike. Those who started to adapt Wang Shuo, the Fifth generation directors, were mostly participants in what Jing Wang describes as the "high-culture fever" of the mid-1980s. With a strong sense of mission, rational critique, and utopianism, these directors had helped cast an intellectual and artistic trajectory "from humanism to the topos of *fansi* (introspection) and on to their fervent search for 'roots' and simultaneous inquiries into *xiandai yishi* (modern consciousness)."[13] In contrast, Wang Shuo claimed no intellectual heritage but recorded pop culture's jeering at the sense of mission, utopianism, and any intellectual rationality. On a figurative level, he presented *pizi*, or cultural rebels, who were mischievous and playful, and who declared no purpose for their rebellion—the Wang Shuo–esque antiheroes. To make such a character be overcome by boredom and pain and then commit suicide may sound difficult. But this is exactly what Huang did in *Samsara*. He reads into Wang Shuo's concluding, drunken scene of the novella his anxiety about China's loss of credible ideals. In a generally frivolous and light-hearted narration of Shi Ba's love life, Wang Shuo does suggest Shi Ba's anxiety about his lack of "consciousness"—in his dream, Shi Ba's "consciousness" looks at his "body," which drags along through life "like a piece of senseless log." This anxiety, however, is limited to the contrast of the materialist pursuit (shown by the dream scene of coins scattered around Shi Ba's body) and the pursuit of happiness in general. Although the tension has a humanist undertone in denouncing materialism in the novella, it is a far cry from what Huang has taken it to. Through the suicide sequence discussed before, Huang has added a clearly defined purpose to Shi Ba's rebellion.

Whereas Huang tries hard to make a statement with Shi Ba in *Samsara*, he retreats from narrative commitment in *Stand Up, Don't Grovel*, as he says: "turning around, retreating in giant strides, hiding, being tolerant, watching from a distance—all this lends *Stand Up, Don't Grovel* its own features of leisure and tolerance."[14] The film's literary basis, Deng Gang's novella *Neighbors* (Zuoling youshe), is a first-person narrative. In adaptation, Huang makes sure that it is turned into the third person to avoid any direct narrative comments. An important feature of Huang's filmmaking after his long break is that he has become more like Wang Shuo—he has stopped his quarrel with life, has abandoned his formalistic experiments, and has picked up the more humorous approach of laughing at life.

Huang's political concern, however, remains despite his laughing at life. The power of money is something new in China's post-Mao life. In *Stand Up*,

Don't Grovel, various characters' adjustment to this power, by overcoming their old-days habits, is presented humorously. Cadre Liu retains much of the older ways of tight political control. His real power in his working unit is kept off-screen, shown only when people come to visit him with expensive gifts. In the everyday life of the neighborhood, which reflects the contemporary widespread aloofness that ordinary people maintain toward Party politics, Cadre Liu's stiff and patronizing attitude toward his neighbors often appears laughable and out of place. Zhang Yunwu's relationship with Cadre Liu would have been one of cat and mouse a few years before or even now if he held a state job and fell into the range of Cadre Liu's power. Yet this unruly character is now empowered by his newly acquired wealth; even his hired help makes more than Cadre Liu does. It is because Cadre Liu is so irritating that his succumbing to the temptation of Zhang Yunwu's wealth becomes amusing. After Cadre Liu fails to incriminate Zhang, he starts to acknowledge Zhang's wealth by doing business with him. When there is a short supply of feeding fish for Zhang's business and Zhang is paying his neighbors to catch fish for him, Cadre Liu steals the deal from the other neighbors: he secretly arranges that a reservoir will become the sole provider for Zhang while he reaps in the profits from this deal. If the audience is uncomfortable that a character like Zhang Yunwu is becoming so rich, it may equally be uncomfortable with the way that Cadre Liu is cashing in. Cadre Liu testifies to the fact that political power is easily corruptible by the power of money it has helped unleash.

Niu Zhenhua, who plays the rascal-entrepreneur Zhang Yunwu in *Stand Up, Don't Grovel*, also plays the leading role in Huang's next film, *Back to Back, Face to Face*, presenting one more person in Huang's character gallery that the audience will both hate and love. This film tells a bittersweet story about the political ambition, intelligence, calculation, and scheming of a petty cadre who craves the top managerial position of a town's cultural center. Having served as the deputy and acting director of the center for years, Wang Shuangli believes that it is time for him to be the real boss. His family, colleagues, friends, and business partners also believe it. His Party bosses, however, are uncertain about his political reliability. The film shows how a new director is appointed but won't be able to stay in the position for long, falling victim to Wang's constant scheming against him. The succeeding new director, the former administrative aide of Wang's direct Party boss, initially controls Wang. but soon he too falls victim to similar schemes by Wang and his folks. By the end of the film, the director's post is still vacant, yet Wang's political future is still vague. Wang has all along refrained from pocketing bribes in order to be in a better position for political scheming. Now he becomes disheartened and cashes in: by exchanging favors with a doctor, he obtains a fake doctor's certificate about a fake disease of his daughter so that his wife may become pregnant again and his father's hope for a grandson may possibly be fulfilled. The ease with which he solves this problem contrasts with what his father has tried before. His father, a shoemaker and an expert schemer himself, has plotted not just for his son's political future but also for the possibility that the family may avoid China's one-child policy to have a male descendant in addition to the current female one. Having no access to political power, he schemes in a crueler way: feeding his own granddaughter tobacco-laced drinks in order to cause her dumbness (so that the birth of another child will be allowed)!

Like *Black Cannon Incident* and *Dislocation, Back to Back, Face to Face* is a critique of the bureaucracy; this time it investigates the subtle mechanism of the system by focusing on the so-called petty politics and by showcasing Wang as a master of *Guanxi xue*, an art (xue) of manipulating the relationship (guanxi) between objects, forces, and persons. *Guanxi xue*, as Mayfair Yang describes in her book-length study, "involves the exchange of gifts, favors, and banquets; the cultivation of personal relationships and networks of mutual dependence; and the manufacturing of obligation and indebtedness."[15] While this art may be universal wherever there are human interactions, it becomes a dominant social phenomenon in a totalitarian culture where the bureaucracy is all-powerful in regulating almost every aspect of people's lives.

The contemporary Chinese discourse about *guanxi xue*, Yang further illustrates, shows an interesting diversity: whereas the official discourse has a monophonic character of condemning *guanxi xue* politically as a negative social phenomenon because of its corrupting influence, the popular discourse displays multifaceted meanings of and varied attitudes toward *guanxi xue*, ranging from, for example, moral rejection, resentment of the political privileges it involves, reluctant acceptance, admiration of its style of operation, and seeing it as a way of beating the system. "By feeding off of official discourse and twisting it for other ends," Yang writes, "popular discourse illustrates how official corruption and popular practices of *guanxi* are related. Both are, in a sense, 'produced' by the distributive economy, which relies on a bureaucracy of distributors to dispense livelihood and discipline."[16]

The case of Wang vis-à-vis *guanxi xue* is interesting because he is an ambiguous character politically and he is equally resourceful in both the popular and official discourses. To start with, Wang is both an insider and outsider on the political map: he is in power (the insiders' circle) but not totally trusted (has not been fully accepted as an insider). This insider/outsider dichotomy itself is an important issue in *guanxi xue*. The meaning of this distinction and the marked difference of how people behave within this distinction can be traced to the roots of kinship-based agricultural society. In one occasion in the film, Wang has a tough problem on his hands. His center has a vacancy, a prestigious job that many would like to get. The daughter of his direct Party boss, Bingbing, has applied for this job. So have the relatives of many other powerful people of the town. For Wang's best political future, the job should go to Bingbing. As a cover-up, he arranges an exam where a panel will interview all the candidates in front of an audience and then pick Bingbing for the job as if it is because of her talents shown in the exam. However, the day before the scheduled exam, he gets a call from his Party boss saying that Bingbing is sick and will not be able to show up for the exam. Not knowing the real intention of his boss, he decides to save this job for Bingbing anyway. In solving this problem, he shows his superb wisdom both in winning sympathy from his peers and in not offending any of the powerful people involved. He makes a speech in front of the panel he picks, denouncing how many powerful people are abusing their power trying to get his job for their relatives, reminding them that they have no clout to disregard these powerful people, and proposing how they may solve the problem by giving all the candidates the same grade as if by chance. Thus, Wang manipulates both official and popular discourses on *guanxi* and secures himself an advantageous position for his boss's next move, whatever that may be.

To emphasize the continuity of Chinese totalitarian politics, ancient and contemporary, in handling *guanxi* and in scheming, Huang selected an ancient compound of palace-like buildings as the primary setting (the location of the cultural center) for his film. This setting also allowed Huang to express his idea of enclosure; his characters are enclosed in these buildings just as their worldviews are set within the given cultural boundaries. The medium shots of walls and the interlocking roofs of the compound lyrically intersect the film at the turning points of the drama. Within the film, the ancient city walls are also frequently chosen as the backdrop to further strengthen the idea of enclosure.

The last film of the second trilogy, *Signal Left, Turn Right*, is a satirical black comedy set in an army-run driving school and is by far the most disturbing and grim film by Huang. The film is remembered for its tight frames (indicating cramped living situations and tense human relationships), littered mise-en-scène (dust-ridden driving school, decaying back alleys, trash, and deserted roads), and low-key lighting. All these features produce a sense of unpleasantness that must be the feeling of the driving students who are coping with a changed, pluralized, and money-oriented society. The film showcases such tainted ways of living as squandering money, immorality, cheating, bribery, and even illicit drug dealing. It is the story of how this group of drastically different driving students—a new millionaire, a laid-off factory worker, a college student, a drug-addicted slacker, and a journalist—constitute a driving class (the five of them share an army jeep for training) and learn to put up with each other until they all graduate.

Signal Left, Turn Right continues two themes of Huang's filmmaking. First, it illustrates inertia and enclosure; the film generates a striking sense of irony as it contrasts an isolated, out-of-date army management team with a group of students reflecting a much-changed world. Second, the film is a sequel study of *guanxi xue* from *Back to Back, Face to Face*. Niu Zhenhua, who played Wang in that earlier film, carries his mastery of *guanxi xue* into the role of the journalist in this film. The narrative of *Signal Left, Turn Right* is a confrontation between these two themes: *guanxi xue*, as popular improvisations, wrestle with the obsolete monopoly of power. A "newly rich" can buy expensive cars, but he has to go through the discipline process of the driving school to get his driver's license. For a few training classes on the road, he has to bribe the instructor to allow him to ride in his Cadillac and follow the beat-up jeep for training. The instructor stands for the corruption of power. He encourages bribery from his students and allows the journalist to use falsified news writing to cover up his negligence in work. The journalist, who uses his access to public discourse to navigate relationships, often for his personal benefit, shows once again the two-sidedness of *guanxi xue*—it is at once how the old-fashioned political power operates and how the general public survives this political power.

Humor in Disenfranchised Cities: Films beyond the Two Trilogies

Beyond the two trilogies, Huang has continued his self-proclaimed urbanism of communal politics. To understand this emphasis, let us start with Huang's *Mr. Wu: A Police Story* (1997), which, similar to *Back to Back, Face to Face*, uses an old resident compound to hint at communal politics. The compound houses a police station, and the major character has changed from the problematic schemer in *Back to Back, Face to Face* to a good police officer that Huang admires. Resembling a Hollywood narrative pattern of a super policeman achieving his goal by not utilizing the force of the squad, *Mr. Wu: A Police Story* depicts how a top city policeman, Wu Jitang, is sent to a neighborhood police station as a disciplinary punishment, how his police work is constantly handicapped by the jealousy and the petty politics at the local station, and how he both has and has not achieved his goal to be a super policeman. *Mr. Wu: A Police Story* often reminds us of Ning Ying's feature film *On the Beat* (Minjing gushi, 1995), which tells similar stories about a community police station. A comparison of these two films may offer some initial observations about Huang's more recent films.

Both films, through depicting the daily job of the community police, present a changed China. Through constant conference scenes of briefings, one knows for sure that the central control is still in position. The famed communal committees consisting of retired residents, mostly the "Grannies," are still relied on by the police for their daily work. Ning's film shows how such helpers aid the police in locating the residents who keep unlicensed pets. Yet, with the new apartment buildings replacing the older neighborhoods of courtyards, with the rise of the market economy and private ownership, and with a new respect for privacy, the old-fashioned central control is also challenged by a great diversity of lifestyles. Even the police station itself, as Huang's film shows, is disfranchised; it receives less funding from the central government and has to become creative in raising some of its own operating funds. In the market economy, the police are also tempted to abuse their power for monetary gain and to usurp funds, such as the fines they collect. In Huang's film, the police have upgraded their station with materials they have confiscated from private business.

Both the films by Huang and Ning also have a similar narrative structure: a young policeman starting his job at a community police station. The audience observes and learns with this new person. The two films, however, differ in style. Ning's film has a documentary approach and represents a slice of life. Its frequent use of long shots indicates, among other things, the neighborhood as part of the changing landscape of Beijing with imposing skyscrapers sprouting out of stretches of impoverished houses. It follows random episodes of the young policeman's routine job, which do not contribute to a consistent drama. Huang's film, on the other hand, is dramatic, even to the point of being melodramatic. The young policeman is soon involved in the petty politics of the station, part of which is the tension between Wu and his station boss, or the good guy and the bad guy. The good guy cares for the ordinary people, cares for the image of the government through his police work, and wants to be professional instead of political. The bad guy cares more about politics and his interests in them. The film's many tear-jerking moments and its depiction of the chief of the city police, who resembles a "savior" in the conventional class-struggle melodrama of the Cultural Revolutionary era, makes this film an old-fashioned one in Huang's oeuvres.

Although not typical of Huang's general film style, *Mr. Wu: A Police Story* indicates some dilemmas that Huang is confronting. To be sure, Huang has never been a director known for long shots. His urban searching for cultural roots is done through drama, a gallery of characters, and carefully designed mise-en-scènes. His earlier films emphasize mise-en-scènes, upon which hinge such themes as enclosure and inertia. Since the second trilogy, his formalist pursuit has retreated and his mise-en-scènes have become less artificial. Instead, he has become more interested in the narrative structure of the film. As he emphasized in my interview with him in the summer of 2002, most of his more recent films have tight structures and a controlled rhythm. Indeed, Huang's current film art is a far cry from his early, formalist ones of absurdity. Since critics often see Huang's formalism as an indicator of his cultural critique, we have to wonder if he has remained a critic as his general film style has changed.

A brief look at one more aspect of Huang's film style, satirical humor, may help answer this question. Through his later films, Huang has made himself into a humorist. His humor refers both to the term's modern usage—the comic quality causing amusement—and to its classic definition—particular moods, inclinations, or peculiarities (humors) that dominate characters. Among Huang's characters, Wang Shuangli's passion for power, Cadre Liu's peculiarity for putting on airs even at home, Author Gao's craze for stories, Xie Yuting's obsession with the marriage certificate (in a film to be discussed later) are some examples illustrating this classic inclination. In this sense, humor has become Huang's conscious effort since his second trilogy, when he claimed that he intended to present a gallery of "hundreds of manners of daily life."

Lin Yutang's cultural view about humor expressed over half a century before may offer an insights about the mellowing of Huang's humorous sense.[17] For Lin Yutang, humor is an integral part of Chinese culture that transcends, complements, and criticizes mainstream ideas and cultural conventions. He, for example, identifies such diverse people as ancient Lao Zi, Zhuang Zi, and more recently Monkey King as humorists; his humorists are cultural critics.

"To be humorous," Lin writes, "one has to have a detached, spacious mentality, to know the mercy of the Buddha, to 'reduce the fire' in the writing, and to align the reader in the same way. A humorist is cool-minded, a detached onlooker whose laughter is often mixed with tears and whose tears are mixed with laughter."[18] In discussing Huang's *Stand Up, Don't Grovel* above, I commented on Huang's change in narrative stance. The change there actually indicates something more. Establishing himself as a critic of China's political culture from the beginning of his film career, Huang also focused primarily on the political mainstream. In a society with reduced central control and with increasingly plural cultural factors at play, Huang has broadened his scope of scrutiny. He has learned the detachment of an observer that has allowed his humor to bloom.

Huang's other films beyond the two trilogies may further help illustrate him as a humorist. *Surveillance* (1996) is a black-humor depiction of an accidental hero, a factory security guard named Ye Minzhu. Ye has a fun relationship with his girlfriend Bai Lin, who runs a record shop. This relationship, however, is upset by two incidents. First, Ye is assigned by a top detective of the city police to a stakeout: from the top of an abandoned water tower, he and an ailing colleague have to keep a twenty-four-hour watch on an empty house believed to be used by criminals who have murdered a family in the course of a big cash robbery. The city police soon change their plan, but the negligence of a factory bureaucrat leaves Ye's stakeout forgotten. The job consumes the life of Ye's ailing colleague and almost starves Ye to death. In the end, his forgotten post turns out as crucial in cracking the case. Second, his enforced absence from Bai Lin's life coincides with the appearance of a rival: a handsome former boyfriend who wants to whisk her away to Tokyo. Ye wins this battle also by chance; he chooses not to compete.

The comic star Feng Gong, who played Huang's Author Gao, now plays the security guard, carrying his underdog image into a more contemporary film, *A Tree in the House* (Meishi tou zhe le, 1998), which offers an intertextual point of reference. In the later film, Feng Gong created an even more popular image of Zhang Damin, a worker at a state-owned factory. Zhang Damin is from an extended family of the urban poor; six members of the family live under the same roof in a crowded and often explosive environment. Both films run along the same line; they are about the lives of underpaid, state-owned factory employees. The laughter elicited by both films resonates and reflects a very broad social problem in contemporary China, that is, whether society can absorb millions of unemployed or underemployed state workers while many state-owned factories are close to bankruptcy, since they cannot transform themselves to suit the changed economic life in China. The laughter of those whose lives are in crisis is mixed with tears.

Another film by Huang, *Something about a Secret* (1999), depicts the life at the other end of the social spectrum and has a different kind of humor, that is, mismatched psychological motives. The film revolves around an accident that happens when He Liying, a successful CEO of a private company, returns home after volunteering her free time to prepare a class reunion. Friends of this class shared some hard times in the countryside during the Cultural Revolution, but now they do not see each other often. Some have emigrated abroad. To bring the friends closer, the reunion asks each participant to reveal a secret. The accident becomes Liying's new secret: she hits a woman bicyclist and drives away in a panic. Her husband, architect Li Guoqiang, sees the aftermath of the accident from the window of their upscale apartment. The incident shatters the peaceful life in this apartment. Liying tries to hide her guilty conscience. The husband also tries to hide his assumption of his wife's guilt. Their eight-year-old son, in the meantime, develops a secret crush on the daughter of Liying's victim. This girl of his age stands vigil outside Liying's apartment complex holding a sign asking for witnesses to the hit-and-run accident. On the night of the reunion, a friend reveals his secret crush on Liying from the old days. The story he tells about their relationship reflects Liying's high moral standards. Liying arrives late, overhears the story, and is encouraged with what she has finally decided to do, that is, to turn herself in.

The mismatched psychological motives of the three members of the family contribute to a skillful use of suspense. The mise-en-scène and the subject of the film, interestingly enough, are a revisit to those of his early film, *Samsara*. The upscale apartment where Huang showcases subtle psychological exchanges among the three family members resembles the apartment in which he dramatizes Shi Ba's sense of alienation. Both He Liying and Shi Ba are in capitalist ventures, although Huang is suspicious of Shi Ba's earlier, less regulated venture but accepts He Liying's more standardized venture. Huang relate both He Liying and Shi Ba to their similar ideological past of high idealism and social catastrophe (e.g., the Cultural Revolution). In *Samsara*, Huang retrieves this ideological past sarcastically and yet, in *Something about a Secret*, he does it with nostalgia. In this latter film, we see clearly the relationship between idealism, high moral standards, and action for a clean conscience; all these are badly in need when a materialist culture is gaining the upper hand in China. The ambiguous roles played by this ideological past are not hard to detect in contemporary films. While Jiang Wen's *In the Heat of the Sun* (Yangguang canlan de rizi, 1994) presents the influence of the ideological past sarcastically (the main character mixes his sexual drive with his memories of heroes from Russian revolutionary literature), Lu Xuechang's *The Making of Steel* (Zhangda chengren, 1996) calls up this same past nostalgically (the main character, early on, finds a role model from Russian revolutionary literature but finds this role model more and more irrelevant in his later life in a materialist culture). Mixed and ambiguous as these roles are, changes in contemporary life—government corruption, widening gaps between rich and poor, and loss of beliefs—have contributed to an increased nostalgia.

In Huang's most humorous *The Marriage Certificate* (2001), this ideological past dances like a specter in a madhouse, shown figuratively in a mental patient's fixation on a role in a Mao-era revolutionary ballet. *The Marriage Certificate* is a gathering of Huang's comedians. Feng Gong (Author Gao in *Stand Up, Don't Grovel* and security guard in *Surveillance*) and Niu Zhenhua (schemer Wang Shuangli in *Back to Back, Face to Face* and the journalist in *Signal Left, Turn Right*) meet for the first time in a Huang film. Lü Liping, who established her reputation for linguistic humor in the multiepisode TV series *The Editors*, comes to their aid. Even director Feng Xiaogang, whose comedies Huang praises, shows his comedic talent in the minor role of a fake-ID maker. A thirteen-year-old girl, Xiaowen, who writes in her diary about her parents' troubled marriage, narrates this lightly satirical portrait of contemporary Chinese life. Her narration, often coupled with her imagination shown in cartoons, adds to the lightheartedness of the film. The girl's mother, Xie Yuting (Lü Liping), is an engineer and her father, Gu Ming (Feng Gong), is a hospital psychiatrist. One day, Yuting's factory announces that it will award a free blanket to any staff member who has been married more than eighteen years. The applicants must submit their marriage certificate as proof. When Yuting can't find theirs, her initial annoyance soon turns to paranoia as she starts to re-examine every aspect of her marital life. This paranoia, coupled with the appearance of an attractive young aide for her husband at work, ruins the harmony of the family and causes the couple to attempt to divorce. The missing marriage certificate, ironically, also saves their marriage; they can't divorce without it.

Fixation is a cause for humor in this film. Dr. Gu's patients illustrate the classical Freudian definition of fixation: "having been 'fixated' to a particular portion of their past, as though they could not manage to free themselves from it and were for that reason alienated from the present and the future."[19] Xie's identity crisis is also fixation. It brings her and her husband back to their roots—their years of exile to the countryside when their coming of age was inspired by the same ballet her husband's patient now is obsessed with. That era and a much-changed China coexist within them and their relationship. When the couple eventually reconcile at the end of the film, they are found among the dancers of *yangge* (sprout-song dance), an aerobic pastime for retired and close-to-retirement urban residents on many city corners. A contemporary urban spectacle, the art form of *yangge* can be traced back to the labor of the peasants and Mao's promotion of it in the revolutionary capital of Yan'an. In a way, *yangge* in today's China is like the mental patient's ballet dancing in Huang's madhouse in this film; they both demonstrate nostalgia. Their daughter's love for writing is not a Freudian fixation. She is the most resourceful person in the midst of the contradictory cultural influences coexisting in contemporary China. In her creative mind, she invokes Lenin's idea about writing and a Hollywood thriller formula equally; she can conjure up her mother's past in drastically different costumes (a Mao uniform vs. contemporary fashion); and she can both play "cool" and be paranoid at her parents' attempt to divorce. She, as the "author character" on screen, demonstrates that Huang's humor is rejuvenating him as a film director.

Huang Jianxin's oeuvre, in a time span of close to two decades, has marked the trajectory of changing political culture in China. His film style has changed. He has altered his way of engaging with this political culture through his cinematic urbanism. He also has to play additional roles in a changed film industry. Huang has long since moved from the legendary Xi'an Studio to affiliate himself with the prestigious Beijing Studio. The business card he gave me at our interview indicates that he is also the deputy general manager of Century Hero Film (Shiji yingxiong), a private investment company in filmmaking. One of the grand projects of Century Hero Film is its joint venture, with an American company, into a series of art films in the Western genre, set in the Chinese West of Ningxia, presenting loosely related stories of Ming Dynasty swordsmen (daoke). Huang himself actually directed one of these films, *Guanzhong Swordsmen II* (Guanzhong daoke xuji, 2003). With all these changes in his life, Huang has never lost his fascination with China's political culture. In the summer of 2002, sitting in his office at Beijing Film Studio, we chatted little about his private company role but primarily on the topic of Chinese political culture. Before we parted, he told me of a film he had in mind.

The title of this projected film is *Praise*. A young man shows up at the editorial office of a local newspaper, demanding praise of himself in print. He alleges that he has just saved a teenage girl from the attack of a rapist and has been wounded by the rapist's dagger. He cannot provide any witnesses to the incident but insists that he needs to be praised for his valor. The editors dismiss him as a lunatic. In a few days, the young man shows up again and provides the identity of the girl he has allegedly saved. A young reporter is assigned to investigate and is stunned by the beauty of the girl, who nevertheless denies the incident. Since the young man continues to demand recognition, the reporter visits his home in a village. In the reconstructed village with the newly acquired wealth of market economy, there is an eyesore of a decayed house. It is the home of this young man. When the reporter enters the house, numerous award certificates hanging on the wall stun him; the young man's father has been a model villager all his life. It turns out that the old man is dying of cancer and has refused government subsidies for rebuilding his house. The only regret he has at this point of life is that his son is a disappointment—this son has never been praised once. The reporter is touched and starts to investigate the alleged incident again. He interviews many people but still cannot build a case. In the meantime, the old man dies and the reporter is asked to drop the case. But then comes the news that the girl is raped.

The story of this film, Huang believes, will reflect much about the Chinese political culture in an age of transition; the old man is both a respectable and pitiful contrast to a changed world. It took Huang three years to turn the story he told me about into the real film, *Gimme Kudos* (Qiuqiu ni, biaoyang wo, 2005). The film continues to be a humorous one, and it further illustrates the Huang ingredients, as in my discussion of his later films. I can see why Huang is fascinated by this story: political representation and its impact on people's identity and lives still occupy his attention. As a roots searcher, Huang Jianxin insists on digging into the political culture in various urban scenes, and he still has many more insights to offer.

3

No One Cheers: The Later Fifth Generation and the Urban "Situation Movie"

Xia Gang's *No One Cheers* (Wuren hecai, 1993) is a peculiar film. A chamber piece presenting four characters in the enclosed space of an apartment, it focuses on these characters' subtle emotional involvements and changes. Yet, unlike Fei Mu's 1948 classic, *Springtime in a Small Town*, which also features enclosure, the characters' nuances in emotion are less expressed in their refrains here than in their competition at talking. The film is a talk-show (*xiangsheng*) kind of film clearly influenced by the linguistic mischief created by bad-boy writer Wang Shuo. The fun the characters have with their slickness covers their anxieties in life. This style, as we are to see, is true to many films discussed in this chapter.

In *No One Cheers* (dir. Xia Gang, 1993), characters keep on bickering about dilemmas in their everyday lives. Do we want to give them a cheer?
Courtesy of China Film Archive, Beijing.

No One Cheers tells the story of a young couple, Keping, a flute player, and her husband, Mianning, an engineer. In order to keep the family together, Mianning quits his engineering job in a remote town to be with his wife in Beijing. He becomes a doorman at the Palace Museum, where he feels bored, and so he seeks excitement at home in playing electronic games. Keping, disheartened by the doldrums of classical music in a changed China, is irritated by those same doldrums at home. The couple gets divorced but must share their apartment. Mischievously wanting to irritate each other, they both bring home their "new sweethearts": a spinster who admires Mianning's apartment and a nouveau riche boyfriend who has worshipped Keping since they were in high school together. Eventually the four get together in the apartment to chat, and their personal stories get unveiled in a humorous exchange of irritations. In various comic tones, a self-satire of these characters emerges, and in this satire, we detect the awkward status of these characters. They are caught in a time of change and between differing value systems. They are undecided and at a loss in facing the contending demands of family and career, individual and state, high art and popular entertainment, the ideal and the real, the past and the present. This awkward in-between-ness is suggestive of many other films of the time. By the end of the film, we feel the pain of the characters and know them better. Their temporary relationships, nevertheless, have not changed. Neither have their dilemmas. They keep on bickering. The question is, do we want to give them a cheer?

Indigenous Conditions and the Situation Movie

Film critics in China gave Xia Gang a big cheer. In 1994 China's leading film journal, *Dianying yishu*, ran two articles on Xia Gang in the same issue, praising him and his style: his persistence with urban subjects, his minute depiction of emotions, his personal style in a seemingly plain film language, his blending of drama and documentary approach, and his resistance to the elaborate allegories that were bringing Chinese filmmaking international glory.[1] This praise for Xia Gang reflected Chinese film critics' anxiety about the further production of Chinese art films in a drastically changed context: the reduced state role in filmmaking funding, the stepping up of the market mechanism, the importing of foreign films and filmmaking investments, the slump in the domestic film market, and a discovery that certain art films fair well in overseas markets.

Another article, written by Zhang Yiwu, in the same year best explains why film critics were cheering Xia Gang when his films were not receiving the same international recognition as those produced by his former classmates, such as Zhang Yimou and Chen Kaige. Zhang Yiwu is among a group of leading Chinese intellectuals who, as Sheldon Lu observed, "sinicized" postmodernism and pushed it to "the center stage of critical discourse in China"[2]. Equally informed in Western postcolonial cultural theories, Zhang Yiwu identified two splitting drives in the Chinese post-new-era (i.e., post-1989) filmmaking. The first drive, he believed, was shown in the fad of representing an ancient or allegorical China to the international film community so that the backwardness of Oriental culture would have its momentary glory on screen. "These films," Zhang observed, "are not the Hollywood kind. They reflect Chinese art films' special objective in a postcolonial and postmodern context, lured by the myth of 'marching toward the world.' These directors rely less on their guts and talents and more on a concise understanding of the tastes of Western audiences and of film festival referees."[3] Zhang assured us that this kind of art film had a special relationship to the Chinese modernist movement seven decades before, that is, the May Fourth critique of Chinese national characteristics. In this relationship, nevertheless, Zhang detected a fundamental difference: "The 'national allegories' produced by the May Fourth 'modernist' discourse were aimed at promoting 'knowledge' for domestic readers about their own status and thus at changing China. Here, the desire to enlighten the masses and speak for them produces a grand narrative of enlightenment. The introduction of Western discourses reinforces the effort to provide new 'knowledge' to the domestic masses. The contemporary 'art film' in this category no longer is aimed at domestic audiences but rather satisfies Western desire and fantasy."[4]

Although Zhang did not claim this clearly, he had proposed the other drive in contemporary production of art films to have the perspective of agency in a postcolonial condition. In other words, this drive was an indigenous voice that had not bypassed indigenous conditions for the sake of Western acceptance. Using films by Xia Gang and several other directors (Zhang Jianya, Hu Xueyang, and directors of the "new image" movement) as examples, Zhang described this other drive as a production of the "situation movie" (zhuangtai dianying). For him, situation here implies a crisis in representation: the audiences' disappointment with the Fifth Generation art film's international adoption, their lack of interest in other conventional Chinese films, and their amazement with other audio-video impacts—MTV, advertisements, soap operas, karaoke, CDs, and satellite TV. This crisis, he believed, has shocked China as a third-world country in the post–Cold War era. "China's situation and that of many individuals," he wrote, "are dislocated. The representational crisis is that of a cultural relocation and that of a renewed understanding of selves. The situation movie is a complex projection of this condition."[5] Zhang believed that the situation movie might regain the indigenous audience because it had merged with the growing mass and popular cultures in China, which were aloof both to official mainstream ideology and to international acceptance. In this chapter, I have decided to borrow the term *situation movie*, as defined here, to refer to a much broader category of films. The term retains Zhang's insight but is no longer used narrowly to refer only to a small group of films by a few directors.

Xia Gang's success in appealing to the indigenous audience was good but still moderate.[6] When Zhang Yiwu was writing about his hope that the situation movie would regain this audience, Feng Xiaogang, a film director who has been a phenomenal success at the box office, had not yet started to bloom on the scene. Feng, nevertheless, suggested the general direction in which the situation movie has been driven. Feng's work is the epitome of profanity in Chinese filmmaking. If Wang Shuo were not already appearing everywhere in films, Feng's influence on filmmaking would be similar to that of Wang Shuo on Chinese literature: playful, lowbrow, tongue-in-cheek, and profane. Feng first won his audience through several TV series, including *Stories from an Editorial Office* (Bianjibu de gushi, 1992), with his streetwise, Wang Shuo–type antiheroes (frequently starring Ge You). Yet, when he first ventured into the film industry, he encountered many setbacks from censorship for his satirical social commentary. He quickly learned to lighten up by doing comedies with no obvious barbs, and he labeled his films "Happy New Year movies" to better link them with popular expectations for entertainment during the holiday season. In 2000, Columbia Pictures Film Production Asia (CPFPA) approached Feng about doing a film for them,[7] telling Feng that they were impressed by his track record at the box office. Indeed, one of Feng's Happy New Year movies, *Be There or Be Square* (Bujian busan, 1998), had earned 34.9 million yuan ($4.36 million) during the 1998–99-holiday season. Feng turned out to be a good bet for CPFPA; his *Big Shot's Funeral* (Dawan, 2002) earned over 35 million yuan in less than four weeks after release.

Feng's success has vindicated many things. One of interest to us here is the triumph of the profane, or the mundane. The profane has become a common characteristic of the situation movie. The idea for *Big Shot's Funeral* goes back to a chat Feng had with director Chen Kaige over a glass of wine. Chen, as we know, has been the epitome of Chinese highbrow art film. The two were talking about the mass turnout in Tokyo for Kurosawa's funeral and how all the roads were blocked. Chen was touched and impressed. Feng, with his usual comedic demeanor, asked Chen not to envy Kurosawa. "If you trust me," he proposed, "when you reach your 'hundredth year' [i.e., die], I will do one for you. I can't guarantee that it will be grander but I am sure that it will make more money." Later, in Feng's meeting with CPFPA, this "funeral" for Chen Kaige became the idea for the film he proposed to them: an agent (to be played by Ge You) has banked on the death of a famous art film director and turned his funeral into an arena of competing bids from advertisers.[8] The allegorical implications here couldn't be more striking: Feng Xiaogang's enterprise for popular entertainment sold the reputation of Chen Kaige, the namesake of art films, in order to declare the triumph of the market.

The difference between Feng and Chen, nevertheless, is not all about the profane. The profane, often seen as a deviation from the revolutionary grand narrative with an emphasis on everyday life as it is, has become a shared pursuit of both popular entertainment and art films. In an article about the Fifth Generation directors' films in a changing time, Ni Zhen, a professor at Beijing Film Academy who once taught the Fifth Generation directors, was impressed by these art film directors' "yearning for the profane": Chen Kaige did *Together* (He ni zai yiqi), Zhang Yimou did *Happy Times* (Xingfu shiguang), Huo Jianqi did *Life Show* (Shenghuo xiu), and Peng Xiaolian did *Shanghai Women* (Jiazhuang mei ganjue). "They caught the last train," Ni wrote, "left behind the laurels for art films, and merged into a torrent to become filmmakers who better merge with the masses." From his initial wording, one would think that Ni was applauding the disappearance of the art film. Reading him more carefully though, we see that Ni was asking the audience to see these as art films that were no longer claiming to be art films: "yearning for the profane and trying to make a profit have become unavoidable realities for filmmakers. . . . [Some directors in their films] puzzle as to the meaning of life in an ambience of the profane and have mixed refined texts into an overall framework of entertainment. . . . [T]he audience, for sure, will tell the difference between decency and vulgarity, refinement and coarseness."[9] Situation movies, in this light, were cultivating new, audience-friendly arts. To appreciate the situation movie, the audience needs to put aside the conventional binaries of art and glorification on one side of the scale and nonart and the profane on the other. The arts are now permeating all of culture in the name of the profane.

The irony of using Feng Xiaogang to illustrate the general drive of the situation movie lies in the uncertainty as to whether his films can be considered art films at all. In Chinese film circles, there has been an undisguised loathing for Feng Xiaogang, and his films are believed to be nothing but popular soap operas. Feng himself, however, has rather enjoyed his marginal position. He has called the Chinese institution for art films a "Sacred Hall" (*baodian*, i.e., Hall of Fame) and humorously described what has happened to it:

> [The sacred hall is] guarded by professionally trained Third and Fourth generation filmmakers. The Fifth Generation didn't go through the gates of the hall but broke in through the windows. However, these Fourth and Fifth Generation directors have now become guardians of the orthodoxy of the sacred hall of Chinese film since they got inside the hall. The Sixth Generation also took over the sacred hall, though not through either the door or the window but by digging in from underground. When I came, I found that not only could I not get into this sacred hall, which was very heavily guarded; but even if I could, there was no longer any space for me inside. So I decided to build a side room (*er fang*) instead. To my surprise, I found that life in this side room was not bad at all.[10]

The issue here concerns an understanding of artistic orthodoxy and what this orthodoxy was guarding as the essentials of an art film. The rise of the situation movie had emphasized diverse styles and rhetoric. In this search for diversity, however, there remained an unchanging fondness for deeper-level meanings. The art of the profane, as mentioned earlier, is informed by an ideology emphasizing the importance of everyday life. Since this new ideology emerged as a negation of the grand narratives of a bygone era, it necessarily retained some critique of the past, which lent depictions of everyday life various political, social, cultural, or existential concerns, be they overt or covert. It was still hoped that a "slice of life," trivial as it might appear, would have some heuristic value while offering moments of entertainment. Any representation, as Chinese traditional wisdom taught, was a vehicle for carrying the Tao, which could be varyingly interpreted as a depiction of the world as it is, the world according to human understanding, and the world based on human ideals. On this point, Feng's films have generally been seen as paying too much attention to the popular taste of the audience to allow his own artistic perception of everyday life, his Tao, to stand out.

Even Wang Shuo frowned on Feng for his catering to the masses. When asked about their similarities, Wang Shuo said that it was a misunderstanding and he was not as "lowbrow (*xialiu*)." It was at first a little stunning to find that the literary rebel Wang Shuo actually cared about cultural status. But one soon realizes that Wang Shuo meant that a rebel did not need to care about mass appeal. The cup of tea Wang Shuo offered to his reader, as his interviewer paraphrased him, mixed bitterness with sweetness. Feng took his cup over, took out the bitterness, and increased the sweeteners to assure its most popular appeal.[11] Wang Shuo also confirmed that his language retained its barbs because it had its targets. He did not clarify these targets, but one can assume that they include the behavior of China's past or present political regimes and particular cultural forces reflected in the various mannerisms of his characters. "Language without a clear target," he assured us, "would lose its power. This target impresses the reader. When it is there and you speak to it, your words also become striking. But if your target has become the wallets of the masses, those same words will lose all their impact."[12] Although the Tao may appear inappropriate to apply to the writing of the iconoclastic Wang Shuo, what he suggested was really his Tao, that is, how social and cultural concerns will allow a writer to remain a critic.

The emphasis on social and cultural concerns in the search for new art films leads us back to the big cheer that Xia Gang received. In addition to his representative role in the situation movie, Xia Gang belongs to a group of directors who are often referred to as the Later Fifth Generation (hou wudai). The Fifth Generation, as we know, has a narrow meaning referring to only the first post-Mao class of graduates from Beijing Film Academy. In its actual usage, the term has also been broadened to refer both to a cinematic movement of the mid-1980s and a group of directors similar in age, that is, those who were born in the first PRC decade of the 1950s. People of this age group all had diverse experiences while coming of age during the Cultural Revolutionary decade (1966–76), not through regular schooling but through working in the countryside, at a factory, or in an army unit. A group of Fifth Generation directors, in the broad sense, who were not involved or recognized in the initial wave of Fifth Generation filmmaking but who have gained more recognition since the 1990s are often referred to as the Later Fifth Generation. They include such directors as Xia Gang (b. 1953), Zhou Xiaowen (b. 1954), Li Shaohong (b. 1955), Sun Zhou (b. 1954), Peng Xiaolian (b. 1953), Huo Jianqi (b. 1958), Ning Ying (b. 1959), and a few others. Their distinction with the regular Fifth Generation directors is not graduation date so much as time from graduation to having filmmaking opportunities. As compared with the post–Fifth Generation directors, who were born in the late 1960s and the 1970s and who came into filmmaking directly from schools, these Later Fifth Generation directors have more beyond-school experience, have witnessed more cultural changes, have personally lived through social dislocations (e.g., sent down to the country and coming back to the city because of the Cultural Revolution), and possess a broader sense of personal experience of history. While one may often detect traces of nihilism or existential boredom, owing to an alleged lack of social engagement, in the post–Fifth Generation films, such feelings are hard to detect in the Later Fifth Generation films. These directors lived a different China. Before they can fit into a drastically changed China, the Later Fifth Generation directors first have to overcome their own selves and their past. Their personal efforts to adjust make them more sensitive to the millions who are doing the same in today's China so as to catch up or fit in.

The urbanism reflected in the Later Fifth Generation films bears testimony to these directors' sensitivity to social and cultural changes. This sensitivity often implies a representational contrast of the current urbanization with the culture's rural past. Xia Gang, for example, had this to say about his urban characters:

> These characters are urbanites to start with, and they have values, ways of thinking, deep-seated desires and media of expression that are totally different from their ancestors. They are high-IQ creatures growing up with modernized transportation, communication, printing, and media. They have abandoned the narrow-mindedness of the peasants but have yet to lose the plain virtues of the peasants. They fill their minds with wisdom but have yet to say farewell to purity. They are often bothered by their helpless weakness and hypocrisy. They secretly miss the ease of living within the crowd when they pursue individuality. These urbanites are complex. Their lives are filled with chances, traps, choices, dilemmas, pains, embarrassments, hopes, and losses. The metropolis ties them together despite their great diversity. In the ocean of city lives, they drift.[13]

The depiction here, obviously, is both about Xia Gang's characters and the director himself. The artistic niche of the Later Fifth Generation directors is their attentiveness in mediating these dilemmas of social change.

Discourse about the Later Fifth Generation reflected a search by Chinese film criticism for an alternative kind of art film; it has created a space for emphasizing social and cultural concerns in filmmaking. This space gave room for a particular structure of feelings that differed from those found either in the films by the early Fifth Generation directors or those by the younger generations. In this chapter, I will discuss some urban-subject films by a few representative Later Fifth Generation directors to present a spectrum of their concerns.

Xia Gang: Sentiments of Comedians

Like Huang Jianxin, Xia Gang is another major Fifth Generation director who has persisted with urban subjects. His personal life has played a role in his favoring of such subjects. When most of his contemporaries were sent down to the countryside in the late 1960s through early 1970s, he was assigned to work in the city of Beijing, as a street mender. He worked the city streets for years until he enrolled in the first post-Mao class at Beijing Film Academy. Xia Gang's film career started late. Although his student film *We're Still Young* (Women hai nianqing, 1982) was highly praised, Xia Gang's directorial debut came as late as 1988. He did not have the chance, as Chen Kaige did, of finding a provincial studio and thus being able to skip waiting in line for a directorial assignment. Instead, he remained an apprentice and waited at the prestigious Beijing Film Studio. Once started, however, his impressive urban-subject films have continued to pour out: *Passionate Encounter* (Zao yu jiqing, 1990), *My Heart's Not Changed* (Woxin yijiu, 1991), *After Separation* (Da saba, 1992), *No One Cheers* (1993), *To Be with You till Dawn* (Banni dao liming, 1995), *Yesterday's Wine* (Yu wangshi ganbei, also known as Youle suiye, 1996), *Life as a Song* (Shengming ru ge, 1997), *A Country Boy in Shanghai* (Boli shi touming de, 1999), *Who Might be Listening* (Shei lai qingting, 2000), and *Love at First Sight* (Yijian zhongqing, 2002).

Compared with Huang Jianxin's interest in urban political culture, Xia Gang has focused more on the emotional lives of urbanites. In this focus, the influence of Wang Shuo is unmistakable. Xia Gang's films as a whole strike us with *qing* (emotion) and *xie* (humor and satire), both of which are also the trademarks of Wang Shuo's writing. In his discussion of the situation movie, Zhang Yiwu saw the success of "Wang Shuo films" (films based on Wang Shuo's short stories and novellas) in the late 1980s as the fountainhead of this artistic trend.[14] Xia Gang's directorial debut, *Half Flame, Half Brine* (1988), has often been considered the best among the initial group of films reflecting Wang Shuo's impact (four films based on Wang Shuo came out within six months). His *No One Cheers* is also based on a Wang Shuo story of the same title.

Wang Shuo's linguistic mischief has influenced Xia Gang's filmmaking greatly. In the summer of 2002, when I visited Xia Gang at his home, we talked about Wang Shuo's impact on filmmaking. Xia Gang first emphasized Wang Shuo's linguistic impact, indicating that Wang Shuo's tongue-in-cheek style had influenced how a whole generation of Chinese youth wrote and talked. Here, Xia Gang was reflecting on the cultural scenes of the 1980s, and he obviously retained his enthusiasm through doing Wang Shuo films. On this point, Wang Shuo himself expressed a more realistic assessment. He believed that his impact was primarily confined to Beijing and the northern part of the country where Beijing dialect was appreciated. He also believed that his impact was temporary, fading while the spoken Chinese of Hong Kong and Taiwan styles were becoming popular.[15] Culturally, Xia Gang believed Wang Shuo to represent a whole generation of young people who grew up in the Mao era—they had Maoist education during their student days, saw this education shattered midway in their lives, and became painfully uncertain if the truth about living lay in their early education or in their later experiences. Xia Gang suggested that Wang Shuo's linguistic mischief reflected anxieties caused by this uncertainty, and it was directed toward Wang Shuo himself as a writer: Wang Shuo was helpless when he saw something beautiful (i.e., ideals) being destroyed; the only thing he could do was to laugh at himself; and Wang Shuo was courageous to make a fool of himself.

Xia Gang's interpretation of Wang Shuo has a distinctive Later Fifth Generation approach, that is, it relates the Wang Shuo–esque self-mockery to a certain identity crisis that accounts for the post-Mao social and cultural changes. It assigns self-mockery an important role in the cultural reflexivity prevalent in the immediately post-Mao China. Self-mockery, part of *xie* (humor and satire) in works by both Wang Shuo and Xia Gang, becomes an important element that keeps the representation of *qing* (emotion) from being sentimental. To me, the best of Xia Gang's films are those in which *qing* and *xie* strike a balance. When they do not, for instance in *Yesterday's Wine* (a film about a teenage girl's emotional attachment to a middle-aged male neighbor), the film becomes sentimental.

Xia Gang's role in the so-called "Wang Shuo fever" (that heated, enthusiastic interest in Wang Shuo) in the late 1980s, in the sense of catching the trend, was purely a coincidence. As an artist, Xia was openly antitrend. He did not even want to become rational about his subjects and characters. For his focus on the emotional life of urbanites, he claimed that he only wanted to relive those unforgettable conditions with his filmmaking but leave all other analysis to the critics. "No art work," he explained, "can be created without being involved in the emotions. I don't like to treat the city I love as an object without life and give it an anatomy, even if it is a most scientific sociological anatomy. I am not willing to force my beloved characters into categories, not even if that may contribute to a seemingly profound social analysis. I also don't call for a simple signifying contrast of the old urban cultures versus the new metropolis in exchange for certain commercial benefits [of selling the films]."[16] Xia Gang's remarks here reflected his artistic fondness for emotion. Different from those for whom conventional, deep-rooted intellectual distrust of emotion was seen as irrational, Xia actually assigned to emotion great cognitive and representational values. His approach to emotion coincides with one credible aspect of emotion that Stephanie Shields describes as "speaking from the heart." As Shields explains, it is "the expressive identification of emotion in everyday life with its 'felt' quality, the sense that emotion is a 'vivid, unforgettable condition which is different from the ordinary condition' in which one finds oneself."[17] Emotions, in this sense, are heightened moments in life that contain rich suggestions of a host of related experiences and conditions. These suggestions invite the sensual ("felt") sharing of the audience but will not be easily exhausted by a rational analysis.

Xia Gang's "felt" approach to emotion characterizes his filmmaking. In the recent development of Chinese film art, Xia Gang has been an advocate for enrichment. Just as he does not want to approach emotions rationally, he also does not want to be restricted by an overt consciousness of any one particular filmmaking style. In his depiction of emotions, he wants to remain resourceful to any style appropriate to his subjects. In an article, Xia Gang wrote, "For my films, I don't close the door on any film techniques. I don't confine myself to a certain theory, trend, or anything before I shoot a film. [I hated to see that] when the 'divorce' between film and play was proposed, all characters became profoundly silent—not uttering a word even when it was needed and dragging the film into confusion. [I also hated to see that] when the long shot was proposed, cuts disappeared and the camera just kept rolling. All this was not about shooting films but about making sure that the films could be talked about easily."[18] Xia has never been noted as a representative of a certain artistic trend, but eventually he was praised for his personal style of concealment—concealing various artistic approaches in his films so naturally that they become barely noticeable.[19] Here, let me use Xia's *After Separation* (1992) and *Love at First Sight* (2002) to illustrate his felt approach and the roles of *qing* and *xie* in this approach.

After Separation is a *When Harry Met Sally* kind of movie. It is about love between two seemingly incompatible characters. The subject of the film is *qing*, that is, the sentiments (love, sense of desertion, loneliness, anxiety, longing, and so on) of spouses left behind by those involved in the contemporary tide of going abroad to pursue education and new lives. The subject, however, is wrapped in a comic cynicism that becomes the film's undertone. The film starts and ends at an airport. After seeing his wife off to Canada, Gu Yan is entrusted with a woman, who has fainted, by her young husband, also heading to Canada. At the hospital, Gu learns that the young woman, named Lin Zhouyun, has lost her pregnancy due to this extreme stress. Owing to this special encounter and their similar situations, Gu and Lin become acquainted. Their obvious difference, Gu's cynicism about migration and Lin's hopefulness about starting a new life abroad, soon alienate them. A year passes. They bump into each other on the street. Learning that Lin is soon to leave for Canada as well, Gu suggests that he host a few days of celebration. The two of them enjoy sightseeing and restaurants together and bid each other farewell. Another year passes. On the eve of the Chinese New Year, Gu and Lin meet unexpectedly at the metropolitan post office[20] where they have both failed to reach their spouses on the phone. It turns out that Lin did not get a visa when she planned to leave the year before. To overcome their loneliness, felt so strongly during the holiday season, Gu suggests that they "play" at being "husband and wife" for a few days to reexperience the warmth of family life. After a few days of role-playing, Lin becomes used to Gu's cynicism. A sense of loss dawns on them when they part, and they decide that they should keep playing this game for all the following holidays. Soon, however, Lin secures a visa to join her husband in Canada and Gu receives divorce papers sent to him by his wife from Canada. In the airport, Lin becomes hesitant as to whether to leave for a new life in Canada or to stay to start a new life with Gu; she even pretends to have lost her passport, by slipping it into Gu's pocket, to delay her trip. When the plane takes off, the film ends with suspense as to whether Lin has left or has stayed.

The difference between Gu and Lin, their respective cynicism and innocence, reflects a narrative pattern in Wang Shuo's love stories. Their roles resemble the "initiator" and "helper" in the traditional Beijing-based comic talk show (*xiangsheng*) in that Gu acts funny to initiate laughter, while Lin keeps an innocent demeanor to contrast the initiator's wit. Keeping this pattern unchanged in his film based on Wang Shuo, Xia Gang focuses on creating a further dichotomy between *qing* and *xie* in the central comedic character, that is, Gu played by Ge You. Instead of always having a helper character to mark Gu's cynicism, *qing* becomes this helper. When Gu enthusiastically intrudes on his best friend's honeymoon, for example, his longing for family life is revealed. This same longing also accompanies his humorous proposal to Lin about playing at being a family. For Gu, *xie* is a mask behind which he may hide his *qing*.

The important element of *xie*, for Gu, is his linguistic mischief. As Xia Gang suggested, this element of *xie* is related to a sense of dislocation and an identity crisis. For this film, the central issue is about people leaving for foreign countries. On this issue, many elements play together to dislocate a character like Gu: the dismissal of Maoist ideology in China as the center of the world revolution, the liberating influences of Chinese travel abroad on a once-closed China, and a postcolonial condition of widespread worship of anything that is foreign, to name just a few. Gu has mixed feelings about being left behind in China, and his cynical remarks about this issue may move anywhere among the above-mentioned elements. On one occasion, Gu suggests eating at a foreign restaurant to bid Lin farewell as she prepares to leave for Canada. They go into a Japanese restaurant. "You will soon have to work in a restaurant to serve foreigners," Gu explains to Lin. "Let them serve you once so that you may balance out your feelings later." Gu does a lot of this balancing game psychologically. His stories about the difficulty of life of Chinese students abroad often sound like "sour grapes." His suggestion to Lin that she should mention Norman Bethune to the Canadian council sarcastically juxtaposes Maoist China, when a Canadian doctor came to China to help with the anti-Japanese war, and post-Mao China, when thousands of Chinese were moving to Canada for new lives. In the Japanese restaurant, however, the table is turned on Gu: an all-Japanese menu and a Chinese waitress speaking Japanese fool him. When Gu laughs awkwardly, we see that his lack of knowledge about foreign countries, as well as changes in his own country, have in effect pulled his leg.

A contemporary film on the same subject of couples being separated by spouses going abroad, by post–Fifth Generation director Hu Xueyang, merits a brief comparison. *The Stay-Behind Wife* (Liushou nüshi, 1991) was Hu's directorial debut at Shanghai studio. The film has a different, lyrical style but tells a strikingly similar story of the friendship between a left-behind wife and a left-behind husband: Nai Qing, whose husband is studying in the United States, falls in love with Jia Dong, a taxi driver whose wife works in Japan. Attentive to minute emotional changes, Hu's film gives the central woman much more depth of character and actually has a more sophisticated understanding of overseas Chinese and their emotional status. Isolation and loneliness are represented as common problems not only among the spouses left behind but of the Chinese abroad. When Nai Qing discovers her husband's affair with a married, rich, and neglected (her husband is constantly on business trips) woman in the States, she soon learns to see herself (her own emotional experiences of being left alone and her nurturing friendship with another man) in that woman. She decides to join her husband in the States even if that means she has to face the challenge of that woman.

The Stay-Behind Wife depicts emotions but does not aim to be romantic. Toward the end of the film, Hu invokes a typical Hollywood romantic scenario for an antiromantic conclusion to the film. In the first snow of the year, Nai Qing remembers that she and Jia Dong once talked about meeting at a particular bridge in Shanghai on that occasion. She goes there, and the film builds up an expectation of high romance. If Jia Dong shows up, the film may end happily. Jia Dong, however, does not show up. He does not forget what they said about meeting at the first snowfall, but his wife, who is back home for a visit, keeps him from going. A perfect romance is marred by Jia Dong's momentary sympathy for his wife, and he never learns why Nai Qing finally decides to join her husband in the United States. Although Hu's film is well directed and has such a sophisticated approach to subtle emotions, it still frequently strikes the viewers as sentimental. Obviously, Hu's film is not a comedy and it lacks the elements of *xie* that have kept sentimentality from emerging in Xia Gang's films. What this further leads us to see is the different speech styles between the two films. While the Wang Shuo–esque *xie* in Xia Gang's films brings its dialogue close to the daily language of the street, Hu Xueyang's film dialogue often sounds bookish and artificial. In Hu's film, Nai Qing's way of talking in particular retains a linguistic artificiality that was typical of many standard studio films of the early 1980s.

Xia Gang's "felt" approach to emotion has kept him young: his *Love at First Sight* invokes youthful feelings and experiences so well that one may easily mistake it for a film directed by a much younger post–Fifth Generation director. Filled with fun and mischief, the film presents a mystery faced by a young man, a handsome computer programmer named Lao Bu. One night Lao Bu encounters a young woman and ends up spending the night with her. The young woman disappears the next morning, but Lao Bu is already infatuated by the encounter, believing it to be "love at first sight." He vows not to let this woman slip out of his life as quickly as she slipped in. He starts his search, involving three of his male friends at his computer company and a curious newspaper reporter. The chance encounter Lao Bu has had with the mysterious woman turns out to be a joke for revenge that this woman has plotted with three of her female friends. These young women, all professional, independent, and single, do not have much trust in men and marriage. When they learned that Lao Bu had dumped a friend of theirs, they decide to teach him a lesson, that a man needs to be faithful and that the taste of being "dumped" is bitter.

Lao Bu, nevertheless, shows an unprecedented faithfulness to the one-night encounter with the woman, whose name he finds out later is Jiujiu (meaning "everlasting"). Although the search gradually unveils the encounter as a joke, Lao Bu still maintains an unwavering faithfulness to what he felt that night. His stubbornness, which is constantly jeered at by all those assisting in his search, eventually turns from funny to touching. The three male colleagues, who befriend three of Jiujiu's female friends in order to conduct counter-revenge, all start to become serious about their new friendships with these women. The curious newspaper reporter also realizes, in the process of this search, that her photographer, who has been so persistent in courting her, has a genuine love for her; she is finally moved to respond. Needless to say, Jiujiu is also touched. The film concludes with a typical Chinese theatrical *da tuanyuan* ending (happy reunions of all involved).

Qing and *xie*, emotion and playfulness, interact to make *Love at First Sight* interesting. Although the film is about *qing*, the narrative is filled with *xie*—in the characterizations, dialogue, drama, and cinematography. Lao Bu's *qing* is joked about throughout. When the journalist decides to set up a hotline for the search for the mysterious woman, the number is misprinted, turning out to be that of a pay phone in front of a public "pay toilet."[21] With a funny scene of her working seriously at the entrance to this restroom on a city square, the comic tone of the search is set. The revelation of the mysterious night when Lao Bu and Jiujiu encountered each other is also presented humorously. In a sequence shot as a fairy tale—involving such elements as fanciful colors, graceful rhythm, mischievous gestures, and striking shadows—the ladies who plot against Lao Bu are presented as nymphs. When *qing* wins toward the end of the film, it is not as much a human effort as "the will of God." God finds his messenger in a clownish, middle-aged company boss who is not experienced with women and who is blind to love (in several scenes he wears sunglasses indoors to hint at this limitation). God's message makes everyone see love and find true love at the end of the film. *Qing* may have won in the story, but the lingering memory of the film is that of *xie*.

The emotional approach of *Love at First Sight* leads Xia Gang into the sensual world of today's youth. Xia's background is evident in the film's mediation between the past and present, between the "old-fashioned" faithfulness to love and the prevailing attitude among the young of "following your momentary feelings" (gen zhe ganjue zou). Yet, just as *qing* can win only with the help of *xie*, the film's mediation has also become overshadowed by its showcasing of the lifestyles of the young. Mixed in the lingering memory of *xie* in the film are the memories of a lifestyle: the ways these characters dress, talk, work, or enjoy leisure; their hairstyles and makeup; their emphasis on individuality or personality; their taste and their playfulness in doing things.

Xia Gang's showcasing of a lifestyle creates a cinematic correspondence with a contemporary fad for "petit-bourgeois literature" (xiaozi wenxue). In a preface to a two-volume anthology containing literary works and critical essays of this literary trend, Ge Hongbing comments on *xiaozi* (petit bourgeois) as a lifestyle:

> Our life has never been so *xiaozi* as it is now.... *Xiaozi* is a lifestyle that is vague, warm, relaxed, content, and joyful.... [It is a lifestyle] with its individuality lost in the fashions and vogues.... The descriptive colors for *xiaozi* are pink, light blue, or light green, whereas red has been the symbol of violent revolutions.
>
> *Xiaozi* consists of a desire that, to a great degree, is produced by certain trends of consumption. This desire, nevertheless, is conservative and introverted. In the metropolis, this desire is turned by *xiaozi* into commodities, which are its regulated and socially sanctioned channels of circulation, and this desire is thus safe and may never lead to disaster.[22]

Ge's approach to *xiaozi* is much the same as that of the Later Fifth Generation directors to their subjects—alert to social change and attentive to historical context. As a scholar, Ge relates *xiaozi* with the collapse of revolutionary ideology, with a certain psychological status, and with the consumer culture of today's metropolis. Not treating it as a subculture isolated in the educated, white-collar urban youth, he regards *xiaozi* as the prevailing feature of today's urban life of the masses: materialistic, everyday, and profane.

It is exactly in this light that Xia Gang has showcased *xiaozi* in *Love at First Sight*. He used the interplay of *qing* and *xie* to keep the less mass-oriented elements of *xiaozi* writing—such as sentimentality, decadence, loneliness, narcissism, and pain—from emerging. The thematic conclusion of the film itself, the triumph of faithfulness to love, is also a deviation from the typical *xiaozi* writers. A critic of *xiaozi* writers, for example, believes that the prevailing theme in most *xiaozi* writing is not faithfulness to love but "love that forever fails": "Vanity triggered by narcissism and the extreme fear caused by possible failure all reduce the courage of *xiaozi* to love.... If love is not short-lived because of the alleged emission of hormones and if love is a relatively long-term relationship between sexes that needs to be obtained through effort, love implies the courage for happiness that is based on sexual attraction and sacrifice. This courage is what is missing with our *xiaozi* friends."[23] With *Love at First Sight*, Xia mixes the old and the new, the other and the self, the faithfulness and the playfulness. In joyful ways, he lends his *xiaozi* protagonist, Lao Bu, what *xiaozi* is most missing—courage and persistence. In doing so, Xia has made the *xiaozi* lifestyle a cultural product for mass entertainment.

Peng Xiaolian: Women in Exile

As most of her contemporaries did, female director and fiction writer Peng Xiaolian had worked in the countryside for nine years before she enrolled in the first post-Mao class at the directing department of Beijing Film Academy in 1978. Upon graduation in 1982, she was assigned to work at Shanghai Film Studio, where she had to do minor chores and wait in line for a turn to direct. In the late 1980s and early 1990s, Peng had a study sojourn on film in New York. Among Peng's films, two feminist features, *Three Women* (Nüren de gushi, 1989) and *Shanghai Women* (Jiazhuang mei ganjue, 2002), stand out as corresponding to each other. The two films are both about women "in exile" from their normal lives, which enlightens their understanding of themselves. There is more than a decade between the two films, and the subject has also turned from the rural to the urban. But the underlying message in both—women's self-empowerment through self-understanding and independence—has not changed. In an interview in 1989, Peng talked about her disgust with the common cultural expectations for women: "Chinese men are very strange. When it comes to work, they think you have to be like a man to do the job; otherwise they despise you. But when it comes to getting a wife, they all say, 'I don't want some superwoman! A woman should be like a woman.' I don't believe the traditional weak image of Chinese women is what women are. I can't stand that. I don't think there's anything beautiful about that at all."[24] Peng's comment was made about *Three Women*, but it still rings true for the more recent *Shanghai Women*; they both illustrate the beauty of weak women becoming strong. Stylistically, the two films also correspond to each other in their plain style, which resembles that of a documentary film. In contrast to Peng's other films produced in-between, such as *Dog Fight* (Quan sha, 1996) and *Shanghai Chronicle* (Shanghai jishi, 1998), the two features on women refrained from cuts, unusual camera angles, and camera motions. *Shanghai Women*'s return to the style of *Three Women*, as Peng herself puts it, was an effort to avoid the influence of commercial films and "to return to something plain and honest."[25]

Three Women uses Peng's own script, based on her observations of and insights into women in the countryside.[26] The film depicts three countrywomen, during the time of the post-Mao economic reform, venturing into the city to sell yarn. In their own poverty-stricken village, they are nobody. Jinxiang, for instance, has been forced to marry a mute in an "exchange marriage," a common local custom arranging two marriages between two families concurrently so that the marriage costs for both families involved are cancelled out. In this particular exchange, Jinxiang carries little weight; the reason for her marriage is that her brother needs to get married to carry on the family line and the right woman for her brother happens to be the sister of the mute. In essence, she is the payment for her brother's marriage. Unwilling to settle into the forced marriage and hearing the other two women's unusual travel plans, she runs away to join them at the last minute. The city and the market economy empower the three of them. They learn to interact with all sorts of people on their own and to forge a sisterhood in their urban adventure away from the village. Their new life lends them a broadened horizon, new values, changed economic status, and self-confidence. When they finally return to the village, they've learned to take their own initiative: they are ready to go to court to pull Jinxiang out of the unfair marriage arrangement.

A haunting parody of the three women's journey of self-discovery in the film is a desperate countrywoman's escape from her village, with no money and no belongings, to give birth to a baby that is not allowed to be born there because of the birth quota. This woman has given birth to girls only and is despised in her village. The three women chance upon her a few times and eventually see her miserable success—haggard but joyously holding a baby boy, ready to make her way home. From their own experience, the three women know this refugee's status in her village is going to change. Success of this kind, nonetheless, only serves to confirm the injustice done to women in the Chinese countryside.

Three Women depicts how two different generations of women (one middle-aged and two younger) differ in their reception of new things and eventually come closer to each other in their process of empowerment; they've all learned that they need first to respect themselves and not to gain this respect through pleasing others, be they husband, sons, or loved ones. *Shanghai Women* further focuses on the communication between generations of women by foregrounding mother-daughter relationships. The script of the film is derived from the composition of a high school student, assuring its perception of a minor in these relationships. Ah Xia, a teenage girl, experiences emotional and physical exile when she moves with her mother, who divorces because her husband is repeatedly unfaithful and refuses to stop. The teenaged girl's sense of security, belonging, and love is greatly challenged as she follows her mother in moving back to live with the grandmother, then into a new household with the mother's remarriage, back to the grandmother's again when the mother's remarriage turns sour, and eventually, with a better mutual understanding between the mother and the daughter, into an apartment of their own.

The empowerment of mother and daughter in *Shanghai Women* comes from an earlier maturity, or sense of femininity, achieved by a minor through family catastrophe. It was this sense of femininity that impressed Peng and made her select the composition as the basis of her film script; she felt that she gained a new understanding of the condition of today's young people and she wanted to emphasize the importance of communication between the generations to ensure the welfare of women and minors in today's urban life.[27] In the film, the mother is depicted as a traditional woman who thinks, first of all, of others. So that her daughter won't be hurt by the loss of a normal family, she forgoes her own happiness and marries someone she does not like. And she keeps denying herself in order to maintain this family. When this "normal" family crumbles with another divorce, she is even willing to resume the marriage with her former husband, who has shown no signs of regret, so that her daughter may still have a presentable place of belonging. The grandmother also endorses this sacrifice. "Being a woman is not easy," she says. "Almost every man has an affair; women must learn to put up with this." The mother being a weak woman has taught the daughter a lesson. Although she has suffered emotional turmoil with the family changes, she eventually realizes, and makes it known to her mother, that they need to challenge the conventional ideal of a normal family and that their own dignity and independence are more important than their vanity about having a normal family.

Li Shaohong: Threats of Materialism

Li Shaohong, another female director, had nine years' service in the army before she became classmates with Peng Xiaolian at Beijing Film Academy. Along with classmate Xia Gang, she waited in line for her chance to direct films at the prestigious Beijing Film Studio. During her film career, she has collaborated with her cinematographer husband, Zeng Nianping, for all the films she has directed.[28] Those films cover diverse subjects: *The Silver Snake Murder* (Yinshe mousha an, 1988), her directorial debut, is a detective/suspense film; *Bloody Dawn* (Xuese qingchen, 1990) showcases cultural violence in a snowbound north China village; *Family Portrait* (Sishi buhuo, 1992) depicts the sense of dislocation of a middle-aged man in modern urban life; *Blush* (Hong fen, 1994) examines sexual politics against the backdrop of prostitution reform in the early years of the People's Republic of China; *Happiness Ave.* (Xingfu dajie, 1998) depicts the life of a working-class family in Beijing; and *Baober in Love* (Lianai zhong de Baobei, 2004) explores the importance of culture and emotional life in urbanization. Interestingly enough, as in the case of Peng Xiaolian discussed earlier, two of Li Shaohong's films, one rural, one urban, and with over a decade in between, also echo each other in theme. This theme, anxiety about the dominance of materialism, demonstrates the director's consistent cultural contemplation and testifies to the Later Fifth Generation's sensitivity to social change in today's China.

Li Shaohong is a unique cultural critic. In her 1990 feature *Bloody Dawn*, she reactivated concerns of the early-twentieth-century cultural critique, such as Lu Xun's anxiety about the devouring nature of Chinese traditional culture—how the vitality of individuals is swallowed up by the apathy, or numbness, of the culturally orthodox. The film is a parody of *Chronicle of Death Foretold*, a novel by Gabriel Garcia Márquez. Roughly following the plot of the Colombian novel, the film portrays a Chinese murder case. A rich carpenter discovers that his bride is not a virgin and returns her to her mother's home. Her two brothers, humiliated by the loss of their family honor, decide to murder the man responsible. One of the brothers has an even more concrete reason for his anger; he will not get his promised bride in the two families' agreement to exchange brides. A schoolteacher, the only one who can read and write in the village, is thought to be the man. The two brothers publicize their intent to murder the teacher but receive no interference from the villagers as they hope for. The villagers sympathize with the carpenter's loss of honor and abhor the education of the teacher, which sets him apart. To them, the carpenter is a respectable person who has earned his wealth and the teacher is a suspicious person with weird behaviors such as writing obscure poems and reading filthy film journals. With such a public sanction, the two brothers cannot help but murder the teacher in front of numerous witnesses.

Bloody Dawn depicts a blind worship of materialism and the villagers' inability to appreciate education, the humanities, and a knowledge of the outside world. By contrasting the villagers' respect for the rich carpenter with the schoolteacher's alienation from them, Li expresses her abhorrence of the ignorance that dominates village life. "Because of ignorance," Li explained, "the entire village, the collective of villagers is the murderer."[29] Li's film, in this sense, becomes a cultural critique. She admits that *Bloody Dawn* is concerned less about drama and more about the collective, society, and history.[30] The film is a product of a time when national culture discourses dominated the intellectual scene and allegorical cultural critique dominated Fifth Generation filmmaking. Studying *Bloody Dawn* in detail, Tonglin Lu noticed how this feature broke away from the early Fifth Generation filmmaking's "pattern of nostalgic portrayal of the countryside" by focusing on the cultural violence "existing in contemporary China in the process of moving toward a market economy."[31] Indeed, *Bloody Dawn* was not like, for example, Zhang Yimou's *Red Sorghum*, which portrayed the folk life of an allegorical countryside with admiration. The nostalgic portrayal of this kind suggested what was missing in the cultural status quo. If *Bloody Dawn* differed from *Red Sorghum*, it was not so different from such contemporary Fourth Generation films as Hu Bingliu's *Country People* or Wu Tianming's *Old Well*. In these films, the closure and backwardness of the countryside were portrayed to show China's need for opening up and for progress. These two different portrayals of the countryside, nostalgic and critical, were equally informed by the national culture discourses of the 1980s. They were either rehearsing the humanist ideals of the discourses in an allegorical landscape or scrutinizing the cultural conditions in a realistic locale. *Bloody Dawn* shows that Li Shaohong was more inclined to the Fourth Generation influence of critical portrayal of the countryside.

The urban-and-rural contrast in such Fourth Generation portrayals of the countryside, as discussed in chapter 1, is not associated with real Chinese cities or any cultural changes of China's post-Mao urbanization. City in this contrast functions primarily as a symbol for such pure ideals as civilization, progress, and open-mindedness. In *Bloody Dawn*, the schoolteacher's association with the urban youth who stayed in the village during the Cultural Revolution has caused his alienation. City is the source of a contrast between knowledge and ignorance, and between open-mindedness and the closed-door resistance to the outside world. Yet when Li Shaohong and many Fourth Generation directors turned to directing films with urban subjects, the city became a reality to them and it could no longer carry the symbolic role of contrasting with the cultural backwaters of the countryside. Li Shaohong's *Baober in Love* best illustrates this point.

Baober in Love uses post-Mao urbanization as its backdrop. In an interview, Li says that she "battled for years on how to convey the feeling that the world we are living in is changing so fast, that things are broken, and that we are struggling to adjust ourselves to this time."[32] "Who would have imagined that we now live by the slogan 'spend money and enjoy life'?" she asks. "As we move rapidly toward development, we should also take care of our world's spirit [soul]. That's what I want to express in this film."[33] Obviously, Li has carried the same anxiety about the dominance of materialism forward from *Bloody Dawn* to *Baober in Love*, from a sleepy village to the fast-changing metropolis.

Baober in Love is less a linear story than a psychological adventure. The story starts with the impact of urbanization on the young child Baober—with a special effect of spinning motion on screen, the alleys of old Beijing are suddenly transformed into today's massive blocks of high-rise buildings and the young child Baober, who spins with the transformation on-screen, screams in confusion. With this spinning transformation, Baober has grown into a young woman living in the modern metropolis. She, nevertheless, searches persistently for the childhood dreams and memories that were lost in the spinning. In this search she befriends a retired literature professor, a lonely person who lives with a huge collection of literary classics. When Baober expresses her admiration for him, the professor falls from the ladder while reaching for books and dies. His falling and the falling of many books from the shelves are shown in another spinning motion on-screen resembling that of the transformation of the cityscape. Urbanization and the collapse of a literary treasure house—its values, tastes, and aesthetics—are juxtaposed. Both changes have traumatized Baober; she clearly behaves like someone who has "freaked out."

Watching a videotape that she picks up off the street, Baober is happy to have found her alter ego. The tape shows a young man confessing how his married, routine, and well-to-do upper-middle-class life bores him. He regrets that his childhood dreams of flying, shown in his collection of toy planes, are not encouraged by his current life. His name is Liu Zhi. Baober is also bored with her life, and she also dreams of flying. Baober tracks Liu Zhi down, causes his wife to kick him out of their penthouse, and makes him fall for her. By now, the camera work has been purposefully erratic, with a mixture of unusual settings, camera angles, lighting, sound, and motion. The audience gradually gets the sense that they are watching many sequences through the fractured point of view of Baober herself. The film has a unique narrative structure: it first freely explores Baober's inner world in a surrealist manner, then informs the audience that Baober is mentally ill, and eventually—when Baober's fanciful worldviews and dreams have inspired Liu Zhi—turns to a grim realism by showing Liu Zhi's failure to bring Baober back to sanity. The film ends with Baober's suicide.

The transition from fanciful surrealism to grim realism is clear when Liu Zhi and Baober decide to settle down in a deserted factory warehouse. Baober loves the emptiness of the huge space, but Liu Zhi insists on remodeling. When Liu Zhi goes ahead to transform the space into living quarters with modern amenities, Baober visualizes the spinning motion of urbanization that has traumatized her before. This is the third time the spinning motion is used in the film. After this point, Baober loses her sanity gradually until she takes her life. The narration of the film, accordingly, retreats from using Baober's point-of-view shots to an objective observation of her insanity.

Baober wants to fly to reach a certain beauty that is free from the materialist world. This beauty, as the film presents it, is elusive and fragile. Baober's childhood, the nonmaterialist, Maoist China, does not seem to have much to offer to this beauty either. Baober's parents hide the fact of human reproduction from her by telling her that she was found in a garbage dump. The film focuses on the effects of how Baober grows up with this lie. She sees beauty in trash. When she first has sex with Liu Zhi, they do it literally in a trash dump that they fall into accidentally; playing hide-and-seek on the top of a building under construction, they slip and fall through an opening used for trash disposal. Although colorful lighting and slow-motion camera work have transformed the trash dump into a crystal palace, it is still a trash dump. Later in the film, before Baober slips into total insanity, we find a sequence with a revealing contrast. It is a most romantic scene of Baober and Liu Zhi making love by the ocean, with the moon rising in the background. Yet the color is cold, the lighting is low, and the effect is chilling. While glorifying romantic love, the film is uncertain whether Baober and Liu Zhi can really reach their ideal beauty of love. Then the film crosscuts to a sunlit beach with loud Maoist music. The child Baober is with her mother and many of her mother's friends. The adults are talking about all kinds of lies they've told their children to disguise the facts of human reproduction. Here the color is bright, the lighting key is high, but a close-range camera purposefully distorts the shapes of all the humans to convey an unpleasant sense. These effects, an indication of Baober's traumatized mind, also point out that the denial of many beautiful things in life has already started in Maoist puritan China. In other words, from the allegorical sense, the death of the literature professor in the film, the collapse of a treasure house that supplies people with diversified senses of beauty,[34] is not caused only by the recent worship of material comfort in urbanization. Romantic love, for example, had long ago been pushed out of everyday life in Maoist China, and that is why Baober has so much difficulty finding it.

In addition to the death of the literature professor, the major allegory of the film is the death of Baober. Here the allegory is twofold. First, Baober is conceived of, in Li Shaohong's words, as the lost soul in today's "overly materialistic, commercialized, 'modern' world."[35] Baober is a marginalized character in the film's showcasing of a contrasting world of luxury and poverty, the new rich and the forgotten. The luxuries of the new urbanites are portrayed with a towering effect. Liu Zhi and his former wife's penthouse (which claims such amenities as transparent stairways, a toilet that flushes to produce the sounds of ocean tides, and a bathroom that has a beachlike floor) overlooks the city. Many of Liu Zhi's earlier gatherings with friends are at the rooftop bars of high-rises. He is often shown urinating in a rooftop bathroom with urinals set against a transparent wall that overlooks the skyline of the city—he pees at the city, he plays with the city, and he enjoys all that the city has to offer. These sequences are shot in warm colors and light. They reflect dreams and reality for many urbanites.

In contrast, Baober finds her ease of mind with other people, the literature professor and a disabled kid in a wheelchair. They allow us to see the drabness of their surroundings, shot by the camera with the colors grayed out. These people have been left out of the new urbanization drive for prosperity. The gym where the disabled kid plays basketball is shabby, and the dust-covered house of the literature professor is decaying. Baober is shown as a kindred spirit to these people. Her inability to connect the two contrasting worlds, her inability to handle the changes caused by drastic urbanization, and her eventual suicide all chill the film.

Secondly, the allegory comments on Liu Zhi's need for love while riding high with urban development. Liu Zhi and his buddy are shown to be love-crazed; they chase girls all the time. "I wish I could be struck by love on the street," Liu Zhi confesses, "and be knocked down." Yet, as Li Shaohong suggests, Liu Zhi confuses his romantic love for Baober with his love for "modernization" and loses her to insanity and suicide when he builds her a modern home.[36] "As we passionately embrace this modern life," Li Shaohong ponders, "what has become of our souls? . . . Like Baober, our spirits have been abandoned."[37]

Baober in Love is by far the most avant-garde film in Li Shaohong's oeuvre. Packed with effects, this film has been described as a work of magical realism, a surrealist fantasy, a roller-coaster ride of fantasy, a fantasy treat that turns darker, and a surrealism that concludes in a grim realism.[38] To adopt the term *magical realism*, a style that uses fanciful material to heighten the intensity of its realistic portrayal of social and political issues, shows that critics again are reminded of the influence of Gabriel Garcia Márquez on Li Shaohong. While *Bloody Dawn* borrowed themes and its plot from Garcia Márquez, *Baober in Love* took on the Colombian novelist's style. With *Baober in Love*, Li Shaohong veered away drastically from her usual style. This film, as Richard James Havis wrote in Berlin, "is the most adventurous film to come from one of China's Fifth Generation directors in a long time."[39] In a way, Li Shaohong broke one of the patterns of Fifth Generation filmmaking, whose general trajectory had long been a turn from experimentalism to classicism—the careers of Chen Kaige, Tian Zhuangzhuang, and Huang Jianxin all testify to it. These young cultural rebels all had their filmmaking breakthroughs with formalist orientations, but when they matured and when the situation of Chinese filmmaking was changing, they all gave up such obvious formal experiments. *Baober in Love* broke this trend and, in doing so, also reactivated the impact of a cultural critique that was strongly felt at the onset of Fifth Generation filmmaking.

The time, however, has changed, and Li Shaohong's stylistic experiment itself now rides on the tides of globalization and market operations. In contrast to the earlier Fifth Generation's low-budget experiments, Li's *Baober in Love* is the most expensive stylistic experiment in Chinese filmmaking ever. Finishing postproduction in France, Li's initial budget for special effects was $1.5 million; however, Li was intrigued by what the French artists could offer and ended up spending over $5 million. (One scene alone, the spinning that shows the magical transformation from old Beijing to new Beijing, and from child Baober to adult Baober, cost $130,000. But Li loved it.[40]) To denounce the dominance of materialism, one has to spend money to attract attention. Market mechanisms also helped the distribution of *Baober in Love*, which offered an interesting case as to how an experimental film can fare much better in a free market than in a centrally controlled distribution system. In the 1980s, Tian Zhuangzhuang's experimental films just could not sell—the audience and the state-monopolized distribution system mutually stalled the film.[41] In 2004 *Baober in Love* had its first-run showing across the country on Valentine's weekend. *China Daily* reporter Zhu Lingyong writes,

> Along with the roses, chocolates, and sweet words, Valentine's weekend crowds in China this year got a surprise in movie theatres, as Li Shaohong's new film *Baober in Love* began its first-run showing across the country.
>
> Thanks to media bombardment and intensive publicity hype, young moviegoers swarmed into cinemas expecting to see a typical "just-for-lovers" film filled with relaxing light-hearted romance, sparkling chemistry, and silly-sweet comedy.
>
> However, many viewers were bewildered by what they saw, and some were even angered.[42]

This reporter further recorded many different opinions of the audience on this film. Although this Valentine's weekend event made viewers feel cheated, Chinese customers nowadays are so accustomed to being cheated that more people surely will watch this film so as to have their own opinion about the hot dispute. In effect, the film was not stalled but got attention. Its first-three-day nationwide box-office revenues reached ten million yuan ($1.2 million US).

Huo Jianqi: Bridging Past and Present

Huo Jianqi graduated from Beijing Film Academy in 1982 as an art designer. He worked as art director on numerous films, including Tian Zhuangzhuang's experimental *Horse Thief*, before he made his own directorial debut in 1995. Huo's earlier films often strike the viewer as conventional. His *Postmen in the Mountains* (Na shan, na ren, na gou, 1998), which won awards in China and overseas,[43] is reminiscent of a government-sponsored political education. A son succeeds his father as postman in a rural, mountainous area in southern China. On a "coaching" tour of the route that the son and the father take together, the son learns to appreciate the job and his father, who has been distant from the son owing to his constant absence from home. Although there are fine pastoral touches, subtle emotional portrayal, and a proselike style, plus the excellent performance of Teng Ruijun in the role of the father,[44] the film still evokes too many prototypes of conventional role models: self-sacrifice, the relationship with one's roots, appreciation of a seemingly unimportant job, and the importance of not complaining.

Huo's recent films on urban subjects have helped erase this conventional impression. His *Blue Love* (Lanse aiqing, 2000) is a stylish depiction of an unusual love affair experienced by an unconventional police detective (he's too fashionable to look like a cop). Huo's *Life Show* (Shenghuo xiu, 2002) presents a tastefully dressed young woman who runs a stand at a food court where she has no lack of admirers. Both films are noted for their evolved suspense and drama, minute emotional portrayal, subtly manipulated camera placement, and well-controlled rhythm. Huo has matured greatly as a film director. To contribute to the Later Fifth Generation art, what Huo did in these two films was bridge the past and the present. Both films are subtle in their artistic negotiation between, on the one hand, older values and ways of life and, on the other, the new styles in a changed world.

Blue Love uses a contemporary love story to retrieve a love tragedy of the past. Tailin, the police detective, thinks that he is stopping a girl from jumping off a high-rise bridge but instead she tells him that he has interfered with her experiment in "behavior art." The girl, Liu Yun, is a stage actress who needs to experiment on people's responses to her unusual behaviors to seek inspiration for an experimental play she is performing. A friendship starts between the two while Liu Yun still experiments with her unusual behaviors. Liu Yun's playfulness makes her relationship with Tailin interesting. Tailin becomes more involved when a more challenging incident occurs. Liu Yun asks Tailin to help her find a person known as "White Horse." She believes that White Horse has had a lot to do with her mother's loss of sanity. Upon checking, Tailin finds that White Horse has been on the most-wanted list of the city police for over twenty years: the uttering of his name was recorded at the scene of the homicide of a city policeman, but absolutely nothing more is known about him. Tailin is asked, against his will, to investigate the case without Liu Yun's knowledge.

White Horse turns out to be Liu Yun's real father. Over twenty years ago, he was in love with Liu Yun's mother, who was then working in the countryside. Unable to arrange her return back to the city, the mother's family arranged for her to marry a city policeman who could assure her return. White Horse and Liu Yun's mother were heartbroken and made love when they knew they had to accept their fate. Years later at a public bath, White Horse chanced to come across the policeman, who was spying on an underground gang. Not knowing the policeman was on duty, White Horse quarreled with him and revealed his official identity, which caused his murder. With the emotional strain of helping White Horse run away from the city and of hiding the truth, Liu Yun's mother lost her sanity.

Liu Yun eventually becomes aware of Tailin's detective work concerning White Horse. When White Horse is arrested, Liu Yun returns to the bridge where Tailin had stopped her from jumping at the beginning of the film. With crowds of people looking on, Tailin confesses his love for Liu Yun and tells her the pain that finding White Horse has caused him. Liu Yun jumps, with a rope that has been hidden from all the onlookers. Tailin jumps after her into the water only to find that Liu Yun is swinging gracefully in the sky right above him.

The contrast between the love stories of the two generations is as distinctive as they can be. They illustrate what David Chaney described as a change from "ways of life" to "lifestyles," which I discussed in the introductory chapter.[45] The older generation's love story in *Blue Love* reflects a prototype of many way-of-life love stories of the past: individuals clash with stable institutions—be they a social norm or a family arrangement—and sacrifice their lives to the passion that they are faithful to. Although these tragedies in love often serve as critiques of the undesirable aspects of the culture, they also testify to the often insurmountable difficulties that these helpless characters have to face to deviate from the shared ways of lives.

China's opening up in a sense, as the film shows, is the older way of life being shattered by a new lifestyle (the masses' access to consumption and leisure). People of the younger generation are given much more room in their pursuit of love. Befitting the allegory of the film, there are no easy norms but only endless experiments (as Liu Yun's experiments for her play) for the younger generations in these pursuits. Love, especially love as detective Tailin and actress Liu Yun experience it, is no longer the prey of stable institutions but the catalyst for social change. Whoever can be more creative, whoever can better express his or her individuality, and whoever can make room for love in a profession is given the credit for defining the new lifestyle. Reminding us of the exploration of the father-and-son relationship in *Postmen in the Mountains*, detective Tailin in *Blue Love* also lives with his father and has succeeded him in his profession (played again by Teng Ruijun). The father in this more recent film, however, plays a much less defining role of indoctrination. The search for a new style, instead, has become the guiding spirit.

Deep down, we must admit that the younger generation's creation of style is not done in a void. We can easily trace many aspects of the new style in *Blue Love*—such as the protagonists' hairstyles, clothing, ways of talking, carefree manners, or professionalism—to foreign influences. These sources may help us see the hybrid nature, the pastiche, as it were, of the new styles. This, however, does not affect the inspiration the younger generation feels in their "freer" creation of love.

Whereas *Blue Love* focuses more on the liberating effects of the new style, another Huo film, *Life Show*, allows the past to weigh heavily on the new style. Shuangyang, the main female character, played by Tao Hong, owns a small food stand that has only one employee. She is stylish—she chooses to live as a single woman, dresses fashionably, and smokes in a stylish manner. While she is faring well in the new business world of private entrepreneurship with her shrewdness and while she nourishes her sense of independence with her new lifestyle, she also has to deal with many things that come to her from the past. She has to play mother to a younger brother since their mother passed away young. The role becomes especially challenging because this artistic younger brother gets addicted to drugs and she has to help him to give them up and start a new life. She has to deal with the older type of bureaucracy to reclaim the housing benefit entitled to her from her retired and remarried father. This job is important, since her economic endeavors are not yet sufficient enough for her to purchase housing. She has to guard her own style of life from exploitive relatives who take advantage of her love for children and use her frequently as a babysitter. The only time she can put aside all these demands is when she sits down at the counter of her food stand for a cigarette. She totally enjoys this moment of being herself, and she often gets lost in an elegant posture of oblivion. This posture, however, also makes her the object of admiration of a self-made rich man, a customer known as Mr. Zhang. Having frequented Shuangyang's food stand for over two years, Mr. Zhang makes his admiration known to her.

Life Show uses Mr. Zhang's silent gaze at Shuangyang at her food stand as a narrative lead-in to gradually reveal all of life's demands on this stylish woman. The film forces us to see the real-life elements hidden under her façade of being stylish. Throughout the film, Shuangyang is encouraged by Mr. Zhang's gaze. She wants to turn him from an admirer of her appearance to a real partner in life. Toward the end of the film, however, she fails and discovers sadly that Mr. Zhang is only drawn by her appearance, is willing to give her some money, but wants to commit himself no further with her than casual sex. She rejects him. Call it old-fashioned, but Shuangyang finds the rejection essential to maintaining her style of life, which, after all, is based on the dignity of independence. *Life Show* starts with a meaningful over-the-shoulder shot of Shuangyang entering her restaurant from the kitchen. In this shot, the camera placement invites the audience to feel Shuangyang's enthusiasm for getting on the stage of life. The film ends with Shuangyang retreating into another smoking oblivion, when an art student stops by to ask her permission to do her portrait. Between her action and her oblivion, Shuangyang showcases the difficulty of a single woman braving her everyday life.

Ning Ying: Cinema Verité and the City of Beijing

When her classmates at Beijing Film Academy were leading the tides of Fifth Generation filmmaking, Ning Ying was studying in Italy. She was admitted to the Centro Sperimentale de Cinematografia in Italy in 1982 and was assistant director to Bernardo Bertolucci in the making of *The Last Emperor* (1987). When Ning Ying returned to China and had her own directorial debut, *Someone Loves Just Me* (1991), she was not eager to catch the tide. Ning Ying's Italian experience has lent her works a flavor different from most of her Fifth Generation classmates; she is less interested in allegorical or epic grandeur and more fond of a documentary approach to everyday life.[46] Her major films, informally referred to as a trilogy about three generations of Beijing natives, have reaffirmed her style of cinema verité. *For Fun* (Zhao le, 1992) is a bittersweet tale of a group of retirees setting up their amateur Peking opera troupe, played primarily by nonprofessional actors. *On the Beat* (Mingjing gushi, 1995) again uses exclusively nonprofessional actors. Instead, a group of police officers at a Beijing local branch play themselves in their everyday life. *I Love Beijing* (Xiari nuan yangyang, 2001) is the story of a Beijing taxi driver. The Chinese title is, literally, *A Warm Summer*; the film follows a taxi driver's fanatic search for love during one particular summer. Our feeling while watching this film, nevertheless, is anything but warm—the warmth of human closeness appears to have been severely damaged by changes that the market economy has brought to Beijing's everyday life. *I love Beijing* is played by lesser-known actors. The actor who plays the taxi driver recalled how Ning Ying set a high standard of performance for them. In a few scenes, they had to do ten to twenty takes so that these professional actors could finally reach "the level of seeming like a nonprofessional actor, totally natural."[47]

For us, *On the Beat* and *I Love Beijing* are good illustrations of Ning Ying's cinematic style and her engagement with the urban culture of Beijing. Both films have unique angles of cutting into the fibers of Beijing's everyday life, and both touch on a wide spectrum of social and cultural change.

On the Beat brings the audience into the cinematic world with a bicycle ride; Yang Guoli (played by a cop of the same name), a senior officer, brings a recruit back to the branch and shows him the area of their governance on the way. Later on, how Yang teaches this recruit everyday police work, a few glimpses of Yang's private life, and a punishment he receives at the end of the film for beating a person lend the film a loose narrative shape. The training lessons Yang manages to pull together, obviously, have not been successful—boredom and fecklessness are shown to dominate everyday police work. The film shows that police work in China at that time was still not clearly regulated. The role of a policeman then fell between an enforcer of laws and a surveillant of community life. In dealing with the violation of certain regulations, police still relied on older ways of political (though they called it legal) education. They often felt that to let violators pay a fine and go was a humiliation to them—"who wants your stinking money? You have to show regret!" In a way, to use Foucault's phrase, the police wanted to see people become docile subjects of the power they instituted.

To suggest the random and chancy nature of police work, and to ridicule its bureaucratic mechanism, the dog becomes a parallel thread of narration in *On the Beat*. The story is set in the Chinese year of the dog, 1994. Tipped off by a phone call, over a dozen police officers of the branch searched for, chased, and then killed a possibly rabid dog. The dog's rabies was confirmed, and the police started to receive routine shots by doctors at their political study sessions—their bodies and minds received treatment at the same time. An award was given to the branch. Compared with the chaotic sequence of casual behavior in chasing and killing the dog, the formalness of the award ceremony appears funny. The elaborate publicity of the award, it turns out, also served another purpose. With the rabid dog as an excuse, the police tightened control on city dogs. To rid their neighborhood of dogs, Yang's branch left many families heartbroken about their pets. Eventually, a dog-owning factory manager refuses to allow his dog to be taken away from his factory. He wants only to pay the fine. He is brought in at night. In a long process of mutual irritation, he badmouths Yang and Yang beats him in return. A minor act of civil disobedience thus irritates the policeman until he is out of the control. Yang's brutal act is punished with an administrative measure. Dogs thus have brought this police branch honor and humiliation at the beginning and the end of the film.

A very affecting scene in *On the Beat* is a lingering overhead shot of a back-alley neighborhood in the city of Beijing (the area of governance of Yang's branch); but, as the camera pans up, the modern buildings of a much changed Beijing fill the screen. With this camera work, Ning suggests that the police work that her film has recorded may soon be wiped out as the older neighborhoods are being torn down. A modern Beijing is rapidly replacing the older city. When Yang and the recruit are riding their bicycles in the neighborhood, gigantic earthmovers shot at a low angle are shown passing them by. Social and cultural changes are also challenging the conventional social and moral surveillance of police work. A peddler they bring in, for example, insists that the nude paintings he sells are not erotic but works of art. The neighborhood team of grannies, a most distinctive Maoist-era feature of residential control that police in this film still rely on, has also been proven to be passé.

I Love Beijing is about a newly emerged social class on the Chinese urban scene—taxi drivers. Anyone who has visited China has had a few words, or a long chat, with them. A driver may be a city kid fresh to the profession, or more likely he'll be a farmer finding a new life in the city or an unemployed state worker finding a new means of supporting his family. Years back who would have imagined that a country known for its bicycle-dominated urban traffic (healthy, economic, and environmentally friendly) would decide to keep its urban population mobile with taxis, and millions of them! Nowadays, most of the Chinese metropolises are like the Manhattan area of New York City—finding a taxi anywhere, anytime is no problem at all. Taxi drivers bear testimony to the drastic urbanization in post-Mao China. Their stories hinge on city traffic, which also reflects cultural and demographic traffic happening simultaneously in Chinese cities. Ning Ying's *I Love Beijing*, a taxi driver's story, is one such story of real and implied traffic in the city. It is an early film on this subject that will surely be followed by many others.

I Love Beijing opens with traffic. It ponders on how traffic suggests patterns of urban culture and how traffic reflects the nature of city life. The opening sequence presents kaleidoscope views: traffic at intersections is shot at different times of the day, from different angles, with different camera ranges, and using different camera speeds. Just as a few pieces of tinted glass, in a confined space with reflections, seem to offer endless patterns of beauty, vehicles in these street intersections have achieved a similar effect. Through this kaleidoscope, we first detect a suggestion of urban everyday life—in the same locale, random and chancy elements will formulate endless patterns of daily activity. Mobility, otherness (people in traffic are often strangers), and coincidence are crucial to this way of life. Through the kaleidoscope, we also detect the nature of the life of the protagonist of the film, Dezi, a taxi driver who moves randomly along the city roads and has opportunistic contacts—which he often hopes to turn into romance—with his clients. He not only makes a living as a taxi driver but also searches for his personal happiness, his emotional life, and a mate.

The narration of *I Love Beijing* assumes an emotive structure, following the emotional experiences of Dezi. The film starts with Dezi posing for wedding portraits with his fiancée, a plain-looking country girl from Henan, a less-developed province whose rural folks populate the service sectors of China's major metropolis and have become second-rate citizens there. The film then flashes back to when Dezi filed for divorce from his first wife, a city girl. Dezi works irregular hours so as to be financially afloat. He keeps his wife well provided for but can spend very little time with her. Divorce soon becomes unavoidable. Single again, Dezi's attraction to girls becomes legitimate. Dezi, as a journalist describes him, becomes "a taxi-driving Don Quixote on his four-wheeled, metered Rocinante, as he pathetically pursues amour."[48] He flirts with girls to make his days happy, and he keeps his eyes open for the right girls to go steady with. He even becomes the friend of a university student after a casual encounter. One of his dates, a country girl working in a restaurant, is undoubtedly pretty. Their relationship, however, soon turns sour when Dezi realizes that his apartment in the city has virtually been turned into the first stop for this girl's relatives to start out from in the city.

The impact of *I Love Beijing* lies less in drama than in the subtle editing of the contrasting experiences of Dezi and his clients. In the film, Dezi's search for pleasure with girls is paralleled by the same search by China's new rich. While Dezi still hopes for friendship to grow out of his casual encounters with girls, the rich people at many ugly Beijing nightclub scenes, where Dezi drives his clients, show no respect for women and they openly display the power of money. An escort girl, for example, is forced to drink numerous bottles of beer to amuse her clients until she collapses. Dezi, feeling in the same rank as the girl in front of the rich people, is sympathetic and offers to take her home. Later in the film, at a high-society gathering where his client brings Dezi, he comes across the same girl, now married to a foreigner—she has achieved the goal of making it that she took on as an escort. The gathering of high society, featuring a mixture of foreigners and China's elite, is presented as a surreal experience for Dezi. He is obviously dazed, finally gets totally intoxicated with the free drinks, and is thrown out into the street. The following sequence shows Dezi driving down Beijing streets with an equally intoxicated girl who hops into his taxi while Dezi is sitting at the wheel trying to regain some sobriety. The sequence is shot as a contrast to the previous one; it is dimly lit in a cold, sobering bluish tone. The beat-up streets and old buildings mixed with construction sites are recorded by a hand-held camera moving with the taxi. It often purposefully shows the modern, neon-lit buildings as the backdrop. The sequence, on the one hand, serves as an emotional unwinding of Dezi from his daze at the gathering. It also, by cinematic contrast, suggests China's uneven development and polarization of the rich and the poor. Dezi, a character from a low social stratum, has a job that often gets him caught in this polarization.

Ning Ying's documentary style of naturalism satirically edits life's own sharp contrasts together. Dezi's mother, for example, must be played by a Beijing native woman of the lower social stratum. The way she talks, her manner, and her protection of her son in the fight of the young, divorcing couple are unmistakably reflective of Beijing's back-alley life. On the other end of the spectrum, the high-society gathering was shot and edited through a big ruse by Ning Ying. Christopher Barden, a journalist, vividly reported how Ning Ying threw a "party" at the pretentious Maxim's de Paris in Beijing and how, with hidden equipment and a hand-held camera, recorded the real Beijing high-society gathering she had in mind for her film.[49] Ning Ying herself, with her Italian husband, belongs to this society. The role she selected for this gathering in the film reflects a definite self-mockery.

The conclusion of *I Love Beijing* is sad. Dezi is again sober after his experience at the high-society gathering. He starts to prepare for his wedding by taking pictures with the girl from Henan. What must be mentioned here is that it is his university girlfriend who has introduced this girl from Henan to Dezi. The moment the two of them are brought together by the university girl, sadness creeps onto Dezi's face; he starts to understand the status difference between him and the university girl. He loses his interests in girls. At the end of the film, a pretty but neurotic-looking girl starts to sing sadly in his taxi and asks Dezi if he has ever encountered any disappointment in love. Dezi smiles sadly but remains silent. Just as the well-known lines from Xin Qiji's poem suggest, when one has encountered too many disappointments, one stops talking about them.[50] What is more, Dezi has not quite recovered from another episode of his love life. He is called to the suicide scene of one of his former girlfriends, the daughter of an unemployed coal miner. While answering the questions of a policeman, Dezi keeps his eyes on a kite hanging on the wall. Toward the end of the sequence, he says, "I bought this kite for her when she first got to Beijing and we were in love. The kite just couldn't fly." Too sad that the kite could not fly. This speaks of the loss of enthusiasm of Dezi and many of his female friends who came to Beijing with the hope of making it here.

In conclusion, the big cheer Xia Gang received from Chinese film criticism in the mid-1990s reflected a cultural anxiety that wondered if the Chinese art film could still be indigenous with the advance of the globalized market in China. The praise of Xia Gang and more critical attention to his contemporary Later Fifth Generation directors in China contained a widespread disappointment of the Chinese with several earlier Fifth Generation directors for their lack of attention to everyday life around them and their effort to meet the Western desire and fantasy to represent an allegorical or ancient China on the silver screen. The urban situation movie produced by the Later Fifth Generation directors testified to China's contemporary cultural relocation, from Maoist collectivist mode of thinking to the diversified possibilities of individual thinking, from nation building to self-definition, and from political totalitarianism to the constitution of a diversified, civic society. Given their own experiences of having lived a changed China, the Later Fifth Generation directors showed more sensitivity to social and cultural changes in their filmmaking than did many post–Fifth Generation younger filmmakers. The general drive of the urban situation movie was shown in a "yearning for the profane." Cultivating an audience-friendly approach, it nourished a new kind of arts that are permeating all of culture in the name of the profane, which, in one perspective, is a deviation from China's sacred, ideology-illuminated past. Throughout this chapter, pairs of films by selected Later Fifth Generation directors illustrated how these directors and their characters mediated many dilemmas of changes in contemporary life. They try new possibilities to deal with their emotional needs. They explore self-discoveries of generations of women and their ways of seeking empowerment. They illustrate the changing roles of city in their lives and in their cultural critique (e.g., from allegory to reality). They worry about their spiritual sanity in a widespread commodity fetishism. They mediate older values and ways of life with the imported new styles of life. They experiment with various styles in a fashion of cinema verité. With diversified cinematic approaches and an artistic maturity, the Later Fifth Generation directors have showcased a changing China. Considering that they have received less critical and scholarly attention in the West, it is my hope that they may be appreciated more and may start to hear some cheers.

4

Beijing Bastards: Century's End Rock Scenes and China's Generation X

The blood of the 1989 Tian'anmen Square massacre cannot be erased from history; this tragedy served as a watershed in China between the cheerful 1980s and the pessimistic 1990s. The politically reticent decade of the *shiji mo*

Dirt (dir. Guan Hu, 1994) uses the agitation of rock music to tell the story of the emotional unsettlement of young urbanites. Courtesy of China Film Archive, Beijing.

(century's end) in China was the moment when the so-called Sixth Generation of filmmaking emerged. Against the vague, less-represented status of the twenty-somethings in that decade, several films from this new generation drew our attention to the contemporary urban youth subculture and to the critical discourses circulating because of these films. This subculture, at first sight, might appear politically aloof and profane in a decade when China was being driven into a materialist culture. Nonetheless, it served as a contrast to the idealistic, involving 1980s and was itself a particular form of protest. "Under the former regimes," as Claire Wallace and Sijka Kovatcheva observed, "youth cultures were a form of 'resistance' because any nonconformist expression of style became an act of defiance, even if it was not intended that way."[1] For these scholars, the idea of youth subcultures developed in a European context helped them "to understand the development of stylistic resistance and small alternative groups under the former regimes, particularly during the latter decades of communism."[2] In this chapter, certain Chinese rock scenes in Beijing and a particular trend of youth subculture, hooliganism, provide a glimpse of a generation of Chinese youth, the contemporary of the Sixth Generation of filmmakers. It is their coming of age on the silver screen, accompanied by a sense of Chinese *shiji mo*.

Beijing Bastards: A Rock Scene and Generational Discourses

Not much happens in *Beijing Bastards*, a rock 'n' roll film produced by Zhang Yuan in 1992. If you are looking for a story, there isn't much of one. However, viewers tend to hang on, just as the characters in the film do: cut into the footage of a rock band rehearsing and performing its music are glimpses into the lives of some of the musicians and their friends. Watching *Beijing Bastards* is a way to experience the boredom of these young characters and to understand the exhilaration of the young audiences at their concerts.

Frequent editing cuts draw our attention from the very beginning of the film. At first, we get a false sense of movement, of progression, with these cuts, but we soon realize that they have only changed our perspective and that we are watching an endless repetition of boredom: the characters repeat themselves, nobody is in a hurry to go anywhere or do anything, and often a sequence contains only a single stationary shot, for instance, of city traffic, suggesting a dulled perspective and what the characters must feel from within it. These cuts also establish the basic scheme of contrast of the film. The concert sequences are usually in warm colors, lit by firelight or strong lamps. They proceed rhythmically with songs and cheering, and they feature frequent close-ups of agitated faces. The nonconcert sequences, those of everyday life, in contrast, are usually in colder, grayish tones with low-key lighting. They contain few close-ups; instead, they are done in a lot of medium and long takes of slow motion. Frames in these sequences often feature something static that checks the sense of movement: for example, when a young man goes into a neighborhood store to make a call, a bemused senior citizen there will remain motionless throughout the sequence, not even once looking at the young man. It's no surprise that the young man's call is not answered.

The young man's search for his girlfriend, Maomao, provides a narrative frame for the film. Not wanting to terminate her premarital pregnancy, Maomao hides away to give birth to the baby, who, presumably, gives the film its title. When the young man finally finds Maomao and learns of the birth of the baby, he seems to be rejuvenated. His hair is cut very short for the first time in the film and he walks down the city streets in high spirits accompanied by songs that merge into the baby's crying. This ending, as Zhang Yuan suggests, confirms the film's searching. "Our generation," Zhang explains, "should not be another beat generation. We should find ourselves in searching. We should stand up."[3] This ending, as I see it, is only a stylistic contrast to the tedium of the whole film; the film's search for a cultural identity remains wishful thinking although it involves the courage of facing confusion. In the film, through the young man's frustrated search for Maomao—his talk with the musicians, his pursuit of other women, and his encounters, which introduce us to other characters such as painters, writers, jobless young urbanites, and college students—we realize that the word *bastard* in the film's title is correctly translated in the plural and that it refers to a decadent Beijing rock community, its subculture, and its relationship to the prevalent *liumang/pizi* cult among the young. The film's narrative is also a plurality: several young characters' stories are woven together through constant cuts, leaving a strong sense of fragmentation. The rock songs are expressions of this fragmentation.

In classical Chinese, *liumang* literally means those unsettled and homeless because of a natural disaster or political chaos. In modern Chinese, the term has become solely derogatory, making it a synonym of *pizi* (a bad guy). In youth cultures, *liumang* and *pizi* are used interchangeably to mean loosely hooligan, loafer, hoodlum, hobo, bum, and punk. In the 1980s, the novels by the Beijing-based bad-boy writer Wang Shuo first drew critics' attention to a cult of *liumang/pizi*. John Minford referred to the young people involved in this cult as a "*liumang* generation" and defined the term broadly: "rapist, whore, black-marketeer, unemployed youth, alienated intellectual, frustrated artist or poet—the spectrum has its dark satanic end, its long middle band of relentless gray, and shining at the other end, a patch of visionary light. It is an embryonic alternative culture."[4] Minford was clearly taking the "*liumang* generation" as ideological emigrants, attributing their decadence to the chaos of the Cultural Revolution, the failure of socialism, "the trauma of disillusionment, and the anarchy to which they were abandoned during the formative years of their adolescence."[5] He believed that the ideological "void" these young people moved into could "give birth to an authentic sense of identity and culture."[6] In the 1990s, however, *Beijing Bastards* suggested that the embryo of the "*liumang* generation" was still growing and had not yet quite formulated an authentic sense of identity and culture.

Some Fifth-Generation film directors had been engaging with this *liumang/pizi* cult. From late 1988 through mid-1989, as mentioned in the previous chapter, these directors created a "Wang Shuo craze." Four films based on Wang Shuo's novellas came out in a few months: *Samsara* (Lunhui) by Huang Jianxin from Xi'an Studio, *Masters of Mischief* (Wanzhu) by Mi Jiashan from Ermei, *Heavy Gasps* (Da chuanqi) by Ye Daying from Shenzhen, and *Half Flame, Half Brine* (Yiban shi haishui, Yiban shi huoyan) by Xia Gang from Beijing. Wang Shuo's hooliganism attracted and perplexed these directors: while they used Wang Shuo–esque *liumang/pizi* as a critique of China's political and cultural status quo, they were also so drawn to these antiheroes that they started to assume a playfulness with life and became more and more estranged from their missionary sense of cultural redemption. Wang Shuo helped these older rebels to grow out of their anger.

Since the Wang Shuo craze, playfulness has started to take root in Chinese filmmaking. In the 1990s, most Feng Xiaogang–directed or Ge You–cast films and TV series suggested a comedic vein, shown, for example, in the high-grossing film *Dreams Come True* (Jiafang yifang, 1997). This comedy repeatedly reminds us of Mi Jiashan's Wang-Shuo-craze film *Masters of Mischief*. Mi's film depicts a company called Three-T, with T representing the sound of the Chinese word for "substitute" (*ti*). The company stands in for their customers involved in serious problems, hit with depression, or facing a penalty. Steeped in black humor, the make-believe endeavors of this fanciful company often invoke tensions caused by the imposition of totalitarian politics in order to provoke our anger. *Dreams Come True* also depicts a fanciful company selling a make-believe product known as "Your dream comes true today": the company does whatever is necessary, primarily through performance, to fulfill the customer's fantasy. The newer young urbanites' similar endeavors, nevertheless, are anger-free: they make us laugh at the various follies and eccentricities of the characters, who are mostly the new rich or new stars of the market economy.

The Fifth Generation's big name, Zhang Yimou, also did not want to be left out of this lighthearted vein and the representation of *liumang/pizi*. His 1997 film *Keep Cool* (You hua haohao shuo), features the comedic narration of a hooligan's passionate search for love and a middle-aged writer's even more passionate search for justice from him: the hooligan breaks the writer's laptop computer when the writer accidentally gets caught up in the hooligan's fight with someone else. While the hooligan plans to fight his rival for a girl, the writer tries to get compensation for the computer, his lifetime investment. Through the bumpy rhythm created by hand-held cameras, distorted viewing angles, and ballad-style music (*dagu shu*), the film uses the idiosyncrasies of the two characters and the unusual friendship they develop in the end to reflect an equally eccentric era.

Keep Cool, however, was being produced at the same moment that critics declared, almost unanimously, that the era of Fifth Generation filmmaking was over. In this generation discourse, the Fifth Generation's engagement with the youth culture was by and large overlooked, and Fifth Generation films became a signifier for the national-culture allegory that was initiated in China's political culture in the mid-1980s but that was soon transferred into a postcolonial context. Rey Chow's critique of the Fifth Generation's cinematic packaging (the cultural production of exotic surfaces for the Western gaze)[7] was warmly embraced by PRC film critics. So was a similar line of postcolonialist arguments from Western academics. They assisted the PRC film critics in their commentary on the Fifth Generation's tedious reproduction of similar national-culture allegories.[8] These critics and academics remarked how the later development of Fifth Generation filmmaking was influenced mostly by overseas investment and how their allegories lacked attention to a changed China, as described by Li Yiming: "The crucial point is that the elite Fifth Generation directors, by producing [these kinds of] films, have given up thinking about [today's] national culture and ethical crisis, removing themselves from humanistic concerns about the reality that the masses are faced with."[9]

Li Yiming's lengthy pronouncement of the end of the Fifth Generation film also contrasted Wang Shuo (how his "deconstructive" writing had provided a new generation with its everyday vocabulary) with the Fifth Generation's lack of concern with reality. This pronouncement, however, did not take into consideration some of the Fifth Generation directors' fascination with Wang Shuo and how this fascination had partially changed Fifth Generation filmmaking. To Li, Fifth Generation films as a cultural movement ended exactly because of its self-imprisonment in "a fabricated history" (yizao [de] lishi). If the directors of this generation had occasionally produced a film not funded by overseas money, not packaged for the Western audience, and not centered on some pieces of fabricated Chinese history, they might well be considered to be not producing anything in their own names but actually contributing to the emerging Sixth Generation of filmmaking, the next cultural movement in cinema.

With the Fifth Generation's international visibility, who would not want to lead people's attention from there to a new kind of Chinese filmmaking? PRC critics first located the Sixth Generation in the later graduates from Beijing Film Academy. They did so primarily because these newcomers stuck to art films while the others had abandoned them either for the sake of box office revenues, overseas investment, or government funding.

Representing the emergence of Sixth Generation filmmaking are *Beijing Bastards* and other titles of the mid-1990s, such as *Weekend Lovers* (Zhoumo qingren, directed by Lou Ye), *Red Beans* (Xuanlian, directed by He Jianjun), *Postman* (Youchai, directed by He Jianjun), *Days* (Dong chun de rizi, directed by Wang Xiaoshuai), *Drowning* (Yanmo de qingchun, directed by Hu Xueyang), *Yellow Goldfish* (Huang jinyu, directed by Wu Di), *Dirt* (Toufa luanle, directed by Guan Hu), and *In Expectation* (Wushan yunyu, directed by Zhang Ming). In subject, these films engage everyday life and the youth culture. Stylistically, they turn their back on elaborate allegories.

Most of the generation-discourse critics, however, were soon disappointed by these directors, feeling that they are too self-enclosed, too devoid of cultural vision, and too immature in filmmaking to make them worthy successors to the earlier generations of directors. Film critic Zuo Shula, for instance, couldn't understand why "the shitty youngsters" (xiao fenqing) in these films complain with no obvious reason about some nameless pains; he was disgusted with the ways these directors copied each other and foreign films in expressing this pain.[10]

The disappointment and discomfort here are partially due to the anger and protest involved in the representation of marginal youth; to be "shitty" is to be provocative and rebellious. In *Beijing Bastards*, a sequence about the nighttime expedition of a youngster is crosscut with an agitated concert sequence. The name of the youngster, Huang Yellow, is a hybrid combining Chinese and English words of the same meaning. While one may attribute this hybrid name to the hybrid influences the young people are exposed to, the name also sounds repetitious, just like the feeling one gets about the sequence—repeated cursing, complaints, and drinking. Huang meets a new friend and starts to drink only moments after being thrown out of a bar for drunken behavior. His night expedition involves meaningless exchanges of rough language, drinking, fighting, throwing up, and peeing in the street. His "shitty" behavior is not only a footnote to the agitation in the concert sequence but is also as provocative. Huang, it is interesting to note, appears on screen with a gesture of challenge. When he is pushed out of the restaurant for being drunk, a close-up captures his back view. This close-up view pauses. Then Huang's head turns around; gazing at the camera, he snaps rudely: "Damn, you bastards are laughing at me!" The comment is misleadingly turned from the on-screen dialogue to a soliloquy: a "shitty" character provokes the audience before he is going to bore them.

In *Dirt*, the female protagonist, a medical student who is guaranteed a good career and a bright future, purposefully mixes with a few rock musicians, who are considered "dirt" by people around them. Her conventional life bores her, and she loves the inspiration she gets from performing the rock songs, feeling that a lot of her nameless anger will only be released in the music.

The discomfort caused by these newcomers forced film critics to reconsider their hope of finding a Sixth Generation. Some critics protested the lack of commanding social concerns in the newcomers, believing that these self-indulgent artists were resisting using social concerns to mark their group identity. Wang Yichuan believed that Chinese filmmaking had entered "a nongenerational era." Zhang Yiwu described the "post-new-era fragmentation" of filmmaking in the 1990s. Han Xiaolei declared the end of Chinese filmmaking generations, claiming that post–Fifth Generation filmmaking had entered a nongenerational, individualistic, and urban-realist era.[11]

In a way, the relationship of most of the generation-discourse critics with the urban youth culture is much like that of the Fifth Generation directors with Wang Shuo. In the mid-1980s, the marketability of Wang Shuo's writing for film adaptation offered a meeting space for high culture (an intelligentsia tradition) and a particular youth subculture (a jeering at any sense of mission, utopianism, and intellectual rationality). Adaptation of Wang Shuo illustrates a difference in the configuration of *pizi*, or antiheroes: a change from the novellas' narrative noncommitment to the films' commitment. Wang

Shuo's change from his earlier first-person novellas to his later third-person writing is marked by the elimination of the narrative voice. Here, we have to realize the subversive nature of Wang Shuo's narrative subjectivity itself; "you mustn't take me as anybody," as his famous saying goes. His narrative is noncommittal to avoid labeling his antiheroes.

The Fifth Generation's adaptation of Wang Shuo hesitated between two tendencies: an imposed "high culture" subjectivity on Wang Shuo–esque antiheroes and a lowbrow subjectivity drawn by these characters, demonstrating the cinematic "Wang Shuo craze" as a cultural buffer between high and pop cultures. Let's take the issue of admission and rejection of pain in these films as an example. A Wang Shuo–esque *pizi* committing suicide because of an unattainable ideal is a most unlikely scenario, but it occurs in both Huang Jianxin's *Samsara* and Ye Daying's *Heavy Gasps*. *Pizi* life is used on both occasions as an example of the political and existential loss contrasting with a heightened humanist ideal, one of the trademarks of high-culture fever. While these two antiheroes signify high-culture messages, Mi Jiashan's *Masters of Mischief* showcases a lowbrow subjectivity, featuring characters who work hard but behave like slackers. The film rejects the pain caused by utopian ideals by taking life as it is: to feel and not to feel pain becomes a political issue showing the character's accessibility or inaccessibility to the ideological orthodox: we don't feel any pain, the slackers tell a Party ideologue, and we don't need you to come and help us.

Here, neither admission nor rejection of pain offended critics, since the pain was given social justification and its representation was a social statement. In post–Fifth Generation films, similar pain is found, for example, in *Yellow Goldfish*. In this film, a college student changes his mind about going to America just as his plane is about to take off, and he stays behind without his family and friends knowing. He starts an anonymous life by selling goldfish but keeps writing and calling home as if from America. His pain at not being able to explain his decision to anyone close to him is a comment on the popular craze of going abroad. The pain of this kind, indeed, is rare in post–Fifth Generation films, which mostly feature a nameless pain of confusion. *Beijing Bastards* is filled with this confusion, with occasional rational comments such as "I've been searching, though not knowing for what" and expressions in songs such as "We don't know the source of our pain.... We don't know why we are so angry, but this anger makes us alive."

Mixed with strong anticultural behaviors, this confusing pain often reflects the emotional stress commonly experienced in adolescence. The young man's search for his lost girlfriend in *Beijing Bastards* leads him to other girls who both attract and confuse him. In one sequence, we find him seeking a girl's comfort, but he courts her clumsily: he assures her that they don't need to do more than talk and she refuses, saying that she has enough trouble herself. Their mutual attraction shows in the long confrontation that ends with the boy's attack on her: the two troubled souls wrestle violently on the floor. Such emotional stress may lend an enclosed perspective to films on this subject. Take *Weekend Lovers*, for example. This film about love among a group of teenagers, mostly high school graduates, indicates a sense of isolation. The mise-en-scène is primarily psychological and consists mostly of indoor spaces and deserted streets in low-key lighting; the frames represent the ways these youngsters feel about the world—their irresistible sense of closure and boredom. The characters are reaching puberty, and their search for sexual gratification is tinted by this boredom: finding and fighting for a partner becomes part of their reckless and disrupted lives. Once again, we find that they are drawn to rock music. This film, like *Beijing Bastards*, also features a group of youngsters rehearsing their music. A few lines of their songs lend us a better sense about this violent but sentimental film:

> Looking at the boring world, I sing.
> My fearful eyes filled with desolation
> ....
> Desire or despair dances all around . . .

The narrator, the central female in the film, tells in retrospect that they were then "filled with pain, feeling that they were not understood by society." Now mature, she concludes for her friends, they are starting to understand that "society hasn't changed. It was not the society that didn't understand them. It was them who didn't understand society." Having no clue how she and her friends are to understand society as grown-ups, we are left only with a strong impression of the troubled adolescent view of the world.

This transient worldview of adolescence didn't appeal to older generations. Most of the generation-discourse critics and the Fifth Generation directors, for instance, were not sympathetic. For them, having spent their adolescent years in the chaotic 1960s and 1970s, often away from home in the remote countryside, the contemporary youngsters' pain was really not their kind of pain. Li Yiming, for example, claimed that the Chinese postsocialist reality had taught him to understand Milan Kundera's "unbearable lightness of being," which Li described as an existence devoid of belief, and which he further paraphrased with a Wang Shuo–esque adage: "Now we are so poor that we've only got money left." Li, nevertheless, was unsympathetic with the younger generation's pain, not seeing it as a substantiation of his understanding of the lightness of being but believing that it was "fabricated reality" (yizao [de] xianshi).[12]

The contrast between the Baby Boomers and Generation X in the United States may better help readers understand the dispute and disappointment here. We know that while the Xers believe that they "are a culture, a demographic, an outlook, a style, an economy, a scene, a political ideology, an aesthetic, an age, a decade, and a literature,"[13] their elders' attitude toward them is reflected in such titles given to them as "the Doofus Generation," "the Tuned-Out Generation," "a generation of animals," "the Blank Generation," et cetera.[14] The age difference between the Fifth Generation and the filmmaking newcomers roughly corresponds to that between Boomers and Xers demographically, whereas the Fifth Generation directors were born in the late 1940s and the 1950s, most of the newcomers were born in the late 1960s and the 1970s.

The Xers realized that while the Boomers had the Civil Rights Movement and the Vietnam War as powerful touchstones for their group identity, they themselves had nothing as exciting. In this respect, the Sixth Generation also believed that they were overshadowed by the Fifth Generation, who had such touchstones for group identity as the Cultural Revolution, the Red Guards, enforced migration to the countryside, and the post-Mao economic reformation, as well as the national cultural critique. While the Fifth Generation's coming of age was accompanied by all these highly idealistic (though often painful, in retrospect) big events, the newcomers' coming of age appears rather insipid. The decade of their growth, especially the latter half of the 1980s, was an age of vagueness, what a film critic described as the "gray ideological syndrome of the century's end" (yishixingtai shijimo huise zonghezheng): "Following 'the death of God,' the [established] altruism-based moral code . . . has collapsed. A new, self-principled moral code has yet to be developed. A value vacuum exists while all conventions are lost."[15]

In such a vacuum, the Sixth Generation grew up with no heroes, no ideals, no government-sponsored jobs, and no grand vision of the country's future. Most of the success stories of self-made *dakuan* (big money) also belonged to their elders, while they themselves seemed to experience only the impact of money worshipping and the depreciation of the humanities. It was an age of depoliticization; people were disgusted by government corruption and would try to fashion an aloofness from the Party. Yet it was politics that gave the Sixth Generation their biggest event in life, the Tian'anmen Square demonstration and massacre, an event that was still so politically sensitive and so brutal that the Sixth Generation could rarely revisit it in their art as the Fifth Generation had done with the Cultural Revolution. On this point, let us look at a sequence in *Beijing Bastards*:

> Frame 1. In the foreground, the musicians chat over beer with a composer friend who brags that every dot he puts on his composition sheet is money in the bank. In the background, a girl watches TV.
>
> Frame 2. A shot from reverse direction shows the girl in the foreground while TV dominates the sound track; it is news about the Russian Vice President demanding an investigation into corruption within the government. In the background, the musician friends continue drinking and in the foreground the girl looks bored: nobody pays any attention to the news that reminds them of the similar situation in China.
>
> Frame 3. The girl enters the adjoining bedroom where she has a long look at herself in the mirror.

This piece of politically sensitive news surely does not find its way into the soundtrack by accident. It, however, is merged into a typical scene in the film that features no political interest, not even the agitation that would be evident in a concert, but instead talk about money accompanied by and wrapped up in a girl's sense of boredom and confusion and self-regard.

Wang Shuo might have paved the way for the emergence of the Sixth Generation's youth films, but he was a transitional figure in the youth culture between the Fifth Generation and the newcomers. While Wang Shuo's narrative attitude was elusive, his character types and patterns of discourses were popular primarily because they reminded readers and viewers of their opposites: conventional heroes and official discourses. In other words, Wang Shuo was popular because he was political, and the emerging Sixth Generation directors were marked by a political aloofness. Even Wang's retrospective look at his adolescent years and his personal appearance in the Jiang Wen–directed film *In the Heat of the Sun* (Yangguang canlan de rizi, 1994) feels different from the Sixth Generation's depiction of adolescence.[16] Glorifying the adolescent recklessness and cruelty of the early Cultural Revolution years, the film indicated, as Dai Jinhua observed, "accumulative yet vaguely directed social feelings and a cultural psyche."[17] The film is a critique of China's political culture. Such political reading, it is interesting to note, is hard to apply to most of the Sixth Generation youth films that have emerged since the 1990s.[18]

The profane lives of the young characters in *Beijing Bastards* offer an interesting contrast to the lines from the rock songs that were written during the 1980s, the last politically idealistic era in China. In "The Last Complaint"[19] from *Beijing Bastards*, Cui Jian sings of the sense of pain associated with the damages done by the Communist campaigns in recent Chinese history:

> I remember that day
> I want to let it all out
> Walking into the wind
> I don't care how far I go
> Dunno know where this rage comes from
> But it inspires me
> Don't wanna think about the past
> Years upon years the wind blows
> Changing form but never going away
> How much pain to how many people
> Revolution after revolution

The young lives showcased in *Beijing Bastards* have no relation to this association of personal feelings and national destiny. These young characters never even mention public affairs, and their most often shared word is *fan* (feeling bored). This contrast makes us think even more of the ghostly impact of the Tian'anmen Square massacre and the trashy feeling it had thrown a whole generation of young people into. This feeling, plus a touch of cynicism, surfaces in the rock song that wraps up *Beijing Bastards*:

> I sing and sing and still can't sing it away
> The pain of this city
> But the pain makes me believe in the good time to come
> I've a smile on my lips
> Like everyone else
> Just living on this earth
> I'm ready for it
> The truth, the lies, the garbage—
> It's all got to come out.

Beijing Rocks: A Rock Band and Two Cinematic Approaches

Two more films about rock 'n' roll further testified how widespread was this trashy feeling and how the political catastrophe of 1989, joined by the advance of commercialism (used as synonyms of urbanization in these films), buried rock music and left great sadness to the generation of young people who grew up with it. These two films, seven years apart, employed the same group of Beijing rock musicians with the band called Overload (chao zai) to dramatize stories of rock music, youth, and China.[20] They are Guan Hu's *Dirt* (1994) and Hong Kong director Mabel Cheung's *Beijing Rocks* (Beijing yue yu lu, 2001). Both films used first-person narratives and featured an outsider visiting Beijing, drawn by the same rock band, becoming part of the band, and finding an emotional resonance in the rock music that the band performs. Both films related rock music with China's contemporary cultural metamorphosis, and both search out the personal stories behind the music. With the same musicians growing angrier, the two films offer us insights into the trajectory of the saddening moods of young people in the 1990s.

Dirt uses the agitation of rock music to tell the story of the emotional unsettlement of Ye Tong, a female medical student in her early twenties. After living in the southern city of Guangzhou for over a decade and bored to death with her daily life, Ye returns to a Beijing back-alley neighborhood, where she spent her childhood, to rediscover happiness. As she rejoins her group of childhood friends, a rock band stationed in the neighborhood attracts her. Emotionally, she finds herself torn between Weidong, a childhood friend who has become a local policeman, and Peng Wei, the lead musician of the band.

Dirt was produced a few years after the Tian'anmen Square massacre. Issued by a state studio and typical of many Sixth Generation films that appeared in the 1990s, *Dirt* appears reticent in its politics.[21] It can only use other public gatherings at the square to hint at the shattering effect of the 1989 tragedy, when the high tide of idealism was also muffled. In one occasion in *Dirt*, to highlight the confused love relationship of Ye with the two contrasting young men, newsreel footage of public gatherings at the Tian'anmen Square for the death of Mao and for the dethronement of the "Gang of Four" are edited in to crosscut with Ye's sex scene and with other glimpses of her everyday life and her emotional confusion. The juxtaposition here, as Zhang Yingjin observes, "suggests the fragmentation of private memory and the seeming irrelevance of public history in postsocialist China."[22] What Guan

Hu wanted to testify with his *Dirt* was that things were falling apart for young people with the loss of idealism.

It is important to know that the Tian'anmen Square massacre, as it affected general culture in China, also served as a watershed in the development of Chinese rock. Featuring a countercultural attitude and lifestyle—with many musicians in long hair, torn jeans, and black leather jackets, and involved in drugs, premarital sex, and an unbridled pursuit of pleasure—it was easy for people to overlook the fact that the development of Chinese rock actually resembled other branches of Chinese high culture in that it valued liberating and enlightening values of art, it sought human integrity, it was concerned about the country's cultural and political status, and it despised commodity fetishism. Chinese rock, for example, saw itself as in defiance of commercial pop music from Hong Kong and Taiwan (gangtai yinyue) and sought its origin in Northwest Wind (xibei feng) style music and songs, which drew heavily on the folk song traditions of China's Northwest region. This style dominated the Chinese music scene in the 1980s and was a musical branch of the nationwide cultural movement of roots searching. Cui Jian's first album, *Rock 'n' Roll on the New Long March* (1987), related his rock songs to the new orientation and economic reforms of the nation. The song that became the de facto anthem of the student protestors at Tian'anmen Square in 1989, Cui Jian's "I Have Nothing," was the most popular rock song to come from the *xibei feng* tradition. The massacre of 1989 chilled China's political mood and depressed a generation of young idealists when a materialist, philistine culture took over the nation. Rock musicians also changed. "Pre-89, we were idealistic," Overload's lead singer Gao Qi reflected. "Post-89, we are realistic. Since 1989, a lot has changed. I've changed. My music has changed. Some people are still writing songs about the government, but I don't see the point. Now I write about how we can live, what our purpose is."[23] The shift was from state to self.

The years around 1989 were when rock had its biggest following. Since the mid-1990s, as rock music has tried to survive the commercialized culture and to cope with the changed political culture, many disillusioned Chinese youth have lost interest in getting agitated and angry and have turned their backs on rock. This was the context in which our film character Ye Tong left Guangzhou for Beijing. Guangzhou in *Dirt* clearly symbolizes the dominance of a commercialized life. Wanting to dispel the dullness of life, Ye is drawn immediately to these rock lines that she heard in Beijing:

> I'm calling out to you.
> Stand up and come with me.
> Take the sword. Feel your life.
> Blood splashes all over me.
> Hatred and death flow together.
> . . . .
> There is no more crowd,
> Just me crying aloud.
> No more tears.
> The sky is no longer blue.
> Come with me.
> Let the flag soar high.
> And cover the sky.
> Tears flow once again.
> Countless souls are waiting.

One is amazed that these lines were not originally written as a depiction of 1989. But undeniably they invoke memories of 1989 and address its aftermath. The film shows the inspiration of such lines at various otherwise tedious gatherings. On one occasion, the audience is primarily older intellectuals. They are first shocked but soon inspired by the youthfulness of the rock songs. The camera here, and in many other occasions throughout the film, captures faces showing appreciation of the rock songs from people of different ages and walks of life.

Dirt shows abhorrence for the dominance of professionalism and commercial culture. Ye is studying to be a doctor; thus she is on a career track that many admire. Yet the "yearning for agitation" she sings about keeps her from being peaceful with her studies. She hates to see how the tyranny of money and commercial culture are transforming the country. When she visits the workplace of a childhood friend who now works for a foreign company in Beijing, she feels almost stiffened by the hushed atmosphere in the huge office building. She comments on what she sees and puts on her earphones; then powerful rock music overtakes the sound track, which offers a sharp contrast between what she enjoys and what she has stumbled into. Among the early group of films produced by Sixth Generation directors, defiance toward commercialism and a sentimental resistance to it were shared cultural feelings. In Hu Xueyang's *Drowning* (Yanmo de qingchun, 1994), which came out the same year as *Dirt*, a college student goes to a southern city to earn his tuition. He falls in love with a rich young woman, whom he coaches in tennis, but is heartbroken to discover that between their love and money the young woman still chooses money. At the end of the film, the young man decides to leave this southern city and starts his life anew—away from the commercial mire.

Dirt presents rock performances in such a way that they reflect not only a yearning for agitation but also confusion with China's post-Mao cultural changes and a nostalgia for the lost innocence of childhood. In a most impressive montage sequence, the rock show is edited with a collage of Beijing street scenes: the changed cityscape, curious foreign tourists, toiling country folk, hands counting money, street vending, and so on. The director is demonstrating that rock music is a response of young people to a changed China. It is as natural or as bizarre a response as, for instance, the popular hobby of ballroom dancing among older folks in the open in many city squares—the sequences emphasize the juxtapositions of rock shows and ballroom dancing, showing that they have both attracted onlookers. Yet before the sequence moves into a quicker rhythm of crosscuts, it features a series of drumbeats when the screen shows still frames of a serene Beijing back-alley shot in a red tone of warm sunlight. This is the neighborhood where Ye grew up and to which she has now returned to search for lost happiness. This is the peaceful life the current urbanization is dismantling. *Dirt* is not saying that life then in Ye's Beijing neighborhood was better. Rather, it is depicting the emotional attachment to childhood in the process of growing up. It is also depicting the emotional unsettlement of all who are involved in the drastic round of urbanization. From this perspective, rock in the film becomes the expression of the confusion of not only the unsettled youth but also of the whole nation.

From this perspective, we also realize that the roots-searching spirit and national cultural discourse still had a lingering impact on this film's approach to rock music. Unlike *Beijing Bastards*, which documented a rock community with no predominant theme and captured more song lines about alienation, despair, and anger, *Dirt* uses rock music to reflect a national dislocation in general and young people's sensitivity to it in particular. *Dirt* even wants to reconcile the countercultural image of rock musicians and the idealism of rock songs. Ye, who is spellbound by rock songs, keeps wondering what singer Peng Wei, who has long hair and wears jeans and a leather jacket, might have looked like before he got into rock. Finally, she gets a glimpse of Peng Wei's past, a photo of a typical Maoist youth. *Dirt* wants the audience to feel all the changes involved in the contrasting images of this young man.

Dirt lets the song lines navigate China's current dislocation, and *Dirt* sings about regaining youthful dreams:

> Push the windows open,
> What is tomorrow going to be like?
> My heartbeats are still the same as before,
> Yearning for agitation.

Seven years down the road. When Mabel Cheung,[24] a Hong Kong director, found Overload and asked its musicians to do her film *Beijing Rocks*, these musicians looked punkier, were singing wilder rock songs, and had sunk into a darker mood. *Beijing Rocks* reminds us of *Dirt*: it is also about an emotionally distressed person, running away from his problems, who comes across the band. Drawn by its music, he develops a friendship with the musicians, has a bumpy ride on the road with the band, but ends this emotional journey in confusion. This time, the distressed person is Michael, an unsuccessful Hong Kong songwriter. His attraction to rock, nonetheless, is not *Dirt*'s idealism but the cynicism of the rock songs and the carefree lifestyle of the rock musicians. His way to deal with his problems, as he confesses, is to keep silent. Now he finds that the rock musicians are not silent about their problems. He becomes best friends with and falls into a love triangle with the band's lead singer Road and Road's girlfriend Yang Yin. Michael's unusual friendship with the band members allows the film to explore the emotional depth beneath the hard rock exteriors of these members. The following is a glimpse of three of the characters:

> Road jumped the train so as not to fall into the same tracks of life as his father, a train conductor, whose job Road could inherit, as promised by the government. He said that he had the sympathy of his parents, who believed that his becoming a rock singer was better than becoming a robber. He became cynical about human nature because he found out that his friends ate the dog he had entrusted them with.
>
> Yang Yin came to Beijing from a provincial town. She was desperate about her lonely life and had become suicidal. She started to date Road and followed the band on the road because she thought this was the coolest way to commit suicide.
>
> A guitarist in the band came from Inner Mongolia. He saw the purpose of life as waiting to die and the process of life as turning from sucker to asshole.

To match the cynicism of such characters, *Beijing Rocks* uses a cinematography that oscillates between documentary and MTV. While the characters talk to the camera, cartoons done in satirical mischief manipulate the screen. Peter Pau, the cameraman for the Oscar-winning *Crouching Tiger, Hidden Dragon*, contributed to this feature and the generally sophisticated cinematography of *Beijing Rocks*.

Unlike *Dirt*'s reticence about politics, *Beijing Rocks* uses the rock scene to express anxiety about Hong Kong's return to China. It focuses on China's chaos and decay to vent anxiety about the kind of China that Hong Kong has returned to. Like *Dirt*, it uses montage editing to showcase rock as part of the many other changes one encounters in today's China. The establishing shots of the film show what Michael sees in a taxi ride through Beijing; it is a collage of varied elements of everyday life that have together changed China's socialist look. The juxtaposition of a rock performance and older folks' street dancing is as noticeable as in *Dirt*. Yet even this similarity is given a political dimension. When Michael and Ping Lu chat about music in Mainland China and Hong Kong, Michael abruptly tells Ping Lu there is no rock 'n' roll in Hong Kong. What Michael means, in other words, is that Hong Kong and Mainland China have totally different political contexts and the angry Beijing rock needs China's political context to be the rock 'n' roll as they know it.

Yet the profound nature of *Beijing Rocks* lies in the fact that it moves beyond a simple political confrontational formula of revealing the darkness of Communist China. In addition to its depiction of China's political corruption, the film is also suggesting that in certain ways China has become just like Hong Kong, controlled by commercialism. On one occasion, the band's rock songs are jeered and the *gangtai* (Hong Kong and Taiwan) love songs are cheered. The film's tragic ending with Road's death in a motorcycle accident caused by his reckless driving is triggered by a music company's rejection of his music.[25] In the company office, Road finds out that the agents there respected the countercultural appearance of rock musicians only because they needed it to package the music for sale. These dramatic details are actually a true allegory of the decline of rock in China due to the triumph of commercialism. This makes *Beijing Rock* echo *Dirt* one more time.

Thus *Beijing Rocks* becomes an elegy to the declining rock in China. Its theme song "Good Night, Beijing," which is used to mourn the death of Road, expresses this feeling best:

> I'll fall asleep in tonight's pattering rain,
> To the sound of Chinese-made road rollers,
> To the roaring of a wound split wide open,
> . . . .
> Good night, Beijing.
> Good night, all you sleepless people.

What is more surprising is that in this mourning salute to rock, the film ends with an image that recalls the embittered worldview of early Chinese rock. Early in the film, Michael explains the meaning of "Mexican Jumping Beans," the name of a Hong Kong music band, to Yang Yin. He assures her that such "magic beans" actually exist. At the end of the film, Michael manages to find some of these beans and present them to Yang Yin, who accidentally discovered that the worms growing within the beans were trying to break out. These beans are Michael's farewell gift to Yang Yin as a souvenir of his friendship with the band and with rock music. The beans become a metaphor of their painful, emotional journey together. The worms first remind us of them, the rock musicians and their friends—they may either break the container to continue to grow or they may be consumed in the violent struggle. The worm also reflects the dark and cynical worldview of the rock musicians. This perspective recalls He Yong's angry song lyrics written in the late 1980s:[26]

> The world we are living in
> Is like a garbage dump
> People are just like worms
> Fighting and grabbing
> What they eat is conscience
> What they shit are ideologies
> Is there hope is there hope
> Is there hope is there hope.

Wrapping itself up in the worm image, *Beijing Rocks* echoes the radical, sarcastic nihilism of He Yong's lines. It also indicates a lack of hope for the further growth of rock in a materialist China.

My Father and I: Rock Lovers Bowing Out

Wang Shuo's feelings for Cui Jian help further illustrate the sadness that rock music had to bow out as materialism advanced in China. In his essays, Wang Shuo has been known for being picky on many popular cultural figures.

He, for example, fought with the martial arts novelist Jin Yong and did not care much of the emerging "beautiful-woman writers" (meinü zuojia) who showcased their sensual and carnal experiences. While he was waging wars on many fronts, in 2000, when he wrote about Cui Jian, his words appeared unusually sincere, and sad. Surprisingly for an iconoclast, he worshipped Cui Jian. He believed that Cui Jian's songs kept his generation "spellbound" (zhaomo) and that they were the generation's birthmarks. This generation, confirmed by Cui's rock lines, wanted to challenge the status quo but also did not want to give up hope.[27] When he wrote, however, Wang Shuo appeared like an old man reminiscing about his life, with regret. To him, in retrospect, Cui Jian's rock music was opium, "he [Cui Jian] tends to make the irresponsible folks like me feel that we did not give up anything; ideals, courage, and hopes still exist. As long as his kind of music is still being played, folks like us do not feel worthless—when the music is over, there is one more round of crashes and an even bigger sense of loss and nihilism."[28] The saddest thing is that rock as opium had stopped working for him when he writes. He confessed that he always fell asleep listening to Cui Jian, and did not even dream of anything. With these songs or without these songs, he knew that he "would sink into the city that has grown newer with taller buildings" and he "would grow old while going from a restaurant to a bar, to a dancing floor, and to all the similar, small rooms."[29] For Wang Shuo, his existential crisis is accompanied by China's contemporary urbanization. From his wording, we see that he perceived current urbanization as a materialist and profane drive that had swallowed his soul (xinling), which he once found in Cui Jian's rock songs.

Cui Jian stopped inspiring such cultural rebels as Wang Shuo and the author's fans. With a general shift in cultural orientation to everyday life and the profane, as discussed in chapter 3, the Wang Shuo kind of cultural rebels found themselves out of date. The public announcement that Wang Shuo was bowing out came with the review of a film. In 2003 Xu Jinglei, a young actress-turned-director made her directorial debut, with herself playing the lead role in *My Father and I* (Wo he baba). Most notable is that older directors Ye Daying, Jiang Wen, and Zhang Yuan offered not only ideas but also service to the film. With these directors playing the roles of the father and the father's friends, the film, behind the scenes and on the screen, tells a story of the love of two generations. College student Xiaoyu (little Yu, played by Xu Jinglei) reunites with her estranged father, Laoyu (old Yu, played by Ye Daying), after her mother dies in a traffic accident. Xiaoyu's parents have been separated for years because the father is considered a *linglei* (alternative, that is, someone who does not have a regular job, is not leading a normal life, is not being responsible, etc.). Xiaoyu, having had no contact with her father in years, has to get to know him anew. In the twists and turns of her own life—marriage, divorce, the birth of her first baby, and the difficulty of finding an ideal job—Xiaoyu finally finds a friend in her father and discovers a warm personality under the façade of a playful cultural rebel.

In his review of this film, Beijing-based cultural scholar Zhang Yiwu saw *My Father and I* as a testimony that a special cultural group of the past two decades, those who had lived as the Wang Shuo kind of antihero, was retiring from history. Since the 1980s, Wang Shuo has published stories and novels, been involved in making films and TV dramas, and become an anticultural fashion leader among the young. In Jing Wang's study of Deng's China, hooliganism, a lifestyle derived from Wang Shuo's writing, is defined as a linkage "between a declining elite and a burgeoning popular culture" and has been vividly described as "a street affair," "a new cult of pleasure seeking and foul play," "the raw libido that society's castaways release and put on exhibit," "the pulse of ... a desublimated era," "the ultimate art of total abandon," "a popular culture that seeks noisy pleasures and mocks self-restraint," "a vocal culture of small alley talk and tall tales," a lifestyle that is "unproductive and totally consumptive," "a narcissistic posture that appeared deceivingly seditious," egotistic characters who "do not live as improvising individuals, only as a collective," and "a celebration of group bondage."[30] Hooliganism, it appears, is a paradoxical phenomenon. It is a breakaway from China's political past, but it also retains a lot of its traits. Its major thrust of anti-intellectualism, for instance, is both a critique and a continuation of China's Communist past (think of the Maoist jeering at the intellectuals). Its antiheroes are among the earliest to quit their state jobs to be among the new individualists who make it on their own. Yet, socially and spiritually, they make sure they don't fall into isolation. They rarely suffer from the existential pain of isolation but remain socially connected enough to let their linguistic mischief shine through. To thrive as an anticultural lifestyle, Wang Shuo–style hooliganism needs a chaotic society, such as that of the immediate post-Mao China, to be its playground. As Zhang Yiwu saw in Xu Jinglei's *My Father and I*, when globalization, a market economy, new-technology industries, urbanization, and professionalism stepped in to further turn China from its Maoist past and to regulate Chinese society anew, hooliganism became obsolete and the hooligans began bowing out of China's cultural stage.

If Lao Yu's giving in to his genuine emotion toward family in *My Father and I* serves as an indication that a hooligan is a hooligan no more, one wonders if such a farewell to hooliganism had really occurred long before. An example that comes to mind is Feng Xiaogang's film *Angels in Black* (Qingyi shizhe, 1994), which was shot about a decade before *My Father and I*. Written and produced by Wang Shuo, the film today is often ignored in Feng Xiaogang's oeuvre, which is curious, especially given the director's rising popularity. Who would imagine that the happy-go-lucky director's collaboration with Wang Shuo, who had stopped writing to take a managerial role in the cultural industry, would result in an artificial film that was unbearably sentimental?[31] Yet, in the sense that Wang Shuo's hooliganism was bidding farewell, this film is a most appropriate example. The film was based on two love stories by Wang Shuo, "Air Stewards" and "A Love Forever Lost." Su Kai, a hooligan involved in black-market sales and delivery of vehicles, makes the acquaintance of two air stewards, Gege and Yang Yan (played by Xu Fan and Ju Xue). His playfulness attracts them both so much that Gege becomes his girlfriend and they build a house together and plan to start their married life there. In addition, Yang Yan becomes his close friend and he confides his troubles to her. Su, however, is soon diagnosed with a terminal disease. So that Gege won't suffer from the pain of his dying, Su fakes a breakup with her and persuades Yang Yan to assist him with a drug-induced peaceful death. The film's artificiality strikes the viewer from the very beginning, when the voice of the deceased Su Kai becomes the first-person narrator, recollecting what happened to him when he was alive. The artificiality lies not only in that the narrator is a dead person but also that he assumes a tone of emotional earnest. This tone corresponds to the elaborate contrast throughout the film of Su Kai's playful mask of defiance and a dignified inner self that both needs and is capable of giving true feelings of love. Critics have long argued that true love doesn't have much room in the hooligans' code of behavior, and it is the Achilles heel of Wang Shuo's hooliganism.[32] To be a hooligan, sentiments of love and playing it cool don't go hand in hand. In Wang Shuo's fiction writing, if ever there were any traces of true selves hidden under the masks of hooligans, the author makes sure that he does not reveal or emphasize them. In this sense, a focused elaboration of the dividedness of self and mask can well be a sign of the author's farewell to hooliganism. In a scene that is presented as a ritual, Yang Yan holds the dying Su Kai while Gege, dressed in a black cape, shows up to the accompaniment of religious music. The camera zooms out to a crane shot of the house and the voice of the dead Su Kai saying, "Thank you, my loved ones, for making me believe, in the last year of my life, in a love that I had never believed in before."

Could it have taken the slow process of a decade for hooliganism to bow out? Why not? Historical changes are constituted of quicksand and slow sand. Yet the change we are looking at may also involve less a bowing out than a mutation in the old-timers who tried to hang on. The three helpers in producing *My Father and I*, Ye Daying, Jiang Wen, and Zhang Yuan, happened to be the biggest fans of Wang Shuo among filmmakers. Ye Daying, who played the father, Laoyu, was among the directors who created a Wang Shuo craze in the 1980s. His films showcased Chinese cinema's initial fascination with Wang Shuo wherein not love but the cultural marginality of hooligans preoccupied the attention of the directors. Jiang Wen, an actor-turned-director, directed what Wang Shuo claimed to be the best among all the films based on his writing, *In the Heat of the Sun*.[33] Unlike the earlier directors who had employed Wang Shuo stories as cultural and political critiques, Jiang Wen showed less concern about any grand themes and more interest in the subjective perception of a teenager growing up in the chaotic era of the Cultural Revolution. The film nostalgically revisits a politically chaotic China that was the playground for a group of teenagers temporarily out of the grip of any institution—family, neighborhood, or school. The film offered an interesting case for studying the group mentality of hooligans, and it illustrated how the Wang Shuo type of antihero grew up in a confused interplay of raw libido, freedom, and the residues of Maoist education. The cases of Ye Daying and Jiang Wen testified to the earlier popularity of Wang Shuo's hooliganism in cinema.

Zhang Yuan indicated what I believed to be mutations of Wang Shuo's impact on more recent cinema. Two of Zhang's films, *I Love You* (Wo ai ni, 2002) and *Green Tea* (Lü cha, 2003), illustrate how an auteur director assimilated a changed Wang Shuo, whose depiction of love had started to merge with the society's general fascination with love, especially the antiromantic emphasis of the everydayness of love and its playfulness as part and parcel of an emerging *xiaozi* (petit-bourgeois) lifestyle that was dominating urban youth. Zhang's two films explored, respectively, two aspects of Wang Shuo's impact, antiromanticism and playfulness in love relations, with differing success.

I Love You is based on Wang Shuo's novella "To Die after a Thrill." Both the film and the novella detail the relationship between a young army nurse with a family history of neurotic violence and a young man she drives into a hasty marriage—how their love life turns into mental and physical violence, how it ends in divorce, and how it produces an unexpected pregnancy. To imply that the film has an extraordinary subject, the real material that films should be made of, overseas reviews have tended to emphasize the neurotic nature of the central female character; how she suffers from claustrophobia and indulges voluntarily in sudden mood swings, hysteria, fits of wild, uncontrollable jealousy, and bouts of deadly rage that alternate with periods of angelic niceness.[34]

The TV series and then Zhang's film, both adapted from the novella, play into the Chinese perception that tends to overlook the neurotic nature of the behavior but focuses on the depiction of a bad marriage. Popular reviews praised the novel's realism in depicting the everyday ordeals of love life. Fiction writer Chi Li even wanted to place Wang Shuo in the camp of neorealism because of this novella.[35] A female scholar, in studying gender roles in Wang Shuo's novels, was not happy that "To Die after a Thrill" depicted a woman's "true emotion" as "female hysteria." She nevertheless was impressed by the realism of this novella: "'To Die after a Thrill' is a portrayal of the family life of an young urban couple, fully revealing their psychological conflicts and emotional crisis: the woman's greediness and the man's aloofness; the woman's attempt to possess and the man's attempt to evade; their sincerity and passion being erased by daily life; their feelings of boredom, vulgarity, profanity, and lowness as if these were fogs in which one lives; their marriage becoming a torturing burden; their family turned into a constant battleground; and the fact that neither of them can find any warmth, peacefulness, or comfort in this kind of family life."[36]

Obviously, what attracted the Chinese audience was the cultural phobia of a bad marriage that reveals human weakness instead of a physical phobia that induces violence. Earlier, Wang Shuo critics had used "To Die after a Thrill" as an example of the contrast in hooligans' personalities—they are passionate and indulgent in carnal love but numb in their emotional lives.[37] To that I would add a related contrast of their loyalty to brotherhood and their aloofness to marriage. In the film, the young man's first beating of his wife is caused by her interruption of his drinking reunion with his former comrades when she returns, exhausted, from work. If you tie such a hooligan down to family life, conflicts and ordeals are to be expected.

By the time Zhang Yuan picked "To Die after a Thrill" for film adaptation, Wang Shuo's cultural image had been revised; he was known less as a hooligan and more as a TV producer of love shows—an eager caterer to popular taste. If his earlier collaboration with Feng Xiaogang in *Angels in Black* (1994) had already confused the audience into thinking that Wang Shuo was turning into a *xiaozi* writer of bad taste in sentiment, his later production of a TV soap opera on the subject of love tended to reinforce that confusion. As fiction writer Zhang Kangkang observed, Wang Shuo's soap operas forced together incompatible components, portraying love and hooliganism, and ended up pleasing nobody—his portrayal of love struck serious writers and the serious audience as shallow and his checked hooliganism stopped feeling fun. Zhang Kangkang believed that Wang Shuo's failure was due to his eagerness to cater to a market of popular taste and that he even abandoned his earlier talent in depicting love. Such a talent, Zhang believed, was shown in "To Die after a Thrill."[38]

Zhang Yuan's film adaptation of "To Die after a Thrill" promoted an unsentimental Wang Shuo. Only the title of the film, *I Love You*, is as banal as Wang Shuo's other soap operas. It, however, is obviously part of the film's sarcasm about love, which is depicted as a human bondage that ties two loved ones together for ceaseless disagreements, frustration, fights, and mutual torture. The film relies on nothing sensational and melodramatic but sticks to Zhang Yuan's trademark style of lyrical realism, a documentary approach punctuated with frequent close-ups. Although based on fiction, the film unrolls like a case study of a relationship through the everyday details of life. This documentary approach, however, does not consist of long shots and long takes but rather multiple cuts and frequent close-ups. The camera closes in all the time to suggest both the claustrophobic nature of the relationship and the subjective engagement of the protagonists, that is, how they are enclosed in the relationship and how this enclosure affected their perception of things. Such a film places a high demand on the acting, and it is worth pointing out that the actress who rendered a superb performance indicating subtle emotions is no other than Xu Jinglei, about whom we opened the discussion in this section.

Green Tea, not based on a Wang Shuo story but with Wang Shuo as the producer, is an effort to instill Wang Shuo's hooliganism and linguistic playfulness into the *xiaozi* lifestyle and into the depiction of love. Wu Fang (played by Vicki Zhao Wei), a bookish graduate student wearing unstylish glasses and formal clothing, goes on many blind dates as a pastime. Over the cup of green tea that she routinely orders, she enjoys telling her dates the chilling tale of the bad marriage of her friend's parents. Then she encounters Chen Mingliang (played by Jiang Wen), a macho hooligan who defies the mysticism she produces over her cup of green tea. Chen is not turned away by

Wu's bookish aloofness, and he is not bothered by her story, either. Chen is so attracted by Wu's difference that he imposes himself on more uninvited meetings with Wu during which she is able to disclose that chilling story of hers in full—how the husband abhors the hands of his wife because she works at a funeral parlor, how he tortures her because of that, and how the wife can't bear the torture and kills the husband. While perplexed by his attraction to Wu, Chen is surprised by his discovery of another woman, Langlang (also played by Vicki Zhao Wei), who works at a bar and who looks astonishingly like Wu. Outgoing and sexy, this other woman easily becomes Chen's friend. Chen, nevertheless, can never be sure that Wu and Langlang are not the same person.

Green Tea appears undecided in many ways. Unlike *I Love You*, it is obviously not concerned with conveying a sense of reality. It is also unlike a contemporary Taiwan film, *The Personals* (Zhenghun qishi, 2003), which uses a woman's blind dates to explore the hidden desires of a culturally diversified society. *Green Tea* is a man's encounter instead of a woman's experience. Is the film one of suspense? The mysterious resemblance between Wu and Langlang, as well as the relationship between Wu's story (one suspects that it is the story of her own parents) and Wu's personality are all elements on which to build the suspense. The film, however, only seems partially interested in developing that suspense. Other than a revelation that Wu and Langlang are actually the same person, the film does not offer much else that the audience may reflect on to tie up the loose ends. The story Wu tells, for example, is hard to apply to the divided personalities; it does not explain why a young woman would play two contrasting roles in experiencing love.

If not totally about suspense, could this film, as a Chinese reviewer suggests, mean to produce an allegory?[39] According to this reviewer, the film is an allegory of love in today's metropolis—Wu embodies the cerebral, or the conservative, attitude toward love, whereas Langlang embodies carnal desire and the need to break the traditional yoke. The difficulty of coordinating the images of these two women indicates the dilemma in love. Without judging whether this reading is a little forced, we still aren't satisfied with this interpretation because we know that allegories, important as they are, are only a secondary product. A film, while conveying an allegory, still needs to be stylistically sufficient in itself.

Could the film, then, be more about mood? The cameraman Zhang secured for *Green Tea* was Christopher Doyle, who is best remembered for his camera work in Wong Kar-wai's mood films. When *Green Tea*, as a reviewer describes it, "is eighty-five minutes of two people just talking,"[40] and especially when the talking is not superbly entertaining or absorbing, the cinematography of the talking becomes more noticeable. Doyle's camera work, from the special-effect close-up of swirling tealeaves that punctuate the scene change to the moody depiction (unique camera angles and movements, unusual frames, and impressive colors) of a series of scenes, has been widely praised. The green tea itself gives many cultural cues indicating peacefulness of mind, good taste in lifestyle, intelligence, and elegance. The swirling tealeaves, while indicating how the green-tea values are disrupted with each encounter of Wu and Chen, also indicate a sense of bewilderment. When this sense starts to build up, the shots of the film move from the use of standard frames and natural color contrasts to more creative frames and more improbable color schemes. If the film cares much about mood, in this case about bewilderment, the camera work has matched it well. In contrast to the film's lack of action and drama, the camera appears unusually active to stress the underlying feelings of the characters. What does not exactly match the mood is the key component of the film, the playfulness of the chatter between Wu and Chen. Wu's story, albeit shocking, contributes little to our bewilderment. Chen's responses and his aggressive gestures, typical of Wang Shuo's hooliganism, are filled with jokes that are at his own expense. As some reviewers observed, when playfulness with words dominates the chatter between Wu and Chen, their true selves and real feelings are hard to determine.[41] The playfulness in this film works well with the mystery and suspense but does not work so well to depict a mood for love.

While each audience surely will have a different response to the combined effects of Zhang Yuan's *Green Tea*, what concerns me here is the film's indication that the Wang Shuo style of playfulness is adapting itself to new moods of love. Except for Zhang Yuan, few younger directors have shown much interest in Wang Shuo when they do romantic films. One reason that has kept Wang Shuo from the younger directors' exploration of love, as I suggested earlier, is that Wang Shuo's characters are not true individualists of a modern society. These characters are often too mischievously playful and cheerful to be existential, isolated, nihilist, or to be in love or lovelorn. Wang Shuo's playfulness, which originated from poking fun at China's political ideology, is also losing its appeal to today's younger generations, who are aloof to traditional political ideology but spellbound by what Benjamin Barber terms "videology," a global hegemony of the McWorld that works through sound bites, film clips, cyberspace, fashion trends, and lifestyles.[42]

A recent news report indicates that today's young people in China are given to being "cute," after years of following all the fashions to be "cool." A code name "Q" has been adopted for this cuteness and a Q-version culture is leading the fashions of the young, affecting what they wear, what they use, how they behave, and what they do. A Q-person typically drives a QQ vehicle, carries a QQ notebook computer, has a Q-version cellular phone, chews Q gum, spends Q money, plays Q electronic games, and has Q toys or wears Q necklaces that come from either Japan or South Korea. A Q-person is usually a loner who socializes through the Internet and communicates through ICQ (short for a chatting tool known as I Seek You). The fashionable playfulness for a Q-person is shown in his love for Cosplay (short for costume play).[43] The Q-persons are now leaving China's Generation X behind, let alone Wang Shuo fans, who are slightly older than the Xers. Although work by Wang Shuo is still being adapted, the nature and origin of his playfulness is a far cry from what Qs are seeking. The emotional culture of today's China, showing the obvious traces of globalization and commercialism, is indeed brushing Wang Shuo aside.

5

Captives of Love: Emotional Styles and the New Urbanites

Captives of Love (Zhengjiu aiqing, 2000), by young director Liu Xin, has mixed emotional effects: it is sentimental but fun, artificial yet genuine, and it brings the audience to tears when love triumphs in the end. It also leaves the audience wondering if the love portrayed in the film can really survive in today's materialist China.

The film is a science fiction of love. Bing'er, a girl who lives on the remote Planet T, stumbles upon a spaceship that has been to Earth and breaks a glass jar containing a goldfish. She starts to feel strange emotions. A sage of the Planet T, whose residents are without sexuality or emotions, decides that the girl is infected by the virus of love from Earth. The treatment: send her there to learn the illusive nature of love and thus be disinfected. Upon her arrival on Earth, Bing'er falls in love with the first man she sees, a self-proclaimed

Dazzling (dir. Li Xin, 2001) mixes fantasy and reality, darkness and light, as well as disappointment with and passion for love.
Courtesy of China Film Archive, Beijing.

musician named Qin Liang. With some initial suspicion, Qin Liang soon gets into a fun relationship with Bing'er. The fun is primarily derived from the innocent love of Bing'er, which appears totally out of place in a society where money and power rule. With his career success, Qing Liang eventually betrays Bing'er, who returns to Planet T "cured." Yet only after her departure does Qing Liang start to realize the importance of her love. He searches for her in vain and becomes blind. Bing'er is moved. She arrives again, bringing light not only to Qing Liang but also to those who doubt the existence of love.

Bing'er strikes the audience as an apparition of innocence and purity roaming in a tainted land. Nothing is more suggestive of the feelings of love of today's urbanites in China. They yearn for love but are also cynical enough to be skeptical of the traditional formulas of "love at first sight" and "love ever after." Love, in keeping with the allegory of this film, can hardly be as pure, as innocent, and as detached as if it were from another planet. Love, as many contemporary films attest, is sacred and not sacred—sacred, because humans value it; not sacred, because it is also part of, and thus as trivial as, everyday life. "Melancholy rather than cheerful," many of these films, as Shuqin Cui observes, "often envelop the audience within a moody aura of anxiety and loss."[1]

A Dionysian Turn, Lifestyles, and the McWorld

The post-Mao Chinese cinema has witnessed an outburst of films representing the private, emotional lives of emerging urbanites. This has been especially true since the mid-1990s. Love, as men and women experience it in their everyday lives, for example, has been the subject of many recent films by younger directors: Zhang Yang's *Spicy Love Soup* (Aiqing ma la tang, 1997), Jin Chen's *Love in the Internet Age* (Wangluo shidai de aiqing, 1998), Fu Jinsheng's *Agreed Not to Separate* (Shuohao bu fenshou, 1999), Huo Jianqi's *Blue Love* (Lanse aiqing, 2000), Feng Xiaogang's *A Sigh* (Yisheng tanxi, 2000), Lou Ye's *Weekend Lovers* (Zhoumo qingren, 1993) and *Suzhou River* (Suzhou he, 2000), Zhang Yuan's *I Love You* (Wo ai ni, 2002) and *Green Tea* (Lü cha, 2003), Zhang Yibai's *Spring Subway* (Kaiwang chuntian de ditie, 2002), Li Xin's *Talk about Love* (Tan qing shuo ai, 1995) and *Dazzling* (Hua yan, 2001), Xia Gang's *Love at First Sight* (Yijian zhongqing, 2002), Liu Xin's *Captives of Love* (Zhengjiu aiqing, 2002) and *Body Temperature* (aka 38 °C; Shanshiba du, 2003), Zhaoyan Guozhang's *A Dream of Youth* (Qia tongxue shaonian, 2002), and Sheng Zhimin's *Two Hearts* (Xin xin, 2002). In 2005 the four best-known young film actresses then—Zhang Ziyi, Zhou Xun, Vicki Zhao Wei, and Xu Jinglei—were each memorable in a role in a film about love: Zhang in *Blooming Jessamine* (Moli hua kai), Zhou in *Beautiful as Ever* (Meiren yijiu), Zhao in *A Time to Love* (Qingren jie), and Xu in *Letter from an Unknown Woman* (Yige mosheng nüren de laixin). Their star status helped promote the visibility of the depiction of love. With the absence of this subject in Maoist cinema as a backdrop, this outburst of romantic love themes impresses us as excessive. We can't help asking if this excess in emotion can play any role in facilitating social or cultural change.

The contrast between emotional absence and excess first brings to mind the different attitudes of Apollonian and Dionysian societies toward emotions. Drawing on Nietzsche, Benedict writes about the difference:

> The desire of the Dionysian, in personal experience or in ritual, is to press through it towards a certain psychological state, to achieve excess. The closest analogy to the emotion he seeks is drunkenness, and he values the illuminations of frenzy. With Blake, [Nietzsche] believes "the path of excess leads to the palace of wisdom." The Apollonian distrusts all this, and has often little idea of the nature of such experiences. He finds means to outlaw them from his conscious life. He "knows but one law, measure in the Hellenic sense." He keeps to the middle of the road, stays within the known map, does not meddle with disruptive psychological states. In Nietzsche's fine phrase, even in the exaltation of the dance he "remains what he is, and retains his civic name."[2]

"The middle of the road" is obviously the decorum of both East and West; the Chinese classical term for decorum, *zhongyong*, translates literally as "treading the middle path." In any emotional culture, decorum is always needed to contrast the Dionysian mode—any frenzy or excess in expressing emotions.[3] This contrast between decorum and excess has many implications to our topic. On the subject of emotion, the distinction here has a twofold implication both for changing Western attitudes toward emotion and for the rekindled Chinese interest in private feelings. Both aspects have significant bearings on this investigation of post-Mao city films about love.

The status of emotion is evolving in the Western mind. Traditionally, the rational, scientific Western mind tended to ignore emotions and emotionality, associating them with irrationality, the flesh, or the baser organs. Since the mid-twentieth century, as psychologists Kurt W. Fischer and June Price Tangney remarked in 1995, "there has been a revolution in the study of emotion."[4] Hundreds of studies on the topic of emotion have emerged in the social sciences and humanities, which has led to a drastically changed perception of emotions.[5] "Emotions," as Candace Clark puts it, "underlie all human experience and social life, shaping all subjectivity, intersubjectivity, everyday interaction, social exchange, social bonds, and social divisions."[6] Emotion has shifted from being on the margin of the culture to being at the center of rekindled academic attention.

If the Western mind tends to approach the subject of emotion in a binary of rationality versus irrationality, the traditional Chinese approach is the cultivation of emotions. The well-known Confucian tenet that human actions are "initiated by emotions but curtailed by rituals" (fa hu yu qing, zhi hu yu li) best explains this approach. The Song Dynasty's neo-Confucian Master Zhu Xi explained how emotions underlie human nature, which, according to traditional Confucianism, is originally good: "Desire emanates from feelings. The mind is comparable to water, nature is comparable to the tranquility of still water, feeling is comparable to the flow of water, and desire is comparable to its waves. Just as there are good and bad waves, so there are good desires, such as when 'I desire to be humane,' and bad desires, which rush out like wild and violent waves. When bad desires are substantial, they will destroy the principle of Heaven, as water bursts a dam and damages everything. When Mencius said that 'feelings enable people to do good,' he meant that the concrete feelings flowing from our nature are originally all good."[7]

Recognizing emotions as indispensable parts of human nature, the traditional Chinese emotional culture institutionalized a wide spectrum of feelings, especially those associated with maintaining the civic order of society in the standard of decorum. The uninstitutionalized feelings, such as romantic love (love not arranged by families), often had to find expression in the less respected, marginal genres of arts and literature, such as ghost stories and popular plays. The emotional culture of Maoist China, reflecting its Utopian ideology of social revolution, also presented its own spectrum of institutionalized feelings. Given the totalitarian nature of the regime plus the fact that it delivered its political agenda by mass campaigns that touched the everyday lives of the people at a grassroots level, Maoist emotional culture was most profoundly regulated, leaving very little room for uninstitutionalized emotions to survive. The Dionysian turn in post-Mao emotional culture, the interest in exploring private feelings, reflects a desire to free human beings from the institutionalized yoke and to enrich human nature.

The contrast between restraint and the Dionysian turn should also be understood in light of David Chaney's discussion of the change from "ways of life" to "lifestyles" that I conferred in the introductory chapter.[8] While a way of life describes Maoist China, post-Mao China has opened up to the flow of lifestyles along with other material commodities. In the globalized, postcolonial, and post–Cold War world of today, *ways of life* and *lifestyles* coexist and interact in an inescapable dialectic. Their tension and conflicts have replaced the former overt ideological warfare among different political regimes to occupy the center stage of the world. Benjamin Barber best describes this dialectic in his book *Jihad vs. McWorld*. For Barber, Jihad (an Islamic zeal denoting religious struggle on the behalf of faith) is used as a generalized name for all kinds of localized cultural forces "in the name of a hundred narrowly conceived faiths against every kind of interdependence, every kind of artificial social cooperation and mutuality."[9] They are the old ways of life. McWorld denotes lifestyles. "McWorld," in Barber's excellent definition, "is a product of popular culture driven by expansionist commerce. Its template is America, its form style. Its goods are as much images as material, and aesthetic as well as product line. It is about culture as commodity, apparel as ideology."[10]

In the early twentieth century, when Chinese youth tried to modernize Chinese culture, they had their eyes on two virtues of Western achievement. The Chinese May 4th new cultural movement of 1919 proclaimed its invitation to Mr. S(cience) and Mr. D(emocracy). While Mr. S has had a relatively easier time making inroads into China, Mr. D has not. Between the May 4th student march in Tian'anmen Square and the 1989 post-Mao student protest in the same square, both prodemocracy and both crushed by military power, the close to the century's history showed a strong political resistance to democracy.

In the post-1989 "depoliticized" economic boom, Western influence has changed its form. The Chinese government today continues to encourage a pragmatic culture that marked the Deng-era economic reform. The government's oppression of ideological dissidents forms a contrast to its leniency around the gap between rich and poor in society. In a profane culture that encourages its members to care more about getting rich and less about the political status of the nation, many have become aloof to democracy. At the same time, they are exposed more to the lifestyles of the McWorld. As Barber describes of China today, "While the struggle against democracy has so far succeeded, the struggle against lifestyle and culture is failing, precisely because the economy's 'own logic' is the logic of McWorld and seems far more likely to bring with it the vices of the West (its cultural imagery and the ideology of consumption as well as a 'logical' tolerance for social injustice and inequality) than its virtues (democracy and human rights)."[11]

The social and cultural bearings of the cinematic boom on private emotions appear to be manifold. The boom should be explored in the context of China's loosened institutional control of emotions, as well as the context of a cultural reengineering of human nature. Western academia's changed perception of emotions does speak to the Chinese new emotional culture. Yet the deepest impact of the West in China is Barber's McWorld—the commercial culture, ideology, and lifestyle that are supported by material and immaterial product lines of the West. If one considers not only the government-sponsored limited import of Hollywood films to China but also the most flourishing Chinese market of pirated DVDs of foreign films, one realizes how amply foreign lifestyles, especially those showcased in Hollywood films, are informing everyday Chinese life. In an era that is advancing McWorld, the Chinese cinematic flourishing of emotions unavoidably shows the hybrid features of outside influences. It has transplanted foreign lifestyles to a Chinese soil that was already breeding new styles of life.

Pirated Copy: Transplanted Emotions and Possessed Lives

Pirated Copy (Manyan, 2004), a film by Sixth Generation director He Jianjun, is a testimony to the coming of McWorld with some twists.[12] Twist number one: pirated products further the advance of McWorld in China. Due partly to indulgence by the government and partly to popular wisdom, the current economic boom in China is fueled by the production of pirated copies of all kinds of Western commodities, from material products like brand-name shirts to cultural products like DVDs. As the world's largest workshop for foreign manufacturers, China is turning the tables on the West by allowing this abundance of pirated products to be sold everywhere to its own citizens. Although the McWorld is taken advantage of in China in economic terms, culturally, it is advancing throughout China with the help of pirated products. The film *Pirated Copy* showcases how the most prosperous markets of pirated DVDs of foreign films are penetrating everyday Chinese life. Just as Wei Hui's fictional characters in her popular *Shanghai Baby* navigate their everyday lives guided by quotes from American popular culture (from Henry Miller to Allen Ginsburg), the characters in He Jianjun's film envision the most striking moments from their favorite movies in the things they do—their lives, in a way, are turned into pirated copies of the West through the billions of disks that one can purchase either in the specialty stores that have mushroomed in Chinese cities or from vendors on street corners.

Twist number two: pirated copies have not just furthered the coming of McWorld but have also led to cultural enrichment. The film *Pirated Copy* vividly illustrates how Chinese intellectuals and university students are exposed to many treasures of world cinema, not just from Hollywood. These intellectuals reach out to the world through disks. The range of films boasted by any DVD shop or vendor in China would easily amaze anyone traveling there today. Often it only takes an educated eye to discover gems with unlikely covers. The DVD cover for *Pirated Copy* itself, for example, shows a sex scene and is labeled as an "X-rated movie" so as to sell better. Many serious films likewise wear the alluring covers of the market.

Pirated Copy uses the vending of DVDs to build a relationship between a variety of characters: a few DVD vendors, several idle youngsters, a university lecturer, a prostitute, an AIDS patient, and an unemployed couple. DVD watching, as a popular front of culture, has become the hobby of urbanites as diversified as the film's characters. Yet, besides the sociological value of being the first film on the subject of DVD watching, *Pirated Copy* continues He Jianjun's favorite style and theme in his filmmaking—a style of psychological realism and a theme of emotional possession. His *Red Beans* (Xuanlian, 1993) depicts a nurse who is struck with love for a neurotic patient. His *Postman* (Youchai, 1995) portrays a shy mailman being drawn into the private doings of the residents of a neighborhood, whose letters he opens and in whose private lives he participates. His *Scenery* (Fengjing, 1999) conveys a strong sense of the paralysis in a small-time attorney's professional and emotional life.[13] His *Butterfly Smile* (Hudie de weixiao, 2001) represents the confusion of a photographer who admires a fashion model, witnesses her hit-and-run accident, and hesitates whether to let his admired beauty accept her responsibility.

Pirated Copy, thus, as a continuation of He Jianjun's favorite psychological exploration, illustrates how foreign films dominate the emotional lives of several central characters. Mei is a young university lecturer on foreign films. She lectures on the cultural implications of the sexual lives of characters in these films. Her private life, however, has been chaste. In contrast, another character, a prostitute of Mei's age, knows the carnal aspect of love but has missed its emotional nuances. Mei seeks these feelings in foreign films. The two young women's love for foreign films brings them to Ming, a master DVD vendor. Ming has quit his university studies and spends most of his time watching and selling foreign films. His collection and his access to disk supplies are more than sufficient to open a specialty store, but he hates to be confined indoors and enjoys reaching out to people to tell them about foreign films and sell them disks. He is like a preacher of foreign films; there is nothing he enjoys more than talking about them to others. For Mei and the prostitute, the handsome Ming becomes a substitute for their beloved film characters. Mei has her sexual encounter with Ming in a classroom, and the prostitute allows Ming to trade DVDs for the sex he has with her. Ming associates with some cultural elites, and he frequents their salons to sell films. The director leads the film audience to see how foreign films are opening new emotional horizons for these characters and how foreign films correspond with these characters for their various "spiritual" needs, like the educated AIDS patient who selects films that may better prepare him for his approaching death.

Parallel to Ming's cluster of acquaintances, another character obsessed by foreign films leads us to see a variety of other characters and the frustrating aspect of the impact of foreign films. An unemployed state worker leads a difficult life. Film watching is a release for his frustrations. Tempted by so many things that he can't pay for, his film-watching experience tells him the solution is to rob a bank. On his way to do that, he encounters a group of idle youths raping a girl. Earlier in the film, the audience has seen these kids selling pirated DVDs and wearing stolen police uniforms to commit petty crimes. Although the unemployed man is not a tough guy, the resemblance of the crime scene to his favorite film *Pulp Fiction* allows him to step into the shoes of an angry film character. He uses film lines to challenge the baffled youngsters and opens fire on them. Instead of robbing a bank, he stops the crime of rape with his crime of murder. Running away from the scene, he wakes up to reality, finds it's too hard to face, and shoots himself. Two prominent social problems in today's China, the frustration caused by unemployment and the petty crimes committed by idle urban youth, both get mixed up here with the business of selling and watching foreign films.

Compared with He Jianjun's other films, *Pirated Copy* is a more enjoyable one to watch. A clear story line organizes much of the footage, especially those about DVD vending, which has a documentary feel. The characters and their personalities come to life through their interactions. The director shows good control of the rhythm of the narrative and demonstrates a humor in editing that is rare in his earlier films. The ending of *Pirated Copy* is a good example. Mei sees Ming on the street not long after their sexual encounter on campus. Ming is running away from the police and does not see Mei. The hand-held camera then cuts to close-range shots following Ming as he runs and then zooms in on his face, which shows his fear and his desperate effort to lose the police. The camera rolls on for minutes without looking back. In this duration, the audience naturally recalls what happened to the other disk dealers who were captured by the police earlier in the film: interrogation and penalty. Finally, when Ming is totally exhausted yet still has not given up, the camera changes direction to show that the police are long gone and the equally exhausted person who is chasing him is the breathless Mei. The film ends here, but the humor it creates lasts. What chases Ming, one thought prompts, is the magic of those disks in his carrying bag that has changed Mei from a restrained person into one who runs for passion. This is a clever and worthwhile use of footage.

In contrast, He Jianjun's earlier films often contain counterproductive sequences. The beginning of *Butterfly Smile* is an obvious example. In about ten minutes, the dialogue-free and low-key opening sequence tries to portray the psychological effects of a fashion model's hit-and-run accident on a hidden witness, the photographer who happens to be her admirer. In an interview, He Jianjun talked about this sequence with some conceit.[14] He did not seem to realize that the sequence occurs at the beginning of the film when the audience knows nothing about the characters and their relationship, and the long confusion in the dark becomes a real ordeal.In *Pirated Copy*, foreign films are both the catalyst for changing lifestyles and a correspondent for many hidden and not-so-hidden desires.

He Jianjun's earlier film *Postman* showcased other kinds of emotional possession before the arrival of foreign films. The film portrayed a more closed world with covert displays of emotion. Xiaodou, an introverted young postman of few words, becomes obsessed by opening letters in his charge that let him peep into the private lives of those in his postal district. Through his peeping, one detects emotional currents hidden under the orderly façade of everyday life—extramarital affairs, prostitution, drug addiction, and suicides. Xiaodou is drawn into these undercurrents. He turns from reading letters to participation. He alters letters, follows letter writers, visits the drug addict, and goes to the prostitute. His participation shows not only the engaging power of voyeurism but also his own particular psychological needs. In a way, the film depicts Xiaodou's voyeurism as his sexual maturity. Orphaned as a small child, Xiaodou grows up with a surrogate mother, his elder sister. His newly discovered channels of peeping are opened at the same time as his sister gets engaged. Emotionally, Xiaodou needs to cut himself off from his attachment to his sister, what we might even call it an Oedipal complex (the film portrays Xiaodou's brother-in-law as an intruder). Throughout the film, Xiaodou's moments with his sister—chatting at dinner, his peeping at his sister bathing, and his climbing into his sister's bed—indicate the nostalgic attachment that he needs to break in his search for new types of emotional gratification.

A powerful leitmotif of hidden desires in the monotony of everyday life in *Postman* is the repeated scene of Xiaodou's female colleague pounding a mail stamp. She is a model worker, but she also grasps at Xiaodou for sex when they find each other alone in the post office. Here the attraction of voyeurism also manifests itself; given the opportunity to go out with his pretty coworker, Xiaodou would rather stay home to read letters and get into emotional communication with the objects of his desire. He wonders why there are certain things that people can only write but can never say to each other face to face. He himself is more attracted to the writing of emotions.

It is interesting to speculate what might have become of Postman Xiaodou if he were to be drawn into the current voyeuristic pastime of disk watching. As a reticent voyeur, how would he participate in the illuminated realm of foreign lives that currently possesses millions of curious eyes in the dark in today's China?

The Wildness: Love and Revenge in Performing the Play

A Dream of Youth is a touching recollection of youthful love and the dreams of a group of actor friends and is, supposedly, semiautobiographical of a group of Sixth Generation filmmakers. Two women, Shanshan and Guo Qing, were once close friends in an acting class at a film school. Now neither of them is performing—Shanshan runs a film investment company, and Guo is married and lives in Japan. A secret between them has kept the two distant from each other. At the beginning of the film, Guo anonymously invests in Shanshan's company for a production. Shanshan turns to a former classmate, Jia Nan, for help with the project. Jia Nan has just abandoned his leading role in a TV series because of a dispute with the director and the disorienting discovery that his newlywed wife is sleeping with the producer of the series. Jia Nan walks out of their apartment, not knowing exactly where to go. In a nearby village, he comes across Chang Bo, an amateur actor who used to work with him in supporting roles. Chang Bo invites Jia Nan to stay with him, and Jia Nan accepts. Later, Jia Nan discovers that Chang Bo is now the boyfriend of Shanshan, who consequently asks Jia Nan to do the film.

Shanshan rejects the investment from Guo as soon as she discovers Guo is the investor. But a new investment from an American documentary filmmaker immediately kicks in to keep the project alive. Shanshan and Guo Qing, with Jia Nan and Chang Bo, are to put together an experimental version of Cao Yu's *The Wildness*. The rehearsals for *The Wildness* are to be the subject of a documentary film by the investor. It turns out that Guo had once betrayed Shanshan by stealing and eventually marrying Shanshan's date. Both Shanshan and Jia Nan have emotional wounds from being abandoned and betrayed by their friends. In rehearsing this play of revenge, they can help heal themselves. Guo, nonetheless, is dying of a fatal disease, and she joins the rehearsal to seek the comfort of being revenged by her friends to allay her guilty conscience. How the Chinese avenge their friends is what interests Fox, the documentary filmmaker. How the performers, with their own emotional entanglements, relate to their roles in *The Wildness* is what the film *A Dream of Youth* explores.

Among Cao Yu's plays written in the 1930s, *The Wildness* was the hardest for the Maoist stage to adapt and thus had been ignored. The play is a revenge story of emotional entanglement. Chou Hu's father lost his property, family, and life to Devil Jiao over a land-ownership dispute. When Chou Hu finally escapes jail and shows up for revenge, he finds that Devil Jiao has died and is survived by his blind wife; his son, Daxing; his daughter-in-law, Jinzi; and a newborn grandchild. In the old days, Daxing and Chou Hu had grown up as brothers and Jinzi was Chou Hu's sweetheart. Believing that a father's debt has to be paid off by his son, Chou Hu kills Daxing and elopes with Jinzi. The newborn baby is also killed by accident in the emotionally charged unfolding of the drama. In the concluding scene, Chou Hu and Jinzi get lost in a dark forest and begin hallucinating. In the meantime, Daxing's blind mother carries the body of her dead grandson and chases them all the way in the wood. The title of the play suggests the roughness of the strong emotion to avenge, which is as primeval as the virgin land. In the play, Chou Hu's reason for revenge is both for the family and for himself—he wants to regain the love of Jinzi. This last point is actually the direct literary source of the title of the play, which is taken from the lines of a Persian poet: "If you were by my side, the wildness would be Heaven."[15] Yet what Cao Yu wanted to show is how this primal emotion of love and revenge is censored by cultural conventions. The forest scene especially indicates the tortures of the guilty conscience that Chou Hu suffers. Jinzi is by Chou Hu's side, but the wildness on the stage is obviously not Heaven. The play is a parody of

Eugene O'Neal's *Emperor Jones*, using such elements as drums, wandering, forest, and hallucination to express the emotional anxiety caused by revenge and the pain left behind by killing. The play also touches upon the taboo of family members killing each other.

In the immediate post-Mao cinematic release from the yoke of social class ideology, *The Wildness* was rediscovered. A film adaptation of *The Wildness* (1982), directed by Ling Zi and played superbly by Yang Zaibao and Liu Xiaoqing, illustrated why this ignored play best met the era's fascination with the ambiguity of human nature. Although the film was banned and held back by the censors for years before it could be distributed, it has now become a classic.

In 2000, when the Chinese soul was being stifled by the profanity of commercialism, a deconstructionist performance of *The Wildness* testified to the era's anxiety.[16] Directed by Li Liuyi, the performance interprets *The Wildness* in postmodern terms. In a collage setting consisting of color TVs (some of which show clips of the 1982 film of *The Wildness*), refrigerators, foreign liquor, flush toilets, old Chinese books and dolls, the play showcases the fragmentation of humanity and traditional Chinese ethics in the postmodern era. In a way, the performance airs the postmodern pessimism about humanity. It emphasizes the failure of humanity to make a real breakthrough. It focuses on the social, cultural, human, and emotional forces that keep Chou Hu and Jinzi, the cultural rebels, from walking out of the dark forest.

A Dream of Youth continues the post-Mao fascination with *The Wildness* and the pessimism of human feelings that make people incapable of walking out of the dark emotional forest of loss and confusion. Yet, indicating a general cultural change in China, the director of this version was less interested in producing any cultural allegories than in showing the emotional forest as an everyday reality that one has to learn to live with. In the film, three of the performers vividly remember their student time rehearsing *The Wildness* and now, more mature in their postschool lives, their understandings of the roles have changed. As students with no particular emotional wounds, they all wanted to play the lead roles in *The Wildness*, to be wild in expressing emotions and to exact vengeance. Now, having tasted some emotional bitterness caused by their close friends, they are learning to appreciate the subtleties of *The Wildness*—the mixed feelings of love and hatred, the emotional dilemmas, the pain caused by revenge, and the split personalities in action. On the level of drama, the film has resolved its problems by eventually turning revenge to understanding and forgiveness among this group of friends. The unfolding of the drama, however, has also showcased a brutal, changed world of distanced human relations where love yields to self-centered personal interests and benefit. The compromise among this group of friends suggests an understanding that love is a blind and chaotic force, and those involved should just accept whatever comes their way. "Life is not as complicated as a play," one character keeps saying in the film. "Let's not confuse a play with real life." All through their rehearsal, these friends cannot find a satisfactory answer to Jinzi's question to her husband in the play: "If your mother and I both fall into a river and both are about to drown, who would you rescue first?" One love always seems to be challenged and checked by another love. The end of the film shows these friends' disbelief that there can be an answer to the question.

Dazzling: To Daydream Varied Fashions of Love

Dazzling mixes fantasy and reality, darkness and light, as well as disappointment with and passion for love. The unique narrative structure of the film—a cinema usher watching love films gazes at the people watching these films and imagines how these cinemagoers' love lives may compare with the films they are watching—offers us a glimpse of the cultural constitution of a generation of young people, the particular visual culture in which they have grown up, their understanding of love, and the cultural range that informs their performance of their love stories. Director Li Xin claims that he is using his "personal means to express a popular subject," his particular ways to "pack" (baozhuang) common feelings, and his experiments with cinematic form to become an indispensable part of the love stories that he is telling.[17] Indeed, Li Xin has left the mark of his generation, those born in the 1970s and 1980s, on the eternal human subject of love. What he uses to pack this subject is a cinematic style that reminds us of MTV, techno music, video games, and cartoons. The style appeals to the taste of the young, who particularly love quick rhythm, a strong sense of motion, and a free manipulation of visual images. The visual impact of this style is a far cry from, for example, the naturalist cinematic style, which avoids unusual camera angles and ranges and avoids cuts. Average cuts in contemporary Chinese films range from seven hundred to eight hundred. *Dazzling* has more than thirteen hundred.

Li Xin emphasizes that his age group is "a generation that needs packages."[18] For now, we can first take his visual style, one that is most compatible with a postmodern culture, as an example of this packaging. Indeed, one of the features of postmodernism is reproduction (packaging) for mass consumption. On this point, however, one quickly thinks of the different cinematic style of Jia Zhangke, a director of the same age group as Li Xin. In representing the young people of a contemporary provincial town, Jia's style is noted for its unobtrusive fashion of realism. One may explain the difference thus: While Li Xin focuses on the big metropolis of today, Jia Zhangke represents the recent past of a provincial town. Jia Zhangke is showcasing a society that is on the threshold of getting into Li Xin's filmic world, and he grapples with small-town modernity, whereas Li Xin plays with postmodernity. One, however, can't deny that Li Xin and Jia Zhangke are both the expressions of an age group, and there are bound to be more expressions of this generation of people. Here we start to see that Li Xin's emphasis on packaging also implies the multiplicity of possibilities—once a love relationship is packaged differently, the nature of it changes as well. *Dazzling* weaves together five love stories of different tastes—they are all part of the inexhaustible dimensions of human love.

One of Li Xin's muses is the German film *Run, Lola, Run* (by Tom Tykwer, 1998).[19] He admits that in the process of directing *Dazzling*, he kept watching this popular film, which indicates that life is like a game—from the same starting point, any incidental factor might lead the game to a different conclusion. Lola receives a phone call from her boyfriend, who has just lost one hundred thousand marks in the subway. "Wait for me. I'm going to get you the money," she tells her boyfriend and starts to run. From there, her running is repeated and it represents three totally different versions of her rescuing her boyfriend: First, she fails to get money from her dad, has to join her boyfriend to rob a supermarket, gets shot by a policeman, and dies in front of her lover. Second, she steals a hundred thousand marks from her father's bank. When she approaches her boyfriend, she realizes that he is on his way to rob the supermarket. She shouts. Her boyfriend changes his mind and turns around to come to her. A truck hits him, and he dies. Third, Lola is almost hit by a truck when she is running aimlessly not knowing where to get the money. She finds herself in front of a casino, goes in to play, and keeps winning. Her boyfriend, in the meantime, finds his lost money. When they finally meet, they laugh. Here are three versions of stories triggered by the same phone call. The film can go on to offer more versions. Although every one of us knows that any slice of our lives may turn out differently due to incidental factors, we also know that one only lives once and can have only one of the versions (and not necessarily the best one). One's unrepeatable life may well be experienced as a letdown when compared with inspiring films with satisfactory endings.

In *Dazzling*, the cinema usher knows and abhors the difference between cinema and real life. As a matter of fact, the film focuses on his confusion with the two—indeed, if anything may happen from the same starting point, how can one determine which is real life and which is cinematic fantasy? The cinema usher is depicted as a parasite of the cinema who is addicted to the darkened room, to the uninterrupted privacy of watching, and to his indulgence with any wild fantasies without taking any action. When he finally braves the broad daylight to seek his own love, he encounters disappointment. "Little Thing," the young woman who appeals to him, is an anticultural wild type, a far cry from any conventional woman of a typical love romance. Here, the influence of *Run, Lola, Run* is still felt; Lola in her running, from a feminist perspective, can be seen as a deviation from the conventions of a traditional woman. She acts quickly instead of being indecisive, she is tough rather than soft, determined rather than weak, an initiator rather than a bystander, willful and wayward rather than obedient. In *Dazzling*, the cinema usher is baffled by his attraction to Little Thing, who has characteristics similar to Lola's, but he is appalled when he learns that Little Thing dies of anticultural behavior, a drug overdose.

This failure in his anticultural encounter, however, is only one version of his experience with love. His fantasy with the love stories of four couples from his cinematic audience accompanies his disappointment in encountering real life. One couple's experience with love is marked by the young man's constant jogging, which is used to indicate the monotonous repetition of the couple's daily routines. Every evening, he sees her at the dock. They greet each other in the same way. They eat at the same place. He accompanies her on the bus ride home, hearing the same, recorded listing of the stops along the way. Then he jogs to a foreign embassy to stand in line overnight for those people who don't want to stand all night but who want a sure chance to be interviewed early for a visa the next day. The film repeats this couple's routine four times until she proposes that they stop seeing each other. He has to jog to deal with the disappointment. Toward the end of the film, he is shown starting a new love relationship.

The second couple is preparing for their marriage, but they also feel the monotony of daily life. They can't find the sparkle of love until one day a sudden downpour catches them unprepared. They embrace each other. What they and the audience take for rain, however, is soon shown to be only an accidental water pipe leakage—the camera zooms out to show the source of the water. This interesting sequence not only shows the cinema's capability of manipulating reality but also suggests the accidental nature of love.

The third story is about the awkwardness and embarrassment of first love. A college student gets so nervous with his wish to express his love to a female classmate that he stammers. His efforts at practicing to overcome the stammering at work, the college's radio station, is accidentally broadcast, which humiliates the young woman and himself. At this point, the cinema usher is getting more accustomed to the sunshine, so that he brings it into his imagining of this story. The images of sunshine warm up the story. The young woman rids herself of the misunderstanding that the boy is making fun of her.

The fourth story is represented as a poetic allegory of searching. The young woman (played by Xu Jinglei) doesn't utter a single word throughout the sequence, but she has yearning eyes and holds a map while walking in the forest where she encounters a woodsman. Later, we see a young family, she and the woodsman and a child, stretching out in the sunshine. In a way, this poetic sequence concludes the cinema usher's imagination, showing the positive impact of the sunshine. The end of the film indicates that the cinema usher gets closer to the world of sunshine in the process of thinking and imagination. According to Deng Guanghui, the conclusion of *Dazzling* testifies to a general change in attitudes of the Sixth Generation directors toward love.[20] Indeed, early Sixth Generation films, such as *Weekend Lovers* and *Dirt*, concern the anxiety of coming of age and are noted for their obvious narcissism, bitterness, and anticultural behaviors. They represent a marginal subculture of youth. *Dazzling* revisits these attitudes and finds compromise for them with ordinary folks' everyday life. *Dazzling*'s attitude, as Deng Guanghui phrases it, "has replaced [this generation's earlier] sharpness, pain, stubbornness, and narcissism with a new understanding and tolerance."[21]

As I have discussed elsewhere in this book, the Sixth Generation's coming of age is accompanied by many general changes of the nation—a turn from the central controlled society to a society of multiplicity, an ideological transition from the grand narrative to a focus on the everyday, and an aesthetic change from the heroic to the mundane. All these changes have influenced how a generation of young people mature and broaden their range of engaging the outside world. The global communication of today makes this generation's broadening of range reach even further. The influence of *Run, Lola, Run* actually leads us to an international case of crosscultural adaptation. *Run, Lola, Run* (1998) is a German adaptation, broadly interpreted, of Polish director

Krzystof Kieslowski's *Blind Chance* (Przypadeck, 1981), which represents three different versions of a medical student's life based on whether he catches or doesn't catch a train. The three versions are typical of the cultural trends in Poland of the 1980s. A year before *Run, Lola, Run*, there was also a British adaptation, *Sliding Doors* (1997), which uses a young woman's catching and not catching a subway train to contrast her different experiences in the realms of life and death. At the end of the film, she meets up with the man who shows up in both realms of her contrasting experiences. *Dazzling*, in this perspective, is an interesting Chinese adaptation in the crosscultural reproduction. A young Chinese director has borrowed an interesting, game-like perspective to life to showcase his maturity in love and in life.

One more muse that Li Xin claims as an influence in directing *Dazzling* is Wong Kar-wai's *Fallen Angels* (Duoluo tianshi, 1995), a film noted for its subtle psychological depiction of five young urbanites—how they are expressive by themselves in their monologues but refuse to be sociable (the film is noted for the multiple monologues of characters), how the rainy nights, the juxtaposition of black-and-white as well as color footage, and other cinematic elements like irregular exposures help bring out their moods and their social aloofness. From Wong Kar-wai, Li Xin has looked for a way of bringing out his generation's feeling of a metropolis, that is, Shanghai. He admits that the aura of a city is hard to grasp because people of different ages, times, and social status all have their different approaches to it. His representation of the city aura needs to project his age group's anxiety with not knowing what to do and what to want in a society fragmented by multiple cultural elements.[22] In Wong Kar-wai, he seems to have found this feel of the urban aura.

Suzhou River: To Question Romance

Lou Ye's 2000 film, *Suzhou River*, portrays romance as the fabrication of wishful thinking. In questioning the possibility of romance in real life, the film also reflects a strong yearning for romance. "What we know as romanticism," Lou says, "and many love stories are totally unreal. But people need this kind of romanticism in order to face the harshness of life."[23]

The film is set in contemporary Shanghai. Flowing through the city is not only a major river, the Huangpu, but also a tributary, the Suzhou. The waterfront of the city, with colossal buildings from the colonial past and the ultramodern present, overlooks the Huangpu. The Suzhou River, on the other hand, flows by the back streets of Shanghai and looks on this city from quite a different perspective. This different angle of view of Shanghai, not just the splendor of a world-class metropolis but a living city connected to everyday life in the back streets—especially that of youth on the margins of society—is for me why Lou Ye named his film as he did.

The film starts with a question. A female asks a male, "If I disappear, will you search for me, as Mardar searched for Mudan? Without any emotion, the man says he will and the woman says that he is lying. The man is the first-person narrator of the film, whom we never have a chance to see. He is a lonely videographer living by the Suzhou River, observing life through his viewfinder. When Meimei, who performs as a mermaid in a huge tank at a bar, falls into his viewfinder, he befriends her and becomes fascinated by the mysticism about her—she will disappear for days and then show up again without a word. Concerning her disappearance, Meimei asks the question that starts and then haunts the film. She brings the videographer's attention to a recent urban legend publicized by the newspapers—the story of Mardar and Mudan.

The videographer starts to make up his version of the story of Mardar and Mudan with a lot of hesitancy as he unfolds his imagined drama, such as "and then, maybe—" These hesitancies clearly mark the substory of the film as fiction. Mardar is a motorcycle courier, who works during the day and, at night, watches pirated DVDs, which become the source of his romanticism. He soon falls in love with Mudan, a girl whom he transports away on his motorcycle from her liquor tycoon father when he entertains prostitutes. Mardar presents Mudan with a toy mermaid to celebrate their love rides together. Mardar is torn with pain when he is asked to kidnap Mudan to get a ransom out of her father, but he does it anyway. Mudan feels betrayed and jumps into the Suzhou River. The newspapers report that people have seen a mermaid in the Suzhou River, but it is the drowned Mudan. A few years later, Mardar gets out of jail, convinced that Mudan is still alive and starts to search for her. The second half of the film has Mardar searching for Mudan. Instead, he first finds Meimei (played by the same actress), who is so impressed by his story that she pretends willingly that she is his Mudan. Just as the videographer worries that he is losing Meimei to Mardar, there comes the tragic news that Mardar has found the real Mudan at a liquor store but the two die together in a drunk-driving accident. Meimei also departs, leaving behind a note asking the videographer to come and find her. Will he? The videographer concludes the film by saying, "I close my eyes, waiting for the next love to arrive." Obviously, the line between reality and fantasy, the times when the videographer opens and closes his eyes, is vague. Yet, in retrospect, the differences of the two realms are also sharp, as sharp as the frame in which a colorful mermaid, bathed in a stream of warm sunshine, is seen on the shore of the murky Suzhou (the effect is like a color image imbedded in a black-and-white picture).

When *Suzhou River* opened at the Toronto International Film Festival, a programmer described the film as Hitchcock's *Vertigo* as if it were directed by Wong Kar-wai, the director of *Chungking Express*. Since then, this resemblance has continually been picked up by various film reviews and scholarly studies.[24] Interestingly enough, Lou Ye insisted that the influence was not at all conscious—he said that he had not even watched *Vertigo* since his graduation from film school. Hitchcock's 1958 classic re-creates *film noir*. In the format of a two-part detective thriller, it portrays a detective's loss-regain-loss of his romantic love associated with two women who are actually the same person involved in an extraordinary murder plot. Obviously, Lou Ye's film is also about a central character's relationship with two identical women in the two parts of a story that involves crime and love. I would suggest that the genre that *Vertigo* belongs to, *film noir*, offers clues to further understand this coincidental resemblance of Lou's film to an earlier masterpiece. As we know, among the fountainheads of the classic period of American film noir is Italian Neorealism, a cinematic tradition that graduates of Beijing Film Academy tend to admire. Problem pictures and semidocumentary crime thrillers influenced by Italian neo-realism in the postwar America led to the formation of a cinematic mood of cynicism, darkness and despair, which in turn produced more crime films and melodramas about an urban jungle of crime and corruption. Mood-wise, Lou Ye's perception of the city resembles those of the film noir; the latter, as summed up by Nicholas Christopher, is to showcase the city as an "urban labyrinth, a place infested with psychosis, anxiety, and existential dread."[25] Lou Ye's Shanghai in *Suzhou River* is a similarly sordid, antiromantic place. It is so not only because it is "a city of criminals, smugglers, and seedy night-clubs"[26] but also, more interestingly, because of the neorealistic approach of the videographer shooting the cluttered banks of Suzhou River—his voice-over tells the audience that the river is the dirtiest in the world, filled with trash and the residues of time.

The image of trash here reminds us of Lou Ye's same perception of Shanghai in his earlier film *Weekend Lovers* (1993), which can help us understand more the anxiety and existential dread harbored in this city. The film portrays the lives of a group of adolescent friends, and it is dominated by a mood of boredom and the pain of coming of age. Rock 'n' roll and street fighting become outlets for this mood. While a girl's boyfriend serves a jail term, she falls in love with a singer of a rock band. When the former boyfriend returns, he wants revenge. To stop his plan of disrupting a rock show, the girl returns to the old boyfriend as required. Enraged, the rock singer fights with and kills the old boyfriend. Feeling guilty, the girl leaves the city. Out of such a brutal and sad conclusion, the film adds a romantic ending. When the rock singer gets out of jail, a limousine carrying all his friends is waiting for him at the street corner. The girl is among them, holding their baby. While the camera pulls up from the scene to end the film, the voice-over says that the couple is later seen living happily in another city. This ending definitely reflects a romantic yearning. Yet when the fanciful limousine is shown in a high angle shot, it occupies only half of the frame. The other half shows a heap of trash, and it stays there till the end of the sequence. The heap reminds us of the sordid and gloomy urban mise-en-scène throughout the film. The story is an episode of growing up, the voice-over at the beginning of the film says, that is painful to recall.

It is ironic that the mood of the coming of age of a generation of urban youth in post-Mao China resembles the dark, cynical mood of the film noir. The film's rock song, which is cowritten by Lou Ye, best paraphrases this mood:

> Have you seen
> Many people are losing their grip,
> Their souls suffocated in the desert?
> Have you seen
> Many people are so indifferent,
> Their feelings dry up in the tribes?
> Holy god, please bestow your food,
> So that your children can get to grow.
> Holy god, please rip the wall between hearts,
> Desire and fantasy will swell.
> Withered Chrysanthemum, mouth wide open,
> Cries out, "Help me!"
> White snowflakes dancing,
> Drizzles drifting, down to this world.
> Looking at this boring world, I sing.
> Fearful eyes full of desolation.[27]

The cynicism of beseeching god in a godless world in post-Mao China is hard to miss in this song. The contrast between boredom and withering on the one hand and desperate singing and cold drizzling on the other is also hard to forget. The gloom of the trashy city matches this mood. Even the reported happiness of the two central characters has to be in another imagined city.

Suzhou River continues the mood of *Weekend Lovers*. Actor Jia Hongsheng, whose real-life story of drug addiction is the subject of a film discussed elsewhere in this book, plays the role of the former boyfriend in *Weekend Lovers* and of Mardar in *Suzhou River*. The first role grows naturally into the second because of the similarity in neighborhoods, cultural atmospheres, and character traits. *Weekend Lovers*, when it is seen as a cultural context, also explains why *Suzhou River*'s videographer is cynical and why he distrusts love. When Meimei is attracted by Mardar's story, the videographer says, "I know we're going to have trouble between us. Shall we say bye-bye now or shall we wait until we have sex one more time?" This aloofness to emotion is characteristic of him all through the film.

The cynical playfulness of the videographer in manipulating the narrative of *Suzhou River* and the same playfulness of the deft handheld camerawork (by cinematographer Wang Yu) to match up with the fanciful nature of the fictional narrative are reasons that people compare Lou Ye with Wong Kar-wai, and *Suzhou River* with *Chungking Express*. What interests us here, however, is how the two directors and the two films compare on the notions of love and romance.

Wong Kar-wai's *Chungking Express*, as David Bordwell's analysis of it shows, has romance printed everywhere on its menu.[28] The film's intertwined love stories of two police officers, 223 and 633, converge at Midnight Express, a fast-food counter in Hong Kong. Food thus becomes an involved metaphor of love.[29] Officer 223, while overcoming the pain of being dumped by his girlfriend, befriends a mysterious blond woman, who turns out to be a drug smuggler. Officer 633 is also abandoned by his girlfriend, an airline hostess. Pining for her, he becomes the object of love of Faye, the girl who works at Midnight Express. When her love becomes known to Officer 633, who asks her out for a date, Faye leaves to become an air hostess herself. Using Bordwell's analysis, we can work out a list of *Chungking Express*'s approaches to love and see how Lou Ye compares.

1. Love is soliloquy and dream. Wong's characters are romantic and devoted to love. Although Wong often emphasizes how characters only keep romantic feelings to themselves and find it hard to communicate these feelings (thus the soliloquy), he still represents a certain belief in and devotion to romance. Lou Ye's films, on the other hand, are half-hearted about romance.

There are always character contrasts. In *Weekend Lovers*, while the rock singer is devoted to romance, the former boyfriend is obviously cynical. In *Suzhou River*, while Mardar is serious about romance, the videographer is not.

2. Love may be experienced as loss, but it also gives characters hope. Wong's characters, while losing the love of someone, regain love with someone else. Love lives on wherever there are human beings. Lou's films are more skeptical about the persistence of love. *Weekend Lovers* ends in the death of one character and the separation of the others. The beauty of the added, imagined reunion of the characters is questioned by putting the scene side by side with a trash heap. *Suzhou River* doesn't even leave any added hope; it ends in death and separation of characters.

3. Love is food. Besides many other hints of this analogy in the film, the owner of Midnight Express encourages his patrons to start anew in love. "Each love, like each dish, is different, but one should broaden one's tastes."[30] Lou Ye is not as matter-of-fact, down-to-earth, or profane. In *Suzhou River*, Mudan will jump into the river for love and Mardar will be obsessed in search of that lost love. Love for them is too sacred to be a changeable pursuit. In *Weekend Lovers*, the rock singer is shy and awkward about dating the girl, whereas the ex-boyfriend is more driven by his sexual desire in seeing the same girl. They, nonetheless, also don't accept the possibility of changing their object of love. Popular urban culture in Hong Kong, which has long mixed the Chinese traditions with the Western and is open to all sorts of influences, has nourished *Chungking Express*'s down-to-earth approach to love. In Mainland China, the culture for love and romance has had a much bumpier ride—from a Maoist puritanical, ascetic, censored, and tightly controlled culture to a fairly sudden post-Mao craving for love and romance that has frequently been infested by the society's loss of control over prostitution, adoption of mistresses and concubines, and pornography. The Chinese emotional culture's puritanical past and its current invasion by carnal desires have left very little room in between for a down-to-earth perception of love and romance to grow.[31] This may partially explain why Lou Ye can't comprise love and romance (still perceived idealistically) with the everyday life he observes through his camera.

4. Love takes time. Here is an important Wong Kar-wai theme: love and life may be experienced in many different ways; they ask for both the patience to wait for the right time and the urgency to catch the slippery moment while you still can. Expiration dates printed on packaged foods and times of flights are some detailed metaphors that work with this theme. Lou's films

are less involved with the concept of time. *Weekend Lovers* is presented as a recollection of past experience. It suggests that the city and the cultural milieu remain the same but the characters have grown and changed—while young, they are angry at life and hostile to society; now grown up, they've learned to compromise. *Suzhou River* plays with time and suggests the possibility that the story may actually be different. Yet it still just presents one definite story. When the videographer closes his eyes at the end of the film to wait for love to dawn on him again, he has no hope that the next love will necessarily be better.

5. Wong's characters in love stories are rewarded with the "Wong Kar-wai epiphanies" of love, the moments that hint at the continuation of love. For Officer 223 it is a birthday message from the blond woman, and for Officer 633 it is the boarding pass Faye gives him. Lou Ye's films have similar moments, but they don't offer much hope for love to continue. In *Weekend Lovers*, the reunion of the lovers and friends, as mentioned earlier, is shown in the contrast between their beautiful limousine and a trash heap by the side of the street. Whether love can continue doesn't depend so much on the lovers; it depends instead more on whether the city will rid itself of its trash. In *Suzhou River*, the note left behind by Meimei asking the videographer to find her could be the start of a beautiful relationship. The videographer, nonetheless, is not equally inspired by the story of Mardar and Mudan. His refusal to follow Meimei indicates that he is going to slip back into his routine life of observing the banal life along the Suzhou River and that he will keep love and romance only in his fanciful mind.

Apparently, Lou Ye's Shanghai is not a sunlit city of love and romance. Thus Lou Ye's ideas are actually not a far cry from those of his Beijing Film Academy contemporaries, such as Jia Zhangke, in promoting a sort of gritty realism. Stylistically, Lou Ye shuns Jia Zhangke–style long takes and long shots. In his films, frequent cuts, special effects, and artificial cinema techniques abound. Yet Lou Ye shares with Jia Zhangke the same culture of urban realism, and he presents a Shanghai as culturally alienating as Jia Zhangke's provincial town in his gloomy stories about love.

Featuring both a yearning for and a cynicism about love, the new urban cinema showcases strong fascination with the private, emotional lives of emerging urbanities in China. A surge of films about love in the 1990s was informed both by the changed Western attitude that started to value emotions more and a rekindled Chinese need to enrich representation of private feelings after decades of Maoist denial of such feelings for the sake of the state and the state's institutionalized feelings. In the context of globalization, this surge reflected negotiation between traditional ways of life and the imported lifestyles. Displaying hybrid features of outside influences, films in this surge transplanted foreign lifestyles in the soil of Chinese everyday life. *Postman* and *Pirated Copy*, the two films by He Jianjun, illustrated differences between a closed China with covert displays of emotions and a new China seeking emotional expressions while possessed by an influx of foreign films. The hidden desires of the past became the new urbanites' open experiments modeled after foreign films. The Maoist denial of unsuitable feelings was shown in the case of Cao Yu's *The Wildness*—how it was ignored in the Maoist time but became popular in the post-Mao era to help promote a renewed emphasis on the ambiguity of human nature and emotion. In *A Dream of Youth*, performing *The Wildness* accompanied the coming of age of a group of Sixth Generation filmmakers and their friends. In *Dazzling*, the same generation of young Chinese fit their love stories into the packages of the imported styles of MTV, techno music, and video games. Here we see the impact of an imported visual culture on the love lives of these young people and on their self-definition, as well as self-expression. In a style of film noir, *Suzhou River* questioned romance, showing it as the fabrication of wishful thinking initiated by mundane urban living. Viewed as a whole, these films have distanced themselves from the myth of love being sacred, and they have drawn love down to earth as part of their commonplace, everyday life. The imported foreign lifestyles have become an integrated part of this everyday life. In a hybrid visual culture of China in the 1990s, which featured the dominance of foreign films, foreign lifestyles also functioned as a mirror that contrasted love with many sordid, antiromantic urban experiences of Chinese young people.

6

Lunar Eclipse: Elusive Urban Realities

In the early summer of 2002, Zhang Xinxin, a Chinese writer who had migrated to the States, was visiting Paris.¹ At a party, she heard all her French friends talking about a Chinese film that had opened in the city after participating in the Cannes Film Festival. She invited her host family in Paris, a senior couple, to watch the film with her, but she felt sorry afterward that she had done so. The film was not a pleasant one. The couple was deeply touched and felt that they needed to update their understanding of China, but Zhang Xinxin felt that they had not been given an accurate picture of today's China nor did they understand the politics that had led to the endorsement of the French opening of this film.

The film was Wang Chao's *The Orphan of Anyang* (Anyang ying'er, 2002). It tells the sad story of an unemployed state worker and a prostitute in a small

Happy Times (dir. Zhang Yimou, 2000) may well be considered a parody of Chaplin's *City Lights*. Courtesy of China Film Archive, Beijing.

provincial town. Feeling the pinch of his unemployed life, the worker finds an abandoned baby at a small noodle shop. He decides to adopt the baby and calls, as instructed by the note found on the child, to claim a monthly allowance. The mother of the baby turns out to be a prostitute, a pretty countrywoman who is trying to make it in the town. The mother is soon touched by the worker's love for the baby, and the three of them start to live together as a family. The worker takes care of the baby and runs a bicycle-repair stand in front of his apartment building. The prostitute takes her customers back to the worker's apartment for her business. The prostitute's former gangster pimp shows up to claim the baby. He has been diagnosed with a terminal disease and worries that his family line will end, since he has no child. The worker, however, is drawn to fatherhood and gets in a fight to defend his right to the baby; unfortunately, he is thrown in jail for the damage caused by the fight. After the worker has gone off to jail, the prostitute has to return to the nightclub to work, but she manages to take the baby with her. During a police raid, though, the prostitute hands the baby to a passerby on the street so that she can run. When she returns in a few minutes, she finds that the passerby has gone and a policeman is waiting for her there. The film ends with uncertainty for this "family": the worker and the prostitute are in jail, and the baby is with a man whose face the prostitute did not even have a chance to look at and remember. The only hope that the film suggests is that the baby may be with a man as kind as the imprisoned worker—a replay of the sequence in which the prostitute entrusts the baby to the passerby shows the passerby to be the worker. Since the replacement of the unidentified passerby with the worker does not raise any doubts as to the validity of the earlier sequence, we naturally take the sequence as a statement from the director: knowing that the baby's earlier, random placement leads the audience to know a kind-hearted worker, the director is hoping that this second unknown person will be equally kind and loving.

The Orphan of Anyang: Does Reality Sting?

Zhang Xinxin was so touched by her Paris experience of watching *The Orphan of Anyang* in Paris that she published an article in China about it in which she raised several issues.[2] First, she questioned the reality shown in the film. Zhang did not deny the validity of everyday life—the unemployment, the prostitution, the shabby streets, the cheap restaurants, and the old apartment buildings. "You also face this kind of reality," she asked herself. "Why can't you make a film like this?"[3] Indeed, the validity of the film is hard to deny. In today's China, the polarity between the rich and the poor, between prosperity and decay, and between the modern and the primitive can hardly be exaggerated. Deep down, however, Zhang resisted the film. She found the reality to be too harsh. "The poor people [in China]," she protested, referring to a fairy tale by Danish writer Hans Christian Andersen, "actually have their clothes on." She labeled this film of exposé and other films of this style, such as several internationally acclaimed features by Jia Zhangke, a sort of cheating by some young Chinese directors hoping to benefit their own careers.

Zhang Xinxin's discomfort with *The Orphan of Anyang*, it appears, has to do with the nationality the film represents at international film festivals. She writes,

> Once home, shaking off the raindrops, the old lady comforted me: "We French need to watch this film. We need to know what the real China is like."
> Hearing this, I felt bad again.[4]

Indeed, like participants in the Olympic games, films at international film festivals are naturally assigned national status and, in the current postcolonial, post–Cold War ideological confrontation between nations, some films may easily be picked up for political reasons. Although Zhang has written about China's decay in her prose since she immigrated to the United States,[5] the presentation of a Chinese film at an international film festival turns out to be too much a public event not to rub her sensitivity about national pride the wrong way.

Zhang is right to note that international politics plays a role in the selection of and awards given to certain Chinese films at international film festivals and that some Chinese art films have been produced "solely for participation in international film festivals and they have almost no indigenous audience."[6] Yet, to use this political reasoning to deny the merits of many internationally awarded films, to forget the Chinese official censorship that had kept these films from reaching indigenous audiences, and to use the alleged motives of the directors to brush aside the reality that these films project makes itself an act of a political nature. Deriving its annoyance and sadness from Nationalism, this fairly popular rejection of a particular kind of film as showcased by Zhang's writing is an integral part of the very same international politics that Zhang's writing refers to.

The style of *The Orphan of Anyang* is the second issue Zhang Xinxin raises. She is not happy that reviewers often compare the style of this and other Chinese underground films with Italian Neorealism. She believes that such a comparison has misled those anxious Chinese directors who are eager for foreign acceptance; it has deprived these directors of other aesthetic choices by leading them to make films only according to the Italian Neorealist formula. Zhang Xinxin suggests that these new films must break the monopoly of the Italian Neorealist style so that they may be accepted worldwide, that is, not just by European film festivals but also by American art cinemas.

Zhang understands the merits of Italian Neorealism. In the case of *The Orphan of Anyang*, she understands that the many long-range shots are supposed to suggest the sense of on-spot shooting and to convey a sense of reality without much artistic mediation. She also understands that the many slow-paced sequences are supposed to convey both a sense of reality and a sense of the mood that the characters are feeling. The sequence showing the closure of a state factory, for example, lasts more than two minutes and contains primarily a frame of the large empty space in front of a deserted workshop. The worker and the prostitute first meet at a cheap noodle shop. After the worker is imprisoned, the prostitute returns to the same place and orders two bowls of noodles, one for herself and one for the absent worker. This sequence lasts close to three minutes and ends with her sobbing over the bowl. This sequence is so long that it gives the audience plenty of time to notice that the last time it was the worker holding the baby caringly and this time he is absent. The audience may also reflect on the brief happiness that the two unfortunate persons shared and how it was so easily crushed. *The Orphan of Anyang* avoids drama and action; the violence and sex are all off-screen. One sequence that Zhang noticed that contrasted with Hollywood melodrama shows the worker at his bicycle-repair stand. He sees the prostitute entering his apartment building, followed by a man who leaves his bicycle at the entrance of the building. The worker grabs a screwdriver and walks toward the building. Zhang wrote that she expected the worker to become envious and to fight the man for his beloved. She was shocked to see that the worker walks quietly to the bicycle, pokes a tire to give it a flat, and returns to his stand and waits for the man to pay him as well. Indeed, such is the shocking effect of *The Orphan of Anyang*'s plain style. It forces the audience to think of the misery contained under the plain surface of this couple's everyday life.

Although she admits the merits of the plain style, Zhang is right that this style is not attracting a wider audience. A middle-aged fiction and prose writer, Zhang writes about her own and many of her American friends' lack of patience with the slow pacing of *The Orphan of Anyang*. My own inquiries of Chinese friends also show that the majority of them, old and young, don't have much patience for a slow movie like *The Orphan of Anyang*.[7] Over half a century away from the era of Italian Neorealism in cinema, with a globalized postmodernity that has quickened the rhythm of urban life, some new elements are unavoidably called for when a director decides to model a film after Italian Neorealism. An interesting film that comes to mind in this regard is Hong Kong director Fruit Chan's *Durian, Durian* (Liulian piaopiao, 2000). The film mixes a plain style of realism with fancy cinema techniques, as well as artistic editing. With this mixture, the film is able to cover a long span of time and to contrast the life experiences of a young Mainland woman who works as a prostitute in Hong Kong on a tourist visa and returns home to snowbound northeast China to invest the money she made in Hong Kong. The alternating fancy and plain sequences of the film reinforce, contrast, and comment on each other, lending the whole film profoundness in social commentary. Unfortunately, Zhang listed Fruit Chan, in the same article, among those directors who are fond of producing films about China using an effect similar to those of *The Orphan of Anyang*, an effect that Zhang sums up with three Chinese characters: *zang, nuan,* and *cha*—dirty, chaotic, and lacking any standard. Once again, Zhang's national pride keeps her from seeing the artistic potential of Italian Neorealism, the possibility of its renovation, as suggested by Fruit Chan.

Does the reality of *The Orphan of Anyang* sting? For Zhang, it does because she is conscious of international politics and she sees opportunistic motives behind its subject and style. The difficulty, however, is that one can hardly hope for a film that is neutral and devoid of any ideology. So far, China's own system of film production and distribution, still monitored by a gradually decentralized censorship, has not presented a picture as raw as *The Orphan of Anyang*. International politics, a reality that must be understood by the audience, have exposed many underrepresented aspects of Chinese lives and have enriched the post-Mao Chinese cinema as a whole.

This opening deliberation has analyzed widely shared feelings against "raw realism," the style shared by a group of emerging directors. In the case of *The Orphan of Anyang*, I want to alert my reader about the post–Cold War international politics present in the production, circulation, and reception of this and many other similar films. With this film I also want to dispel the misconception that reality is an object out there for films either to get close to or to distort. In the sense of cinematic representation, Chinese urban lives are intertextually projected, negotiated, and maintained by various cinematic approaches. "There can be no 'real' reality," Hungarian critic Miklós Haraszti cautioned us, "when there are many realities."[8] The films involved may definitely subscribe to international politics in a more globalized urban culture. They, nonetheless, are tightly woven in a Chinese texture and are related to a particular epistemic status, a concept of reality, and a shared emotional structure. Wang Chao, for example, has an emotional statement about how his *Orphan of Anyang* relates to its characters: "What right do you have to arrange plots for them? What right do you have to script dialogue for them? What right do you have to declare their salvation as your theme? . . . And what right do you have to assert our moralist stance?"[9] This statement and other similar cinematic approaches themselves are part of realities of contemporary Chinese urban lives. In the remainder of this chapter, I continue to focus on the new cinema's fascination with the underrepresented aspects of urban lives. Here the thing to emphasize is how the officially conducted public discourses had kept certain areas of lives hidden and our films, in venturing into these areas, would challenge cultural decorum and cause discomfort.

Beijing Bicycle: Retrieving Western Cinematic Counterparts

To pin down the elusive nature of city lives and to explore their underrepresented aspects, Chinese directors have several Western cinematic traditions to turn to. A few pairs of corresponding foreign and Chinese films help to specify how these Western traditions inscribe themselves in various structures of feeling that the Chinese directors are exposed to.

Chaplin, Blind Girls, and Sympathy. Zhang Yimou's *Happy Times* (Xingfu shiguang, 2000) may well be considered a parody of Chaplin's *City Lights* (1931). In Chaplin's film, an unemployed tramp falls in love with a blind flower girl and goes through a series of misadventures, including robbery and a jail term, to raise money for the operation that can restore her sight. In Zhang's film, an unemployed state worker wants to change his life and starts to do so by dating a plump woman. Since the woman appears aloof, he tries hard to please her, including promising to take care of a blind girl, a relative who lives with the woman and who is obviously a burden. He and his pals, all state workers forced into early retirement, get a wonderful business idea to help the girl, that is, to make her a masseuse. They, however, don't have any money or place to start the business. A series of misadventures abort the state worker's business plan, but the idea has already inspired the blind girl. So that she won't be heartbroken, the worker is forced to set up a fake hotel with a massage room in an abandoned factory building. He hires the girl, and all his pals play the roles of hotel customers to keep the girl in business. The tragicomic nature of the film is best shown in this kind-hearted make-believe. All the while, the audience can see that the wall of the massage room is made of flattened carton boxes that they have not even bothered to cover, since the girl can't see, and there is no ceiling. They see the "customers" of the hotel tipping the girl with pieces of paper that feel like money. They also see the girl working seriously, dreaming of making enough money to see an eye doctor. All the bizarreness of this business contains much sadness for all involved, both the girl and all these state workers who don't have much else to do. In the process, the unemployed worker develops a fatherly love for the girl. Although he is soon abandoned by the big woman and his life is not changed much, a beautiful relationship with the blind girl is established. The film ends with him reading a letter he fakes in the name of the girl's runaway father to keep the girl's spirits up. Then, the two of them talk about their dreams of a better tomorrow.

Happy Times started as a side project for Zhang. He had been half-hearted about it until three things happened.[10] First, the addition of the blind girl, who was not present in the original script, inspired him greatly because he felt, through her, he could better depict the "life of ordinary folks." Second, he talked Zhao Benshan, a nationally admired comedian, into playing the leading role of the unemployed worker. Zhao's popularity assured the best reception of this black comedy by audiences. Third, Zhang Yimou was touched by the end of the script, wherein the two miserable persons, "the tramp and the blind girl," share their dreams about the future. "Dreams," Zhang Yimou explained, "are what filmmakers search for. . . . Humans can give up all but their dreams. . . . In everyday life, what allows unfortunate characters to go on with their lives and to be optimistic about their miseries is that they still have dreams."[11] These were the three crucial elements that make *Happy Times* into a parody of, and an homage to, *City Lights*: a blind girl, a popular clown, and sympathy for unfortunate social outcasts.

This film shows a peculiar influence of Chaplin on Chinese cinema. Chaplin, who criticized the ills of capitalist modernity, had long been favored in China, and he remained an emphasis in Beijing Film Academy's curriculum. Between Chaplin and the young post-Mao film directors, there was one more affinity that may further explain Chaplin's appeal. As we know, Chaplin's vision of the world was colored by a youth of economic deprivation, and he felt deeply sympathetic toward the underprivileged all of his life. The young Chinese directors' visions of the world were also colored. The coming of age of Zhang Yimou's generation occurred during the Cultural Revolution, in either the country villages or state factories; these directors mingled with the people of the Chinese grassroots when they were formulating their understanding of the world. This peculiar social experience, like Chaplin's own youth, would always orient these directors' social sympathy, making them particularly sensitive to how the drastic social changes in the post-Mao era might influence the lives of many ordinary Chinese, be they underpaid state employees, unemployed state workers, or farmers forced to migrate into the cities to make a living.

The Fifth Generation's special experience in coming of age has become a legacy that affects not only them but also the next generation. An example is *Chen Mo and Meiting* (Chen Mo yu Meiting, 2002), an independent film produced by a recent graduate of Beijing Film Academy who was born in the 1970s. Resembling many leftist productions of the 1930s, the film depicts the lives of people of the lowest social stratum, especially those coming to the big metropolis from the countryside or provincial towns. Meiting works at a beauty salon and is considered a small-town girl even though she speaks the Beijing dialect flawlessly. It turns out that her parents were forced to migrate to the small town during the Cultural Revolution and never got back. Now their daughter joins the millions of outsiders who try to make it in Beijing. Many directors born since the 1970s are the contemporaries of the Fifth Generation's sons and daughters. This connection may be one more reason, in addition to international politics, why many younger directors also show strong sympathy for the social outcast. Wang Xiaoshuai's *Beijing Bicycle* (Shiqi sui de danche, 2001) and Wang Chao's *The Orphan of Anyang* are good examples.

China's new economic boom contains a lot of human misery, and it has produced new hotbeds for social, ethnic, gender, and economic inequalities. A major impact on this economic boom from the developed West, labeled by Benjamin Barber as the "McWorld," would not always bring with it the virtue of the West, that is, human rights and democracy but was more likely to bring the ideology of consumption and a logical tolerance for social injustice and inequality.[12] When there were cultural factors that tended to dull the sensitivity to social injustice, the correspondence between Chaplin and the social past of many of the Chinese directors became especially valuable in promoting sympathy and the emotive power of films. Many recent titles bear testimony to this sympathy and present a realist gallery of ordinary folks and underdogs with everyday lives—those underpaid or unemployed state workers, plus taxi drivers, parking attendants, street venders, schoolteachers, and the second-class citizens of country folks trying to make it in the cities. A few impressive titles among many are Ah Nian's *Call Me* (Hu wo, 2000), An Zhanjun's *The Parking Attendant in July* (Kancheren de qiyue, 2003), Li Shaohong's *Happiness Ave.* (Xingfu dajie, 1998), Lu Xuechang's *Cala, My Dog* (Kala shi tiao gou, 2003), Ning Ying's *I Love Beijing* (Xiari nuan yangyang, 2001), Peng Xiaolian's *Shanghai Women* (Jiazhuang mei ganjue, 2002), Shi Runjiu's *A Beautiful New World* (Meili xin shijie, 1998), Tang Danian's *City Paradise* (Dushi tiantang, 1999), Xia Gang's *A Country Boy in Shanghai* (Boli shi touming de, 1999), and Wang Guangli's *Go for Broke* (Heng shu heng, 2001).

Italian Bicycle and Beijing Bicycle. Wang Xiaoshuai's 2001 film *Beijing Bicycle* calls to mind Vittorio De Sica's 1948 film *The Bicycle Thief*, a classic that everyone attending Beijing Film Academy would have studied. In De Sica's film, a man who has been unemployed for two years finally finds a job as a municipal bill poster. Since the job requires him to provide his own transportation, he pawns the family's sheets and buys a bicycle, which is stolen his first day out. He and his son search the city in vain for the thief. In the end, the man is driven to steal a bicycle himself but is caught in the act. The film was shot on location in Rome with nonactors in the leading roles (the protagonist was played by a factory worker coached by De Sica). If the Italian film portrayed the dilemmas of the working poor in the postwar economy of hard times, its Chinese counterpart depicts the similar difficulty of Chinese villagers who are forced to leave the farm to work in the cities in the post-Mao economic boom. In Wang's film, a new migrant, Guei, finds a job as a courier. The job requires him to use portions of his salary to purchase the bicycle provided by the company. The very day Guei purchases the bicycle, it is stolen. Desperate to regain his lost job, this seventeen-year-old country boy searches the city, which must have millions of bicycles and, amazingly, finds it (he had put a secret mark on the bicycle). The new owner of the bicycle, who purchased it from a flea market, is a city boy of his own age. Since they both have invested in this bicycle, they can't think of anything better to do than share it. In the rest of the film, through their sharing of this bicycle, through the contrast of the differences in their daily lives, the hardship of new urban migrants is portrayed.

The impact of Italian Neorealism on post-Mao cinema, as shown in this parody of Beijing bicycle to Italian bicycle, was not coincidental. The reasons for its attraction definitely go beyond the opportunistic motives discovered by

Zhang Xinxin. The identical historical efforts in post-Mao and post-Fascist societies to deviate from the yoke of totalitarian ideologies encouraged an homage by post-Mao filmmaking in China to Italian Neorealism, which dictated abolishing contrived plots, avoiding professional actors, and taking to the streets for its material to establish direct contact with contemporary social reality. It was precisely the respect for the "everyday life" of ordinary people, so alien to the heroic ideal of Fascism, that Italian Neorealism was recapturing. On-location shooting, the use of nonprofessional actors, and improvisation of script were among the means that Italian Neorealism used to reinvent Italian daily life. In the post-Mao art films, the same trend has been unmistakable; similar efforts have been used to break the centrally controlled Maoist engineering of reality. Along with the development of a star system in the new market economy of film production and distribution, many directors, especially those working independently or with low budgets, produced films in an Italian Neorealist style. Later in this chapter, we shall see how, at the onset of his film career, Zhang Yuan often coached people to perform their own stories, a single mother with her retarded child, a neurotic father interacting with his alcoholic sons, and so on. This approach, plus his initiation in exploring the underrepresented subjects—retardation, mental illness, alcoholism, and homosexuality—lent these films a raw sense of reality.

Many contemporary directors shared this approach. He Jianjun (aka Zhao Jisong), a Sixth-Generation director, used lesser-known actors to perform in his *Postman* (Youchai, 1995) and *Scenery* (Fengjing, 1999). He avoided contrived plots, dialogue, and unnecessary cuts, preferring long shots and natural lighting and creating both a raw sense of everyday ambience and the psychological effect of stiffening and paralysis in portraying two of his antiheroes, the postman who peeks into others' lives by stealing and reading their mail and an attorney who can't pull himself together to get anything done. Zhang Ming and Jia Zhangke, two more Sixth Generation directors (discussed in chapter 7), also used an Italian Neorealist style to portray the kind of small-town lives that cinemagoers of the metropolis would not be familiar with. And Wang Guangli, a self-made director, invited a group of unemployed state workers to perform their own story of private business ventures and how these ventures affected their lives.

If the examples above involved primarily independent, underground, unconventional, low-budget, and beginning-of-career projects, there are also examples of more established directors favoring this approach. Zhang Yang, a Sixth-Generation director who had commercial success with his earlier films, such as *Spicy Love Soup* (Aiqing ma la tang, 1997) and *Shower* (Xizao, 1999), and who was well funded by Imar Film Studio,[13] ventured into a documentary approach to explore an unfamiliar subject: drug use. In his 2001 film *Quitting* (Zuotian), he coached a drug-using actor, Jia Hongsheng, to perform his own story of quitting with his real parents and sister. The subtlety of generational difference and communication, the blurring of fantasy and reality, and the difficult process of self-recovery are all captured with a touching sense of reality. Then there was Sun Zhou, a Fifth Generation director, who let superstar Gong Li interact with a real developmentally delayed child in *Breaking the Silence* (Piaoliang mama, 1999) to depict the emotional difficulty of a single mother educating her child. Zhang Yimou, the most established Fifth Generation director, in *Not One Less* (Yige dou buneng shao, 1997), coached a group of village kids to perform their own story of education, or rather the lack of it.

The enemy of the Italian Neorealist style in post-Mao cinema was not only the former Maoist engineering of reality. The economic boom and the dominance of the market also promoted the box office, the star system, and capitalist control, which often go contrary to the spirit of Italian Neorealism. Just as Italian Neorealism could never have outlasted the prosperity and affluence of the Italian economy of the 1950s, how the influence of Italian Neorealism may fare in the post-Mao economic boom had yet to be revealed.

Citizen Kane and the Performance of Reality. In *Quitting*, Zhang Yang uses interviews and performances to reconstruct the difficult process by which Jia Hongsheng, a real-life actor, gives up drugs. Zhang Yang acknowledges that *Citizen Kane* is his model, although he has to admit that there is a major difference; that is, his subject is alive and he participates in the process of reconstructing his own life.[14] Indeed, Zhang Yang's *Quitting* may not be as involved and mysterious as *Citizen Kane*. Yet it does reconfirm *Citizen Kane*'s concept that reality is a compromise through multiple perspectives and that a certain performance will reconstruct a certain fashion of reality. This concept is essential for the discussion of this chapter.

Zhang Yang's theater background has contributed to the appeal of *Citizen Kane* to him. As a graduate of the Central Academy of Theater in Beijing, Zhang Yang has always wanted to bring the concept of performance into his film narration. Admiring Brecht, he does not want to hide the traces of performance in those films. Knowing Pirandello, he wants his characters to search for their authors.[15] *Quitting* is a good example of this effort, in which Zhang Yang yields the authorship of the film to the interaction between various comments on and performances of Jia Hongsheng's life. Although the film has many engaging, dramatic sequences, they are intersected by soliloquies of many different people commenting on Jia Hongsheng as a person. These "vis-à-vis" communications often tend to alienate, in a Brechtian sense, the audience from a full identification with the emotive drama.

In *Quitting*, what corresponds to the "Rosebud" mystery of *Citizen Kane* is the question of why Jia Hongsheng would confuse himself with John Lennon, the British Beatles star. This is the most intriguing part of the film. Drug use and quitting drugs may have caused physical discomforts that account for Jia's frequent loss of temper and may also have contributed to the difficulty others have in living with him. His identity confusion with John Lennon, however, is much more of a cultural issue. It involves his discomfort with his mundane life, his disappointment with life away from the limelight, and his anxiety over his everyday identity. Ever since he played Keke, an anticonventional youth in Zhang Nuanxin's *Good Morning, Beijing* (Beijing ni zao, 1990), Jia has been almost an icon for a generation of marginal, rebellious, angry, nihilistic, and rock 'n 'rolling youth.[16] In *Good Morning, Beijing*, the song that marks his characterization is the rock star Cui Jian's "Fake Minstrel."[17] The song portrays him as a cultural rebel—mysterious, free-spirited, dashing, individualistic, and filled with expectations. In a way, this song also explains why his role in real life, modeled after this song, strikes us as that of an eccentric loner (duxing xia).[18] Chinese rock youth worship the Beatles. Jia, as an icon of this generation, needs only a little devotion to confuse himself with a Beatles star. He confuses his cinematic roles (shown as a fixation with John Lennon, his role model) with his everyday self.

Jia's family has to send him to a mental hospital to rid him of his fixation with Lennon. The sequences showing Jia at the hospital further illustrate that Jia's problem concerns his cultural orientation. As Zhang Yang suggests, Jia may appear insane in normal life but he is absolutely sane in a mental hospital.[19] In an enlarged mental ward resembling the one in *One Flew over the Cuckoo's Nest*,[20] Jia's courage to stick to the identity of Lennon is soon undermined by intimidation. He decides to step back from Lennon, a character he is now playing, to admit that he is only an actor; he has to make a compromise with his mundane life to escape the humiliation of the mental hospital.

To compromise is the theme of *Quitting*. Zhang Yang and Jia Hongsheng selected the Beatles' "Let It Be," a song that Jia listened to a lot during his real-life process of quitting drugs, as the theme song for *Quitting*, and mixes it with Chinese rock music by Cui Jian, Zhang Chu, Dou Wei, and the Tang Dynasty Band. "Let It Be," as the song title suggests, encourages the listener to leave behind any anger and anxiety. The interaction of this song with the angrier Chinese rock music provides tension in the musical dimension of the film. "Man protests in life and strives," Zhang Yang explains. "In the end, there is no escape but to go with nature."[21] "To go with nature," a Chinese colloquialism bearing the mark of Taoist influence, often indicates a pessimistic view of man's inability to understand and control his fate. It is a close translation of "let it be."

Among his contemporaries, Zhang Yang may not be the best choice of a director to do a film about compromise. In comparison with films by more marginal directors like Jia Zhangke, Zhang Yang's films have little anger and fewer critical edges. Their different family backgrounds have an undeniable role in this difference; while Jia Zhangke must have felt alienated growing up in a small provincial town before attending Beijing Film Academy, Zhang Yang grew up in a family of the cultural elite in Beijing and thus has quarreled less with his life. Zhang Yang's view of the angry youth subculture, however, is typical among his contemporaries. Anger, this view holds, is an age thing—life is never ideal; young people tend to express more anger, but they will eventually grow out of it. Lu Xuechang, a Sixth Generation director, expresses it best: "Shooting films young, it's very likely that you will feel at odds with society. But you have to grow up. You can't always pretend to be not an adult. . . . You tend to ask yourself why can't you merge into the society? Do you want to? And changes come along [in your films with these questions]."[22] Lou Ye's *Weekend Lovers* (Zhoumo qingren, 1993), also with Jia Hongsheng playing a major role, vindicates this view. At the end of this rock 'n' roll film about love among a group of teenagers, the first-person narrative voice of a female character, now a grown-up and years away from the action of the film, draws the conclusion: "During those days, my friends were filled with pain, feeling that they were not understood by society. Now grown up, they have realized that society has not changed. It was not the society that didn't understand them; it was they who didn't understand society."

Lou Ye's film career is also a case of growing out of youthful anger. He established his reputation with *Weekend Lovers* and *Suzhou River* (Suzhou he, 2000), two films that obviously grew out of his personal youthful experiences. Famed and favored with much more generous investments, Lou Ye's recent films, such as *Purple Butterfly* (Zi hudie, 2003), claim a grander scope, better-known stars, and interesting technical exploration. Yet, to compare

Lou Ye's work once again with Jia Zhangke's persistence, film after film, in digging into his coming of age in a small town—Lou's later films are hard to relate to any experiences of angry youth; rather, Lou is a director who, with a sudden wealth of funds, has been trying hard to make his films pay. His commercial responsibility has obviously reduced the artistic immediacy one feels in his earlier films. Again, as we are uncertain about how the impact of Italian Neorealism may fare in the advance of commercialism in China, we are equally uncertain whether the "raw realism" of these young directors may hold their ground in the face of similar lures.

Mother: Zhang Yuan and Documentary Lyricism

In the early 1990s, Zhang Yuan was among a group of young directors whose films signaled the coming of a new generation. An explorer interested in experimenting in various film styles, Zhang has been an unpredictable director; his films have shown rather drastic changes in style, especially the more recent ones. His *Green Tea* (Lü cha, 2003), for instance, uses a highly artificial cinematography. In contrast, the beginning of Zhang's film career, shown in his earlier features such as *Mother* (Mama, 1990), *Beijing Bastards* (Beijing zazhong, 1992), and *Sons* (Erzi, 1995), was unmistakably marked by a documentary style. These films were not done by professional actors, as mentioned earlier, but by real people performing their own stories. They were predominantly shot with hand-held cameras, the mise-en-scènes were less artificial, and they avoided conventional narrative lines and the intensity of drama.

The low-budget situation of Zhang and of other emerging directors was an immediate reason for the documentary approach. Ironically, a widely shared opinion holds that many new-generation directors then produced artistically better films—films with a raw sense of reality and an immediacy of feeling. The low-budget situation turned out to be a blessing for these directors. For Zhang, his initial way to finance his filmmaking was also culturally significant. Since his graduation from Beijing Film Academy in 1989, Zhang has created an unconventional career. Rejecting a government job assignment to an army film studio, he managed to produce films outside the state-monopolized studio system. To finance this expensive endeavor, he produced videos of musical performances by those bands who were not favored by the state musical industry but who had a popular following among the young. Eventually, he became a primary producer of musical performances by Cui Jian, who has been indisputably considered the initiator of the Chinese rock movement and who is an icon of a spectacular youth subculture. Zhang's connection with Cui offered him a special niche that put him in touch with the pulse of the young. His music productions not only helped finance his production of art films but have also assured him a rebel's consciousness.

Zhang and the other emerging directors in the 1990s had a clear conviction that they needed to break away from a convention established by directors who only a year before, in the immediate post-Mao China, were rebels themselves. This convention, somewhat simplified, was to project various versions of an allegorical China for the sake of cultural critique. Not too surprisingly, the onset of the breakthrough of these earlier rebels was also a documentary-ism, known as *jishi meixue* (documentary aesthetics), which featured proposals of *danhua* (antimelodramatic) and *jishi* (not to beautify but to depict reality in a plain style). The prevalent intellectual spirit of a national cultural scrutiny in the 1980s, however, quickly led these directors away from their documentary approaches so that they might have freer hands to build film allegories.

Zhang picked up the previous rebels' weapon for another breakthrough. In his hands, documentary-ism was adopted to draw attention to the less represented margins of a gradually decentralizing Chinese culture and society—he explored alcoholism and neuroticism, a decadent rock community, homosexuality, and the life of a single mother taking care of a mentally retarded child. His candid camera was the rebels' camera, using what was real (what was less represented) to challenge what was artificial (overrepresented). Zhang's adoption of documentary-ism, however, faced a new problem. In the last cinematic wave, directors had not had much problem with audience perception, since they were dealing not with marginal lives but with the popularly shared sense of reality that had been ignored by the Maoist ideological hyperbole. Where the earlier directors could easily win over the audience because they were depicting a familiar reality, Zhang's awkward, unfamiliar reality on the margins of the society often caused discomfort for the audience. To deal with this discomfort, Zhang had to blend in touches of lyricism to cue certain emotional responses.

Zhang's first feature-length film, *Mother*, involves a young woman's frustration in caring for and raising her retarded son without social help or sympathy (lacking proper representation, the issue of mental retardation is usually ignored by ordinary people in China). Shot in black and white and interspersed with color footage of interviews with other mothers of mentally disabled children, the film has a documentary scope and raw emotional effect. Strong lyricism is also mixed structurally into the documentary style of the film. The film begins with the young mother massaging her son, choreographed in close-ups of the hands of the mother and eyes of the child. A sense of frustration—confusion caused by love that is not returned—also builds from here. All through the film, one feels the love of the young mother to her child; all through the film, the child is not responding—he does not even know how to address his own mom. In several stressful moments, the same stationary shot of the naked child sleeping under a loose sheet is shown. It is a shot in soft lighting of the gracefully posed body of the child, in the effect close to that of a classical painting focusing on the beauty of the human body. The frame prompts the audience to share the mother's love for the child and to understand the mother's frustration in not finding this beauty in the child's waking life. With this film based on the real-life experiences of actress Qing Yan, who also plays the title role, Zhang Yuan established his cinematic style of minute emotional exploration through real-life characters and experiences.

Although mostly an individual effort, *Mother* was not yet an independent film, since it was produced within the studio system with the help of Xi'an Film Studio. The documentary lyricism of this feature about an ignored aspect of Chinese urban life was not initially well received in China. After being banned, *Mother* was smuggled out of China and won a Special Jury Prize at the 1991 Nantes Film Festival in France. As had happened with many other Chinese films, foreign recognition led to attention at home; *Mother* was eventually broadcast on Beijing cable television in 1997.

Zhang's 1995 film *Sons* was not just one more example of his documentary lyricism but also an important annotation to *Beijing Bastards*, a rock 'n' roll film about a young man in search of his girlfriend-in-hiding (see chapter 4). *Sons* explores the real family life of *Beijing Bastards*' on-screen character, the searching young man. As Zhang Yuan's downstairs neighbor, this young man urged the budding director to do a film about his family, which was torn by alcoholism and insanity. When Zhang Yuan eventually worked out a script and "borrowed" the father back from the mental hospital, the four members of the family, playing themselves in the film, reenacted the family's troubles, loosely following Zhang Yuan's script and direction.[23]

Watching *Sons* is much like watching Nicolas Cage's performance of an alcoholic man in *Leaving Las Vegas* (1995); you feel awkward sharing the sense of paralysis caused by alcohol and you have a constant sense of disappointment. In Chinese culture, alcoholism is often indulged when it can generate visions and creative energies (e.g., where liquor becomes the muse to Li Bai's poetry writing). Yet when liquor deepens disappointment and induces destruction, it becomes intolerable, and that is why *Sons* could never become a mainstream film. In *Sons* the parents are retired professional dancers. Their boredom with life and their constant bickering, which leads to divorce, contrasts with the youthful ideal they once had. The father not only indulges in liquor but also displays symptoms of schizophrenia. The two unemployed sons indulge equally in alcohol, not only because of their unemployment and their own boredom with life but also because of the constant embarrassment their neurotic father causes them inside and outside the apartment.

The alcoholic father, who believes that "only some men are fathers but all men are sons," suggested the title of the film. His suggestion rings true when we consider the film from certain perspectives. First, the two generations of alcoholics under the same roof are both "sons" to their political cultures: the father faces the letdown of the high idealism of his youth, and the sons face the lack of any idealistic inspirations in life. They mirror each other with their drinking problems. Second, although the father's neurotic acting up seems to occupy the foreground of the film, the camera often registers this foreground through over-the-shoulder shots in the perspective of the two sons. In one intense sequence, the already-drunk father returns home and imposes himself on the peaceful drinking of the sons. One of the sons feels so distressed that their fun with the bottle is being destroyed that he hits his father on the head with one. The blood calms both of them down but solves none of their problems. While the father is in the hospital, we see the son leaving a bar with his girlfriend. He then collapses on the street, obviously having drunk too much.

Years after the production of the film, Zhang Yuan reported that the sons had finally left their unemployed lives behind; they opened a bar in Beijing known as the Hidden Trees.[24] Drinking, it seemed, was still an important part of their life, and drinking, as a social problem, was still much of a hidden issue, as suggested by the name of the bar.

Go for Broke: A Stroke of Luck for Documentary Realism

When Zhang Yuan turned to other cinematic styles, Wang Guangli picked up his documentary style, this time, met with a surprising official endorsement. Wang was not known among the small circle of young feature film directors, most of whom were graduates of China's few film or theater schools. In 2001, nonetheless, Wang's feature film *Go for Broke* not only obtained official approval for distribution but was also selected to participate in the competition for the official Golden Rooster Awards.[25] For him and for the contemporary documentary movement he came from, this good fortune was similar to what happens to his characters in the film, a group of unemployed state workers who win a big lottery.

Wang Guangli, who was born in rural Sichuan Province in 1966, started as an outsider. He studied psychology at college and secured a decent university teaching post in the same field. In 1992, however, he left his job to pursue his dream of becoming a film director. In Beijing he produced a politically sensitive documentary film *I Have Graduated* (Wo biye le, 1992), which chronicled post–Tian'anmen Square massacre changes in student life at six prominent Beijing universities by interviewing graduating seniors. The film showed Wang's film talent; it is a documentary but is also avant-garde in its cinematic expressions. It mixes long shots and long takes with montage, camera motions, and other special effects. This film, along with such films as Wu Wenguang's *Bumming in Beijing: The Last Dreamers* (Liulang Beijing: zuihou de mengxiangzhe, 1990), became one of the pioneering works of a cinematic trend known as "the new documentary movement" (xin jilu yundong), which emphasized objectivity, auteurism, and the filmmaker's independence from the state ideological monopoly and production control. This film was also blacklisted by the Chinese government in 1994, along with a penalty on several directors who had sent their films to international film festivals without government permission.

In *Cinema and Desire*, Dai Jinhua vividly describes the unique nomadic artists' community out of which the new documentary movement emerged. She notes how a group of artists—painters, rock stars, avant-garde poets, art photographers, unknown writers, experimental theater directors, and dedicated yet scantily financed would-be film directors—lived on the outskirts of Beijing with no household certificates (thus no benefits of any social services), no steady jobs, no secure residence, only a dream of artistic independence, of doing the things they cared to do.[26] Wang Guangli's decision to give up the steady income and social status of a university professor for freelancing jobs with television stations is a good illustration of the artistic devotion of the members of this community. The lives of these artists were literally on the margins of mainstream society in Beijing. Their rhetoric naturally followed suit. Cui Zi'en, a columnist on Chinese independent filmmaking, clarified his understanding of center and margin: "We run toward the margins from the center. We had to. The center is decaying, just like a heart that is not functioning. We are escaping. We are finding areas on the margins that are not as decaying to pause and to get ready to run toward the new margins. The times urge us to run; we are the vanguard of the era."[27]

Wang's first effort in feature films, *Maiden Work* (Chunü zuo, 1998), may also be considered a portrayal of the Beijing artistic community and fringe culture. It has an experimental plot that confuses a character's dreams and an artist's process of projecting his artistic vision on-screen. Sandwiched by surrealist episodes and a docudrama of behind-the-camera work, the film portrays a lesbian liaison in a milieu of nude canvases and Mao folk tunes. Xue, an aspiring female journalist, approaches Jinian (Memory), a painter of nudes, for an interview. She unexpectedly recognizes a female friend among Jinian's painting subjects and starts an intensive sexual tryst, driven by an emotion that is shown as deep and mysterious. *Maiden Work* was produced independently. Like most of these kinds of films, it was screened in film festivals in Rotterdam, Vancouver, and San Francisco, but it has not been accepted for public screening in China.

Knowing that none of Wang's films were officially accepted in China before *Go for Broke*, one understands why it is interesting that this particular film received favor. In this film, Wang returned to his specialty of docudrama. He tracked down a group of formerly laid-off workers after reading their story in a 1998 newspaper and invited them to play their own lives. Shot with a 35-millimeter camera in an intimate, straightforward style, the film uses no special lighting, no special costumes, no set design, and no make-up. The real-life characters speak their own Shanghai dialect and remain themselves, though often a little tense in front of the camera, which is, almost all the time, held on the hip, without using stabilizers, tracks or tripods. The film follows the fate of Zhang Baozhong, who loses his job at a state-owned shipbuilding company in Shanghai, becomes disoriented in life for a few years, but finally borrows a bundle of cash and persuades several fellow laid-off workers to join him in establishing and running a construction company. From there the audience follows this group of friends to see their difficulties in business (how they are taken in by scams, slip to the brink of bankruptcy, and refinance and rebuild from scratch), to glimpse their personal lives (how a father with a disabled daughter has to manage the family's difficulty in daily life, how a single mother offers emotional support to Zhang, and how Zhang has to hide from loan sharks), and to share their exhilaration in winning a Shanghai Welfare Lottery prize of fifty thousand dollars.

Winning the lottery is not only a stroke of luck; the Chinese government likes the positive idea that the lottery has rewarded a group of laid-off workers who don't rely on government subsidies but work hard to make it on their own. In China's wrenching transition to a market economy, unemployment of state employees has become a national tragedy that director Wang Guangli describes as "extremely widespread and deeply disturbing." He compares it with war with Japan in the 1930s and the Cultural Revolution in the 1960s.[28] Although the six friends in Wang's film get lucky, the spotlight on them does not erase their hardships. In Wang's film, the contrast is especially emphasized: when we see the six friends all wearing red shirts of celebration as they go on the media show at a glittery TV studio, we are reminded of the contrasting footage showing the gritty streets, cramped housing conditions, littered construction sites, and dim offices where these characters live and work every day.

For us, Wang's case illustrates the constructive influence of the new documentary movement on the filmmaking of the new generations. The documentary approach played a certain role in Fifth Generation filmmaking. Among earlier directors, one can think of Tian Zhuangzhuang and his *On the Hunting Ground* (Liechang zhasa, 1985). Among the later directors, one thinks of Ning Ying, who does both docudrama-style feature films and real documentaries.[29] But for the younger generations, this amphibiousness in documentary and feature films has been common. Zhang Yuan is primarily known as a feature film director. He, however, is also among the initiators of the new documentary movement; an informal meeting at his home in 1992 is now often considered among the starting events of the movement.[30] His *Square* (Guangchang, 1994), *Crazy English* (Fengkuang yingyu, 1999), and *Golden Star Miss* (Jinxing xiaojie, 2000) are important titles in documentary filmmaking. Shi Runjiu, now a well-known feature film director, also directed such documentaries as *North Shannxi* (Shanbei, 1992), *Northeast* (Dongbei, 1993), *Shanghai* (1994), *Home* (Jia, 1996), and *China-on-fire Concert* (Zhongguo huo yanchanghui, 1997). Jia Zhangke's film career is noted for his parallel production in feature and documentary films; his documentaries include *One Day in Beijing* (You yitian, zai Beijing, 1994), *In Public* (Gonggong changsuo, 2001), and *Conditions of Dogs* (Gou de zhuangkuang, 2001). Lou Ye's award-winning *Suzhou River* is derived from a project of a documentary series; the observation of real life triggered his and his first-person narrator's fantasy in the film.[31]

The documentary approach has lent many distinctive features to the younger generations of film directors. It gives them a political sense of moving away from the political mainstream to explore various underrepresented cultural and social margins. It enhances their aesthetic preference for the antistudio, antiprofessional, and antibeautification style that has often been described as gritty urban realism. The documentary approach has not limited the younger directors in their stylistic explorations. But often what they need to defend are not their styles but the validity of their screen images. Liu Guangyu, a Chinese film critic, noticed an interesting contrast in the titles of two books that reached his desk at the same time. One book is a Chinese translation of Fellini's autobiographical writings, titled *I'm a Born Liar*.[32] The other is a collection of interviews of the new Chinese generation of film directors, titled *My Camera Does Not Lie*.[33] Liu noticed that Fellini's "lies" concern primarily his aesthetic manipulation in filmmaking that he can afford to joke about, whereas the younger Chinese film directors have to justify what they do ethically. Liu believes that the younger Chinese directors have only a limited freedom in stylistic manipulation, since they are dealing with "heavy images" (raw images from real life that may often be taboos themselves).[34]

East Palace, West Palace: To Understand Queer Lives

Homosexuality presented "heavy images" on the Chinese screen. When we consider three post-Mao films on this subject, Zhang Yuan's *East Palace, West Palace* (Dong gong xi gong, 1996), Liu Bingjian's *Men, Men, Women, Women* (Nan nan nü nü, 1999), and Li Yu's *Fish and Elephant* (Jinnian xiatian, 2001), we realize how difficult it was for Zhang Yuan's film, as the initial one in the post-Mao cinema on this subject, to deal with the public unfamiliarity with the issue. Whereas Zhang Yuan's film had to resort to allegory to present a challenging critique, the other two films, with homosexual writers and actors involved in the production, started to treat the subject more from an everyday-life approach, depicting homosexual love relations in more detail and merging the character with friends, family members and everyday folks.

As mentioned earlier, Zhang Yuan started his film career by turning several untouched "stones" in contemporary society to expose lives of socially disenfranchised groups. For a director who might not always be familiar with these lives, the processes of making these films were those of education and discovery. His documentary approach went well with these processes, and it set a track record for his film career. In 1996, when he directed *East Palace, West Palace*, he obviously was continuing to turn the social stones. As with his earlier films, he was drawn to the issue of homosexuality with sensitivity for injustice. He read about how police rounded up homosexual men in parks in Beijing to facilitate medical research on AIDS. This story prompted his desire to meet gay people to "find out what (if anything) is different about them."³⁵ This time, however, Zhang was not so lucky to have a neighbor or friend who could lead him into the life he wanted to discover. Instead, he collaborated with novelist Wang Xiaobo and worked on his script. The result of their collaboration was a drastic stylistic change from Zhang's earlier films.

Palace is set in a park which is part of the Forbidden City. Xiaoshi, a policeman whose job is to keep homosexual men from dating in the park, has a habit of interrogating suspected gay men when he is on night duty, primarily for his own amusement. One night, he captures Ah Lan, a gay writer who openly showed his love for Xiaoshi in an earlier, chancy encounter. The film focuses on the night of interrogation. Xiaoshi's abuse of his power is met with Ah Lan's masochistic fantasy. The interrogation is turned into a seduction. Eventually, the policeman is lured into sexual intimacy with the gay writer. The film is allegorical, since it is interceded by an opera performance of a female convict falling in love with her executioner. While gay love is assigned a criminal association, Ah Lan's seduction of the policeman also implies a desperate plea for understanding.

We wondered why Zhang would resort to allegory, a style that he and his so-called Sixth Generation directors were conscientiously turning their backs on. The political reason was the most obvious; Zhang had a critique of the government's treatment of the homosexual people. This was Zhang's understanding of the issue: "Although there are many stories recorded about gays in Chinese culture, after the Liberation of 1949 and especially during the Cultural Revolution (1966–76), the very word 'homosexual' disappeared from all newspapers, books, and even public discussion."³⁶ Indeed, scholars' accounts of the tradition of same-sex love in ancient China appeared irrelevant to the everyday reality of the immediate post-Mao China.³⁷ What Zhang's film dealt with was a historical discontinuity and a political culture that saw homosexuality as an import from the decadent West. When the channels for public representation of homosexuality were closed, homosexuals were hounded in everyday life as "hooligans" (liumang), the same name that has been given to decadent youth.

As Zhang had no access to homosexual life, he could hardly use his by now well-crafted weapon of a documentary approach. To initiate public discourse on this issue, he had to do a reading of a story about homosexuality with the hope that many other readings would follow to support his critique. When it comes to reading and critique, allegory becomes the best option. "Allegory," as Jerome Silbergeld, citing Paul de Man and others, argues, "stimulates 'reading' but allows no *particular* reading, distributing authorship among the audience. As such, it remains the best rhetorical antidote to the intended ideological monopoly of totalitarian government."[38]

The distribution of authorship among the audience has all the more importance here, since Zhang Yuan's critique could not be carried out, assuming a simplistic confrontation between the government and the people. The ideological monopoly informs the public. To dismantle this monopoly and to understand homosexuality, the audience had to understand the political culture they lived in, to understand themselves, and then to understand an issue rarely talked about. The film stimulated the audience to do so with an allegory that not only protested the government's policy on homosexuality but also invited the audience to reflect on themselves—the policeman relates to government by his job but relates to the audience as an average guy. Wang Xiaobo's story, on which the film script is based, is a piece of black humor that suggests fluidity in a person's sexual orientation.[39] It echoes an ancient Chinese assumption that a person's sexual identity might not be as fixed as it appears, and an individual was capable of enjoying a wide range of sexual acts.[40] Just as the policeman can be seduced on-screen, many among the audience can be seduced. One logic follows here is that anyone has the possibility of being gay but it takes some trauma or some abnormal experiences for someone to fix the sexual identity as being homosexual. To be homosexual is just like being sick; others should be sympathetic with them but not persecute them. This understanding is the take of the film, in which one sees the mismatch of how Ah Lan likes to recap his personal history, whereas the policeman is more interested in knowing about the gay writer's sexual acts. The uncertain sexual orientation of the policeman, while serving as a narrative suspense, is also a sarcastic comment that a straight person is potentially capable of gay love too.[41]

Owing to a lack of representation, the gays in this initial film on homosexuality in post-Mao China could hardly interact with other realms of life on an equal footing, as, for example, in Ang Lee's *Wedding Banquet*, a comic depiction of cultural differences, the generation gap, and light-hearted interactions between gays and straights in the United States. On the contrary, the representation of gay men in *East Palace, West Palace* was focused on persecution and protest. This accounts for the lyrical intensity of *Palace*.

Three years after *Palace*, when Liu Bingjian directed *Men, Men, Women, Women*, he collaborated with a gay scriptwriter and some homosexual actors and actresses. The film showcased the lighthearted relationship between gays and lesbians in contemporary Beijing and subtly depicted their interactions with straight people. Especially impressive is the film's depiction of Xiao Bo, a gay country boy who is trying to make it in Beijing. This handsome young man's innocence functions like a mirror that reflects, through all the kinds of persons he encounters, the varied understanding, misunderstanding, sympathy, and apathy toward a gay person. Although Liu's approach to his subject is often fun and accessible, the eccentric endeavors of his two central gay characters—Chongchong, who edits a magazine of toilet literature,[42] and Guigui, who hosts a radio program known as " public toilet time"—still prompts the audience's perception that gay people are sick. These characters' odd interests appear as countercultural as their sex lives.

Fish and Elephant, by first-time director Li Yu, started to present homosexual love among more ordinary folks. The story relates four women: Xiaoqun, a young woman from Sichuan, is the elephant trainer at a big-city zoo. She lives with her lesbian partner, Xiaoling, the owner of a clothing shop. The two of them keep a tank of tropical fish in their apartment and enjoy feeding the fish together. One summer, their peaceful life is tested by the arrival of two other women.

Xiaoqun's mother, who worries that her daughter remains unmarried, travels from their hometown to live with her, wanting to speed up the process of finding her a spouse. Xiaoqun's father had abandoned her mother years earlier for another woman. In the process of arranging dates for her daughter, Xiaoqun's mother falls in love with an older man, Mr. Zhang, who was originally sought out as a potential spouse for the daughter. When the mother confesses to the daughter that she is going to get married, the daughter confides to her that she is lesbian, has a partner, and has no need for dates. Although both women find their confessions difficult to make, the mother is obviously much more shocked by what her daughter tells her than the daughter is by her mother's engagement.

Next, Junjun, Xiaoqun's former lover, sneaks into the elephant room at the zoo to meet with Xiaoqun. Junjun is involved in a homicide case, and the police are after her. Xiaoqun hides her in the elephant room. Xiaoling discovers Xiaoqun's secret meetings with Junjun in the elephant room and suspects that Xiaoqun has changed in her feelings for her. In a rage, she poisons the whole tank of fish and leaves the apartment. Xiaoling's distressed odyssey in the city, which often attracts men seeking the company of women, further saddens her. She returns to the apartment, where Xiaoqun explains her sympathy for Junjun, who is in hiding because she has killed her rapist father. Xiaoqun's own bad relationship with her father makes her understand the actions of her former lover. She, nonetheless, reassures Xiaoling that her emotional relationship with Junjun is in the past and they are lovers no more. Xiaoqun and Xiaoling reconcile.

With the help of old Mr. Zhang, Xiaoqun's mother learns to accept her daughter's sexual orientation and they plan their wedding. At the zoo, Junjun is discovered and surrounded by the police. She kills two police officers before she is arrested. In Xiaoqun's apartment, the reconciled couple makes love more passionately than ever. At the wedding, with lots of guests, Xiaoqun's mother expects the arrival of her daughter with her partner. Will they arrive? The film ends in expectation.

This expectation suggests that just as the film could not be openly issued in China, the director is still not sure if a homosexual relationship could come into the open in China, but she is hopeful. What's most impressive about the film is its depiction of the mother-daughter relationship. The mother, a down-to-earth woman, learns to accept her daughter, seeing how her own second marriage is understood by the younger generation. The film also impresses the viewer with its everyday-life approach to depicting the lesbian relationship: how Xiaoqun gets to know Xiaoling with just one visit to the clothing shop and how they live in harmony, shown in the ways they look at each other, eat together, read together, and light cigarettes for each other. The director tells us in a remark about the film that the two women playing Xiaoqun and Xiaoling are lovers in real life and they have presented their true feelings on-screen.[43]

Li Yu's hope for the acceptance of a homosexual relationship was not even imaginable to Zhang Yuan when he directed *East Palace, West Palace* in 1996. Zhang's mind-set was more focused on persecution. From Ah Lan's seduction and protest, to Chong Chong and Hui Hui's eccentric cultural endeavors, and to Xiaoqun and Xiaoling's unspectacular everyday life, we witness a spectrum of representations of homosexuality, a process in which authorship moves from straight writer writing about homosexual people to homosexual writers writing about themselves, and a consistent call for understanding and sympathy.

Lunar Eclipse: The Moonstruck Reality

If director Wang Quan'an is not a familiar name to you but you have watched *Good Morning, Beijing* (1990), discussed in chapter 1, the fact is that you've met the director. As his graduation work at Beijing Film Academy, Wang played bus driver Zou in that influential early post-Mao urban-subject film directed by Zhang Nuanxin. *Good Morning, Beijing* concludes with an uncertainty about the future of its young characters, all riding in the same bus. Years later, when Wang Quan'an made his own directorial debut in *Lunar Eclipse* (Yueshi, 1999), he further explored dilemmas faced by young people in their everyday lives.

Lunar Eclipse leaves a strong impression of light, which, as a photographer character in the film comments, is the soul of any good picture. The narrative structure of the film is best described as following the light. Although not all lunar, the impressionistic lighting effects of the film on the whole convey a moonstruck feeling of the surreal. Bing, a taxi driver spellbound by his love of photography, finds in his camera's viewer a woman skating on a frozen pond in winter twilight. She bears an uncanny resemblance to his former girlfriend. Bing later discovers that the woman is a musician who has just given up her performing career to marry a wealthy CEO. A friendship starts between Bing and the newlywed musician, who is fascinated to learn of Bing's earlier friendship with her look-alike, an unsuccessful actress, who frequents a privately owned photo studio where Bing works. The owners of the studio, an amusing couple of an older husband and younger wife, are Bing's good friends. Bing's current friendship with the musician recalls his earlier friendship with the actress. Although the film ends with the musician witnessing a traffic accident that kills her look-alike, the mysticism of the relatedness of the two women is already established. The two women not only look alike and act alike, but they have also both married older men for financial benefit.

Filled with frequent close-ups, many cuts, constant camera movement, and a creative use of lighting, the film focuses on the surreal relationship between the experiences of the two women, between a sense of self and alter-ego, between being awake and dreaming, and between the present and the past. To add humor to the parallel story lines, the story of the studio-owning couple functions as a foil, or parody, to the central relationship of the film, allowing it to showcase three couples of younger women marrying older men, leading the audience to think of the similar problems faced by these women. The film's title both indicates the film's surreal effects and, as director Wang suggested, symbolizes the situation of women being overshadowed by men. The moonstruck eccentricity of the women shows their pain at not being able to find themselves in their married life.

In 2001, at a Harvard film series on Chinese cinema and society in transformation, with most of the selections showcasing a plain, less interventional style of realism, Wang's *Lunar Eclipse* stands out as a stylistic black horse.[44] Wang was confident about his style; both popular perception and critical reviews back home had been enthusiastic about the ways in which he edited his first film.[45] Film's reality, Wang commented when he showed up at the screening of his film at Harvard, should be different from what you watch on the street. "Film is about the mysticism of life," Wang said. "We don't understand it totally, but we are touched here and there. Film is like a dream, which is part of us that we don't totally understand." Wang's emphasis on mysticism reminded the Harvard audience of another film that was then showing in the Boston area—*Suzhou River* by Wang's classmate Lou Ye. Both *Lunar Eclipse* and *Suzhou River* feature subjective approaches, and both hinge on a narrative mysticism puzzling the relatedness of two identical-looking women.[46]

In chapter 5, while discussing Lou Ye's *Suzhou River*, I suggest that Lou, who stands on the other end of a paradigm of film styles from Jia Zhangke, actually shares with Jia the same cultural cynicism, and they both contribute to the urban realism that distinguishes the new generation's filmmaking. This suggestion, strictly speaking, breaks some commonsense boundaries of film styles. Louis Giannetti, in his widely used textbook *Understanding Movies*, offers a chart of film styles: with classical cutting (a film language that emphasizes dramatic intensity and emotional emphasis) sitting at the middle of the chart, less manipulative styles of "sequence shots" and "cutting to continuity" fall into the "realism" side of the chart, and more intrusive and interpretive editing such as "thematic montage" and "abstract cutting" find themselves on the other side of the chart labeled "formalism."[47] Whereas Jia Zhangke generally relies on less manipulative long takes and long shots, Lou Ye, as well as Wang Quan'an, prefer manipulative close-ups, a moving camera, and frequent cuts (only some of them abstract). How do we reconcile the stylistic distance between these two extremes and consider them both as contributing to a blooming of urban-realist cinema?

To begin with, realism as the general cultural spirit of the Chinese new urban cinema exceeds the restricted stylistic denotation of realism. To capture elusive urban realities calls for sensual, subjective, and even surreal experiences. When people recall the urban aura of Hong Kong, for example, many impressions contributed by Wong Kar-wai's manipulative film techniques naturally come to mind. To exclude them, one's reality of Hong Kong would be missing something. The same is true of post-Mao Chinese cultural reality.

Many subjective image manipulations found in the films by Wang Quan'an, Lou Ye, and Li Xin must accompany the more naturalistic early films by Jia Zhangke and Zhang Yuan to make our feeling for China more complete. Especially for the younger generations, images and the manipulation of images have become more and more their daily reality. In my interview with film director Huang Jianxin, we talked about generational changes in today's China, from language-oriented ones to image-oriented ones.[48] Huang suggested that the younger generations, in dealing with much enriched visual input in their daily lives and in playing electronic and computer games, have formulated their sense of reality more from images or rather their manipulation of images. Young people today, dubbed by Zhang Yiwu as "a disk-watching generation," also watch more films than they read books. Image-wise, the opening of Li Xin's *Dazzling* reminds the viewer of both electronic games and science fiction films. While an older audience complained about its artificiality, the younger audience did not seem to care. And whereas one critic believed that *Dazzling* showed "a crisis in creating images,"[49] another believed that the film best represented a generation's (including those born in the late 1960s and the 1970s) ways of seeing the world: "they [director Li Xin and his contemporaries] organize their sensual experiences according to their 'game-generation' lifestyle."[50]

Considering as a whole the films that have emerged since the 1990s, few have ventured far into the formalist end of Giannetti's style chart. Films by Wang Quan'an, Lou Ye, and Li Xin, though rich in their active use of various film techniques, are not formalist as far as the general film narrative is concerned. The overall style of these directors, at best, falls on the middle point of classicism, with only an occasional inclination toward the formalist side. Here probably also lies the clue to the coincidence that both Wang and Lou used the mysticism of identical-looking women, a Hitchcock narrative formula, and a form of suspense that requires the film to have a clear narrative line. Both Wang Quan'an and Lou Ye draw the audience's attention to the narrative itself by exposing its make-believe nature and challenging its reliability. Nonetheless, they both also rely on clear story lines and dramas with some emotional intensity. This prevailing stylistic restraint contrasts with the stylistic indulgence showcased at the onset of the last cinematic high tide of Fourth and Fifth Generation filmmaking. In the mid-1980s, formalism and absurdity, as represented by Tian Zhuangzhuang's *Horse Thief* (Daoma zei, 1986) and Huang Jianzhong's *Questions for the Living* (Yige sizhe dui shengzhe de fangwen, 1987), were in vogue. Directors then did not have to worry about the market, and formalist experiments often helped the films pass the censors because of the obscurity of their social message. Directors who have emerged since the 1990s cannot afford to ignore the market, both domestic and overseas. Lou Ye's *Weekend Lovers* (1993), widely claimed to represent the arrival of the Sixth Generation, captured critical attention in China. His *Suzhou River* (2000) first succeeded by going the international film festival route and then receiving critical attention in China. Both films fall primarily into the category of classicism in their use of editing. In contrast, Lou's formalist film, a grotesque, surreal thriller *Don't Be Young* (Weiqing shaonü, 1994), has been ignored.

Social and cultural concerns, as well as a contemporary urban subject, are also called for to tie films of different styles into a bundle called urban realistic cinema. Film criticism in China also prefers stylistic experiments with these elements rather than experiments devoid of them. The reasons why Lou Ye's *Don't Be Young* has been ignored definitely include an element shown by the film's opening caption: "a different time and a different place." Filled with surreal uncertainty in the general narrative and a grotesqueness of image, the film is set in an ahistorical time and place and is about a young woman's search, in nightmares and nightmarish daytimes, in a haunted house and abandoned streets, for clues to the disappearance of her father and the suicide of her mother. The film is a sophisticated work with controlled performances, superb camerawork, and thrilling psychological effects. Yet, when social, cultural, and historical associations are purposefully discouraged, the film excludes the general audience and the socially and culturally oriented film critics who are not used to this gamelike execution of horror and mysticism.

Half a decade later, in Wang Quan'an's contemporary urban subject *Lunar Eclipse*, film critics and scholars were excited that they found an appropriate (experimental as it is) film language that is addressing a reality that everyone living in today's China would be familiar with. Huang Shixian, a professor at Beijing Film Academy, believed that Wang's style would be as influential as that of Zhang Yuan, whose films then featured a documentary-ism.[51] Dai Jinhua, a professor at Beijing University, praised *Lunar Eclipse* as "an auteur film, an art film, and a film whose language is not a package but the film itself."[52] Chen Xiaoming, from the Chinese Academy of Social Sciences, suggested this cultural significance of Wang's style: "Wang's fragmented narration—with its constant deconstruction and reconstruction, with its shattering cuts and camera movements, with its use of lighting that suggests brokenness—is related to the dilemmas faced by contemporary people in their lives and their efforts to rid themselves of dilemmas. [Wang's] restless forms of expression themselves are a part of contemporary life."[53] Obviously, Chinese academia was ready and eager to theorize about the kind of stylistic exploration exemplified in *Lunar Eclipse*. The film also lent me a case, as a conclusion of this chapter, to show the artistic richness displayed by the new cinema while it engages the elusive everyday life of the city.

7

City Paradise: Urbanization Looms over an Old Land

He held this allegory in a film script for years. Lu Chuan, a young man fresh from Beijing Film Academy, had knocked on the doors of many different film companies. Many executives recognized the merits of the script but did not want to invest in him, an unknown name in the film circle then.

The script tells the story of a small-town policeman who wakes up one morning to find that his gun is missing. Recalling that he had become drunk at the wedding of his sister the previous night, he visits all who attended the wedding, hoping to retrieve the missing gun. This private search reveals a lot about the policeman's connections in the town but yields no clue for finding the gun. The missing gun causes an identity crisis for the policeman; in great

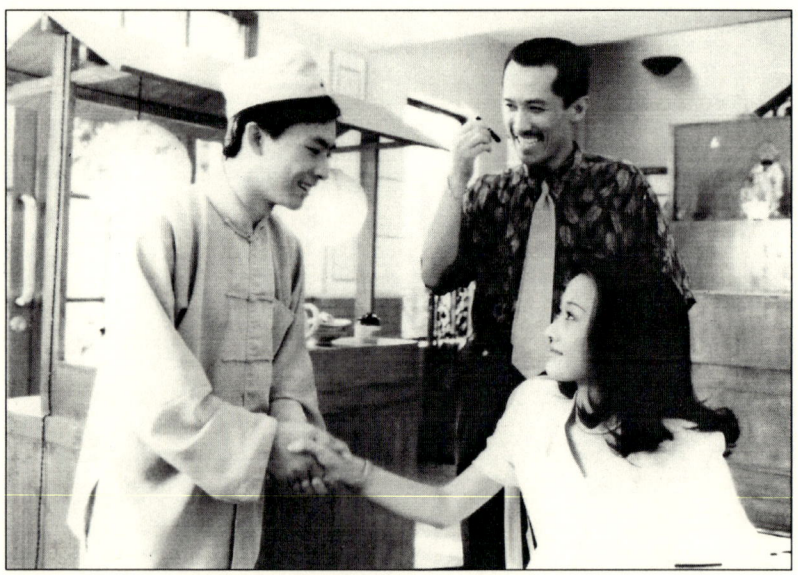

In a society where everyone is trying to make it on his or her own, one's "rice bowl" (Chinese for financial income) is always more attractive than one's "home." *A Country Boy in Shanghai* (dir. Xia Gang, 1999).
Courtesy of China Film Archive, Beijing.

anxiety, he feels alienated from his institution, family, lover, friends, and the town. All he has taken for granted and all that was once natural around him start to appear strange. The government also gets involved in the search. The script suggests that the film should rely on camera motions and cuts both to indicate the sense of insecurity felt by the protagonist and to tell a suspenseful story of how drug trafficking affects the peaceful life of the small town.

This script was *The Missing Gun*. In his long search for an investor, Lu Chuan merged his own sense of anxiety with that of the protagonist in his script and pushed the psychological intensity of the script to the utmost. When the superstar Jiang Wen eventually showed interest in the script, Lu Chuan finally got the chance to have his directorial debut. Although Jiang Wen's preference for dramatic acting obviously diverted the film somewhat from Lu Chuan's preference for visual expression,[1] the film's strong sense of anxiety, rich allegorical implications, and psychological realism resembling the style of Edward Yang impressed film critics.[2] Considering the cultural implications of the film, a critic noticed how the missing gun kept gaining allegorical richness in the long process of a vain search, and he compared the process of this search to that of waiting in Samuel Beckett's *Waiting for Godot*—"when both 'searching' and 'waiting' can't obtain their objects, the tragic sense of absurdity concerning human action is felt."[3]

The Missing Gun: An Allegory of Urban Mobility and Otherness

Among various allegorical readings of *The Missing Gun*, Wang Yichuan's reading has a particular bearing on the topic of this chapter, that is, how post-Mao urbanization has fragmented the former sense of self that is tied to a particular piece of land.[4] This sense of self is often known as one's roots, the importance of which can't be overstated in the traditional, self-sufficient life. The ancient Chinese philosopher Lao Tzu emphasized the security one feels with their roots. "Heaviness is the root of lightness," his *Tao Teh Ching* states. "To be light is to be separated from one's roots."[5] To feel light, in a sense, is to feel alienated from the accustomed sense of self one develops at a particular place; it is to be in the air and not on the ground. The modern Western philosopher Heidegger also pointed out that a particular place has a role in human cultural identity—it describes both one's "external bond" and the "depths of his freedom and reality."[6] In the ancient, self-sufficient model of life, one's identity (the "immobile" personality) was related to how one might best benefit from the resources of a particular, isolated place. In the globalized, urbanized model of life today, one's identity (the "mobile" personality) is constituted by a constant search for a better place and a circulation of resources. The philosophy of the immobile personality emphasizes the natural connection of things, and its idealized mentality is one of content; on the other hand, the mobile personality holds the individual accountable for their understanding of the allocation of resources and their own movements, according to this understanding. It tends to generate anxiety. *The Missing Gun*, according to Wang Yichuan's reading, testifies to the tension caused by the transition from a self-sufficient isolation to connection, from the immobile personality to the mobile personality, and from content with existential isolation to the anxiety caused by searching and mobility.

Ma Shan, the local policeman, has lived in the changed society for a long time without realizing it. He does not learn to relate his home, a seemingly isolated sleepy town, with the outside world until the search for the missing gun fragments his sense of roots and forces him to see the connection. In his identity crisis, Ma Shan becomes especially sensitive to the contrast of the two women in his love life—his wife and his former girlfriend. His wife epitomizes the immobile society and shows little sympathy for Ma Shan's negligence. His former girlfriend personifies the mobile mentality—she started as Ma Shan's first love in the small town, left for a better job and got involved in another love relationship, and then returns to the town to cohabit with still another man. Her sympathy for Ma Shan and her social connection eventually become crucial for finding the gun. Ma Shan has long considered his wife to be on the side of Self and his former girlfriend to be on the side of Other. In his identity crisis, the solidarity of self is lost and what his former girlfriend personifies, otherness and mobility—the two essential characteristics of urban life—become educational. Ma Shan's fear of the flirtatious relationship he finds with his former girlfriend adds an intensity and unsteadiness throughout this educational process.

What resonates for the audience in the anxiety shown in *The Missing Gun*, from one perspective, is the loss of roots in post-Mao urbanization. This cultural change affects almost everyone in contemporary China, since it is witnessing the greatest of mobility of population between small towns and the metropolis, between the countryside and the cities, as well as between China and abroad. Such mobility and otherness have become increasingly true in the changed social life. Nostalgia for home, for one's sense of belonging, is also becoming commonplace. It has become an appealing theme in popular culture, appearing in songs, stories, TV series, and films. Yu Jin's 1999 book on Chinese popular music has a section on this theme, offering us plenty of examples of its appeal.[7] One of the best-selling CDs of the 1990s was a collection of songs titled *Away from Home* (Chumen zai wai). The theme songs for the TV series *An Out-of-Town Girl* quickly sold more than twenty thousand copies: It is about homesickness ("Year after year I return home in dreams / You're far away but you're always in my heart"). Gan Ping's songs became popular because of lines such as "This metropolis does not have the moon of the hometown. You want to cry but you also want to hold back your tears." Hou Dejian's "On the Road" (Chuzou) goes, "My home is really far away / So far that I don't know where it is / I find it only at midnight in dreams." Hou's song became so popular that it even induced Cui Jian to write a song of the same title, further elaborating the feelings of being away from home and on the road. Li Chunbo's song, "A Letter Home," does not have especially touching lines but does have an admission of homesickness. It sold a record eight hundred thousand copies. Banking on his popularity with songs, Li Chunbo directed a well-received film, *Don't Cry, Girl* (Nühai bieku, 2002), which also features the emotional life of a young white-collar woman trying to make it away from home in a big metropolis.

In 2003, a most popular "happy-new-year" film was titled *Far from Home* (Wo de meili xiangchou). The film follows three characters as they start their lives anew in a metropolis—a country girl who finds a job in a restaurant, a white-collar girl who follows her job there, and a Hong Kong professional who is seeking business opportunities in the city. In their stories, we encounter even more outsiders who are trying to make it in this city. All the characters are struck by homesickness. but they are also all inspired by the changes this city has brought to their lives. One characteristic of this popular genre of cinema, a holiday season social event, is its wide appeal to viewers of different age groups, social backgrounds, ethnicities, and gender. The fact that homesickness can become the subject of a happy-new-year film indicates how mobility and the choice of where to live have touched many layers of today's society and thus have also touched the souls of all kinds of people. Xia Gang, the director and scriptwriter for *A Country Boy in Shanghai* (Boli shi touming de, 1999), another popular film about contemporary migration, comments on home and roots profoundly: "Migration is to live away from home. It also indicates a mental condition that one has temporarily lost his spiritual orientation and has to adjust to the fact of wandering. In a society where everyone is trying to make it on their own, one's 'rice bowl' [Chinese for financial income] is always more attractive than one's 'home.' In people's search for their 'rice bowls,' they are searching for [a new] sense of 'returning home.' The fact that 'rice bowls' and 'homes' can't always remain together is what this film is about."[8] This writer's juxtaposition of searching for one's "rice bowl" and searching for "home" indicates a new conception of home in urbanized China. Home is not where you were born and where you know everyone else. Home is mobile and it needs to be reconstructed in otherness, that is, in new urban environments with accidental social combinations.

A Country Boy in Shanghai: Glass Walls and Urban Newcomers

As discussed in chapter 1, the advance of a new era of urbanization and the rise of a new urbanism in Chinese cinema since the 1990s drew a conclusion to the brief period of Fourth Generation allegorical urbanism, in which the city stands for the allegorical implications of reformation, openness, science, education, and civilization in contrast to the countryside, which is often associated with the inertia of history, closure, ignorance, antihumanity, and decay. In the newest city films, the city/country contrast based on these humanist and enlightenment values has stopped functioning. The country migrants in cities rarely invoke generalized city/country contrasts but find themselves mixing with other less fortunate urban residents, such as unemployed state workers, to become victims of various aspects of a drastic urbanization that is affecting the lives of millions. It is true that the country folks who try to make it in cities find it particularly hard to establish new homes. Like laborers from developing countries now living in developed countries, the country folks are second-class citizens in the cities, supplying cheap labor primarily in the service sector. Many of them don't wish to stay in the city; they only hope to make enough money to ensure a better life once they return home. For those who wish to stay, the transition from being a country person to being an urbanite is not smooth at all.

Disassociating with the city/country allegory, the representation of rural migrants testified to the new cinema's plunge into the flow of everyday life. The figure of rural migrants, as Zhang Zhen observes, "is hardly an icon for a national cinema" and the cinematic stories of the rural migrants have lent Chinese new cinema "a distinctive social urgency as well as a formal rigor."[9] To understand the changes initiated by the representation of rural migrants, let us visit a gallery of them in cities through several films.

Xia Gang's film *A Country Boy in Shanghai* offers us an interesting perspective of Shanghai today, in relation to the contemporary influx of rural population to cities. The film's title is literally "glass is transparent." It reflects the film's allegory that portrays Shanghai as a city with many glass walls built between different social groups. Shanghai, as the country boy's father tells him before the boy leaves his Sichuan village, is the busiest port for all kinds of vessels to harbor. Indeed, Shanghai, in its colonial past, was a vanguard Chinese city that was open to all kinds of influx, cultural and social. The influx was not only from overseas. It was also from across the land in China. People migrated to Shanghai to "make it." After being closed a few decades in the Maoist era, Shanghai was quickly restored to its role of a big seaport and a city of immigrants. Is this city a melting pot for immigrants? While melting to a certain degree may unavoidably happen, *A Country Boy in Shanghai* depicts the new immigrants' feeling about the glass walls. The transparency of the glass offers them a glimpse of other peoples' lives, making them conscious of their differences. However, when one forgets about these glass walls and wants to trespass into the others' sphere, they hit the walls.

In this film, the country boy, known as "Little Sichuan," is the first-person narrator. From the labor market, Miss Wang, the manager of a restaurant, picks him to become the tea boy of the restaurant. The job requires him to look "cute" when he serves the tea from a bronze teakettle that has an extremely long serving spout, a distinctive feature of the restaurant. Miss Wang becomes Little Sichuan's first idol in Shanghai; he admires and fears her, knowing that she had migrated to Shanghai a few years before from a smaller city to the northeast and is now the boss. Little Sichuan soon also learns that the real boss, the owner, is Mr. Su, a builder from a southern town, who handles construction projects in Shanghai. Living in a side room at Mr. Su's temporary residence in Shanghai, he later learns of Mr. Su's love relationship with not only Miss Wang but also another young woman working at the restaurant, "Shannxi Lass." Before this discovery, Little Sichuan is a bosom buddy of Shannxi Lass. He is drawn to her because of their similar status and backgrounds. By the end of the film, Mr. Su decides that Shannxi Lass is a better partner in life, divorces his wife in his hometown, plans to marry Shannxi Lass, and promotes her to be the manager of the restaurant. Miss Wang backs out of the relationship, sells her shares in the restaurant, finds another man, and moves on to own her own flower shop. Witnessing all this, Little Sichuan thinks that he now has a better future in the restaurant. Shannxi Lass, nonetheless, tells Little Sichuan that he must leave—she does not want anyone who knows how she has made it to be in her new life. Although director Xia Gang makes a special effort to give depth to the character of Mr. Su, depicting him not as a villain, one realizes that what draws Shannxi Lass to him obviously is not love but a desire to change her social status. The actress who plays the role of Shannxi Lass had this to say about her role: "Through the glass, we can observe closely the world beyond but we can never touch, smell, or taste the real flavor of that world. The glass in between remains cold. Your struggle may break the glass. That, however, will also break your head and break your hopes. Differences of social status have distanced us. Let's remain observing behind the glass walls. That way you can still keep your hope alive."[10]

Glass walls deter people from moving beyond. They hinder communication among urbanites and strengthen such undesirable aspects of urban culture as Otherness—the accidental combination of urban communities in which residents don't need and don't bother to know their next-door neighbors. *Call Me* (Hu wo, 2000), a film that presents unforgettable images of rural migrants in the city, explores how people communicate in today's city, where people live closer together but feel more distant. The film uses a beeper-messaging center in Beijing to connect some unrelated stories happening over seven summer days. For a decade or so, the telephone beeper was a cheap and thus popular way for Chinese city residents to communicate. Especially for rural migrants who didn't have a fixed place to live and who couldn't afford a cell phone, beepers were important. People called the messaging center to leave a brief message, which was then relayed to a beeper.[11] In the film, the daily work of the beeper-messaging center is unmistakably shown as the pulse of the city. Here we hear all kinds of messages from, for example, anxious business dealers, desperate lovers, and concerned parents. The messages reflect the varied personalities and mentalities. Given the diversity of its stories and their relatedness to the pulse of the city, as the director suggests, the time of seven days suggests a symbolic process of genesis—"these stories are less about slices of life but more about a depiction of Chinese contemporary daily life that repeats itself."[12] In other words, the beeper-messaging center offered the director a good angle for creating a generalized understanding of urban cultural conditions—people's wish to get closer to each other and their reality of living in isolation.

Two country migrants offer us contrasting stories. The first one, coming from northwest China, has been selling his blood to an underground blood bank. He is diagnosed with AIDS. Knowing that he is going to die, he wants to find the person who first got him into selling blood in order to stop him from doing more harm to others. He also walks Beijing streets posting a notice that reads, "I am Zhang Shun from Shannxi. Whoever received my blood, call me." No one ever responds by leaving messages on his beeper. The frames in which he talks to his goldfish while washing himself in his shabby room are filled with an isolated sadness. To contrast this tragedy, the second migrant's story is more comical. He is a flower seller who enjoys singing. When his singing is jeered at by a music teacher, he is not hurt but persists in receiving some tutoring from her. With his comic stubbornness, he gets what he asks for. Although the flower seller breaks the glass wall in reaching out, his comic acceptance releases little of the pain for the viewer that has been caused by the AIDS victim, who is facing death all alone. The AIDS epidemic has been out of control in China, with many victims among rural migrants who get infected through selling blood. Ah Nian's film was the first to touch on the issue, showing the misery of the patient and the dismal conditions of the underground blood bank.

The image of glass walls is also crucial in another city/country film, Tang Danian's *City Paradise* (Dushi tiantang, 1999). The film tells the story of Dasheng, a new transplantee who makes a living in Beijing by washing office-block windows. His work offers him a spectacular view of Beijing as a modern metropolis, and he constantly sees the city as a reflection from a single window or from a whole wall of glass, accompanied by constant traffic noise. The sense of mobility and horizons and the money he earns inspire Dasheng to leave behind his wife and a neurotic mother. He obviously has made an effort to build a new social life in the city, and he even finds his foster parents, going to their apartment regularly to do their housework. These visits present human warmth in urban apartment life, where Dasheng is obviously favored for his diligence, obedience, and trustworthiness. However, when he develops a relationship with a pretty neighbor, who is also from the country and who works in the building as a household helper, it becomes harder for Dasheng to keep his favored image. Eventually, when Dasheng is caught sleeping with this neighbor by her host family after he makes a mess of the apartment, he is quickly labeled as one of those country folks who take unfair advantage of the kindness of their hosts. All of a sudden, his foster parents and people he knows turn a cold shoulder to his ousting from city life. City people are harsh to newcomers when the latter forget about their second-class-citizen status and attempt to go beyond the traditional boundaries. The moment of Dasheng's ousting is a time when these boundaries, or glass walls, reassert themselves.

A realistic film attentive to detailed character portrayal, *City Paradise* is also a sad allegory of city/country contrast, a rare generalized reflection on this issue in the new urban cinema. Following Dasheng's city life and home visits, the difference between city (glass-surface buildings, dense communities, and busy traffic) and the countryside (captured by the camera in a pastoral serenity) amazes the audience. For urban cinemagoers, why someone would leave behind the quiet country for the chaotic city might remain a mystery. Dasheng's house in the country may be old, but it looks so harmonious with it natural setting. His mother, who chases creatures invisible to others, is definitely demented, but her missing of her son is also unmistakable. Midway through the film, when Dasheng's mother traces her lost son to the city, loses her way, and rests her aching feet next to a glass-surface building to look at the bewildering world around her, no one can resist the allegorical implications of the scene: the rural past of the ancient country, represented by the mother, is searching for her lost son—the confused rural migrant to the city—as a drastic urbanization pulls all possible laborers into its high tides.

The director of *City Paradise*, Tang Danian, is a Sixth Generation graduate from the script writing department of Beijing Film Academy.[13] In Sixth Generation filmmaking, he is better known as a scriptwriter, having written scripts for such films as Zhang Yuan's *Beijing Bastards* and Wang Xiaoshuai's award-winning *Beijing Bicycle*, which received a Golden Bear from the 2001 Berlin International Film Festival. This latter work is another city/country contrast film. *Beijing Bicycle*, as discussed in the previous chapter, uses a bicycle to connect two seventeen-year-olds, Guei from the countryside and Jian from the city. The bicycle that the two teenagers are forced to share leads us to see their different lives, which otherwise might not have crossed. Guei's city life as a humble migrant has been reduced to work only—he focuses on his income, to which is tied all his dreams and his identity. Jian is not from a wealthy family, but just being an urban resident makes him look superior. He is studying at a trade school and can afford to join his friends at video game outlets for after-school entertainment. Guei is far away from his family, making his own living and earning the bicycle, whereas Jian still thinks it is natural that his father should buy him the bicycle.

In Wang Xiaoshuai's film, the city/country contrast shown in the differences between the two teenagers is actually aimed at showing their similarity—their attachment to the bicycle, or their alienation in today's materialist culture. At the beginning of the film, when Guei joins others from the country to become a city courier, the company manager encourages them to be "rickshaw boys of the new era." The image is invoked from Lao She's 1937 novel *Rickshaw*, in which the protagonist is drawn into the devotion behind working hard to earn ownership of a rickshaw. On the immediate story level, Wang Xiaoshuai's film and Lao She's novel are comparable: The protagonists' similar journeys toward ownership are interrupted by various incidents that are not always within their control. Here pathos is aroused about the fragile personal destinies confronting social chaos. Many dramatic downfalls in Lao She's novel eventually turned the rickshaw puller into a beggar, whereas Wang's film concludes with a badly beaten Guei carrying his destroyed bicycle and walking against the busy traffic of Beijing streets. Yet neither Lao She nor Wang Xiaoshuai wants their work to be a tearjerker. Among other themes, *Rickshaw* is about fetishism and alienation; it is about how human beings are turned into slaves to their means of living, be it a rickshaw or an occupation. In his later stories, Lao She's sarcastic narrators discuss the idea that "if you are crazy about something, you will end up paying your life for it" ("Predilection," 1943), or "if things force one to get into a certain track, he moves along it just as a train has to move along its rails" ("This Life of Mine," 1947).

As in Lao She's *Rickshaw*, the bicycle in Wang's film, as an object of desire, is often described as a woman or is involved with the characters' desire for women. Guei's hope for acceptance in city life depends on the bicycle. His idol of worship is a "city girl" whom he can see in an apartment balcony overlooking his brother's food stand and who frequents the stand. When Guei finds his missing bicycle and rushes back to his brother's, he bumps into the girl. On the screen, his idols of love, the bicycle and the girl, collapse. The sarcasm here, however, is that Guei's idol turns out to be a country girl working for an urban family; Guei and his brother have been fooled by all the borrowed clothes she changes into just to impress them.

Jian's attachment to the bicycle is also confused with the friendship of a girl. With the bicycle, Jian earns the privilege of riding home with her. The girl remarks to him that his bicycle is nice. The bicycle, like the Western sports jacket that the girl's next boyfriend wears, is a status symbol that satisfies adolescent vanity. When Jian's ownership of the bicycle becomes questionable, he is dumped by the girl and gets into a fierce fight with the girl's next boyfriend. The fighting occurs when Guei comes to pick up the bicycle; Guei also becomes a victim.

Although they are similarly involved in the fetishism of the same bicycle, it is still rather disturbing to see that Guei, an innocent country boy, becomes the victim of adolescent crime on the urban scene. The country/city contrast makes us realize better how the idle lifestyle of urban youth has contributed to their boredom, anger, petty crimes, and street fighting. Likewise is the effect of an earlier film by Wang Xiaoshuai, *So Close to Paradise* (Biandan, guniang, 1997), in which an innocent rural migrant becomes the narrator of a crime film. Typical of the emerging Sixth Generation films then, *So Close to Paradise* has a pseudo plot, a slice-of-life feel, and characters who live on the margins of society. The main character, Dongzi, is trying to make it in the city of Wuhan but ends up joining many other country folks by using the carrying pole he brings from the countryside to carry passenger luggage at the dock to make a minimal living. People call these workers "carrying poles," and they remain peasants in the city. Dongzi's fellow villager, Gao Ping, with whom Dongzi lodges, is more ambitious; he takes up a life of crime and becomes a small-time con man in the town. He pays Dongzi to follow him now and then.

Assuming the atmosphere of a Hollywood gangster flick, the film follows a rough plotline relying on such elements as searching (Gao Ping searches for Ruan Hong, a Vietnamese girl who may lead him to find the person who has taken his money), a love triangle (both Gao Ping and Dongzi fall in love with Ruan Hong, whom they abduct), and fighting (Gao Ping dies in a fierce fight when the local gangster boss finds that Gao is sleeping with his woman). The Hollywood resemblance, however, is only superficially invoked to package a confused sense of social change experienced by those living on the margins of society, a prostitute and a rural laborer in the city.[14] The pseudo nature of the plot lies in the fact that it has no twists and turns, it creates no suspense, it is not hurrying much to happen. In essence, it merely provides a scope for the audience to experience the random happening of things. The love triangle also dissolves by the end, as Ruan Hong shows her love for the dead Gao Ping. Although Dongzi's narrative voice relates episodes of the film, he remains a passive, silent onlooker. And when Dongzi's awkward smile at the Vietnamese girl wraps up the film, we realize why the film's Chinese title is literally *The Carrying Pole and the Girl*: Dongzi and Ruan Hong are equally helpless in the film, they are less the lovers or characters in action than the onlookers, and the two of them relay the audience's emotional response to this particular slice of life they live and tell. The English title of the film, *So Close to Paradise*, is the name of a song that Ruan Hong sings at a sultry nightclub. The life shown in this film, clearly ironic, is far from paradise.

A more disturbing city/country contrast is found in an independent film, *Two Hearts* (Xin xin, 2002) directed by Sheng Zhimin.[15] Tingting, a country girl, is employed by a small company in Beijing to provide sexual service on the telephone to adult callers. She is confined to a room where she lives and works—to talk dirty and to moan. Luckily, to show the destination of the incoming calls, she has a computer terminal that allows her to surf the Internet, on which she becomes a good friend of Xinxin, a city girl who is supposed to have left for Canada to study yet secretly delays her trip, since she wants to have her first sex with her boyfriend before she leaves the country. The boyfriend, however, has changed his mind about dating her. In the film, Xinxin's search for her boyfriend showcases a teenage lifestyle of rough talk, fighting, sexual promiscuity, and consuming time in "Internet bars," game rooms, and parties. It is a lifestyle closer to that of Jian in *Beijing Bicycle*, only rougher, idler, and more decadent. This showcasing of teenage lifestyle is juxtaposed by Tingting's work for two effects. First, a poor country girl's confined and exploited life is a sharp contrast with the lives of her city counterparts, who indulge in their idle lives. Second, the teenage decadence reflects the decadence in adult culture. The vulgar sex talks the adults have with Tingting contrast the sexual promiscuity of the teenagers. In her search for her boyfriend, Xinxin discovers her father at a nightclub accompanied by girls of her age. When Xinxin is fed up with the search for her boyfriend, she has her first sex with her boyfriend's father. These shocking twists in the film are indeed symptoms of a sick culture. At the end of the film, Tingting and Xinxin decide to meet. Yet, since Tingting presented herself as a male when she chatted with Xinxin on the Internet and does not have a chance to explain this fact to her, they stand not far from each other at their arranged meeting place but do not recognize each other. Lives for the country and city girls will continue to be kept apart and different.

Let's conclude our visit to this gallery of country folks by returning to the city of Shanghai, where a countryman, after several strikes at the glass walls, establishes himself with his earnest work. The film is Shi Runjiu's *A Beautiful New World* (Meili xin shijie, 1998). Among the school-trained art film directors, Shi Runjiu is more inclined to commercial success. This film, with superb acting from Jiang Wu and Tao Hong, and with a humorous love story in which a country person is first sneered at but eventually loved by his pretty relative, gave the production company Imar an early success in investing in low-budget films that might sell both in China and overseas.[16] Film scholar Ni Zhen hailed this film as a turning point for the younger directors to heed everyday life around them, to know the demands of the box office, and to push art films closer to popular entertainment.[17] Incidentally, the film is presented as a story told in the style of the Shanghai dialect ballad that is popularly enjoyed at teahouses. This metanarrative frame lends the film a local flavor, an everyday feel, and an added humorous touch. Shanghai fiction writer Wang Anyi once commented on the Shanghai dialect ballad as an art form that is nosy about the current happenings in the neighborhood; it may appear shortsighted and profane, she said, but it is also a practical Shanghai approach to everyday life.[18]

A Beautiful New World is an art film that assumes a popular appeal. The star power of the film, nonetheless, has made its country folk image artificial and thus less powerful than other stories we have seen in this section. In the film, Zhang Baogen (Jiang Wu) comes from the countryside to Shanghai to claim a luxury apartment won through a lottery drawing, only to find that it is a futures commodity that he has to wait for years to get. In the meantime, people in his village who are looking for donations out of his lottery winnings make it impossible for him to return. Deciding to find a job in Shanghai and wait for his apartment to materialize, he is forced to move in with a distant relative, a younger woman he calls "Auntie" (Tao Hong). His first surprise comes when his auntie insists on charging him a few dollars a day for lodging with her. From here develops the unlikely romance between the country bumpkin and his aggressively modern auntie. Unlikely indeed. The film, as a comedy, does not need to make its ending of Baogen's winning of his auntie's love feel convincing. The lasting impression is how Baogen, a down-to-earth country person, contrasts with his opportunistic auntie and how he ends up teaching her a few lessons about basic human decency. Baogen does not change throughout the film. Neither does the city. Baogen's later success in business does not erase the pain of his earlier failures or eliminate the possibility that they will happen again. The humor in a country bumpkin encountering cynical, contemporary Shanghai leads us to see clashes between materialism, the new market economy, opportunities, traditional values, and human desires. The country folk in this film, like other country folk in films discussed here, mirror the social change in cities and among urbanites.

In Expectation: Zhang Ming, Jia Zhangke, and Provincial Backwaters

In Expectation (Wushan yunyu, 1996) is Zhang Ming's directorial debut. In this film set in a small Yangtze River town, Zhang Ming likes to let his camera pause on the plastic pails that local residents use to store the live fish they will cook later. In his film language, these pails become an allegory of the capsules of local lives both isolated from and also greatly affected by the mainstream of contemporary Chinese urbanization. Lives of the small-town people in Zhang's films are like water and fish taken from the Yangtze,

China's number-one river—they are part of the mainstream, but they are also thrown into containment (represented by the plastic pails) to become local backwaters. The red color of the pails suggests a certain anxiety in this relationship between connection and detachment. Such an allegory imbedded in the psychological realism of Zhang Ming's films is highly suggestive of many contemporary films about provincial lives, especially those by Zhang Ming and Jia Zhangke, two Sixth Generation directors trained by Beijing Film Academy in the late 1980s and early 1990s.

Born in 1961, Zhang Ming grew up in a small town on the banks of the Yangtze's scenic Three Gorges. He had already become a talented fine arts student at China's Southwest Normal College when he was accepted, in 1988, by the graduate program of Beijing Film Academy to major in directing. As a student, he witnessed the glory enjoyed by a few prize-winning Fifth Generation directors in the international limelight. He also experienced the rapid decline of art film production at home when filmmaking lost government sponsorship and had to survive on its own in the market. By the time he graduated in 1991, it was already exceedingly difficult for filmmakers to find investors. From 1991 to 1994, Zhang Ming taught classes in audiovisual language at Beijing Film Academy and looked for chances to direct. In 1995, with help from friends, he invested in his first film, *In Expectation*. He named his film production company Earth Workshop (nitu gongzuozu) and was determined to bank on his own life in the small river town on the Yangtze.

In Expectation is the best translation of the title of Zhang Ming's first film, which is literally "Rain clouds over Mt. Wu," a Chinese idiom suggesting the foggy mountain scenery where heaven and earth touch. This union of heaven and earth is often used as a literary euphemism for the human sexual act. The story of the film, in a general atmosphere of expectation, is indeed the union of a man and a woman. Mai Qiang, the man, is the signal operator at a lighthouse on the Yangtze River Gorges. He is a shy single man expecting changes in his private life but not knowing how to make them happen. His work is one of expectation; he awaits the passing ships and displays various signals for them. Chen Qing, the woman, is the front-desk receptionist of a state-owned hotel in the town. Her job is to expect daily tourists to stay at her hotel. A single mom with a little boy, she is expecting to remarry. She yearns for it, because she does not want to become the mistress of her boss, who helps her financially and demands sex in return. The suspense in the film starts when Chen Qing's boss reports to the local policeman, Wu Gang, that an unidentified person has raped Chen Qing. Wu Gang, who is expecting to get married soon, starts the investigation reluctantly; he can't quite understand why Chen Qing denies the allegation but her boss keeps pressing the case for her. When the investigation unfolds, the unidentified person turns out to be Mai Qiang. Earlier on, the film shows Mai Qiang's friend bringing a prostitute to the lighthouse, hoping that the prostitute will overcome Mai Qiang's shyness and offer him some experience with women. That effort obviously does not work; Mai Qiang shows no interest in the woman. Later on, this same friend pulls Mai Qiang's leg when they are shopping in the town—he randomly identifies Chen Qing from the crowd and tells Mai Qiang that she is a prostitute. He dares Mai Qiang to follow her home. Mai Qiang is obviously attracted to Chen Qing and readily follows her home. When the investigation has discovered this much, it has to figure out why Mai Qiang leaves Chen Qing with a whole lot more money than what people normally pay a prostitute and why Chen Qing still refuses to charge Mai Qiang with rape. In the end, we are happy to realize that the suspense of the film becomes a process through which the two lonely people find each other. They have come to realize their mutual need, and they are ready to start a new life together. While their private expectations have yielded good results, we are still a little uncertain about what their new life is going to be like. The film also deals with the town's expectation of being inundated—with the construction of the Three Gorges Dam as the backdrop, this ancient town is scheduled to go underwater. The town's people all expect to move and to start anew.

In Expectation is remarkable in its portrayal of the emotional nuances of the major characters. Take Chen Qing's boss, for example. He has some genuine concern for Chen Qing's welfare. In the meantime, he is also a despicable married man seeking sexual gratification from his unfortunate employee. In pressing the case for Chen Qing, he is trying both to protect her and to protect his own interest. The hypocrisy of his earnestness throughout the investigation of the case is unmistakable. In telling its story, so charged with subtle emotions, the film also documents the daily life of a small town that is soon to disappear. Policeman Wu Gang cuts Mai Qiang's hair while talking with him about the case. On his way to investigate, he stops by a goldsmith to make his wedding rings and to chat. In his interview with Mai Qiang's friend, this friend soon breaks the formalness of the interview and offers to sell the policeman a refrigerator for his new home. These instances of the human touch in small-town life are hard to find in the contemporary metropolis.

Zhang Ming's next film, *Weekend Plot* (Miyu shiqi xiaoshi, 2000), is also set on the banks of the Yangtze River. Four high school friends have a weekend reunion by the river. One has stayed in town to become a policeman, and the others are now residents of a big metropolis. Although the policeman is married and the others have their significant others, their reunion brings back memories of the old days and vague relationships of love, especially that between the policeman and a young woman in the group. During their gathering, they accidentally discover a note that reads "I will love you till death." The speculation of who may be the writer of the note causes tension among the group, and many traces of mutual affections among the group members or their emotional relations with others are explored. At the end of the film, a phone call from a metropolitan customer of the young woman solves the mystery—it is this customer's joke with this young woman. In retrospect, one learns not only the delicacy of emotional relationships and the many possibilities of emotional changes but also a contrast between the small-town earnestness and the metropolis lightheartedness about emotions.

Both of Zhang Ming's films are noted for the excitement that the characters show in seeing big ships passing by on the Yangtze. This excitement reflects the isolation of the place and the impact of the outside world. In the first film of Jia Zhangke's "Shanxi Trilogy," films about the landlocked, coal-mining area of China's heartland, we see an identical excitement in characters watching a passing train. Fenyang, in Shanxi Province, is Jia Zhangke's hometown. In an interview, he recalled how when he was fourteen, when he first learned to ride a bicycle, he took a long ride with friends to see the train for the first time: "We saw a freight train carrying coal, and had an intimation of the wider world. This was a memory I carried with me during my years at the Beijing Film Academy."[19]

Jia's film career, in a way, testifies to Levi-Strauss's dictum that one goes to others to better understand the self—Jia's education in Beijing in the literature department of Beijing Film Academy has led him to scrutinize his hometown. He always had a strong desire to leave home to see the outside world. But he also believed in roots—"Your emotions and anxieties can never depart from the place of your birth." And he sees his hometown as showing "the original face of China"—the awkward, harsh conditions of the provincial backwater washed up on the margins of the economic boom. Like his marginalized characters "who struggle in life and are failures," Jia's artistic return to his hometown reflects a similar "feeling of insecurity and anxiety" that many experience in the midst of China's contemporary economic reforms, which Jia portrays very negatively: "It's often said that the Cultural Revolution was a great disaster that made victims of all of us, but I think the economic changes during the '80s were tantamount to a great revolution that was quite destructive. It's not reformist, it's a top-down movement; it remains a movement, just as the Cultural Revolution was a movement. In such a movement, an individual confronts many new things psychologically and emotionally and he loses his or her original ideals.... Through running its course, it [the economic reform of the 1980s] has harmed a lot of individuals."[20] Jia portrayed the lives of these individuals from the perspectives of the young people in the trilogy: *Xiao Wu* (1997), *Platform* (Zhan tai, 2000), and *Unknown Pleasures* (Ren xiaoyao, 2002).[21]

Xiao Wu has the unfinished look of a low-budget film, with shooting completed in just twenty-one days. The unfinished look, however, is also intentional on the part of the director, who wanted to emphasize "a down-to-earth, on-the-spot mood," the "bystander" status of the camera, and "many rough edges" that he purposefully kept with the hand-held camera that accounts for two-thirds of the film's camera work.[22] The film starts with Xiao Wu ("Little" Wu) boarding a bus headed for his hometown of Fenyang, a dusty provincial town not likely to be found in any tourist brochures. He avoids paying the fare by claiming that he is a cop. Chain-smoking, ill-postured, monosyllabic, and wearing a Western-style suit: all this and his mean demeanor are convincing enough to allow Xiao Wu to get on the bus. From this point on, the camera follows him through his life in the town, yet presenting no drama and no clear-cut narrative lines.

Xiao Wu is the head of a group of pickpockets. The local police know his style of taking cash and then depositing the victim's ID cards in a mailbox for return. Skilled as a pickpocket, Xiao Wu is also a shy person. He has his own need for love, his own moral compass, and a set of values he believes in. One of Xiao Wu's former partners in crime is now a respectable businessman of the town, and his wedding is getting a lot of media attention. Not wanting to be reminded of his past, he does not invite Xiao Wu to the wedding. Xiao Wu, nonetheless, wants to keep his childhood promise of presenting his friend with a nuptial gift of cash. He shows up at the wedding preparation and is quickly led to a side room where the two have an awkward conversation. Their meeting is typical of Jia's nondramatic film style. "In the traditional method," Jia explains about this meeting, "there would be a conflict. The drama would unfold from this moment. But in my treatment, nothing happens. They say a few words and take their leave." Jia attributes this to a Chinese way of crisis management—people bury things in their hearts to avoid conflicts.[23] In one long, unbroken take, the weight of the emotional history of the two is captured not only without drama but also without much verbalization.

The film as a whole is put together by similarly approached moments: Xiao Wu befriends a prostitute; Xiao Wu follows the fashion by buying a pager for the prostitute; Xiao Wu washes himself in a public bath; Xiao Wu visits his family; Xiao Wu is taken in by the police as the city starts a campaign to keep petty crime under control. The unhurried bystander camera follows Xiao Wu in such moments of his life with no obvious effort to force them into any particular narrative direction. Often the audience gets an insight into Xiao Wu's character between scenes. In one sequence, for example, Xiao Wu visits the sick prostitute at her shabby dorm shared with other girls. They smoke, chat, and ask each other to sing songs. Xiao Wu is shy and too embarrassed to sing. In another sequence, when Xiao Wu is all alone and undressing to take a bath, he starts to sing the song the prostitute asked him to sing before and he chuckles. Toward the end of many moments like these, the audience gets to know Xiao Wu as a person, not just the pickpocket. They see how Xiao Wu has come through his random life with his values intact. Although there is no clear narrative orientation, the film as a whole is still Jia Zhangke's comment on China's economic boom. Xiao Wu, Jia explains, "may be a more nonconformist character, but his spirit is traditional and his sense of values is a throwback to the past. The economic reform movement has put all these things at risk. He believes in honor and trust between friends and loyalty between lovers, and that blood is thicker than water between family members, but he discovers all these notions have fallen apart."[24]

The success of *Xao Wu* as it circulated through the international film festival circuit assured Jia better conditions for continuing with his more involved projects.[25] First, he completed *Platform*, a realist epic that he had long before conceived. The setting is still his—and Xiao Wu's—Fenyang. The lead role is still played by Jia's alter ego, Wang Hongwei, who also came from a provincial town to Beijing to study and who brings the role of Xiao Wu alive.[26] The time is the first decade of the post-Mao era, 1979–89. The group of people the unhurried camera follows this time work for the town's "troupe of cultural workers," a group of government-sponsored singers, dancers, and musicians who travel the province for the sake of propaganda. Minliang (played by Wang Hongwei) is a sullen troublemaker who catches on to such fashions as bell-bottomed pants, once denounced as the symbol of a decadent bourgeois lifestyle, by asking his mom to make him a pair. More drastic changes are down the road. The troupe gradually loses government sponsorship and has to adjust to the popular tastes of the market to survive. How Minliang and his group of young friends in the arts troupe live through these changes, their adjustments and their tours, offers glimpses into how China was transformed from pure "communism" to the most acquisitive and corrupt kind of state capitalism.

"Platform" was a Chinese rock song popular during the 1980s. Jia believes it is a song about expectation and chose it as the title of his second film in the trilogy to indicate hope in everyday life. "The platform," Jia says, "can be both the starting point and the finish. We are always expecting, searching. Always on the road to somewhere."[27]

Indeed, *Platform* is an on-the-road film. The landscape of the Yellow River and nearby Mongolian territory, where the arts troupe tours, is evoked in all its dusty severity. This land sustains the bizarre changes in the performances, symbolized by Jia's fondness for trains—here to indicate cultural traffic. The film starts with the troupe performing a propaganda piece, a dance about a train heading for Mao's hometown, or China being monopolized by Maoist ideological railroads. In the middle of the film, the characters have many conversations at the town's bus platform (there is no train station in the town) and they stop by the tracks to cheer the passing trains. Confusing messages are coming in from the outside world. Their performances also turn into Chinese versions of all kinds of Western pop culture. The film ends with the sound of the train—in a character's home, the teakettle's whistle becomes that of a train and the whole film fades out. China is still on the road to an unknown destiny.

A glimpse of today's China through small-town life is found in Jia's third feature, *Unknown Pleasures*. Although the setting of the film is not exactly Fenyang but a bigger, neighboring city with a train station, Jia continues to provide the same geocultural feel and does not want his audience to notice the change. He even brings in Xiao Wu from his earlier film as a money-lending gangster, to strengthen the sense of continuity. The film portrays the unlikely friendship between Qiaoqiao, an actress who is not with any arts troupe but who works as a dancer for promotional events for Mongolian King Liquor, and two idle youngsters of the town, Xiao Ji and Bingbing. Outwardly, the twenty-something Qiaoqiao is tough, and this toughness attracts the feckless Xiao Ji and Bingbing. Qiaoqiao's toughness actually contains a lot a pain that she has to suffer in dealing with both bureaucrats and gangsters to keep her dancing job. In one sequence, we see that she has to take "hugging" pictures with all the bureaucrats (a subtle sequence that shows the vulgarity and hidden erotic desires of the men) when she inadvertently walks in on one of their meetings. In another scene, we see that she has to flirt with a gangster controlling her dance show. The friendship between Qiaoqiao and Xiao Ji (Bingbing already has a college-bound girlfriend) causes a fight between Qiaoqiao and the gangster. She consequently loses her dancing job. Xiao Ji wants to get a gun to take revenge on the gangster for Qiaoqiao, but before he can do that, the gangster dies in a traffic accident. Feeling bored, Bingbing wants to join the army, but he is found to have contagious hepatitis. He even has to distance himself from his girlfriend because of this illness. With a backdrop of China's joining the World Trade Organization and Beijing's selection as the host city of the 2008 Olympics, all of which is shown on TV screens at various moments during the film, *Unknown Pleasures* draws a sharp contrast between China's growing prominence on the world stage and the bored, tedious life of a group of small-town youth who wish to have fun but don't seem to be able to find it in their lives.

"*Ren xiaoyao*" (Unknown pleasures) is the title of a dance that Qiaoqiao does for Mongolian King Liquor. It is also a popular song that Xiao Ji and Bingbing grow up with. The song reflects the sources of inspiration for the young people from folk literature, such as Yue Fei[28] and the Monkey King stories. Clips of the Monkey King cartoon, for example, are used several times in the film to show the youngsters' wish for freedom from all constraints. "*Ren xiaoyao*" also refers to the Taoist oblivion of social identity and its ideal pleasure of moving with natural forces. Taoist master Zhuangzi once dreamed of being a butterfly in blissful dances and did not want to wake up to a clear distinction between himself as human being and himself as butterfly. Qiaoqiao has a butterfly tattoo, which inspired Xiao Ji to get one as well. None of them, however, can find the Taoist blissful dance; they deal with societal forces in their boredom. Qiaoqiao loves dancing but has to spend most of her time and energy dealing with her problems in life. Xiao Ji and Bingbing love mobility. The film starts with Bingbing driving a motorcycle through the town. It arouses the expectation that the film is going to be like *Easy Rider* and that it is going to have some action. Yet not much action occurs. Over a meal at a restaurant, Xiao Ji tells Qiaoqiao of an American movie (*Pulp Fiction*) he watched from a pirated DVD. He is fascinated with the commotion a bank robber arouses when he shouts out that he is a robber. "I am a robber!" he imitates the American movie and shouts to the rest at the restaurant. At this point, Jia's film cuts to motion: Xiao Ji, Bingbing, and Qiaoqiao disco to loud music and revolving lights with a huge crowd of youngsters. Suddenly, some gangsters pull Xiao Ji out, hit his face repeatedly, and ask if he is having fun. Bearing the pain of the slaps, Xiao Ji affirms repeatedly that he is having fun. In the general style of an unhurried camera following the characters without interference, this heavily edited sequence shows an artificial bizarreness of the action the bored youngsters can conjure up. Here we also need to know that this scene is "a loan" from *Pulp Fiction*, from which Xiao Ji and Qiaoqiao get their specific dance moves.[29] In reality, when Xiao Ji and Bingbing really go to rob a bank and Bingbing reveals the fake bomb that he has tied to his body and shouts that he is a robber, this causes no commotion at all. A security guard sees through Bingbing right away and gets him arrested. Xiao Ji gets scared and escapes on the motorcycle. Corresponding to Bingbing's ride at the beginning of the film, Xiao Ji rides the motorcycle until it is out of gas and abandons it on the road. The long take of the abandoned motorcycle on the side of the road makes us think of the inertia of Xiao Ji and Bingbing and their desire for motion. Discussing *Unknown Pleasures* in detail, Tonglin Lu explains the disappointment due to globalization (which to Jia is a connotation of Americanization and in this film is a critical reference to *Pulp Fiction*) having added more pain to folks living in the provincial backwaters in China because, to them, "the dazzling effect of globalization remains an unknown or unknowable pleasure."[30]

On the whole, Jia's cinematic style in the trilogy is noted for his fondness for long takes. The tedious passage of time, in which nothing significant happens, is an aspect of reality that, according to Jia, can only be conveyed through time. "The deadlock," Jia reflects, "exists between humans and time, the camera and its subject. Everybody experiences the monotony of time passing where nothing that is noteworthy occurs."[31] For Jia, whose characters so far are those living on the margins of the economic development of contemporary China, his long takes guarantee that he engages with these characters' reality. From his preference for long takes, it seems Jia is also meticulous about structures—those of narrative, imagery, and sound. The train from *Platform*, for example, leads the viewer to see the structures of narrative (tours and cultural changes), imagery (the simulated train and the real train), and sound (the simulated whistle and the real whistle) that subtly weave together the naturalist materials of the film.

After the trilogy showcasing his folks from Shanxi, Jia brought some of them into Beijing to "work" in *The World*, the name for both his 2004 film produced within the system (at Shanghai studio) and a grand theme park in Beijing that boasts replicas of over one hundred landmarks from around the world. Tao (Zhao Tao, who also played Qiaoqiao in *Unknown Pleasures*) works as a dancer among many migrants who staff the workforce of the park. The fantasy that the park promises its visitors is that they've seen the whole world while that they have not even left Beijing. The immediate irony for those who work in the park is exactly this captivity of not having to leave the park. The mental transfer of seeing the world has stopped working for them through the repetition of watching on daily basis. They don't care to see the world anymore, but they still have to stay in the park. "I've turned into a ghost," Tao complains about her working and living at the park, not getting to see what happens outside. Hoping that working at the World is to ensure a brighter future, she hangs on, emotionally seeking the sense of security from her boyfriend Taisheng who, also from Shanxi, works as a security guard at the park. Taisheng's work allows him to leave the park frequently. As in Wang Xiaoshuai's *So Close to Paradise*, Taisheng allows us to see petty crimes and lowlife characters among the rural migrants in the cities.[32] He has learned to be an opportunist in his newfound urban life, and his failure to remain faithful to Tao vindicates what he tells her in the film: "You can't count on anyone these days. Don't think much of me."

The World (Shijie, 2004) is an appropriate film to wrap up this chapter, since it juxtaposes globalization and urbanization with rural and small-town migrants in a particular historical context: in his long-shot view that covers a broad range, Jia places his migrant characters against the vast spaces. The juxtaposition is symbolized in a striking frame at the beginning of the film: against the skyline of the park in twilight is the silhouette of a country person carrying a big basket of trash. To Jia, the country folks pick up the "trash" (that is, they are exploited as cheap labor, they are relocated by the millions as migrants, and thus they experience a sense of insecurity) caused by China copying the world. They "sacrifice their lives" so that China may look modern from the outside.[33] Several parallel correspondences emerged in the loosely related, naturalistic narration of the film. These correspondences resemble montage in shot structure—a shot and a countershot initiate mental, commentary synthesis from the audience. In *The World*, the montage is the correspondence of the sequences. They comment on the central relationship between Tao and Taisheng in the film, they require the audience to come up with their commentary synthesis, and they substantiate Jia's critique of modernization.

A Wenzhou woman, whom Taisheng has an affair with, lets us see several of these correspondences. Just as the representation of the world in the theme park may be ridiculed for its falseness and derision, the Wenzhou woman does the same as a fashion designer; she copies foreign brand-name styles for her customers. Hearing her talking about her copying, we realize that the theme park has unfortunately become a symbol for China's rampant copying of the foreign in every aspect of life (movies, songs, fashions, and lifestyles). Migration accompanies copying as part of this globalization process. In China, in certain towns, people don't just migrate to the Chinese metropolis; they traditionally go overseas to make their money. Wenzhou is such a town, and the Wenzhou woman's husband has already settled down in the Chinatown of Paris. Her going there is the next step of their plan. Whereas most Chinatowns around the world can't shed themselves of the ghetto image, since undocumented workers gather there, their parallel relationship with the theme park in the film becomes a sting. It reminds us not only of the shabby underground dorm and change rooms where performers gather but also the similar situation that the country folks find in the metropolis and what Chinese undocumented workers encounter overseas. To further stress the relatedness of these migrations, we also see the less fortunate folks in former socialist-camp countries migrating among themselves: Tao's former boyfriend goes to Ulan Bator to study, and several Russian women come to the theme park to make money. In these unsettling processes of being away from home and away from one's roots, the Wenzhou woman's opportunistic value of seeking temporary love from Taisheng and Tao's traditional lifestyle of hoping to establish some stability by marrying Taisheng specify the moral dilemmas migrants faced within their changed lives.

The shows in the theme park go on; the park receives about 1.5 million visitors annually. Juxtaposed with the shows at the park are several quasi-Brechtian-alienation cartoon passages in the film as unspectacular mental shows of his tiny human dramas. *The World* is an unresolved film, which depicts globalization looming over the ancient land of China, and which indicates that the park's shows and the related human drama shows are bound to unfold further.

Conclusion

The Concrete Revolution (Qianru routi de chengshi, 2005), Guo Xiaolu's personal essay in the form of a documentary on urban reconstruction in Beijing,[1] comments on the visual contrast between the glamorous, colorful television clips of contemporary urban-subject soap operas and the realities of the

Contemporary cultural concerns about everyday lives and profanity have become the shared features of both popular entertainment and art films. *I Love Beijing* (dir. Ning Ying, 2001).
Courtesy of China Film Archive, Beijing.

Beijing skyline—with its grit, smog, and smokestacks—a major eyesore that the soap operas manage to avoid. With a journalist's candor, Guo wanted to engage herself with this contrast between a commercial façade on the one hand and, on the other, her acquaintance with the urban builders who represent a floating population from rural China and an important part of today's urbanization. The contrast here is important. The new urban cinema that I discuss in this book also confronts this difference. This cinema's initial rebel edge, far from shunning eyesores, tackles taboo subjects and unearths underrepresented aspects of urban lives. This cinema is fascinated with the new glossy façade of the metropolis. But it focuses more on human dilemmas living changed lives behind this façade. The auteur works of this cinema claim a full spectrum of styles. Some feature an aesthetic sense of immediacy, a raw realism distant from studio effects, the authentic roles aloof to the star system, and the many long takes that avoided cuts. Some emphasize the sensual packaging of emotions, the surreal perceptions created by frequent close-ups, many cuts, constant camera movement, and creative lighting. Some maintain the middle-of-the-road approach of classicism. Whatever the style, the artistic candor of our directors has helped draw a line between the art films and the gilded, artificially lit urban façade projected by some of the contemporary soap operas and jeered by writer/filmmaker Guo Xiaolu.[2]

The line between our scope of investigation, the urban-subject art films, and the popular urban soap operas has become harder to draw. The cultural status of art films does not guarantee that some of them (e.g., those engaging *xiaozi* subjects) may not just look like soap operas. As discussed in chapter 3, the meaning of art film has been culturally redefined. In China, *Tao* had long been considered a grand discourse from which any artwork was supposed to be dictated; Tao informed artworks as if they were its vehicle. Today, this Tao in art films has been downgraded from being "sacred" (contributing to the grand discourses of either an ideological indoctrination in Maoist China or a cultural redemption in the immediate post-Mao era) to being "profane" (testifying to a personal experience of a slice of everyday life). The redefined Tao (as a testimony to the fragmented human conditions) is still considered by many critics an essential point that distinguishes art films from popular entertainment. One way to look at it is that whereas popular soap operas often tend to sacrifice the Tao to cater to popular tastes without much auteur discretion, art films negotiate their auteur perception of lives with the audience and resist the lure of commercialism. However, one should never overemphasize this contrast. Soap opera is a whole field of study by itself.

We are only using the commercial façade of some of them to help illustrate the art films we discuss. The point I make is about similarity rather than difference: the contemporary cultural concerns for "everyday lives" (richang shenghuo) and "profanity" (shisu) have become the shared features of both popular entertainment and art films.

It is difficult to see the burgeoning cinematic urbanism, as surveyed in this book, as the result of one cinematic movement, comparable, for example, to the Fifth Generation's break from Maoist didacticism in filmmaking. It is a more pluralistic cinema containing different artistic and ideological orientations. Directors of different age groups, and with varied backgrounds, contributed to the genesis of the new urban cinema. Focusing on an early group of underground films in the 1990s may allow one to better depict the artistic immediacy, the marginal subject matter, and the rebels' edges of a new urban cinema. This approach, however, lacks the scope of understanding the emergence of urban cinema broadly, and it may also indulge an overemphasis on political confrontation.

Indeed, political censorship in Chinese filmmaking has been notorious. Every post-Mao filmmaking generation has developed certain strategies to cope with censorship. The Fifth Generation's use of formalism—such as *Yellow Earth*'s narrative feature of concealment (image over plot, symbolism over story, songs over dialogues, and ambiguity over didacticism)[3] and *Horse Thief*'s ritual elaboration—was the earlier case of how films with politically sensitive messages managed to get past the censors. Adding the international film festival circuit to their resources, the Newborn Generation has begun using independent (underground) filmmaking as a strategy in dealing with censorship. Yet, as Valerie Jaffee has insightfully pointed out, considering the Newborn Generation's filmmaking as a whole, underground filmmaking remains more "a procedural or tactical decision than a moral, political, or aesthetic one."[4] With Chinese society becoming more and more decentralized and film censorship gradually disintegrating and slackening with it, many films with sensitive subjects and problematic styles also manage to pass the censorship.[5] Looking at the filmmaking trajectories of many directors—Zhang Yuan, Wang Xiaoshuai, Jia Zhangke, and so on—they have been moving under- or above-ground as the situation required. "Independent filmmaking in China," Chris Berry argues, "never was a dissent culture."[6] Berry proposes that we adopt "a Foucauldian approach" that looks at power as productive and that investigates issues in "the changing power dynamics."[7] "The more active they [Chinese independent filmmakers] become and the more opportunities they explore," he explains, "the more complex are the negotiations and relationships they have to develop with others in the matrix of power in order to remain independently Chinese."[8] Focusing on being independent or underground alone, obviously, is not a broad enough category for us to select films.

Broadening the scope, we may also see that political censorship is not the only enemy to the new urban cinema. As I have discussed in several instances throughout this book, the availability of international funding and box-office expectations have not always played positive roles in the film careers of some of the young Chinese directors. With some of their most profitable films populated by all-star casts, shining with expensive special-effect camera work, and pursuing grander subjects, one starts to miss the plain artistic immediacy that these directors once contributed to the rise of new urban cinema. In chapter 6, while discussing the influence of Italian Neorealism on Chinese new urban cinema, I express the concern that China's contemporary economic boom (promoting box-office success, the star system, and capital control) may devour the plain, new urban cinema as the affluence of the Italian economy of the 1950s had swallowed its Neorealism. In the introduction and in chapter 5, when I discuss the rise of *xiaozi* culture, although I attend more to how this culture disintegrated Maoist life, I am also well aware of the commercial effects of the *xiaozi* culture—its interest in commodities and in how commodities help to define fashion, style, and taste. *Xiaozi* culture is growing with the new urban cinema, but it is potentially the enemy of the plain, artistic immediacy for which this cinema was recognized in the first place.

With respect to the scope of my survey, I also need to explain how I have used the framework of filmmaking generations in this book. My feeling about this framework is ambivalent. I see its historical role. I see that it refers to a few broadly categorized historical personalities and structures of feelings. I see its acceptance by critics and popular readers as common knowledge—a way of cutting Chinese cinema into a few historical periods. But I have also seen its oversimplification, as well as the fact that it has lost its historical relevance to be pushed further. I feel that it is not up to me to discard the framework but to point out the difficulties of continuing to use it in describing today's urban cinema in China. Although I still retain the framework for easier reference, I also don't want to overemphasize its importance.

The framework of five generations of Chinese filmmaking was proposed in the early 1980s to identify a cinematic movement initiated by some members of the first post-Mao graduates of Beijing Film Academy. Zheng Dongtian, a professor and director from Beijing Film Academy recalled how the impact of the screening of *Yellow Earth* at a film conference in 1984 in Beijing led the participants to talk about "generational differences" among the Chinese film directors, and how the conference became the fountainhead for the "five-generation" discourse and framework.[9] So as to define the emerging Fifth Generation at the time, the framework focused on distinguishing this group of directors from their teachers' generation—those trained in the PRC's formative years, with careers delayed by the Cultural Revolution, but leading the immediate post-Mao filmmaking tide in China (such directors as Wu Yigong, Zhang Nuanxin, Xie Fei, and Wu Tianming). The rest of the framework refers to broader periods of time: First, the pioneers who started the Chinese filmmaking industry in the late teens and the 1920s (such directors as Deng Zhengqiu and Zhang Shichuan); Second, the left-wing filmmakers of the 1930s and 1940s (such directors as Sun Yu, Cai Chusheng, Shen Fu, and Fei Mu); and third, the directors who produced Maoist cinema in the first two decades of the PRC (such directors as Cui Wei, Shui Hua, and Xie Jin). The framework served a historical role of introducing a group of directors and their cinematic breakthrough in relation to the nation's earlier filmmaking culture. When many films by the so-called Fifth Generation directors started to win international attention and awards in the 1980s, the framework of five generations of Chinese filmmakers helped curious international, as well as Chinese, audiences to get a quick sense of the history of Chinese filmmaking.

The framework has since been widely used in Chinese film criticism. Reflecting the Chinese mind of synthesis, *generation* has been a favorite Chinese intellectual concept. In his *Discussion of Chinese Contemporary Intellectual History*, Chinese cultural scholar Li Zehou emphasizes that the study of generations may reveal some "historical personalities," that is, how groups of people with common social experiences will form dynamic communities showing some common characteristics in values, social behaviors, ways of thinking, emotional inclinations, and moral standards.[10] Here lies the reason why I favor this framework. In this book, as I am still using the framework, I think of it primarily as a reference to the time of a certain historical personality and not necessarily to a group of people for all of their lifetimes—directors outlive a historical period or generation and don't need to be the same to belong to dynamic communities. This understanding of generation refers more to a "structure of feelings," to borrow a Raymond Williams term. Williams uses this term to characterize historical periods for their particular patterns of interests, impulses, and restraints. He also uses it to discuss the influences between generations, that is, how the impact of the early generations has to relocate in a new structure of feeling.[11]

To depict the new urban cinema, while still referring to the generational framework, I discussed films primarily by the Fifth (emphasizing the Later Fifth) and the post–Fifth Generation directors. The comparison of urbanism across Maoist cinema, in chapter 1, is that between films by the Second Generation on the one hand and those by the Fourth and the Fifth Generations on the other. The second chapter focuses on one particular Fifth Generation director, Huang Jianxin, to point out the similar cultural roles played by the early post-Mao city films and the rural roots-searching films. This chapter also uses the long film career of Huang Jianxin and his persistence on city genre to pinpoint the changes a Fifth Generation director has undergone. In chapter 3, I broaden the meaning of "status movie" to include more directors and films and to further describe the historical change of the Fifth Generation. Here I focus especially on a group of late-emerging Fifth Generation directors to describe their contributions to the new urban cinema. In chapter 4, the post-Fifth Generation directors are ushered in in a discussion of the Chinese *shiji mo* (century's end). But from here, I have also started to downplay the film generation framework and to mix the films by different generations while investigating various aspects of the new urban cinema: its depiction of rock scenes and youth subculture, its understanding of emotions, its engagement with the elusive reality of urban lives, its view of the subaltern class of country folks in the metropolis, and its picture of many small towns across the vast land of China in relation to drastic urbanization.

The book's earlier encounters with the Fourth, the Fifth, and the Later Fifth Generations occurred by following a rough chronology, since I wanted to explore how the post-Mao urban cinema was related to such ideological discourses as cultural retrospect (roots searching), social reform, market orientation, China's opening up to the outside world, and China's marching onto the global stage. Many films in these chapters represent a cinematic participation in these socially orchestrated discourses. The generation framework here offered two different structures of feelings in dealing with urban subjects. First of all, in the time of the immediate post-Mao cultural critique, there was the Fourth Generation's allegorical urbanism. Contrasting the backwardness of the countryside that stands for the closed-door China, the city becomes an allegorical index of modernity, science, progress, reformation, and hope. Although Fifth Generation directors do not seem to belong to this camp, they share this structure of feelings. It was only that they are not dealing with contemporary subjects nor allegorizing the city. Rural roots search and urban allegory are two sides of the same story of a cultural/political critique. Among the early Fifth Generation directors, Huang Jianxin was an exception in that he insists on contemporary urban subjects. His films waver between the Fourth generation urban allegories plus roots searching on the one hand, and, on the other, the spirit of the Later Fifth Generation filmmaking characterized by an effort to bridge the past and the present while starting to engage contemporary urban subjects. Intended as roots searching in urban scenes, Huang's early films attack the Party's bureaucratic culture. His depiction of the city is partially real and partially allegorical, serving his deliberation on such issues as the impact of Western science, the persistence of the Party orthodox, the difficulty in the emergence of individualism, and the effects of alienation.

The Later Fifth Generation, as I discuss in chapter 3, grew up in Maoist China. They need to overcome themselves in living and projecting a changed China. Although the contrast may not be absolute and should not be overstressed, I am still deeply impressed by how the Later Fifth Generation directors' approach to the new urban China involves more of their own adjustment to it, while the younger directors tend not to invoke this comparison of the past with the present. Take *Blue Love* and *Suzhou River*, for example. Both films were issued in 2000 on the subject of love. Whereas *Blue Love*, by a Later Fifth Generation director, uses new fashions of love to retrieve and contrast a tragedy in love in Maoist China caused by the political dominance of everyday lives, *Suzhou River*, by a post–Fifth Generation director is all about today, and it communicates with Hollywood in showcasing a mystery of the identities of the leading female role. These directors of different age groups subscribe different structures of feelings.

The reason that I downplay the role of generation framework midway in my survey is to reflect that the framework itself encountered difficulty. In chapter 4, while describing a post-Mao rock scene, I investigate how the generational discourses in the post–Fifth Generation film culture are eager to identify a succeeding generation to be responsible for the new orientations in cinema, and I discuss the disappointment it caused among both the critics and the aloof younger generation of directors. The chilling stories told by these younger directors, testifying to a cultural fragmentation—accompanied by despair, decadence, and alienation—disappointed and baffled the critics in China. Instead, as I discuss in the introduction, these critics started to suggest that Chinese filmmaking had entered a nongenerational, individualistic, diversified, and urban-oriented era. What this proposal suggests, diversity rather than shared social concerns, describes both the emerging new directors and the burgeoning urban cinema. There is no hope of pushing the film generation framework further to formulate a Sixth Generation, although the term is widely used for easy reference, and it would not be right to attribute the new urban cinema as the sole product of a single group of directors.

The Fifth Generation, as we know, all came from one school: the Beijing Film Academy. Some belonged to the first post-Mao class of four-year formal training, and some attended special training classes of different lengths in the early 1980s. Among the late-emerging Fifth Generation directors that I discuss, Xia Gang, Li Shaohong, Peng Xiaolian, Jiang Xiaozhen, and Ning Ying all belonged to the first post-Mao class. They were the classmates of Zhang Yimou (trained as a cinematographer at school) and Chen Kaige. Huo Jianqi also belonged to this class. He was trained as an art designer, assigned to work as a designer but later turned into a known director. Huang Jianxin was a special student sponsored by the Xi'an Film Studio for two-year training at Beijing Film Academy at a time when the first post-Mao class had just left. Returning to the Xi'an studio in 1985, however, he was just in time to catch the tide of the early Fifth Generation filmmaking but persisted on urban subjects when others favored allegories set in the countryside.

The making of the Fifth Generation reflected an older China of tight institutional control. The younger directors, those born since the 1960s, added a few more schools to the educational backgrounds of Chinese filmmakers, as shown in the following list:

Beijing Film Academy: Cui Zi'en, Guan Hu, Guo Xiaolu, He Jianjun (2-year class), Hu Xueyang, Jia Zhangke, Jin Ge, Li Hong, Li Xin, Liu Bingjian, Lou Ye, Lu Chuan, Lu Xuechang, Tang Danian, Wang Chao, Wang Quan'an, Wang Rui, Wang Xiaoshuai, Wu Di, Zhang Ming (graduate program), Zhang Yuan

Beijing Central Theater Institute: Jin Chen, Shi Runjiu, Zhang Yang

Shanghai Institute of Theater: Liu Xin

Beijing Institute of Broadcasting: Ah Nian

Beijing University of Radio and TV: Sheng Zhimin

As the new city films started to reinvent a diversified China on the silver screen, we at least have also started to see some diversity in the making of film directors.

Most directors discussed in this book are still in the prime of their creative lives. Culturally, the grandest urbanization in China has also yet to peak. In years to come, Chinese urbanization and its exploration by film artists will continue to push the momentum of urban cinema sketched in this book. The urbanism these films project, as I experienced throughout the writing this book, and as my readers will continue to witness, is still expanding.

■

NOTES
SELECTED BIBLIOGRAPHY
SELECTED FILMOGRAPHY, BY DIRECTOR
INDEX

NOTES

Introduction

1. Following common usage in Chinese film studies, six chronological generations are used to refer to film artists of different eras: the First Generation refers to China's pioneers of the silent films of the 1920s; the Second Generation, the leftist filmmakers of the 1930s and 1940s; the Third Generation, mostly Yan'an-trained filmmakers who became important in the early PRC (People's Republic of China) cinema of the 1950s; the Fourth Generation, those trained in the early 1960s but who had to wait until the post-Mao late 1970s to start making films; the Fifth Generation, the first post-Mao graduating class from Beijing Film Academy and several other young directors who joined them in the post-Mao cinematic new wave; and the Sixth Generation, also known by several other group names and including the post-1989 (Tian'anmen Square massacre) young film artists in an urban-focused era.

2. The representative titles of early new city films include primarily works by the Fourth and Fifth Generation directors: Huang Jianxin's *Black Cannon Incident* (1985), *Dislocation* (1986), and *Samsara* (1988); Huang Jianzhong's *Questions for the Living* (1986); Song Jiangbo's *Masquerade* (1986); Zhang Zeming's *Sunshine and Showers* (1988); Sun Zhou's *Add Sugar to Coffee* (1988); Zhou Xiaowen's *Price of Madness* (1988); Tian Zhuangzhuang's *Rock Kids* (1988); Zhang Junzhao's *Arc Light* (1989); Zhang Liang's *A Woman's Street* (1989); Xie Fei's *Black Snow* (1989); and Zhang Nuanxin's *Good Morning, Beijing* (1990).

3. See Richard Sennett, ed., *Classic Essays on the Culture of Cities* (Englewood Cliffs, NJ: Prentice-Hall, 1969). This anthology offers a concise introduction and the essential writings of the German School of urban studies.

4. See Dai Jinhua, "Xin zhongguo dianying: Disanshijie piping de biji" (New Chinese film: A note on third-world criticism), *Dianying yishu* 1 (1991): 46–54. My brief account in this paragraph is loosely based on Dai's discussion in this article, and on my own observations. The Fourth Generation films referred to here include Ding Yinnan's *A Back-lit Picture* (1982), Wu Tianming's *The Story of Life* (1984) and *Old Well* (1986), Teng Wenji's *A Village in the Metropolis* (1982) and *On the Beach* (1985), Hu Bingliu's *Country People* (1986), Yan Xueshu's *In the Wild Mountains*, (1985), and Zheng Dongtian's *Young Couples* (1987).

5. Ibid., 49.

6. Some basic ideas of Oswald Spengler's *Decline of the West* became known to Chinese film critics through Fei Xiaotong's anthropological study of Chinese earth-bound society, *Xiangtu zhongguo* (Earthbound China), which was reprinted in 1985 by Sanlian Shudian in Beijing.

7. Wang Hui, "Dangdai dianying zhong de xiangtu yu dushi" (City and countryside in contemporary films), *Dianying yishu* 2 (1989), 18.

8. See, for instance, Long Haiqiu, "Paihuai dushi: Tan jinqi de chengshi ticai yingpian" (Wandering in the city : On recent city films), *Yishu guangjiao* 2 (1989): 56–61; Wang Liaonan, "Shisu shenhua: Muqian chengshi dianying de pingge pinggu" (Worldly mythology: An evaluation of the present city films), *Yishu guangjiao* 2 (1989): 49–55; Wei Xiaolin, "Bianyuan ren: Yizhong xinde yinmu zhurengong xingxiang" (Marginal hero: A new image

of the screen protagonists), *Yishu guangjiao* 2 (1990): 70–75; and Chen Xiaoyun, "Gudu de chengshi: Chengshi dianying yanjiu zhiyi" (Lonely city: A study on city films), *Wenyi pinglun* 4 (1990): 88–89.

9. Chen Xiaoyun, "Gudu de chengshi," 88–89.

10. Chen Xiaoyun, "Gudu de chengshi," 84, 89.

11. See Dai Jinhua, *Wuzhong fengjing: Zhongguo dianying wenhua 1978–1998* (Foggy sceneries: Chinese cinematic culture, 1978–1998; Beijing: Beijing daxue chubanshe, 2000): 380–82.

12. The bargain that Deng Xiaoping offered at the start of his reform and which the state learned to appreciate after the Tian'anmen Square massacre, as Perry Link describes, was "Shut up and I'll let you get rich." See Perry Link, "The Old Man's New China," *New York Review of Books* 9 (June 1994): 31–36.

13. Zhang Zhen, "Bearing Witness: Chinese Urban Cinema in the Era of 'Transformation' (*Zhuanxing*)," in *The Urban Generation: Chinese Cinema and Society at the Turn of the Twenty-first Century*, ed. Zhang Zhen (Durham, NC: Duke University Press, 2007), 13.

14. The early titles include Zhang Yuan's *Beijing Bastards* (1992), Lou Ye's *Weekend Lovers* (1993), He Jianjun's *Red Beans* (1993), Wang Xiaoshuai's *Days* (1993), Hu Xueyang's *Drowning* (1994), Guan Hu's *Dirt* (1994), Wu Di's *Yellow Goldfish* (1996), and Zhang Ming's *In Expectation* (1996).

15. See, for instance, Wang Yichuan, "'Wudaiqi' zhongguo dianying" (Non–generation era Chinese cinema), *Dangdai dianying* 5 (1994): 20–27; Han Xiaolei, "Dui diwudai de wenhua tuwei: Hou wudai de geren dianying xianxiang" (Getting beyond the Fifth Generation culture: Post–Fifth Generation individual filmmaking), *Dianying yishu* 2 (1995): 58–63, and Lü Xiaoming, "Jiushi niandai zhongguo dianying jingguan zhiyi: 'Diliudai' jiqi zhiyi" (An aspect of Chinese filmmaking of the 1990s: "The Sixth Generation" and challenges to this label), *Dianying yishu* 3 (1999): 23–28.

16. In 1993 an article appeared in *Shanghai yishujia* (Shanghai artists), a literature journal, with a collective authorship referring to all the students of Beijing Film Academy's class of 1985 (the year they entered the school). Titled "Zhongguo dianying de hou *Huangtu di* xianxiang" (The post–*Yellow Earth* phenomenon in Chinese film), this article has been seen by some critics as a landmark document for the new group of film artists. Concerning filmmaking generations, this article reads, "A generational framework caused categorization of aesthetics and styles [between generations], which was a heavy burden that the situation of filmmaking at times could hardly bear." See detailed quotation and discussion of this article in Jia Leilei, "Shidai yingxiang de lishi dipingxian" (The Sixth Generation directors and the images of the era in their films), *Dangdai dianying* 5 (2006): 6–31.

17. My idea on this point was supported by Sheldon Lu, *China, Transnational Visuality, Global Postmodernity* (Stanford, CA: Stanford University Press, 2001), especially 31–47.

18. Michael Foucault, *Power /Knowledge* (New York: Pantheon Books, 1980), 126.

19. Ibid.

20. The antiurban feature of Mao's China has been discussed by many sources. See, for instance, L. J. C. Ma, "Anti-Urbanism in China," *Proceedings of the Association of American Geographers* 8 (1976): 114–18; C. P. Cell, "De-urbanization in China: The Urban-Rural Contradiction," *Bulletin of Concerned Asian Scholars* 11.1 (1979): 62–72; M. B. Farina, "Urbanization, de-urbanization, and class struggle in China, 1949–79," *International Journal of Urban and Regional Research* 4 (Dec. 1980): 487–501; R. J. R. Kirkby, *Urbanization in China: Town and Country in a Developing Economy, 1949–2000 A.D.* (New York: Columbia University Press, 1985); and Victor F. S. Sit, ed., *Chinese Cities: The Growth of the Metropolis since 1949* (Oxford: Oxford University Press, 1985).

21. Martin King Whyte and William L. Parish, *Urban Life in Contemporary China* (Chicago: University of Chicago Press, 1984), 358.

22. In a comparison of Western Europe and China, Rhoads Murphey emphasized the importance of Chinese cities as administrative centers. "The city has been a center of change in western Europe," he observed, "while it has been the reverse in traditional China, despite the broad similarity in urban economic functions in both areas." See Murphey, "The City as a Center of Change: Western Europe and China," *Annals of the Association of American Geographers* 44 (1954): 349–62.

23. Whyte and Parish, *Urban Life*, 1–2.

24. See, for example, Tang Danian's *City Paradise* (1999), Xia Gang's *A Country Boy in Shanghai* (1999), Ah Nian's *Call Me* (2000), Wang Xiaoshuai's *Beijing Bicycle* (2001), and Wang Guangli's *Go for Broke* (2001).

25. See, for instance, Homi K. Bhabha, *The Location of Culture* (London: Routledge, 1994), 241, for "contramodernity"; Enrique Dussel, "Beyond Eurocentrism: The World-System and the Limits of Modernity," in Fredric Jameson and Massao Miyoshi, eds., *The Cultures of Globalization* (Durham, NC: Duke University Press, 1998), 3–31, for "trans-modernity" (emphasizing cross-cultural exchanges against one-way imposition); Aihwa Ong, *Flexible Citizenship: The Cultural Logics of Transnationality* (Durham, NC: Duke University Press, 1999), 35, for "alternative modernities"; N. Garcìa Canclini, *Hybrid Cultures: Strategies for Entering and Leaving Modernity* (Minneapolis: University of Minnesota Press, 1995), for "hybrid" modernization.

26. Edward Gibbon, *The Decline and Fall of the Roman Empire*, abridged by D. M. Low (London: Chatto and Windus, 1960), 11.

27. Xiaobing Tang, *Chinese Modern: The Heroic and the Quotidian* (Durham, NC: Duke University Press, 2000), 279.

28. Ibid, 283.

29. See Raymond Williams, *Culture and Society, 1780–1950* (London: Penguin, 1961) and *The Long Revolution* (London: Penguin, 1965). See also Alan Swingewood's discussion of Williams in *Cultural Theory and the Problem of Modernity* (New York: St. Martin's Press, 1998).

30. Tonglin Lu, *Confronting Modernity in the Cinemas of Taiwan and Mainland China* (Cambridge: Cambridge University Press, 2002), 1.

31. See, for instance, Han Xiaolei, "Dui diwudai," and Zuo Shula, "Cong 'diliu dai' dianying dao *Wushan yunyu*" (From "Sixth Generation" film to *In Expectation*), *Dianying yishu* 3 (1996): 80–83.

32. Li Yiming, "Shiji zhimo: Shehui de daode weiji yu diwudai dianying de shouzhong zhengqin" (Century's end: Ethical crisis and the funeral for Fifth Generation filmmaking), *Dianying yishu* 1–2 (1996): 9–13, 24–28.

33. Li Yiming, "Cong diwudai dao diliudai" (From the Fifth Generation to the Sixth Generation), *Dianying yishu* 1 (1998): 15–22.

34. Ibid., 15.

35. Paul Willis, *Common Culture* (Boulder, CO: Westview Press, 1990), 129.

36. Ibid, 27.

37. Examples include Huo Jianqi's *Blue Love* (2000) and *A Time to Love* (2005); Xia Gang's *Love at First Sight* (2002); Wang Rui's *After Divorce* (1995); Zhang Yuan's *I Love You* (2002) and *Green Tea* (2003); Zhang Yibai's *Spring Subway* (2002); Li Chunbo's *Don't Cry, Girl* (2002); Li Xin's *Dazzling* (2001); Liu Xin's *Captives of Love* (2000) and *38°C* (2003); Zhaoyan Guozhang's *A Dream of Youth* (2002); and Sheng Zhimin's *Two Hearts* (2002). For more examples and further discussion of this topic, see chapter 6.

38. Richard Sennett, *The Fall of Public Man* (New York: Knopf, 1977), 337.

39. Zhizhu Yi, "Youxiu xiaozi de ruogan qingjie" (Random episodes about a good *xiaozi*), in *Fengse de biaoqing: shi xiaozi nüzuojia jiexi* (Pink expressions: Analysis of ten female *xiaozi* writers), ed. Ge Hongbing (Beijing: Wenhua yishu chubanshe, 2002), 1:50. Nüwa is the legendary Chinese goddess who created human beings. Zhizhu Yi, the critic's name, is obviously a mischievous pen name and Internet login name meaning Spider 1. The emphasis in the quote is mine.

40. See Geng Li, "Chengshi bianfu: hei keke jiexi" (City bats: An analysis of writer Black Coco), in *Ganshang de landiao: shi xiaozi nüzuojia jiexi* (Sentimental blue tones: Analysis of ten female *xiaozi* writers), ed. Ge Hongbing (Beijing: Wenhua yishu chubanshe, 2002), 2:105–8. A partial list reads as follows:

1. Successful persons (one has to be at least "economically decent")
2. Bar (dizziness + dimness + a particular feel of it)
3. Sentimental (that is to learn to be so)—to a Chinese, this is an art of life that derives from drama and transcends drama
4. Despise success (not want to congratulate one's own success but assumes the attitude of wanting to abandon it as soon as possible)
5. Euphonious music (this can bring memories but has nothing to do with love)
6. First person (reality is what I feel)—dreams are means of desires and "I" is the means of daydreams for becoming a writer
7. High-rise buildings (a successful *xiaozi* needs to look down at the working masses, if not physically, at least psychologically)
8. . . .
9. Jokeless (*xiaozi* is fond of sentiments but resists senseless humor)
10. Knight errant (that is, your love definitely leads to nothing)
11. Lyrics (even if you cannot sing the whole song, you have to learn to quote a line or two)
12. . . .
13. *Norwegian Wood* (the novel, a favorable topic of conversation for *xiaozi*, even though nobody understands it)
14. Fashion
15. Foreign languages
16. Clothing that reflects one's personality
17. Quiet evenings (believing that romance will emerge here and real life will not intrude)
18. Classic movie
19. Solitude
20. Train (the soft rhythm and archaic taste makes it the ideal place for expressing *xiaozi* feelings)
21. . . .
22. Valentine's Day (a special day for a *xiaozi* to seek romance and express a taste)
23. . . .
24. Party
25. YSL perfume
26. Ailing Zhang ("new independent woman" is invoked by this name for a female *xiaozi* who needs love and special care in equal parts)
27. Coffee and red wine

For entry 13 of this list, *Norwegian Wood* is a novel by Japanese author Haruki Murakami. Set in Tokyo during the late sixties, the novel depicts a college student trying to find himself, to grow up, to make a commitment to someone, and to be true to that commitment. The novel ponders such issues as junk information, signs, symbols, living reality, and existentialism and is rich in urban sensibility. Many names of songs, albums, writers, directors, musicians, and movies appear in this novel, which itself is named after a well-known song of the Beatles, "Norwegian Wood." There is a Chinese translation of this novel by Lin Shaohua (Shanghai: Shanghai yiwen chubanshe, 2001).

41. Although her writing is not included in this anthology, Wei Hui is considered the most influential, pioneering *xiaozi* writer. Her name is often mentioned by critics edited in this anthology. See Wei Hui, *Shanghai baobei* (Shanghai baby; Shenyang: chunfeng wenyi chubanshe, 1999). The subtitle for this semiautobiographical novel is "a novel written by a woman for women about her body and heartfelt experiments in life."

42. Born in 1968, Ge Hongbing is known as a "new-born generation" literary scholar in China.

43. Ge Hongbing, preface to both *Fense de biaoqing* and *Ganshang de landiao*, ii.

44. Ge Hongbing, preface, i.

45. Sheldon H. Lu, "Chinese Film Culture at the End of the Twentieth Century: Case of *Not One Less* by Zhang Yimou" in *Chinese-Language Film: Historiography, Poetics, Politics*, ed. Sheldon H. Lu and Emilie Yueh-yu Yeh (Honolulu: University of Hawaii Press), 120.

46. Ibid. By "cultural fast food," Lu refers to karaoke, television dramas, soap operas, best sellers, and tabloid journalism.

47. Mian Mian and Wei Hui have caught the attention of Western readers as China's bad girls of letters. The two of them, however, are only part of a fashionable trend in today's urban youth subculture in China. It's really the tip of an iceberg—the tip is two female writers and their books in print, and the iceberg is the abundance of similar writings circulating on the Internet. With less control and censorship, a large and highly participatory young readership, and no need for publishing editors, cyber-fiction in the style of Wei Hui and Mian Mian has been proliferating.

48. See David Chaney, "From Ways of Life to Lifestyle: Rethinking Culture as Ideology and Sensibility," in *Culture in the Communication Age*, ed. James Lull (London: Routledge, 2001): 75–88.

49. Michael Foucault's 1967 lecture notes, "Des Espaces autres," as quoted in Edward W. Soja, *Postmodern Geographies* (London: Verso, 1989), 17.

50. For an excellent discussion of the *"guangchang* (square) complex" in Chinese mass culture of the 1990s, see Dai Jinhua, *Cinema and Desire,* ed. Jing Wang and Tani Barlow (London: Verso, 2002), 213–34.

51. See Deborah S. Davis "Introduction: Urban China" in *Urban Spaces in Contemporary China*, ed. Deborah S. Davis et al. (Washington, DC: Woodrow Wilson Center Press; Cambridge, UK: Cambridge University Press, 1995), 7–8.

52. Linda Chiu-han Lai, "Whither the Walker Goes: Spatial Practices and Negative Poetics in 1990s Chinese Urban Cinema," in *The Urban Generation: Chinese Cinema and Society at the Turn of the Twenty-first Century*, ed. Zhang Zhen (Durham: Duke University Press, 2007), 207.

53. Ibid., 211.

1. *X-Roads*: Old and New City Films

1. In actuality, both Bai Yang and Zhao Dan lived in Shanghai in the PRC era. Zhao died in 1980, and Bai in 1996.

2. See, for example, Christopher Howe, ed., *Shanghai: Revolution and Development in an Asian Metropolis* (New York: Cambridge University Press, 1981); Leo Ou-fan Lee, *Shanghai Modern: The Flowering of a New Urban Culture in China, 1930–1945* (Cambridge,

MA: Harvard University Press, 1999); Sherman Cochran, ed., *Inventing Nanjing Road: Commercial Culture in Shanghai, 1900–1945* (Ithaca, NY: East Asia Program, Cornell University, 1999); Hanchao Lu, *Beyond the Neon Lights: Everyday Shanghai in the Early Twentieth Century* (Berkeley: University of California Press, 1999); Yingjin Zhang, ed. *Cinema and Urban Culture in Shanghai, 1922–1943* (Stanford: Stanford University Press, 1999); Shu-mei Shih, *The Lure of the Modern: Writing Modernism in Semicolonial China, 1917–1932* (Berkeley: University of California Press, 2001); Andrew F. Jones, *Yellow Music: Media Culture and Colonial Modernity in the Chinese Jazz Age* (Durham, NC: Duke University Press, 2001).

3. *All about Shanghai and Environs: A Standard Guide Book*, 1934–35 ed. (Shanghai: University Press, 1935), 43–44. Quoted in Xiaobing Tang, *Chinese Modern: The Heroic and the Quotidian* (Durham, NC: Duke University Press, 2000), 100.

4. Since the 1980s, especially as pioneered by director Feng Xiaogang, the "Chinese New Year film" has become a genre of fun-filled, celebratory comedies that the general audience expects during China's holiday season.

5. *Shen bao*, October 15, 1933. Quoted in Laikwan Pang, *Building a New China in Cinema* (Lanham, MD: Rowman & Littlefield, 2002), 178.

6. Shu-mei Shih nicely summed up this perception in her study of modernism in Shanghai. See *The Lure of the Modern* (Berkeley: University of California Press, 2001), 235. The primary sources for this perception are Hendrik De Leuuw's *Cities of Sin* (1933), Ernest Hauser's *Shanghai: City for Sale* (1940, translated into Chinese in 1941), and G. E. Miller's *Shanghai: Paradise of Adventurers* (1937).

7. Yang Binhua, ed., *Shanghai weidao* (The aura of Shanghai; Changchun: Shidai wenyi chubanshe, 2002).

8. Gu Huaming, "Bianhou ji" (Postscript) in *Richang Zhongguo: Wushi niandai laobaixing de richang shenghuo* (Everyday China: Ordinary people's everyday lives in the 1950s), ed. Wu Liang et al. (Nanjing: Jiansu meishu chubanshe, 1999), 1:165.

9. See Cheng Naishan, "Ah Fei zhengzhuan" (A biography of *Ah Fei*) and "Shanghai tan shang 'lao kele'" (Colorful old guys of Shanghai) in Yang Binhua, ed., *Shanghai weidao*, 213–44 and 245–66.

10. Cheng Naishan, "Ah Fei zhengzhuan."

11. This depiction is used in Theodore White's video narration of modern Chinese history, *China: A Revolution Revisited* (Metromedia Producers Corporation, Chicago; Films Incorporated, 1971).

12. For the guns (i.e., political and military powers) that the ideals could attach to, the Nationalist revolution was also an option and was even ideologically closer to the May Fourth ideals. In addition to many historical factors, the Communist triumph in China also included an ideological victory by presenting the Nationalist government as a corrupt establishment with problems identical to many social problems of modern China and thus hostile to the youthful spirit of May Fourth.

13. Here *Crossroads* leads us to see the façade of entertainment that Leftist filmmaking often adopted to contain its critique of social ills and oppression. *Street Angel*, a contemporary film also starring Zhao is another example. In *Street Angel*, the two central females, a singer and a prostitute, allegorize Chinese womanhood. The singer is portrayed in high-key lighting and a lively acting style to allow her innocence to suit the film's comic style and Utopian dream. The prostitute, staying in the shadows and suffering all the personal pains, violations, and death, has "ghostly" expressionist makeup and serves to remind the audience what a grim reality this comic film is addressing.

14. The ten-per-year film import quota was maintained in the 1990s. By the early

2000s, especially since China's entry into the World Trade Organization, the quota has been raised significantly.

15. In a discussion after the Harvard screening of this film (Nov. 24, 2002), the director assured me that there is a Mandarin version of the film with English subtitles. She, nevertheless, says that she has no problem with issuing the all-English version to the overseas market. Months later, after viewing the Mandarin version of the film, I was further assured of the failure of the all-English version of the film. The attraction between Yang Shao and Zhao Ming through an intimacy only detectable through their mother tongue is not conveyed at all in the all-English version. The comic effects of Zhao Ming's American friends speaking Chinese with accents are also lost.

16. The questions from the audience at the Harvard screening of this film focused on its language problem, as well as the elite status of the protagonists (e.g., their close contacts with foreigners in China).

17. See Dai Jinhua, "National Identity in the Hall of Mirrors" in *Cinema and Desire: Feminist Marxism and Cultural Politics in the Work of Dai Jinhua*, ed. Jing Wang and Tani E. Barlow (London: Verso, 2002), 189–212. I have paraphrased Dai rather freely. The Chinese diaspora literature in her study refers primarily to *A Chinese Woman in Manhattan*, *Beijinger in New York*, *I Am a Lawyer in America*, and so on.

18. Zou and Keke, as to be discussed soon, contrast each other on screen. In real life, they both will have significant involvements with the so-called Sixth Generation filmmaking. Wang Quan'an, who plays Zou, graduated from the acting department of Beijing Film Academy in 1991. After working for Xi'an Film Studio for years, he turned to film directing, debuted with *Lunar Eclipse* (1999), followed by *The Story of Ermei* (2003). Jia Hongsheng, who plays Keke, appeared in many important Sixth Generation films, such as Ah Xi in Lou Ye's 1994 film *Weekend Lovers*, Mardar in Lou's 2000 film *Suzhou River*, and an artist who presents fake suicides in Wang Xiaoshuai's 1997 film *Frozen*. In 2001 Jia Hongsheng's real life story of quitting drugs becomes the subject of Zhang Yang's film *Quitting*. Jia played his own story in collaboration with his parents.

19. *The Lower Depths*, a play by Russian writer Maxim Gorky, had a strong appeal for left-wing Chinese artists and received stage (in the "orphan-island era" in the city of Shanghai) and screen (1947 by Wenhua Studio) adaptations, both titled *Night Lodge* (Yedian) and directed by Zuo Ling. The "lower depths" (diceng) became a frequently used term referring to the lower social strata. The influence of Gorky's play on Chinese film artists of the 1930s may also be due to Jean Renoir's 1936 adaptation *Les Bas-fonds*. Working amidst the rise of Hitler and the Popular Front in France, Renoir had his special need to take license with the dark nature of Gorky's play. In 1957 the Japanese director Akira Kurosawa also adapted Gorky's play, titling it *Donzoko*. Referring to the postwar social reality in Japan, Kurosawa focused on the conflict between illusion and reality—a theme he would return to over and over again.

20. See Zhang Wei, "Nüxing guishu yu lishi qianyi: *Beijing, ni zao* de yuyanxing chanshi" (The position of women and historical transformation: An allegorical interpretation of *Good Morning, Beijing*), *Dangdai dianying* 39 (1990): 55–60.

21. For a discussion of some aspects of Xiao Hong's allegorical role, see Ma Ning, "The Textual and Critical Difference of Being Radical: Reconstructing Chinese Leftist Films of the 1930s" in *Celluloid China*, ed. Harry Kuoshu (Carbondale: Southern Illinois University Press, 2002): 97–109.

22. These lines are from Cui Jian's "Jia xingseng" (Fake minstrel [traveling monk]), which is used as a theme song in *Good Morning, Beijing*.

23. See Fredric Jameson, "Third-World Literature in the Era of Multinational Capitalism," *Social Text* 15 (1986): 65–88.

24. See Dai Jinhua, "Xin zhongguo dianying: Disanshijie piping de biji" (New Chinese film: A note on Third-World criticism), *Dianying yishu* 1 (1991): 46–54.

25. Raymond Williams, *The Country and the City* (Oxford University Press, 1973), 1.

26. Fei Mu, "Daoyan, juzuozhe: Xie gei Yang Ji" (Director and script writer: A letter to Yang Ji), *Dagong bao*, Oct. 9, 1948.

27. In 1941 Fei Mu wrote, "I tried time and again with no success to turn my film mise-en-scène into the style of Chinese paintings. It has proven difficult for me." Fei Mu, "Zhongguo jiuju de dianying hua wenti" (On the issue of filming Chinese old plays), in *Qingqing dianying haowai—Gu Zhongguo zhige tekan*, minghua yingye gongsi, Dec. 1, 1941.

28. Luo Yijun, *Zhongguo dianying pinglun gaishuo* (Outlines of Chinese film criticism), quoted in Wen Wu "*Ping Xiaocheng zhi chun*" (On *Springtime in a Small Town*), *Dianying yishu* 1 (1990), 128.

29. See for example, Jian Zunxu, "Shuqing xieyi yun yiuyiu" (Flavors of depicting feelings and meanings), *Dianying xinzuo* 6 (1988); Wen Wu "Ping *Xiaocheng zhi chun*" (On *Springtime in a Small Town*), *Dianying yishu* 1 (1990); Ying Xiong, "*Xiaocheng zhi chun* yu dongfang dianying" (*Springtime in a Small Town* and oriental film), *Dianying yishu* 2 (1993); Li Shaobai, "Zhongguo xiandai dianying de qianqu: Lun Fei Mu he *Xiaocheng zhi chun* de lishi yiyi (A pioneer in Chinese modern films: On the historical significance of Fei Mu and his *Springtime in a Small Town*), *Dianying yishu* 5-6 (1996); Taiwan, National Film Archive, ed., *Xiaocheng zhi chun de dianying meixue: Xiang Fei Mu zhijing* (Aesthetics of *Springtime in a Small Town*: Saluting Fei Mu), Caituan faren dianying ziliaoguan, 1996; Hong Kong Film Critics Association, ed., *Shiren Fei Mu* (Fei Mu as a Poet), Dianying pinglun xuehui, 1998; Qiu Feng, "Dianying shiren Fei Mu" (Film poet Fei Mu), *Dianying wenxue* 3 (2001).

30. Cheng Jihua et al. *Zhongguo dianying fazhan shi* (History of Chinese film development), vol. 2 (Beijing: Zhongguo dianying chubanshe, 1980), 271.

31. Founded by the merging of three small studios (Huabei, Minxin, and Da zhonghua) in 1930 by Luo Mingyou, Lianhua was a leading film studio in Shanghai in the 1930s. The studio showed a split in the political tendencies of its production: Luo Mingyou, having close ties with Nationalist government, encouraged conservative films, while left-wing film artists, such as Sun Yu and Shi Dongshan, produced politically controversial films. After 1936, the year before the studio dissolved with the Japanese occupation of Shanghai, left-wing production gained the upper hand at Lianhua. Lianhua produced such classics as *Three Modern Women*, *Big Road*, *Fisherman's Daughter*, and *Goddess*.

32. The English titles for these films are *City Night* (1933), *Life* (1934), and *A Nun's Love* (1934).

33. The English titles for these films are *City Night* (1933), *Wolf Hunting* (1936), and *Confucius* (1937).

34. On March 12, 1994, the Chinese government issued a directive banning a group of directors from film directing as a penalty for their participation in international film festivals without government permission. Tian Zhuangzhuang was among the directors listed in this directive. The other directors were Zhang Yuan, Wang Xiaoshuai, Wu Wenguang, He Jianjun, and Ning Dai.

35. Ian Haydn Smith's review of *Springtime in a Small Town*, Kamera.co.uk, http://www.kamera.co.uk/reviews_extra/springtime_in_a_small_town.php (accessed September 20, 2003).

36. Shelly Kraicer, "Chinese Films at the 27th Toronto International Film Festival—a Report," *Senses of Cinema* 23 (2002), http://archive.sensesofcinema.com/contents/festivals/02/23/toronto_chinese.html (accessed May 6, 2010).

2. *Dislocation*: Huang Jianxin's Urban Searching for Roots

1. See Linda Chiu-han Lai, "Whither the Walker Goes: Spatial Practices and Negative Poetics in 1990s Chinese Urban Cinema," in *The Urban Generation: Chinese Cinema and Society at the Turn of the Twenty-first Century*, ed. Zhang Zhen (Duke University Press, 2007), 216–17. Referring primarily to Anke Gleber's *The Art of Taking a Walk: Flânerie, Literature, and Film in Weimar Culture* (Princeton, NJ: Princeton University Press, 1999), Lai discussed how Huang Jianxin's vision of the city recalls the standard descriptions of a *flâneur* (walker). "*Flânerie* and *dérive* ('drifting')," Lai explains, "are forms of spatial practice adopted, primarily among European intelligentsia, as subversive tactics to combat alienation in urban life in the West" (205).

2. Lai, "Whither the Walker Goes," 215.

3. Chai Xiaofeng, "Huang Jianxin fangtan lu" (An interview with Huang Jianxin), *Dangdai dianying* 2 (1994), 37.

4. I wrote this before interviewing Huang Jianxin in the summer of 2002, when Huang said almost exactly the same thing about this film. He, nevertheless, confided to me that he seldom had the same feeling (ganjue) on set about this film as he would with his other, urban-subject films.

5. Huang Jianxin, "Dianying de meili" (Attraction of films), in *Huang Jianxin: Nianqing de yanjing* (Huang Jianxin: Youthful eyes), ed. Chai Xiaofeng et al. (Changsha: Hunan wenyi chubanshe, 1996), 407.

6. Paul Pickowicz, "Huang Jianxin and the Notion of Postsocialism," in *New Chinese Cinemas: Forms, Identities, Politics*, ed. Nick Browne et al. (Cambridge, UK: Cambridge University Press, 1994), 63–64.

7. H. C. Li, "Color, Character, and Culture: On *Yellow Earth*, *Black Cannon Incident*, and *Red Sorghum*." *Modern Chinese Literature* 5.1 (1989), 107.

8. Zeng Desheng, "Success in the West: New Chinese Film Exhibition in Los Angeles," *China Screen* 3 (1987), 35.

9. Chai, "Huang Jianxin fangtan lu," 38.

10. See Eugene Yuejin Wang, "The Rhetoric of Mirror, Shadow, and Moon: *Samsara* and the Problem of Representation of Self in China," *East-West Film Journal* 5.2 (1991): 69–92.

11. See Zhao Fei, "Lunhui de zaoxing chuli" (Image productions in Samsara). *Dianying yishu* 5 (1989): 42–44.

12. Chai, "Huang Jianxin fangtan lu," 38.

13. Jing Wang, *High Culture Fever: Politics, Aesthetics, and Ideology in Deng's China* (Berkeley: University of California Press, 1996), 4–5.

14. Chai Xiaofeng et. al., eds., *Huang Jianxin: Nianqing de yanjing* (Huang Jianxin: Youthful eyes; Changsha: Hunan wenyi chubanshe, 1996), 418.

15. Mayfair Mei-hui Yang, *Gifts, Favors, and Banquets: The Art of Social Relationships in China* (Ithaca, NY: Cornell University Press, 1994), 6.

16. Ibid., 189.

17. See Lin Yutang, "Lun youmo" (On humor), in *Lin Yutang jindian zuoping xuan* (Selected classics by Lin Yutang; Beijing: Dangdai shijie chubanshe, 2002), 32–43.

18. Ibid., 39.

19. Sigmund Freud, *Introductory Lectures on Psychoanalysis* (New York: Norton, 1966), 273.

3. *No One Cheers*: The Later Fifth Generation and the Urban "Situation Movie"

1. Ge Fei, "Chongjian wenqing: Xia Gang dianying pingshu" (Reconstruct warmth: A comment on Xiangang's films), *Dianying yishu* 3 (1994): 22–28. Ying Xiong, "Cong fengge dao pingpai: Guanyu Xia Gang dianying" (From style to quality: On Xia Gang's films), *Dianying yishu* 3 (1994): 17–21.

2. Sheldon H. Lu, *China, Transnational Visuality, Global Postmodernity* (Stanford, CA: Stanford University Press, 2001), 46.

3. Zhang Yiwu. "Hou xinshiqi Zhongguo dianying: Fenlie de tiaozhan" (Chinese film in post-new era: The challenge of fragmentation). *Dangdai dianying* 5 (1994), 7.

4. Ibid., 8.

5. Ibid., 10.

6. Xia Gang's films achieved a decent selling record: *Encounter Passion* (1990) sold 99 prints, *My Heart's Not Changed* (1991) 90 prints, and *After Separation* (1992) 148 prints. Most other art films usually did not sell more than fifty prints. Yet, compared with the so-called "entertainment films" (yule pian), Xia's success was moderate. The best-selling Chinese films, ten for each year from 1987 to 1991, present a selling record ranging from 215 to 379 prints. See Ni Zhen, ed., *Gaige yu Zhongguo dianying* (Reform and Chinese cinema; Beijing: Zhongguo dianying chubanshe, 1994), 166–69.

7. Columbia Pictures Film Production Asia, a subsidiary of Hong Kong–based Columbia Asia, is best known as the coproducer of the multiple-Oscar-winning international hit *Crouching Tiger, Hidden Dragon*.

8. See Feng Xiaogang et al., "Dawan tan *Dawan*" (Big shots talk about *Big Shot*), *Dianying yishu* 2 (2002), 47. "The hundredth year" means the limit of one's natural life, that is, death.

9. Ni Zhen, "Kewang shisu" (Yearn for profanity), *Dianying yishu* 6 (2002), 31.

10. Feng Xiaogang, "I am the Outsider of the Sacred Hall of Chinese Cinema," speech delivered Nov. 16, 2000, at Beijing Film Academy. *Beijing Youth Daily*, November 24, 2000. Quoted and translated by Shuyu Kong in "Big Shot from Beijing: Feng Xiaogang's *He Sui Pian* and Contemporary Chinese Commercial Film," *Asian Cinema* 14.1 (2003), 179.

11. Wang Shuo and Lao Xia, *Meiren zeng wo menghanyao* (The beauty presents me with the knockout drug; Wuhan: Changjiang wenyi chubanshe, 2000). For comments by Wang Shuo and his interviewer, Lao Xia, on Feng Xiaogang and popular culture, see especially 11–30.

12. Ibid., 14.

13. Xia Gang, "Guanyu dushi de huati" (On topics about metropolis), *Dangdai dianying* 4 (1997), 89.

14. Zhang Yiwu, 9.

15. See Wang Shuo and Lao Xia, *Meiren zeng wo menghanyao*, especially 227–34.

16. Xia Gang, "Guanyu dushi de huati," 90.

17. See Stephanie A. Shields, *Speaking from the Heart: Gender and the Social Meaning of Emotion* (Cambridge, UK: Cambridge University Press, 2002), 4. Shields's elaboration of the "felt" quality of emotion is derived from E. Duffy, "An explanation of 'emotion' phenomena without the use of the concept 'emotion,'" *Journal of General Psychology* 25 (1941): 283–93.

18. See Xia Gang, "Dianying buneng shuo chulai" (A film is not made by talking), *Dianying yishu*, 1 (1993), 53.

19. See Ge Fei, "Chongjian wenqing," and Ying Xiong, "Cong fengge dao pingpai," for such comments.

20. In the mid-1980s, for ordinary Chinese citizens, foreign phone numbers could not be dialed by any phones but the designated ones in certain metropolitan post offices.

21. In contemporary Chinese cities, there are certain public restrooms that the clients need to pay a fee to use. These bathrooms are usually better maintained with a janitor guarding the door, to collect the fee, and to keep the place clean.

22. See Ge Hongbing's preface, which is printed in both volumes of the two-volume anthology that have the same subtitle: *Shi xiaozi nüzuojia jiexi* (Analysis of ten female *xiaozi* writers). The titles of the two volumes are, respectively, Ge Hongbing, ed., *Fense de biaoqing* (Pink expressions; Beijing: Wenhua yishu chubanshe, 2002), and Ge Hongbing, ed., *Ganshang de landiao* (Sentimental blue tones; Beijing: Wenhua yishu chubanshe, 2002).

23. Leng Jing, "Qige ci he yige cizu: Yingying jiexi" (Seven words and a phrase: An analysis of Yingying), in Ge Hongbing, ed., *Ganshang de landiao*, 193–94.

24. Chris Berry, "Interview with Peng Xiaolian," *Camera Obscura* 18 (1988), 31.

25. Peng Xiaolian, "Guanyu *Jiazhuang mei ganjue* de chuangzuo" (About the production of *Shanghai Women*), *Dianying yishu* 4 (2002), 96.

26. In her interview with Chris Berry, Peng Xiaolian talked about this film: "The first thing I did in working on this film was to write the script for *Three Women*. Why did I do that? It's rural. I spent nine years in the countryside, didn't I? I was even the head of a women's brigade there. So, while I was there, I spent all my time with women. And the story was about women." She also talked about many revisions she had to make so that the film would pass the censors. See Chris Berry, "Interview with Peng Xiaolian," *Camera Obscura* 18 (1988): 26–31.

27. See Peng Xiaolian, "Guanyu *Jiazhuang mei ganjue* de chuangzuo," 95–96.

28. Zeng Nianping was a young assistant professor of cinematography when Li Shaohong enrolled at Beijing Film Academy. Li often talks about the pleasure of having Zeng as her cinematographer and about the ease of communication between the two of them on set.

29. Zhang Wei and Ying Xiong, "Zouchu dingshi: Yu Li Shaohong tan Li Shaohong de dianying chuangzuo" (Getting away from the fixed model: Talking with Li Shaohong about her filmmaking), *Dangdai dianying* 35 (May 1995), 50.

30. See Zhang Wei and Ying Xiong, "Zouchu dingshi," 47.

31. Tonglin Lu, *Confronting Modernity in the Cinemas of Taiwan and Mainland China* (Cambridge, UK: Cambridge University Press, 2002), 173.

32. "A Director's New Wings," posted March 1, 2004, http://www.china.org.cn/english/features/film/88844.htm (accessed August 30, 2004).

33. "A Director's New Wings."

34. The books mentioned in this treasure house are primarily the literary classics of the May Fourth cultural movement of the early twentieth century and the world literary classics introduced to China during the May Fourth era.

35. Quoted in Zhu Linyong, "*Baober in Love* Draws Raves, Rants, and Crowds," posted February 24, 2004, http://www.ChinaDaily.com.cn (accessed August 30, 2004).

36. "The twenty-first-century Chinese are infatuated with modernization," Li Shaohong says, "like a love-struck man craving for his lover." See Zhu Linyong, "*Baober in Love* Draws Raves, Rants, and Crowds."

37. Zhu Linyong, "*Baober in Love* Draws Raves, Rants and Crowds."

38. See, for example, "A Director's New Wings"; Meng Ye, "Review of the Week: *Baober in Love*," posted February 15, 2004, http://www.MonkeyPeach.com (accessed August 30, 2004); Zhu Lingyong, "*Baober in Love* Draws Raves, Rants, and Crowds"; Derek Elley "Review: *Baober in Love*," posted February 24, 2004, http:// www.variety.com (accessed 30 August 30, 2004); and Richard James Havis, "*Baober in Love*," posted March 2, 2004, http://www.HollywoodReporter.com (accessed August 30, 2004).

39. Richard James Havis, "*Baober in Love*."

40. See "A Director's New Wings."

41. In the state-monopolized distribution system, filmmakers make money not by box office sales but by selling prints to state-run theaters. In the 1980s an average film sold about one hundred prints. Tian Zhuangzhuang's *On the Hunting Ground* sold two prints and *Horse Thief*, seven.

42. Zhu Linyong, "*Baober in Love* Draws Raves, Rants, and Crowds."

43. The film won Best Film, Best Director, and Best Male Actor at the nineteenth Gold Rooster Awards in China. It also won the Air Canada Award (public favorite) at the 1999 Montreal World Film Festival.

44. Teng Ruijun also played, for example, in Huang Jianxin's *Surveillance* (1996) and *Mr. Wu: A Police Story* (1997) in similar roles of honest and self-sacrificing characters.

45. See David Chaney, "From Ways of Life to Lifestyle: Rethinking Culture as Ideology and Sensibility," in *Culture in the Communication Age*, ed. James Lull (London: Routledge, 2001), 75–88.

46. A film critic records a humorous, somewhat cynical, comment on Ning Ying's patience to explore her film subjects and her lack of motivation to catch the tide in filmmaking to become famous. "I recall the comment of a well-known director," this critic writes, "about the total difference between Ning Ying and Wang Xiaoshuai. Ning Ying is a woman. She has made films. She has made money. She is married to an Italian. Her husband is nice. She travels between the two worlds [of China and Italy]. She does not need to strive and to catch any tide. She can afford to settle down to explore the lives of her local police [referring to her documentary approach shown in *On the Beat*]. Wang Xiaoshuai, in contrast, has to produce commercials to pay his car loans." This film critic further contrasts Ning Ying's ease in developing her film career with some other directors, including Wang Xiaoshuai. "When they do films," he writes, "they are driven by a lot of eagerness: eager that the film will come out, be seen, be recognized, be awarded, be used to compete with others, be profitable, and eager that one film will lead to the chance to do another one." See Zhao Zhiguo, "Dapai daoyan: Chaoqian yu luohou" (Big directors: Ahead or behind the time), *Dianshi, dianying, wenxue* 2 (2003): 4–11.

47. See Christopher Barden, "A Beijing Cabbie's Summer of Love: Veteran Film Director Ning Ying Documents Changing Beijing through the Eyes of a Philandering Taxi Driver," *Beijing Scene* 6-3 (October 29–November 4), http://www.beijingscene.com/v06i003/feature/feature.html (accessed August 15, 2004).

48. Ibid.

49. See Barden, "Beijing Cabbie's Summer of Love." Barden vividly depicted what happened while Ning Ying's camera was rolling for *I Love Beijing*: "Two old Italian Maoists, who first arrived in China in 1968, get drunk with nostalgia, bemoaning, 'No one cares about politics anymore, only making money.' A Chinese person asks a Yugoslav to explain his country to him. 'Sure,' the Yugoslav fellow replies. 'Just let me know when you have a couple days of spare time.' French discuss Chinese law, Germans talk of banking, and two Spanish expert on the Taoist sage Zhuangzi drink wine and ponder the ceiling as

they quote from the master: 'Everyone knows the use of useful things, but few know the use of the useless things.' . . . Ning Ying, you might argue, is the most Taoist of Chinese filmmakers and the most Italian of Chinese filmmakers."

50. Xin Qiji (1140–1207) is a Song Dynasty poet. The poem I refer to here reads (my own translation): "While young, I knew not the taste of disappointment. I enjoyed the views on high towers. To produce new poems, I searched for disappointment. . . . Now that I'm filled with disappointments, I hesitate to touch on them. I say, instead, 'What a cool day of autumn!'"

4. *Beijing Bastards*: Century's End Rock Scenes and China's Generation X

1. Claire Wallace and Sijka Kovatcheva, *Youth in Society: The Construction and Deconstruction of Youth in East and West Europe* (New York: St. Martin's Press, 1998), 170.

2. Ibid.

3. Quoted in Ning Dai, "*Beijing zazhong* juqing jianjie" (A synopsis of *Beijing Bastards*), *Dianying gushi* 5 (1993), 9.

4. John Minford, "Picking Up the Pieces," *Far Eastern Economic Review* 8 (August 1985), 30. I also borrowed Minford's phrases in this article to translate the meanings of *liumang*.

5. Ibid.

6. Ibid.

7. See Rey Chow, *Primitive Passions: Visuality, Sexuality, Ethnography, and Contemporary Chinese Cinema* (New York: Columbia University Press, 1995), 58.

8. To further understand Chinese film critics' interest in postcolonialism, see Wang Yuechuan, *Houxiandai houzhimin zhuyi zai Zhongguo* (Postmodernism and postcolonialism in China; Beijing: Shoudu shifan daxue shubanshe, 2002).

9. See Li Yiming, "Shiji zhimo: Shehui de daode weiji yu diwudai dianying de shouzhong zhengqin" (Century's end: Ethic crisis and the end of the Fifth-Generation filmmaking), 2 pts., *Dianying yishu* 1 (1996): 9–13, and 2 (1996): 24–28. The quote is from 2 (1996), 25.

10. See Zuo Shula, "Cong 'diliu dai' dianying dao *Wushan yunyu*" (From the Sixth Generation to *Rain Clouds over Wushan*), *Dianying yishu* 3 (1996): 80–81.

11. See Wang Yichuan, "'Wudai qi' zhongguo dianying" (Chinese film in a nongenerational era), *Dangdai dianying* 5 (1994): 20–27. Zhang Yiwu, "Hou xinshiqi zhongguo dianying: Fenlie de tiaozhan" (Chinese film in the post–new era: The challenge of fragmentation), *Dangdai dianying* 5 (1994): 4–11. Han Xiaolei, "Dui diwudai de wenhua tuwei: Hou wudai de geren dianying xianxiang" (Getting beyond the Fifth Generation culture: post–Fifth Generation individual filmmaking), *Dianying yishu* 241(1995): 58–63.

12. See Li Yiming, "Shiji zhimo," 2 (1996), 28.

13. Douglas Rushkoff, *The GenX Reader* (New York: Ballantine Books, 1994), 3.

14. Geoffrey T. Holtz, *Welcome to the Jungle: The Why behind "Generation X"* (New York: St. Martin's Press, 1995), 1.

15. Huang Shixian, "Yishixingtai zhenghou: Wang Shuo shi 'fanban wenhua' de shimaoxing yu huihuaixing" (Ideological symptom: On Wang Shuo's "anti-culture" style), *Dianying yishu* 6 (1989), 41.

16. The film is based on Wang Shuo's novella *Dongwu xiongmeng* (Vicious animals). Wang Shuo plays the role of a gangster "Godfather" in the film.

17. Dai Jinhua, "Geren xiezuo yu qingchun gushi" (Personal writing and story of youth), *Dianying yishu* 3 (1996), 12.

18. Some Sixth Generation directors depicted the Fifth Generation life experience. Lu Xuechang's *The Making of Steel* (1998) was a good example. The film contrasted the protagonist's inspirations when he was a teenager (in the 1960s and 1970s) and his disappointment with life when he entered adulthood (in the 1980s and 1990s).

19. "Zuihou de baoyuan" (The last complaint), according to the film credit, is a song of Dou Wei's Zuomeng (Dream) Band. Although Dou Wei also appears in *Beijing Bastards*, it is Cui Jian who sings this song in the film.

20. Having its debut show in 1991, Overload is the first thrash metal band of Chinese rock.

21. As practiced by several other independent filmmakers, Guan Hu got his film issued by purchasing a state studio logo, this time it was from the Inner Mongolian Studio.

22. Zhang Yingjin, "Rebel without a Cause? China's New Urban Generation and Postsocialist Filmmaking," in *The Urban Generation: Chinese Cinema and Society at the Turn of the Twenty-first Century*, ed. Zhang Zhen (Durham, NC: Duke University Press, 2007), 59.

23. Steven Schwankert, "Beijing Rocks: Rockin' in the Not-So-Free World," posted September 1995, http://www.sat.dundee.ac.uk (accessed January 10, 2005).

24. Mabel Cheung worked as a director for Radio and Television of Hong Kong prior to obtaining a master's degree in film studies from New York University. Her feature film debut *Illegal Immigrant* (1985) won her the best-director award at the Hong Kong Film Awards. Her *An Autumn's Tale* (1987) won the best-director award at the Hong Kong International Film Festival. Her other films include *The Soong Sisters* (1997) and *City of Glass* (1998). *Beijing Rocks* received a best-picture nomination at the 2002 Hong Kong Film Awards.

25. Here the film may be alluding to the tragic death of Tang Dynasty (a rock band) bass player Zhang Ju in a 1995 motorcycle accident.

26. These lines are from his song titled "Garbage Dump." Quoted by Jeroen de Kloet in the article "Marx or Market: Chinese Rock and the Sound of Fury," in *Multiple Modernities: Cinemas and Popular Media in Transcultural East Asia*, ed. Jenny K. W. Lau (Philadelphia: Temple University Press, 2003), 28.

27. See Wang Shuo, "Cui Jian yinxiang" (Impressions of Cui Jian), in *Suibi ji* (Random essays; Kunming: Yunnan remin chubanshe, 2004): 213–14.

28. Ibid., 213.

29. Ibid., 214.

30. See Jing Wang, "Wang Shuo: 'Pop Goes the Culture?'" in *High Culture Fever: Politics, Aesthetics, and Ideology in Deng's China* (Berkeley: University of California Press, 1996): 261–86.

31. Wang Shuo became the manager of a consulting firm in cultural affairs (Beijing shishi wenhua shiwu zixun gongsi) in 1992; and in an interview in 1994, he talked about the isolation of a writer's life and how his managerial job responded to his need to get closer to other people (ren qun). See Ding Xiaobai's interview with Wang Shuo in *Dianying yishu* 2 (1995): 43–49.

32. See Jing Wang, "Wang Shuo," 282–83, and see Zhang Yi, ed., *Kankan Wang Shuo* (Chatting about Wang Shuo; Beijing: Huzxia chubanshe, 1993).

33. See Ding Xiaobai's interview with Wang Shuo.

34. See, for example, Maria Barbieri, "The Other Half of Heaven: Women in Chinese Cinema" (Courtesy of the Far East Film Festival), http://www.asianfilms.org (accessed March 15, 2005), and Lee Alon, "Movies: *Infernal Affairs, I Love You*, and *Naked Weapon*," http://www.cityweekend.com.cn/beijing/articles/cw-magazine/reviews/Movies_CW02 (accessed March 15, 2005).

35. For a spectrum of popular perception of Wang Shuo, including Chi Li's comment, see *Pizi yingxiong: Wang Shuo zai pipan* (A hooligan hero: More critiques of Wang Shuo; Beijing: Zhonghua gongshang lianhe chubanshe, 2000).

36. Han Xuelin, *Chong bu chu de fanli: Wang Shuo xiaoshuo de nüxing shiye* (Barriers: Female perspectives in Wang Shuo's novels; Zhengzhou: Henan wenyi chubanshe, 2002), 52.

37. See Zhang Dexiang and Jin Huimin, *Wang Shuo pipan* (A critique of Wang Shuo; Beijing: Zhongguo shehui kexue chubanshe, 1993), 91–95.

38. Zhang Kangkang, "Wan de bushi wenxue" (It's not literature that is played with), in *Pizi yingxiong*, 420–26.

39. See Di Fei, "Yibu youxiu de dushi aiqing yuyan" (A brilliant allegory of love in a metropolis), in *Wenyi bao*, Sept. 18, 2003, 4.

40. See Kozo's review of Green Tea, posted 2004, http://www.lovehkfilm.com/panasia/green_tea.htm (accessed March 15, 2005).

41. See Su Hongjing, "Zaqizaba dianying yuansu de dapingpan" (Mismatched film elements), in *Wenyi bao*, Sept. 18, 2003, 4.

42. See Benjamin R. Barber, *Jihad vs. McWorld: How Globalism and Tribalism Are Reshaping the World* (New York: Ballantine Books, 1996), 17.

43. See a series of news reports under the general title of "Q ban shenghuo" (Q version life) in *Boston Chinese Report* (March 18–March 24, 2005), B2 and B5.

5. Captives of Love: Emotional Styles and the New Urbanites

1. Shuqin Cui, "Working from the Margins: Urban Cinema and Independent Directors in Contemporary China" in *Chinese-Language Film: Historiography, Poetics, Politics*, ed. Sheldon H. Lu and Emilie Yueh-yu Yeh (Honolulu: University of Hawai'i Press, 2005), 99.

2. R. Benedict, *Patterns of Culture* (London: Routledge & Kegan Paul, 1935), 78–79.

3. Candace Clark defines emotional culture thus: "Every culture and subculture includes its own emotion labels, definitions, feeling rules, role values, knowledge, and social logics pertaining to emotions and emotionality. Together, these make up emotional culture." See Candace Clark, "Taming the 'Brute Being': Sociology Reckons with Emotionality," in *Postmodern Existential Sociology*, ed. Joseph A. Kotarba and John M. Johnson (New York: AltaMira Press, 2002), 166.

4. See Kurt W. Fischer and June Price Tangney, "Introduction: Self-Conscious Emotions and Affect Revolution—Framework and Overview," in *Self Conscious Emotions*, ed. June Price Tangney and Kurt W. Fisher (New York: Guilford Press, 1995), 3.

5. William M. Reddy, in his book *The Navigation of Feeling* (Cambridge, UK: Cambridge University Press, 2001), documented many major studies in the above-mentioned "revolution in the study of emotion."

6. Clark, "Taming the 'Brute Being,'" 155.

7. See William Theodore de Bary, ed., *Sources of Chinese Tradition*, vol. 1 (New York: Columbia University Press, 1960), 500–501.

8. See David Chaney, "From Ways of Life to Lifestyle: Rethinking Culture as Ideology and Sensibility," in *Culture in the Communication Age*, ed. James Lull (London: Routledge, 2001), 75–88.

9. Benjamin R. Barber, *Jihad vs. McWorld: How Globalism and Tribalism Are Reshaping the World* (New York: Ballantine Books, 1996), 4.

10. Ibid., 17.

11. Ibid., 186.

12. He Jianjun, aka both He Yi and Zhao Jisong, was born in 1960 in Beijing. He did his apprentice filmmaking with such directors as Chen Kaige, Zhang Yimou, and Tian Zhuangzhuang. After two years of study at Beijing Film Academy (1988–90), he embarked on his own career of film directing. *Pirated Copy* was shown at the Thirty-third International Film Festival in Rotterdam, Holland.

13. *Scenery* (Fengjing), a 114-minute film in a surrealist style, toured America in 2001. It was included in New Chinese Cinema: Tales of Urban Delight, Alienation, and the Margins, UCLA Film and Television Archive's ten-film presentation prepared by Berenice Reynaud. It was also part of the Boston Museum of Fine Arts' "New Films from China" series. In He Jianjun's interviews published in China, however, he never mentions this film. In his interview with Taiwan film scholar Jiao Xiongping in 1997, he does mention it, then titled *Attorney* (Lüshi), and discussed his general plan of doing a city series of various urban professions, with *Postman*, already done, to be followed by *Attorney, Teacher,* and *Taxi Driver*. See Jiao Xiongping, *Fengyun jihui: Yu dangdai Zhongguo dianying duihua* (Random meetings: Dialogues with contemporary Chinese filmmakers; Taibei: Yuanliu chuban gongsi, 1998), 269–75.

14. See Zhang Huijun and He Jianjun, "*Hudie de weixiao* duitan" (A dialogue on *Butterfly Smile*), *Dianying yishu* 6 (2001): 105–8.

15. See Cao Shujun and Yu Jianmeng, *Shehun: Xiju dashi Cao Yu* (To capture souls: Master dramatist Cao Yu; Beijing: Zhongguo qingnian chubanshe, 1990), 230.

16. The performance was part of a series of events planned as a celebration of Cao Yu's ninetieth birthday. Cao Yu's three major plays, *The Sunrise, The Thunderstorm,* and *The Wildness* were all performed in August and September. Among these performances, only *The Wildness* was experimental and naturally caused a lot of controversy. See, for example, Tian Benxiang "Ye tan xinban *Yuanye* he *Richu*" (More thinking about new versions of *The Wildness* and *The Sunrise*), *Zhongguo xiju* 10 (2000): 14–16, and Sun Jie, "Jiegou zhuyi de zhexiubu: Yi shiyan xiju *Yuanye*" (Deconstruction as an excuse: Comment on the experimental play *The Wildness*), *Zhongguo xiju* 10 (2000): 17–19.

17. See the interview by Zhang Yu and Ding Yilan with Li Xin, "Yong lingyizhong fangshi kan dianying" (Watching film in a different way), *Dangdai dianying* 1(2002): 33–35.

18. See Zhang Yu and Ding Yilan's interview, 35.

19. Tom Tykwer's *Run, Lola, Run* has fascinated Chinese film lovers. In 2002 China's leading film journal *Dangdai dianying* (second issue of the year) ran a special section consisting of three articles to discuss the director and the film.

20. See Deng Guanghui, "Xin dianying de huo yu ai: *Huayan* de wenhua zidai" (New film's confusion and love: The cultural attitude of *Dazzling*), *Dangdai dianying* 1 (2002): 50–53.

21. Ibid., 52.

22. See Zhang Yu and Ding Yilan's interview, 34 and 35.

23. Quoted in Matt Langdon's review of *Suzhou River*, posted February 22, 2001, http://www.geocities.com (accessed February 10, 2005).

24. For an insightful scholarly study, see Jerome Silbergeld's *Hitchcock with a Chinese Face: Cinematic Doubles, Oedipal Triangles, and China's Moral Voice* (Seattle: University of Washington Press, 2004).

25. See Nicholas Christopher, *Somewhere in the Night: Film Noir and the American City* (New York: Holt, 1997), back cover.

26. In www.FilmFestivals.com, reporter Fanfan Ko writes, "Lou Ye has said that although Shanghai in *Suzhou River* is a city of criminals, smugglers, and seedy night-clubs,

he considered that every city, like every person, wears different masks. Who is to say which one is the real one?" Lou Ye obviously needed the mask of Shanghai that he selected to suit the mood of the film. See Fanfan Ko's review of *Suzhou River*, http://www.filmfestivals.com/paris_00/film_suzhou.htm (accessed February 10, 2005).

27. The English subtitles of this song appear on screen in a VCD version of the film (by Beijing dongfang yingyin gongsi), presumably provided by China Film Archive's dubbing service. I changed a few words for a more accurate translation.

28. See David Bordwell, "Romance on Your Menu: *Chungking Express*," in his *Planet Hong Kong: Popular Cinema and the Art of Entertainment* (Cambridge, MA: Harvard University Press, 2000), 282–89.

29. See Bordwell, "Romance on Your Menu" for an explanation of food metaphors in this film.

30. Bordwell, "Romance on Your Menu," 285.

31. As an interesting case of how the carnal intruded on emotional culture in post-Mao China, see "Yellow Peril" in Jianying Zha's *China Pop: How Soap Operas, Tabloids, and Bestsellers are Transforming a Culture* (New York: New Press, 1995). This chapter discusses emotional culture by focusing on the 1993 dispute about Jia Pingwa's *The Abandoned Capital*, a best-selling novel that is abundant with sex scenes but is also seen as a fatalistic, apocalyptic, and fin de siècle vision of China as an abandoned, spiritless, and decadent culture given to carnal desires. Lou Ye's 1993 film *Weekend Lovers*, one must note, was produced in this cultural context.

6. *Lunar Eclipse*: Elusive Urban Realities

1. Zhang Xinxin emerged in the immediate post-Mao era as a fiction and nonfiction writer. Her major works then include *The Dreams of Our Generation* (1986), *Beijing People* (1986), and *Chinese Lives: An Oral History of Contemporary China* (1987).

2. See Zhang Xinxin, "Dongfang buliang, xifang liang?" (To make it not in the East but in the West?), *Wenyi zhengming* 1 (2004): 63–66.

3. Ibid., 64.

4. Ibid., 64–65.

5. See, for example, Zhang Xinxin's book *Liulang shijie de fangshi* (My ways of bumming in the world; Shenyang: Shenyang chubanshe, 2002).

6. Zhang Xinxin, "Dongfang buliang, xifang liang?" 65.

7. Like many other independent films that do not officially open in China, the DVD of the French edition of *The Orphan of Anyang* is readily available at China's many video shops and thus is known to many among the educated audience.

8. Miklós Haraszti, *The Velvet Prison: Artists under State Socialism* (New York, 1987), 121.

9. Wang Chao's statement appears in *Wode sheyingji bu sahuang: Xianfeng dianyingren dangan—shengyu 1961–1970* (My camera doesn't lie: Dossiers of avant-garde filmmakers born between 1961 and 1970), ed. Cheng Qingsong and Huang Ou (Beijing: Zhongguo youyi chubanshe, 2002), 165, 173. This English translation is Yingjin Zhang's quote when he studies issues of truth, subjectivity and audience in China's independent filmmaking. See Yingjin Zhang, "My Camera Doesn't Lie? Truth, Subjectivity, and Audience in Chinese Independent Film and Video" in *From Underground to Independent: Alternative Film Culture in Contemporary China*, ed. Paul G. Pickowicz and Yingjin Zhang (Rowman & Littlefield, 2006), 31.

10. See Zhang Jiuying, *Fanpai Zhang Yimou* (To photocopy Zhang Yimou; Beijing: Zhongguo mangwen chubanshe, 2001), 184–99.

11. Zhang Jiuying, *Fanpai Shang Yimou*, 191.

12. Benjamin R. Barber, *Jihad vs. McWorld: How Globalism and Tribalism Are Reshaping the World* (New York: Ballantine Books, 1996), 186. See chapter 5 for more discussion of the impact of the McWorld on the lifestyles of the Chinese young urbanites.

13. A New Yorker in Beijing, Peter Loehr, founded Imar Film Studio in 1996. A graduate of Georgetown University, Loehr produced TV programs in Japan and Taiwan for a few years before landing in China. His Imar Studio has been a success story, both in profits and in tapping into and developing young Chinese filmmaking talents. Zhang Yang was among the earliest young directors that Imar invested in. His *Spicy Love Soup* (1997) made over 3 million RMB, and his *Shower* (1999) earned 20 million RMB in China and $2 million in the United States.

14. Zhang Yan's interview with Zhang Yang, "*Zuotian*: Let It Be" (*Quitting*: Let It Be), *Dianying yishu* 1 (2002), 41.

15. I had a brief interview with Zhang Yang during the summer of 2001 in which we exchanged ideas about the role of theater in his filmmaking.

16. Some of the roles that Jia Hongsheng played include Ah Xi in Lou Ye's 1993 *Weekend Lovers* and Mardar in Lou's 2000 *Suzhou River*. "Jia is strangely reminiscent of John Cusack," film reviewer Sean Weitner writes of Jia's performance in *Suzhou River*, "warm but pensive, charming but socially awkward." See Sean Weitner's review of *Suzhou River*, http://www.flakmag.com/film/suzhou.html (accessed April 30, 2010). Jia is also well remembered for his performance in Wang Xiaoshuai's 1997 film *Frozen*, in which he portrays the artist who plays with suicide as an exploration of performance art.

17. The reader may find the lyrics of this song in my discussion of *Good Morning, Beijing* in chapter 1.

18. The interviewer expressed this impression on behalf of the audience she knows. See Zhang Yan's interview.

19. Zhang Yan's interview, 42.

20. Chinese mental wards usually accommodate three to six patients. Zhang Yang had to work out a special scene to allow a dozen mental patients to interact with Jia Hongsheng.

21. See Zhang Yan's interview, 42.

22. Miao Ye, "Diliudai de ganjue hen fuza: Lu Xuechang duihua lu" (Mixed feelings of the Sixth Generation: An interview with Lu Xuechang), *Zhongguo guangbo yingshi* 4 (2003), 44.

23. Zhang Yuan reminisced that during the shooting of the film, the four members often altered their lines as dictated by the mood of a scene.

24. Notes taken at a panel discussion with Zhang Yuan about his films shown at Harvard Film Archives, November 4, 1999, at Yenching Institute of Harvard University.

25. In August 2002, while in Beijing, I was at the screenings of films that had been invited to participate in the competition. Several other younger directors' films, such as Lu Xuechang's *A Lingering Face*, Zhang Yang's *Shower*, and Wang Xiaoshuai's *Suburban Dreams*, were also selected for competition.

26. Dai Jinhua, *Cinema and Desire: Feminist Marxism and Cultural Politics in the Work of Dai Jinhua*, ed. Jing Wang and Tani E. Barlow (London: Verso, 2002), 85.

27. See Cui Zi'en's writing on initiating a column on Chinese independent filmmaking in *Yinyue yu biaoyan* 1 (2001), 13. It is interesting that in five issues in 2000 through 2001, Cui Zi'en managed to run a column discussing Chinese independent filmmaking in this unlikely journal (*Music and Performance*) of Nanjing Arts Academy while other major film journals were mostly silent on the subject.

28. See "Director's Statement" in the publicity materials for this film distributed by East Line Entertainment and Media, which was posted online at Asian Film Archive, http://www.usc.edu/isd/archives/asianfilm/china (accessed December 10, 2004). The posting is not available any more.

29. *Railroad of Hope* (2002) is a well-known documentary by Ning Ying. Each year during August and September, thousands of peasants leave their home villages in Sichuan and travel by train for a long trip of more than three thousand kilometers to the Chinese Muslim area of Xinjiang to become seasonal workers for the cotton harvest. Ning Ying took a three-day journey with these peasants on the road, mostly women, to document their trip, their lives, and their hopes. This documentary has toured America and several European countries.

30. Over a dozen film artists, documentary filmmakers Wu Wenguang, Duan Jinchuan, Shi Jian, and Jian Yue among them, had an informal meeting at Zhang Yuan's home in Beijing and focused their discussion on independence in filmmaking. This gathering ended with the hope that the participants would keep in touch with each other to further promote the idea of independent filmmaking. See the introduction of Lu Xinyu's *Jilu Zhongguo: Dangdai zhongguo xin jilu yundong* (Documenting China: New documentary movement of contemporary China; Beijing: Sanlian shudian, 2003).

31. *Suzhou River* is part of a ten-film documentary, *Super Cities*, which Lou planned to produce. Lou Ye wrote about the creative process for *Suzhou River*, "I started to shoot the film as a documentary. I started by shooting the real river. I would go with my mini-8 camera, wandering by the Suzhou River every day. In a month's time, I became very familiar with the lives on both banks of the river. From there I entered the story, entered the 'I' of the story, and started to fabricate." See Lou Ye, "Zai yingxiang de heliu shang" (On the river of images), in Cheng and Huang, *Wode sheyingji bu sahuang*, 258.

32. See Federico Fellini, *I'm a Born Liar: A Fellini Lexicon*, ed. Damian Pettigrew (New York: Abrams, 2003).

33. See Cheng and Huang, *Wode sheyingji bu sahuang*. For a scholarly discussion of several assertions made in this book, see Yingjin Zhang, "My Camera Doesn't Lie?"

34. Liu Guangyu, "Ziyou de shuxie yu chenzhong de yingxiang" (Free writing and heavy images), in *Duoyuan yujing zhong de xinshengdai dianying* (Newborn generation film in the context of multiple discourses), ed. Chen Xihe and Shi Chuan (Shanghai, Xuelin chubanshe, 2003), 255–67.

35. Tony Ryans, "Provoking Desire," *Sight and Sound*, July (1996), 28.

36. Chris Berry, "*East Palace, West Palace*: Staging Gay Life in China," *Jump Cut* 42 (1998), 88.

37. See, for example, Bret Hinsch, *Passions of the Cut Sleeve: The Male Homosexual Tradition in China* (Berkeley: University of California Press, 1992).

38. Jerome Silbergeld, *China into Film: Frames of Reference in Contemporary Chinese Cinema* (London: Peaktion Boos, 1999), 111.

39. See Wang Xiaobo's story, "Sishui rouqing" (Love tender as water), in *Wang Xiaobo quanji* (Complete works of Wang Xiaobo), vol. 8 (Kunming: Yunnan chuban jituan gongsi, 2007), 281–312. This story is the base for a script that Zhang Yuan worked on.

40. See Hinsch, *Passions of the Cut Sleeve*, especially 169.

41. Hu Jun, who played the policeman in *East Palace, West Palace*, later played the title role of a gay man in Stanley Kwan's award-winning *Lan Yu*, a Hong Kong film about homosexual life in contemporary China. Zhang Yuan's sarcasm about a cultural enforcer of sexual codes is thus intertextually maintained.

42. To edit this culturally marginal magazine, which publishes writings found on the walls of the city's public toilets, is shown as an eccentric endeavor in the film. What is interesting is that Hong Kong director Fruit Chan was seriously inspired by similar "toilet culture" of different nations and did a film on this subject titled *Public Toilet* (Renmin gongce, 2002).

43. The director's remark was printed on the cover of this film's VCD (video compact disk), published by Dayan wenhua gongsi of Guangzhou.

44. Organized by Zhang Zhen and Zhijie Jia, *The Urban Generation: Chinese Cinema and Society in Transformation* (February 2001) screened He Jianjun's *Postman*, Zhang Ming's *In Expectation*, Jia Zhangke's *Xiao Wu*, Zhang Yuan's *Sons*, Ah Nian's *Call Me*, Ning Ying's *On the Beat*, Wang Quan'an's *Lunar Eclipse*, Lu Ye's *Mr. Zhao*, Lu Xuechang's *The Making of Steel*, Wang Xiaoshuai's *So Close to Paradise*, and Shi Runjiu's *A Beautiful New World*. See *Harvard Film Archive Bulletin* (January/February 2001) for more details.

45. *Dazhong dianying* (Popular cinema), for example, documented a panel discussion of leading film scholars praising the film. These scholars were trying to understand why the unique film style of Wang Quan'an could cater to both popular taste and intellectual interest. See Zhang Suyan, "Xinren xinzuo *Yueshi*" (New film *Lunar Eclipse* by a new director), *Dazhong dianying* 4 (2000): 12–13.

46. The pity was that Wang, when he visited Harvard, had not seen *Suzhou River* and could not comment on the similarities. One of the organizers of the event, Zhang Zhen, later wrote an excellent scholarly essay on China's contemporary art cinema via a comparison of *Lunar Eclipse* and *Suzhou River*. See Zhang Zhen, "Urban Dreamscape, Phantom Sisters, and the Identity of an Emergent Art Cinema," in *The Urban Generation: Chinese Cinema and Society at the Turn of the Twenty-first Century*, ed. Zhang Zhen (Durham, NC: Duke University Press, 2007), 344–87.

47. Louis Giannetti, *Understanding Movies*, 8th ed. (Upper Saddle River, NJ: Prentice Hall, 1999), 133.

48. I interviewed Huang Jianxin in the summer of 2002 in his Beijing film studio office.

49. Zhang Donggang, "Kan *Huayan* tan renwu xingxiang" (A discussion of character images in *Dazzling*), *Dianying yishu* 4 (2002), 65.

50. Deng Guanghui, "Xin dianying de huo yu ai: *Huayan* de wenhua zitai" (New film's confusion and love: The cultural attitude of *Dazzling*), *Dangdai dianying* 1 (2002), 52.

51. See Zhang Suyan, "Xinren xinzuo *Yueshi*," 13.

52. Ibid.

53. Ibid.

7. *City Paradise*: Urbanization Looms over an Old Land

1. See Wu Guanping's interview with Lu Chuan about *The Missing Gun*, "Xun qiang er san shi" (A few issues about *The Missing Gun*), *Dianying yishu* 2 (2002): 43–46.

2. *Dianying yishu* and *Dangdai dianying*, two leading PRC journals in cinema studies, carried several articles on *The Missing Gun* in the first half of 2002.

3. See Li Daoxin, "Wulian beiju yu shengcun huanxiang: Yingpian *Xun qiang* de wenhua dujie" (The tragedy of fetishism and mirage of existence: A cultural reading of *The Missing Gun*), *Dianying yishu* 3 (2002), 46.

4. See Wang Yichuan, "Wudi jiaolü he liuti xingge de shengcheng" (The genesis of rootless anxiety and personality of mobility), *Dangdai dianying* 3 (2002): 23–26. Wang Yichuan is a professor at Beijing Normal University.

5. Lao Tzu, *Tao Teh Ching*, translated by John C. H. Wu (New York: Barnes and Noble, 1997), 53.

6. M. Heidegger, "An Ontological Consideration of Place," in *The Question of Being* (New York: Twayne, 1958), 19. Quoted in Wang Yichuan.

7. See Yu Jin, *Kuanghuan jijie: Liuxing yinyue shiji biaofeng* (Carnival: A century's storm of popular music; Guangzhou: Guangdong renmin chubanshe, 1999). The section is titled "Music for those away from home: I want to go home."

8. Xia Gang et al. "Shanghai shi ge tan: *Boli shi touming de* paishe sanji" (Shanghai is a seaport: Shooting notes on *A Country Boy in Shanghai*), *Dianying yishu* 1 (2001), 65.

9. Zhang Zhen, "Bearing Witness: Chinese Urban Cinema in the Era of 'Transformation' (*Zhuanxing*)," in *The Urban Generation: Chinese Cinema and Society at the Turn of the Twenty-first Century*, ed. Zhang Zhen (Durham, NC: Duke University Press, 2007), 6.

10. Ma Yili, "Boli houmian kan shijie" (To observe the world from behind the glass), *Dazhong dianying* 7 (2002), 25.

11. At a 2001 screening of *Call Me* at Harvard University's Carpenter Center for the Visual Arts, Ah Nian said there were about 3 million migrants working in Beijing at the time when he shot the film and nearly all of them had beepers.

12. Ah Nian, "*Hu wo* daoyan chanshu" (Director's note about *Call Me*), *Dianying yishu* 1 (2001), 31.

13. Tang Danian, Zhang Yuan, and Wang Xiaoshuai were schoolmates at Beijing Film Academy. They all belong to the class of 1985 (the year they entered BFA).

14. See Jian Xu "Representing Rural Migrants in the City: Experimentalism in Wang Xiaoshuai's *So Close to Paradise* and *Beijing Bicycle*," *Screen* 46, no. 4 (winter 2005): 433–49. Having written about *So Close to Paradise*, I found the author confirming my idea here. Xu believes that Wang Xiaoshuai invoked the film noir lexicon to purposefully let down the audience's genre expectation. Encountering a formal failure, the audience is forced to be more attentive to the social boundaries of the Chinese urban scenes that have kept a gangster-romance from emerging.

15. Sheng Zhimin, born in 1969, graduated from Beijing University of Radio and TV. He had run rock bands and directed experimental plays and TV plays before he got into filmmaking. He was involved with the production of Jia Zhangke's *Platform* and some of Fruit Chan's films. *Two Hearts* was his own directorial debut in feature films.

16. Shi Runjiu and Zhang Yang, both trained at Beijing Central Institute of Drama, are two notable younger directors that Imar Company invested in. Shi's *A Beautiful New World* and Zhang's *Shower* are Imar's success stories, since they both had good box-office income in China and abroad.

17. Ni Zhen, "Shouwang xinshengdai" (Expecting the new generation), *Dianying yishu* 4 (1999): 70–73.

18. See Wang Anyi, *Xunzhao Shanghai* (In search of Shanghai; Shanghai: Xuelin chubanshe, 2001), 128–30.

19. See Tony Rayns' interview with Jia Zhangke, posted August 2000, http://www.usc.edu/isd/archives/asianfilm/china/zhantai/interviews.html (accessed April 30, 2004). The posting is not available anymore.

20. See Stephen Teo's interview with Jia Zhangke , posted June 2001, http://www.archive.sensesofcinema.com/contents/01/15/zhangke_interview.html (accessed April 30, 2004).

21. Jia Zhangke made *Xao Wu* (1997) ahead of *Platform* (Zhan tai, 2000) for financial reasons. Chronologically, *Platform* is the first of his Shanxi trilogy.

22. See Stephen Teo's interview.

23. See Stephen Teo's interview.

24. See Stephen Teo's interview.

25. *Xiao Wu* garnered the 1998 Berlin Film Festival's Wolfgang Staudte Award, the 1998 Vancouver International Film Festival's Dragons and Tigers Award, and the San Francisco International Film Festival's ten-thousand-dollar best-film prize, and it was selected by the New Directors/New Films series, jointly presented by New York's Museum of Modern Art and the Lincoln Center.

26. Wang Hongwei was Jia's classmate at Beijing Film Academy. He was a student of film theory and was not trained as a professional actor. He was from a small town in Henan province. In Stephen Teo's interview with him, Jia laughed at the comment that Wang was his alter-ego and admitted that there was something of himself in the characters of Xiao Wu and Cui Mingliang, the leading man in *Platform*.

27. See "Director's Statement" about *Platform*, published together with Tony Rayns' interview online.

28. Yue Fei was a Song Dynasty general, a loyal and patriotic character in popular folk literature.

29. See my discussion of *Pirated Copy* in chapter 5 to see another instance where *Pulp Fiction* is referred to in a Chinese film.

30. See Tonglin Lu, "Trapped Freedom and Localized Globalism" in *From Underground to Independent: Alternative Film Culture in Contemporary China*, ed. Paul G. Pickowicz and Yingjin Zhang (Lanham, MD: Rowman & Littlefield, 2006), 139.

31. See Stephen Teo's interview with Jia Zhangke.

32. For a discussion of the similarity of these two films, see Li Xuewu's "Zuowei fangxiang huo xushu de 'shijie': Cong yingpian *Shijie* he *Biandan guniang* tanqi" (In a copied/narrated "world": Comparing *The World* and *So Close to Paradise*"), *Dangdai dianying* 4 (2005): 121–23.

33. See David Walsh, "Interview with Jia Zhang-ke, Director of *The World*," *World Socialist Web Site*, posted September 29, 2004, http://www.wsws.org/articles/2004/sep2004/int-s29.shtml (accessed May 23, 2008).

Conclusion

1. In 2005, Guo Xiaolu brought this film to Harvard where I discussed it with her. *The Concrete Revolution*, which won the Grand Prix at the International Human Rights Film Festival in Paris and the Special Jury Prize at the EBS International Documentary Film Festival in Seoul in the same year, explores the hardships of rural seasonal workers behind the glossy new façade of Beijing, which they built for China to present to the world.

2. Guo Xiaolu is also a versatile writer on many subjects. Her novels include *Village of Stone* (Random House, 2004) and *A Concise Chinese-English Dictionary for Lovers* (Random House, 2007).

3. For this narrative feature of concealment, see Mary Ann Farquhar, "The 'Hidden' Gender in *Yellow Earth*" in *Celluloid China: Cinematic Encounters with Culture and Society*, ed. Harry Kuoshu (Carbondale: Southern Illinois University Press, 2002), 220–32.

4. Valerie Jaffee, "Bringing the World to the Nation: Jia Zhangke and the Legitimation of Chinese Underground Film," *Senses of Cinema*, no. 32 (July–September 2004), http://archive.sensesofcinema.com/contents/04/32/jia_zhangke.html (accessed May 5, 2010).

5. Using Jaffee's examples, in 1993, while Zhang Yuan's *Beijing Bastard* and Wang Xiaoshuai's *The Days* inspired their contemporaries to go underground, Guan Hu's *Dirt* (1994) and Lou Ye's *Weekend Lovers* (1993) were produced within the system.

6. Chris Berry, "Independently Chinese: Duan Jinchuan, Jiang Yue, and Chinese Documentary," in *From Underground to Independent: Alternative Film Culture in Contemporary*

China, ed. Paul G. Pickowicz and Yingjin Zhang (Lanham, MD: Rowman & Littlefield, 2006), 119.

7. Ibid., 111.

8. Ibid., 120.

9. See Zheng Dongtian, "Dai yu wudai: Dui Zhongguo daoyan chuantong de yizhong miaoshu" (Generation and nongeneration: A depiction of Chinese film directing tradition), *Dangdai dianying* 1 (2006): 10–12.

10. See the postscript of Li Zehou's *Zhongguo xiandai sixiangshi lun* (*Discussion of Chinese contemporary intellectual history*; Hefei: Anhui wenyi chubanshe, 1999). Chinese film scholar Ni Zhen cited this idea of Li Zehou in his *Story of the Beijing Film Academy* (Beijing: Zuojia chubanshe, 2002) to justify the usage of filmmaking generations.

11. See Raymond Williams, *The Long Revolution* (London: Penguin, 1965), 63–88, and *Politics and Letters: Interviews with New Left Review* (London: New Left Books, 1979), 157–68.

SELECTED BIBLIOGRAPHY

Barbalet, Jack, ed. *Emotions and Sociology*. Oxford, UK: Blackwell Publishing, 2002.
Barber, Benjamin R. *Jihad vs. McWorld: How Globalism and Tribalism Are Reshaping the World*. New York: Ballantine Books, 1996.
Berry, Chris, ed. *Perspectives on Chinese Cinema*. London: BFI Publishing, 1991.
———. "*East Palace, West Palace*: Staging Gay Life in China." *Jump Cut* 42 (1998): 84–89.
Berry, Chris, and Mary Ann Farquhar. "Post-Socialist Strategies: An Analysis of *Yellow Earth* and *Black Cannon Incident*." In *Cinematic Landscapes: Observations on the Visual Arts and Cinema of China and Japan*. Ed. Linda C. Ehrlich and David Desser, 81–116. Austin: University of Texas Press, 1994.
Berry, Michael. *Speaking in Images: Interviews with Contemporary Chinese Filmmakers*. New York: Columbia University Press, 2005.
Bordwell, David. *Planet Hong Kong: Popular Cinema and the Art of Entertainment*. Cambridge, MA: Harvard University Press, 2000.
Chai Xiaofeng. "Huang Jianxin fangtan lu" (An interview with Huang Jianxin). *Dangdai dianying* 59 (1994): 37–45.
Chai Xiaofeng et al., eds. *Huang Jianxin: Nianqing de yanjing* (Huang Jianxin: Youthful eyes). Changsha: Hunan wenyi chubanshe, 1996.
Chaney, David. "From Ways of Life to Lifestyle: Rethinking Culture as Ideology and Sensibility." In *Culture in the Communication Age*, ed. James Lull, 75–88. London: Routledge, 2001.
Charney, Leo, and Vanessa Schwartz, eds. *Cinema and the Invention of Modern Life*. Berkeley: University of California Press, 1995.
Chen Kaiyan, ed. *"Heipao shijian": Cong xiaoshuo dao dianying* (*Black Cannon Incident*: From novella to film). Beijing: Zhongguo dianying chubanshe, 1988.
Chen Xiaoyun. "Gudu de chengshi: Chengshi dianying yanjiu zhiyi" (Lonely city: A study of city films). *Wenyi pinglun* 4 (1990): 84–89.
Chen Xihe, Shi Chuan, eds. *Duoyuan yujing zhong de xingsheng dai dianying* (New-born generation films in the context of complex discourses). Shanghai: Xuelin chubanshe, 2003.
Cheng Qingsong and Huang Ou, eds. *Wode sheyingji bu sahuang: Xianfeng dianyingren dangan—shengyu 1961–1970* (My camera doesn't lie: Dossiers of avant-garde filmmakers born between 1961 and 1970). Beijing: Zhongguo youyi chubanshe, 2002.
Chow, Rey, ed. *Modern Chinese Literary and Cultural Studies in the Age of Theory: Reimagining a Field*. Durham, NC: Duke University Press, 2000.
———. *Sentimental Fabulations, Contemporary Chinese Films*. New York: Columbia University Press, 2007.
Christopher, Nicholas. *Somewhere in the Night: Film Noir and the American City*. New York: Henry Holt and Company, 1997.
Connor, Steven. *Postmodernist Culture: An Introduction to Theories of the Contemporary*. Oxford, UK: Blackwell, 1989.

Cui, Shuqin. *Women through the Lens: Gender and Nation in a Century of Chinese Cinema*. Honolulu: University of Hawaii Press, 2003.

Dai Jinhua. "Xieta: Chongdu disidai" (Slanting tower: To reread the Fourth Generation). *Dianying yishu* 4 (1989): 3–13.

———. "Sisuo yu jianzheng: Huang Jianxin zuopin" (Contemplation and witnessing: Huang Jianxin's oeuvre). *Dangdai dianying* 59 (1994): 46–52.

———. "Geren xiezuo yu qingchun gushi" (Personal writing and story of youth). *Dianying yishu* 3 (1996): 10–12.

———. *Wuzhong fengjing: Zhongguo dianying wenhua 1978–1998* (Foggy sceneries: Chinese cinematic culture, 1978–1998). Beijing: Beijing daxue chubanshe, 2000.

———. *Cinema and Desire: Feminist Marxism and Cultural Politics in the Work of Dai Jinhua*. Ed. Jing Wang and Tani E. Barlow. London: Verso, 2002.

Davis, Deborah S., et al., eds. *Urban Spaces in Contemporary China: The Potential for Autonomy and Community in Post-Mao China*. Washington, DC: Woodrow Wilson Center Press; Cambridge, UK: Cambridge University Press, 1995.

Donald, Stephanie Hemelryk. *Public Secret, Public Spaces: Cinema and Civility in China*. Lanham, MD: Rowman & Littlefield Publishers, Inc., 2000.

Fei Xiaotong. *Xiangtu Zhongguo* (Earthbound China). Beijing: Sanlian shudian, 1985.

Foucault, Michel. *Language, Counter-Memory, Practice*. Ed. Donald F. Bouchard, 113–38. Ithaca, NY: Cornell University Press, 1977.

———. *Power/Knowledge: Selected Interviews and Other Writings*. Ed. Colin Gordon. New York: Pantheon Books, 1980.

Ge Fei. "Chongjian wenqing: Xia Gang dianying pingshu" (Reconstruct warmth: A comment on Xiangang's films). *Dianying yishu* 3(1994): 22–28.

Ge Hongbing, ed. *Shi xiaozi nüzuojia jiexi* (Analysis of ten female *xiaozi* writers). Vol. 1, *Fense de biaoqing* (Pink expressions); vol. 2, *Ganshang de landiao* (Sentimental blue tones). Beijing: wenhua yishu chubanshe, 2002.

———. *Wo de N zhong shenghuo* (My N-type life). Rev. ed. Haikou: Nanhai chubanshe, 2004.

Guo Xiaolu. *Dianying ditu* (A map of films). Shanghai: Shanghai wenyi chubanshe, 2001.

———. *Dianying lilun biji* (Notes on film theory). Guilin: Guangxi shifan daxue chubanshe, 2002.

Hall, Peter. *Cities in Civilization*. New York: Fromm International, 1998.

Han Xiaolei. "Dui diwudai de wenhua tuwei: Hou wudai de geren dianying xianxiang" (Getting beyond the Fifth Generation culture: Post–Fifth Generation individual filmmaking). *Dianying yishu* 2 (1995): 58–63.

———. "Tuwei hou de wenhua piaoyi" (Cultural disorientation after a breakthrough). Pts. 1 and 2. *Dianying yishu* 5 (1999): 58–65; 6 (1999): 51–54.

Harré, Rom, ed. *The Social Construction of Emotions*. Oxford, UK: Basil Blackwell, 1986.

Hinsch, Bret. *Passions of the Cut Sleeve: The Male Homosexual Tradition in China*. Berkeley: University of California Press, 1992.

Holtz, Geoffrey T. *Welcome to the Jungle: The Why behind "Generation X."* New York: St. Martin's Press, 1995.

Huang Jianxin. "*Heipao shijian* chuangzuo sikao" (Thoughts on shooting *Black Cannon Incident*). In *Heipao shijian: Cong xiaoshuo dao dianying* (*Black Cannon Incident*: From novella to film). Ed. Chen Kaiyan, 211–24. Beijing: Zhongguo dianying chubanshe, 1988.

———. "Dianying de meili" (Attraction of films). In *Huang Jianxin: Nianqing de yanjing* (Huang Jianxin: Youthful eyes). Ed. Chai Xiaofeng et al., 397–423. Changsha: Hunan wenyi chubanshe, 1996.

———. "Wo kan xijupian" (My understanding of comic film). *Dianying yishu* 3 (1999): 44–47.
Huang Shixian. "Yishixingtai zhenghou: Wang Shuo shi 'fanpan wenhua' de shimaoxing yu huihuaixing" (Ideological symptom: On Wang Shuo style "anti-culture"). *Dianying yishu* 6 (1989): 40–44.
Jiao Xiongping. *Fengyun jihui: Yu dangdai Zhongguo dianying duihua* (Meetings in wind-driven clouds: Dialogues with contemporary Chinese filmmakers). Taibei: Yuanliu chuban gongsi, 1998.
Jones, Andrew F. *Like a Knife: Ideology and Genre in Contemporary Chinese Popular Music*. Ithaca, NY: Cornell University Press, 1992.
Kirkby, Richard J. R. *Urbanization in China: Town and Country in a Developing Economy, 1949–2000 A.D.* New York: Columbia University Press, 1985.
Kotarba, Joseph A., and John M. Johnson, eds. *Postmodern Existential Sociology*. New York: Altamira Press, 2002.
Kuoshu, Harry. *Lightness of Being in China: Adaptation and Discursive Figuration in Cinema and Theater*. New York: Peter Lang, 1999.
———, ed. *Celluloid China: Cinematic Encounters with Culture and Society*. Carbondale: Southern Illinois University Press, 2002.
Lapsley, Robert, and Michael Westlake. *Film Theory: An Introduction*. Oxford, UK: Manchester University Press, 1988.
Lau, Jenny Kwok Wah, ed. *Multiple Modernities: Cinemas and Popular Media in Transcultural East Asia*. Philadelphia: Temple University Press, 2003.
Lee, Leo Ou-fan. *Shanghai Modern: The Flowering of a New Urban Culture in China, 1930–1945*. Cambridge, MA: Harvard University Press, 1999.
Lewis, John Wilson, ed. *The City in Communist China*. Stanford, CA: Stanford University Press, 1971.
Li Yiming. "Shiji zhimo: Shehui de daode weiji yu diwudai dianying de shouzhong zhengqin" (Century's end: Ethical crisis and the funeral for Fifth Generation filmmaking). Pts. 1 and 2. *Dianying yishu* 1 (1996): 9–13; 2 (1996): 24–28.
Li Zehou. *Zhongguo xiandai sixiangshi lun* (On the history of Chinese contemporary thought). Hefei: Anhui wenyi chubanshe, 1999.
Lim, Song Hwee. *Celluloid Comrades: Representations of Male Homosexuality in Contemporary Chinese Cinema*. Honolulu: University of Hawai'i Press, 2006.
Long Haiqiu. "Paihuai dushi: Tan jinqi de chengshi ticai yingpian" (Wandering in the city: On recent city films). *Yishu guangjiao* 2 (1989): 56–61.
Lynch, Kevin. *The Image of the City*. Cambridge, MA: Technology Press, 1960.
Lu, Sheldon H. *China, Transnational Visuality, Global Postmodernity*. Stanford, CA: Stanford University Press, 2001.
Lu, Sheldon H., and Emilie Yueh-yu Yeh, eds. *Chinese-Language Film: Historiography, Poetics, Politics*. Honolulu: University of Hawai'i Press, 2005.
Lu, Tonglin. *Confronting Modernity in the Cinemas of Taiwan and Mainland China*. Cambridge, UK: Cambridge University Press, 2002.
Lu Xinyu. *Jilu Zhongguo: Dangdai Zhonguo xin jilu yundong* (Documenting China: New documentary movement of contemporary China). Beijing: Sanlian shudian, 2003.
Lull, James, ed. *Culture in the Communication Age*. London: Routledge, 2001.
Lyotard, J. F. *The Postmodern Condition*. Manchester, UK: Manchester University Press, 1984.
McGrath, Jason. *Postsocialist Modernity: Chinese Cinema, Literature, and Criticism in the Market Age*. Stanford, CA: Stanford University Press, 2008.
Miles, Malcolm, et al., eds. *The City Cultures Reader*. London: Routledge, 2000.

Ni Zhen. "Shouwang xinshengdai" (Expecting the new generation). *Dianying yishu* 4 (1999): 70–73.

——. *Beijing dianying xueyuan gushi: Diwudai dianying qianshi* (Beijing Film Academy story: The early history of the Fifth Generation filmmaking). Beijing: Zuojia chubanshe, 2002.

Pang, Laikwan. *Building a New China in Cinema: The Chinese Left-Wing Cinema Movement, 1932–1937.* Lanham, MD: Rowman & Littlefield Publishers, Inc., 2002.

Pickowicz, Paul. "Huang Jianxin and the Notion of Postsocialism." In *New Chinese Cinemas: Forms, Identities, Politics*, ed. Nick Browne et al., 57–87. Cambridge, UK: Cambridge University Press, 1994.

Pickowicz, Paul, and Yingjin Zhang, eds. *From Underground to Independent: Alternative Film Culture in Contemporary China.* Lanham, MD: Rowman & Littlefield Publishers, Inc., 2006.

Qiu Zhengyi, ed. *Shanghai shishang ditu* (Fashion atlas of Shanghai). Shanghai: Hanyu dacidian chubanshe, 2002.

Reddy, William M. *The Navigation of Feeling.* Cambridge, UK: Cambridge University Press, 2001.

Rowe, Colin, and Fred Koetter. *Collage City.* Cambridge, MA: MIT Press, 1978.

Rushkoff, Douglas. *The GenX Reader.* New York: Ballantine Books, 1994.

Sennett, Richard, ed. *Classic Essays on the Culture of Cities.* Englewood Cliffs, NJ: Prentice-Hall, 1969.

——. *The Fall of Public Man.* New York: Alfred A. Knopf, 1977.

Shields, Stephanie A. *Speaking from the Heart: Gender and the Social Meaning of Emotion.* Cambridge, UK: Cambridge University Press, 2002.

Shih, Shu-mei. *The Lure of the Modern: Writing Modernism in Semicolonial China, 1917–1932.* Berkeley: University of California Press, 2001.

Silbergeld, Jerome. *Hitchcock with a Chinese Face: Cinematic Doubles, Oedipal Triangles, and China's Moral Voice.* Seattle: University of Washington Press, 2004.

Sit, Victor F. S., ed. *Chinese Cities: The Growth of the Metropolis since 1949.* Oxford, UK: Oxford University Press, 1985.

Soja, Edward W. *Postmodern Geographies: The Reassertion of Space in Critical Social Theory.* London: Verso, 1989.

Stam, Robert, Robert Burgoyne, and Sandy Flitterman-Lewis. *New Vocabularies in Film Semiotics: Structuralism, Post-Structuralism, and Beyond.* London: Routledge, 1992.

Stokes, Lisa Odham, and Michael Hoover. *City on Fire: Hong Kong Cinema.* London: Verso, 1999.

Swingewood, Alan. *Cultural Theory and the Problem of Modernity.* New York: St. Martin's Press, 1998.

Tang, Xiaobing. *Chinese Modern: The Heroic and the Quotidian.* Durham, NC: Duke University Press, 2000.

Tangney, June Price, and Kurt W. Fisher, eds. *Self Conscious Emotions.* New York: Guilford Press, 1995.

Wallace, Claire, and Sijka Kovatcheva. *Youth in Society: The Construction and Deconstruction of Youth in East and West Europe.* New York: St. Martin's Press, 1998.

Wang Anyi. *Xunzhao Shanghai* (In search of Shanghai). Shanghai: Xuelin chubanshe, 2001.

Wang, Jing. *High Culture Fever: Politics, Aesthetics, and Ideology in Deng's China.* Berkeley: University of California Press, 1996.

Wang Liaonan. "Shisu shenhua: Muqian chengshi dianying de pingge pinggu" (Worldly mythology: An evaluation of the current city films). *Yishu guangjiao* 2 (1989): 49–55.

Wang Hui. "Dangdai dianying zhong de xiangtu yu dushi" (City and countryside in contemporary films). *Dianying yishu* 2 (1989): 12–19.

Wang Shuo. *Wang Shuo wenji* (Selections of Wang Shuo). Ed. Sun Bo and Du Jianye. 4 vols. Beijing: Huayi chubanshe, 1992.

———. *Wang Shuo zi xuan ji* (Wang Shuo's self-selected novels). Beijing: Huayi chubanshe, 1998.

———. *Wuzhizhe wuwei* (One who has no knowledge has no fear). Shengyang: Chunfeng wenyi chubanshe, 2000.

———. *Suibi ji* (Random essays). Kunming: Yunnan reming chubanshe, 2004.

Wang Shuo and Lao Xia. *Meiren zeng wo menghanyao* (The beauty presents me with the knockout drugs). Wuhan: Changjiang wenyi chubanshe, 2000.

Wang Yichuan. "'Wudaiqi' zhongguo dianying" (Chinese film in a nongenerational era). *Dangdai dianying* 5 (1994): 20–27.

Wang, Yuejin. "The Rhetoric of Mirror, Shadow, and Moon: *Samsara* and the Problem of Representation of Self in China." *East-West Film Journal* 5, no. 2 (1991): 69–92.

Wei Hui. *Shanghai baobei* (Shanghai baby). Shenyang: Chunfeng wenyi chubanshe, 1999.

Whyte, Martin King, and William L. Parish. *Urban Life in Contemporary China*. Chicago: University of Chicago Press, 1984.

Williams, Raymond. *The Long Revolution*. London: Penguin, 1965.

———. *The Country and the City*. New York: Oxford University Press, 1973.

———. *Problems of Materialism and Culture*. London: Verso, 1981.

Willis, Paul, et al. *Common Culture: Symbolic Work at Play in the Everyday Cultures of the Young*. Boulder, CO: Westview Press, 1990.

Wu Liang et al., eds. *Richang Zhongguo* (Everyday China). 5 vols. Nanjing: Jiangsu meishu chubanshe, 1999.

Xia Gang, "Guanyu dushi de huati" (On topics about the metropolis). *Dangdai dianying* 4 (1997): 89–90.

Yang Binhua, ed. *Shanghai weidao* (The aura of Shanghai). Changchun: Shidai wenyi chubanshe, 2002.

Yang, Mayfair Mei-hui. *Gifts, Favors, and Banquets: The Art of Social Relationships in China*. Ithaca, NY: Cornell University Press, 1994.

Ying Xiong. "Cong fengge dao pingpai: Guanyu Xia Gang dianying" (From style to quality: On Xia Gang film). *Dianying yishu* 3(1994): 17–21.

Yu Jin. *Kuanhuan jijie: liuxing yinyue shiji biaofeng* (Carnival: A century's storm of popular music). Guangzhou: Guangdong renmin chubanshe, 1999.

Zha, Jianying. *China Pop: How Soap Operas, Tabloids, and Bestsellers Are Transforming a Culture*. New York: New Press, 1995.

Zhang, Li. *Strangers in the City: Reconfigurations of Space, Power, and Social Networks within China's Floating Population*. Stanford, CA: Stanford University Press, 2001.

Zhang Yingjin. *The City in Modern Chinese Literature and Film: Configurations of Space, Time, and Gender*. Stanford, CA: Stanford University Press, 1996.

———, ed. *Cinema and Urban Culture in Shanghai, 1922–1943*. Stanford, CA: Stanford University Press, 1999.

Zhang Yiwu. "Hou xinshiqi Zhongguo dianying: Fenlie de tiaozhan" (Chinese film in the post-new era: The challenge of fragmentation). *Dangdai dianying* 5 (1994): 4–11.

———. "'Kandie de yidai' de jueqi" (The rise of the "disc-watching generation"). *Dangdai dianying* 5 (2002): 20–21.

Zhang Zhen, ed. *The Urban Generation: Chinese Cinema and Society at the Turn of the Twenty-first Century.* Durham, NC: Duke University Press, 2007.

Zuo Shula. "Cong 'diliu dai' dianying dao *Wushan yunyu*" (From the Sixth Generation to *In Expectation*). *Dianying yishu* 3 (1996): 80–83.

SELECTED FILMOGRAPHY, BY DIRECTOR

The names of state film studios are shortened. *Beijing*, for example, stands for Beijing Film Studio. Names of newly incorporated state film companies, of private film companies associated or affiliated with the state studio system, and of international film corporations are recorded in full. Producers of some films made outside the state studio system later purchased the endorsement of state studios (and submitted to state censorship conducted through these studios) to get into the official distribution system. For these films, I first list them as "independent" and then list, if available, any studios or companies that have either invested in or purchased the distribution of these films.

Ah Nian
A Chinese Moon (Zhongguo yueliang, 1995), Fujian
Love in the Winter (Dongri aiqing, 1997), Zhejiang
Call Me (Hu wo, 2000), Beijing / Zhongguo dianying gongsi

An Zhanjun
The Ordinary People's Life (Meili de jia, 2002), Beijing Forbidden City Film
The Parking Attendant in July (Kancheren de qiyue, 2003), China Film Group

Chen Yusu
Shanghai Panic (Women haipa, 2001), independent (based on Mianmian's Internet novel of the same title)

Cheung, Mabel
Beijing Rocks (Beijing yue yu lu, 2001), Media Asia Group (Hong Kong)

Cui Zi'en
The Old Testament (Jiu yue, 2002), independent (digital video [DV])
Feeding Boys, Ayaya (Aiyaya qu puru, 2003), independent (DV)

Feng Xiaogang
Angels in Black (Qingyi shizhe, aka Yongshi wo ai, 1994), Beijing
Dreams Come True, aka *Party A, Party B* (Jiafang yifang, 1997), Beijing
Be There or Be Square (Bujian busan, 1998), Beijing Youth Film / Forbidden City Film
Sorry, Baby (Mei wan mei liao, 1999), Forbidden City Film
A Sigh (Yisheng tanxi, 2000), Beijing
Big Shot's Funeral (Dawan, 2001), China Film Group / Huayi Brothers & Taihe Film Investment Co. / Columbia Pictures Film Production Asia Limited
Cellphone (Shouji, 2004), China Film Group / Huayi Brothers & Taihe Film Investment Co. / Columbia Pictures Film Production Asia Limited

Fu Jinsheng
Agreed Not to Separate (Shuohao bu fenshou, 1999), Shanghai Paradise Film and Television Group

Gao Xiaosong
Where Have All the Flowers Gone (Nashi hua kai, 2000), Xi'an / Beijing DMVE Culture Development Co.

Guan Hu
Dirt (Toufa luanle, aka Zangren, 1994), independent: Neimeng
The Street Rhapsody (Langman jietou, 1996), Beijing
Midnight Walker (Yexing ren, 1998), Dream Factory
Farewell Our 1948 (Zaijian women de yijiusiba, 1999), Beijing / Liaoning Beifang Film Studio
Eyes of Beauty (Xishi yan, 2002), China Film Group / Tourist Development Company of the City of Zhuji

Guo Xiaolu
Concrete Revolution (Qianru routi de chengshi, 2005), independent, documentary

He Jianjun (aka He Yi, Zhao Jisong)
Self Portrait (Zihua xiang, 1991), a short documentary
Red Beans, aka *Suspended Love* (Xuanlian, 1993), independent: Fortissimo Film Sales
Postman (Youchai, 1995), independent: Hubert Bals Fund
Scenery (Fengjing, 1999), independent
Butterfly Smile (Hudie de weixiao, 2001), Beijing / CCTV Movie Channel / China Film Group Co.
Pirated Copy (Manyan, 2004), independent: Hubert Bals Fund of International Film Festival Rotterdam

Hu Xueyang
The Stay-Behind Wife (Liushou nüshi, 1991), Shanghai
Drowning (Yanmo de qingchun, 1994), Shanghai

Huang Jianxin
Black Cannon Incident (Heipao shijian, 1985), Xi'an
Dislocation (Cuowei, 1986), Xi'an
Samsara (Lunhui, 1988), Xi'an
Stand Up, Don't Grovel (Zhan zhi le, bie pa xia, 1992), Xi'an
Back to Back, Face to Face (Bei kao bei, lian dui lian, 1994), Xi'an / Senxin yule gongsi
Signal Left, Turn Right (Da zuodeng, xiang you zhuan, aka Hongdeng xing, lüdeng ding, 1995), Xi'an
Surveillance (Maifu, 1996), Xiaoxiang
Mr. Wu: A Police Story (Shui bu zhao, 1997), Xi'an
Something about Secret (Shuochu nide mimi, 1999), Zhejiang
The Marriage Certificate (Shei shuo wo bu zaihu, 2001), Xi'an / Forbidden City Film / Shanxi Jinhua
Gimme Kudos (Qiuqiu ni, biaoyang wo, 2005), Media Asia Films / Beijing Forbidden City Film / Taihe Film Investment / Happy Pictures Culture Communication

Huo Jianqi
The Winner (Yingjia, 1995), Beijing / Hongzhou
Postmen in the Mountains (Na shan, na ren, na gou, 1998), Xiaoxiang / Beijing / Hunan Postal Office

Blue Love (Lanse aiqing, 2000), Beijing / China Film Group / Dianying pingdao jiemu zhongxin
Life Show (Shenghuo xiu, 2002), the Second Studio of China Film Group
A Time to Love (Qingren jie, 2005), Beida xingguang jituan / China Film Group

Jia Zhangke
Xiao Shan Goes Home (Xiao Shan huijia, 1995), independent
Xiao Wu, aka *Artisan Pickpocket* (Xiao Wu, 1997), independent: Hutong Communication / Radiant Advertising
Platform (Zhan tai, 2000), independent: distributed by Ad vitam (France) and Primer Plano (Argentina)
Unknown Pleasures (Ren xiaoyao, 2002), independent: distributed by e-picture (France), Bitters End and Office Kitano (Japan) and New Yorker Films (USA)
The World (Shijie, 2004), Shanghai / Xinghui Inc. (Hong Kong)

Jiang Wen
In the Heat of the Sun (Yangguang canlan de rizi, 1994), Hong Kong Dragon Film / China Film Coproduction Corporation

Jiang Xiaozhen
X-Roads (Xin shizi jietou, 2001), Shanghai

Jin Chen
Love in the Internet Age (Wangluo shidai de aiqing, 1998), Xi'an
Chrysanthemum Tea (Juhua cha, 2000), Xi'an / Shan'xi Hengtai Group Production

Jin Ge
Wilderness of Youth (Qingchun kuangye, 2003), Xiaoxiang / Beijing Today's Generation Co.

Li Chunbo
Don't Cry, Girl (Nühai bieku, 2002), China Film Group / Beijing

Li Shaohong
Bloody Dawn (Xuese qingchen, 1990), Beijing
Family Portrait (Sishi buhuo, 1992), Beijing / Era (Hong Kong)
Blush (Hong fen, 1994), Beijing / Ocean Film Corp.
Happiness Ave. (Xingfu dajie, 1998), Beijing
Baober in Love (Lianai zhong de Baobei, 2004), Beijing rongxinda yingshi yishu zhongxin

Li Xin
Dazzling (Hua yan, 2001), Shanghai / New Generation Film and TV Co.
Master of Everything (Ziyu zile, 2004), Shanghai / Yindu jigou Co. / New Generation Film and TV Co.

Li Yang
Dead Wells, aka *Blind Shaft* (Mang jing, 2003), independent: Li Yang-Tang Splendour Films Limited / Bronze Age Films Co.

Li Yu
Fish and Elephant (Jinnian xiatian, 2001), independent: Cheng Yong Productions

Liu Bingjian
Men, Men, Women, Women (Nan nan nü nü, 1999), independent: The Apsaras Film & TV Production Company

Liu Hao
Chen Mo and Meiting (Chen Mo yu Meiting, 2002), independent: Liu Hao and Zero Film

Liu Xin
Captives of Love (Zhengjiu aiqing, 2000), Shanghai Paradise Film and TV Group / Beijing Yingda Cultural Communication Co.
38°C (Sanshiba du, 2003), E'mei / Jiangsu Cultural Products Development Co. / Beijing Jinma Visual Culture Co.

Lou Jian
Fathers (Hongse niandai, 2001), Beijing Gudu / Nanjing / Changzhou TV

Lou Ye
Weekend Lovers (Zhoumo qingren, 1993), Fujian
Don't Be Young, aka *The Girl in Danger* (Weiqing shaonü, 1994), Shanghai / Longwei zhipian gongsi
Suzhou River (Suzhou he, 2000), independent: Essential Film / Dream Factory
Purple Butterfly (Zi hudie, 2003), Shanghai Film Group / Shanghai / Dream Factory

Lu Chuan
The Missing Gun (Xun qiang, 2002), China Film Group / Huayi Brothers

Lu Xuechang
The Making of Steel, aka *How Steel Is Forged* (Zhangda chengren, aka Gangtie shi zheyang liancheng de, 1996), Beijing
A Lingering Face (Feichang xiari, 1999), Beijing / Zhongguo dianying gongsi / Dianying pingdao jiemu zhongxin
Cala, My Dog (Kala shi tiao gou, 2003), Huayi Brothers / Taihe Film Investment Co. Ltd.

Ma Ling
Don't Go, I Love You (Bie zou, wo ai ni, 2003), Yunnan television / Beijing Ma Ling wenhua yishu youxian gongsi

Meng Jinghui
Chicken Poets (Xiang jimao yiyang fei, 2002), Shanghai

Mi Jiashan
The Trouble Shooters, aka *Masters of Mischief* (Wanzhu, 1988), Emei

Ning Ying
For Fun (Zhao le, 1992), Beijing / Vanke Film and Television (Hong Kong)
On the Beat (Minjing gushi, 1995), Beijing / Eurasia Communications Ltd.
I Love Beijing (Xiari nuan yangyang, 2001), Beijing
Railroad of Hope (Xiwang zhi lü, 2002), independent: Eurasia Communications Ltd., documentary

Peng Xiaolian
Three Women, aka *A Story of Women* (Nüren de gushi, 1989), Shanghai
Shanghai Women (Jiazhuang mei ganjue, 2002), Shanghai

Shanghai Story (Meili Shanghai, 2004), Shanghai dianying jituan gongsi / Shanghai Tangchen

Sheng Zhimin
Two Hearts (Xin xin, 2002), independent

Shi Runjiu
A Beautiful New World (Meili xin shijie, 1998), Xi'an / Imar
All the Way (Zou dao di, 2000), Xi'an / Imar

Sun Zhou
Add Sugar to Coffee (Gei kafei jia dian'r tang, 1988), Zhujiang
Breaking the Silence (Piaoliang mama, 1999), Zhujian / Guangdong sanjiu yingye

Tang Danian
City Paradise (Dushi tiantang, 1999), independent

Teng Huatao
Sky of Love (Qing qian yixian, 2003), China Film Corporation / Beijing / Hong Kong One Hundred Year Co.

Tian Zhuangzhuang
Rock Kids (Yaogun qingnian, 1988), Beijing Qingnian
Blue Kite (Lan fengzheng, 1993), Beijing / Longwick Film (Hong Kong)
Springtime in a Small Town (Xiaocheng zhi chun, 2002), Beijing / China Film Group / Beijing rongxinda yingshi yishu zhongxin

Wang Chao
The Orphan of Anyang (Anyang ying'er, 2002), independent: Les Films Du Paradoxe

Wang Guangli
I Have Graduated (Wo biye le, 1992), independent, documentary
Maiden Work (Chunü zuo, 1998), independent
Go for Broke (Heng shu heng, 2001), Shanghai / East Line Entertainment and Media

Wang Quan'an
Lunar Eclipse (Yue shi, 1999), independent: Beijing
The Story of Ermei (Jingzhe, 2003), Xi'an / Beijing Silk-Road Production

Wang Rui
After Divorce (Li le hun jiu bie lai zhao wo, 1995), Beijing Qingnian / Wanzhong jituan
The Flying Leopard (Chongtian feibao, 1999), Beijing Qingnian / Movie Channel

Wang Xiaoshuai
The Days (Dong chun de rizi, 1993), independent
Frozen (Jidu hanleng, 1997), released under the pseudonym Wu Ming (anonymous), independent: Winstar Cinema
So Close to Paradise (Biandan, guniang, 1997), independent: Beijing / Beijing jindie yingshi yishu zhizuo zhongxin
Suburban Dreams, aka *The House* (Menghuan tianyuan, aka Fangzi, 1999), Beijing / Movie Channel / China Film
Beijing Bicycle (Shiqi sui de danche, 2001), independent: Arc Light Films / Pyramid Productions
Drifters (Er di, 2003), independent: People's Workshop / Purple Lights Film (Hong Kong)

Wu Di
Yellow Goldfish (Huang jinyu, 1996), independent: Vancouver International Film Festival

Xia Gang
Half Flame, Half Brine (Yiban huoyan, yiban haishui, 1988), Beijing
Passionate Encounter (Zao yu jiqing, 1990), Beijing
My Heart's Not Changed (Woxin yijiu, 1991), Beijing
After Separation (Da saba, 1992), Beijing
No One Cheers (Wuren hecai, 1993), Beijing / Yanming guoji youxian gongsi
To Be with You till Dawn (Banni dao liming, 1995), Beijing / Beijing Biaoqi
Yesterday's Wine (Yu wangshi ganbei, aka Youle suiyue, 1996), Beijing
Life as a Song (Shengming ru ge, 1997), Beijing
A Country Boy in Shanghai (Boli shi touming de, 1999), Beijing
Who Might be Listening (Shei lai qingting, 2000), Beijing
Love at First Sight (Yijian zhongqing, 2002), Beijing Forbidden City Film / Beiying jituan gongsi er fenchang

Xie Fei
Black Snow (Benming nian, 1989), Beijing Qingnian

Xu Jinglei
My Father and I (Wo he baba, 2003), Beijing yinian wenhua fazhan gongsi / Beijing huayi lianmeng wenhua chuanmei touzi gongsi / China Film Group
Letter from an Unknown Woman (Yige mosheng nüren de laixin, 2005), Asian Union Film and Media

Yang Yazhou
A Tree in the House (Meishi tou zhe le, 1998), Xi'an

Yu Zhong
Far from Home (Wo de meili xiangchou, 2003), Forbidden City Film / Beijing sihai zongheng wenhua fazhan youxian gongsi / Beijing tianshi wenhua youxian gongsi

Zhang Ming
In Expectation, aka *Rain Clouds over Mount Wu* (Wushan yunyu, 1996), Beijing / Beijing dongfang dadi wenhua fazhan youxian gongsi
Weekend Plot (Miyu shiqi xiaoshi, 2000), Nei Menggu / Earth Film (Nitu dianying gongzuo zu) / Guangdong Juxing Film Co.

Zhang Nuanxin
Good Morning, Beijing (Beijing ni zao, 1990), Beijing Qingnian

Zhang Tielin
The Chair (Yizi, 2002), Sunfair Production Limited

Zhang Yang
Spicy Love Soup (Aiqing ma la tang, 1997), Xi'an
Shower (Xizao, 1999), Imar
Quitting (Zuotian, 2001), Imar

Zhang Yibai
Spring Subway (Kaiwang chuntian de ditie, 2002), China Youth / Beijing Electric Orange Entertainment

Zhang Yimou
Keep Cool (You hua haohao shuo, 1996), Guangxi
Happy Times (Xingfu shiguang, 2000), Guangxi

Zhang Yuan
Mother (Mama, 1990), independent: Xi'an
Beijing Bastards (Beijing zazhong, 1992), independent: Beijing Bastards Group / Hubert Bals funds of the Film Festival Rotterdan
Sons (Erzi, 1995), independent
East Palace, West Palace, aka *Behind the Forbidden City* (Dong gong, xi gong, 1996), independent: Quelqu'un d'Autre Productions
Crazy English (Fengkuang yingyu, 1999), documentary
Seventeen Years (Guonian huijia, 1999), Xi'an
I Love You (Wo ai ni, 2002), Xi'an / Jewel Film Investment Co. / Beijing Asian Union Film Ltd.
Green Tea (Lü cha, 2003), Beijing Asian Union Film Ltd.

Zhaoyan Guozhang
A Dream of Youth (Qia tongxue shaonian, 2002), China Film Group / Beijing jialan yingshi wenhua yishu youxian gongsi

Zheng Dongtian
Mandarin Ducks (Yuanyang lou, 1987), Beijing Qingnian

Zhu Chuanming
Working for Films (Qunzhong yanyuan, 2001), independent, documentary

INDEX

Page numbers in italics denote illustrations.

Abandoned Capital, The, 239n.31
After Separation (Da saba), *1*, 80–82, 232n.6
Ah Nian, 166, 194–95, 218
Ah Q, 52
American complex, 33–34
An Zhanjun, 166
Andersen, Hans Christian, 160
Angels in Black (Qingyi shizhe), 127–28, 129
Apollonian, 2–3, 136

Back to Back, Face to Face (Bei kao bei, lian dui lian), 47, 59–61, 62
Bai Yang, 23–24, 227n.1
Baober in Love (Lianai zhong de Baobei), 89, 91–95
Barber, Benjamin, 132, 138–39, 165
Barden, Christopher, 103, 180n.49
Be There or Be Square (Bujian busan), 73
Beautiful as Ever (Meiren yijiu), 136
Beautiful New World, A (Meili xin shijie), 166, 199–200, 243n.16
Beckett, Samuel, 189
Beijing Bastards (Beijing zazhong), 17, 106–17, 121, 171, 173, 196
Beijing Bicycle (Shiqi sui de danche), 165, 166–68, 196–98, 199
Beijing Rocks (Beijing yue yu lu), 20, 118, 122–24
Benedict, R., 136
Berry, Chris, 213–14, 233n.26
Bertolucci, Bernardo, 21, 99
Bethune, Norman, 82
Bicycle Thief, The, 166–67
Big Shot's Funeral (Dawan), 20–21, 73–74
Black Cannon Incident (Heipao shijian), 46, 48, 49–53, 56
Black Snow (Benming nian), 39
Blind Chance, 150

Bloody Dawn (Xuese qingchen), 89–91, 94
Blooming Jessamine (Moli hua kai), 136
Blue Kite (Lan fengzheng), 42
Blue Love (Lanse aiqing), 96–98, 217
Blush (Hong fen), 89
Bordwell, David, 154–56
Breaking the Silence (Piaoliang mama), 11, 168
Bumming in Beijing: The Last Dreamers (Liulang Beijing: zuihou de mengxiangzhe), 175
Butterfly Smile (Hudie de weixiao), 140, 142

Cala, My Dog (Kala shi tiao gou), 166
Call Me (Hu wo), 166, 194–95
Cao Yu, 144–46, 238n.16
Captives of Love (Zhengjiu aiqing), 134–35
Center Stage (Ruan Lingyu), 33
Chan, Fruit, 162, 242n.42
Chaney, David, 18, 97, 137
Chaplin, Charlie, *158*, 163–65
Chen Kaige, 42, 72, 73–74, 78, 94, 218
Chen Mo and Meiting (Chen Mo yu Meiting), 165
Chen Xiaoming, 186
Chen Xiaoyun, 4
Cheng Bugao, 27
Cheng Naishan, 29
Cheung, Mabel, 20, 118, 122–24, 236n.24
Chi Li, 129
Chicken Poets (Xiang jimao yiyang fei), 14
Chinese (Happy) New Year film, 26, 73, 191, 228n.4
Christopher, Nicholas, 152
Chronicle of Death Foretold, 89
Chungking Express (Chungqing senlin), 152, 154–56
Citizen Kane, 168–71

city (chengshi, dushi), 3, 4, 8, 9, 15, 19, 21, 37–39, 47, 55–56, 90–91, 93, 125, 150, 152, 154, 156, 191, 192, 194, 200, 216; of Beijing, 19, 78, 99, 162; and countryside, 2–4, 8, 13–15, 16, 26–27, 37–39, 90, 192, 195–96, 198; of Guangzhou, 118–19; of Shanghai, 8, 25–26, 27–28, 33, 150, 193, 199, 227n.2; of Wuhan, 198
City Lights (Chaplin), *158*, 163–65
City Night (Chengshi zhi ye), 26, 41
City Paradise (Dushi tiantang), 166, 195–96
City Scenery (Dushi fengguang), 26–27
Clark, Candace, 137
comic talk show (xiangsheng), 70, 81
common culture, 7, 10–13, 14
Concrete Revolution, The (Qianru routi de chengshi), 211–12, 244n.1
Confucius (Kong fuzi), 41
Country Boy in Shanghai, A (Boli shi touming de), 78, 166, *188*, 191, 192–94
Country People (Xiangmin), 38–39, 90
Crossroads (Shizi jietou), 23–24, 25–26, 28, 30–32, 39, 228n.13
Cui Jian, 37, 117, 119, 124–26, 170, 171–72, 191
Cui, Shuqin, 135
Cui Zi'en, 175–76, 240n.27

Dai Jinhua, 3, 4, 33, 38, 115–16, 175, 186
Davis, Deborah, 21
Days (Dong Chun de rizi), 111
Dazzling (Huayan), *134*, 146–50, 185
De Sica, Vittorio, 166
Deng Gang, 58
Deng Guanghui, 149
Dionysian, 136, 137
Dirt (Toufa luanle), 20, *106*, 111, 112, 118–22, 149, 236n.21
Dislocation (Cuowei), 45, 46, 48–49, 56, 57
documentary aesthetics (jishi meixue), 11, 172
Dog Fight (Quan sha), 87
Don't Be Young (Weiqing shaonü), 186
Don't Cry, Girl (Nühai bieku), 191
Donzoko, 229n.19
Dou Wei, 170
Doyle, Christopher, 131–32
Dreams Come True (Jiafang yifang), 109

Dream of Youth, A (Qia tongxue shaonian), 143–46
Drowning (Yanmo de qingchun), 120–21
Dumas *fils*, 31
Durian, Durian (Liulian piaopiao), 162

East Palace, West Palace (Donggong xigong), 178–82, 241n.41
elite culture, 6, 17, 27, 42, 126
Emperor Jones, 145
everyday life, 7–15, 22, 28–29, 33, 38, 47, 59, 74, 75, 80, 93, 99, 101, 104, 108, 111, 123, 125, 135, 149, 151, 157, 167, 182, 192, 200, 213

Fallen Angels (Duoluo tianshi, 1995), 150
Family Portrait (Sishi buhuo), 89
Far from Home (Wo de meili xiangchou), 191
Faustian, 2–3
Fei Mu, 24, 26, 39–42, 43, 70, 215, 230n.27
Fei Xiaotong, 223n.6
Feng Gong, 57, 65, 67
Feng Xiaogang, 20, 67, 73–76, 109, 127–28, 129, 135
film noir, 152–53, 157, 243n.14
Fischer, Kurt W., 136
Fish and Elephant (Jinnian xiatian), 178–82
flâneur, 47, 231n.1
Flowers of Shanghai (Hai shang hua), 43
For Fun (Zhao le), 99
Foucault, Michel, 6, 19, 100

Gao Qi, 119
Ge Hongbing, 16–17, 85, 227n.42
Ge You, 73, 74, 81, 109
Generation, of Chinese filmmaking, 6, 214–16, 223n.1, 224n.16; Fourth, 3, 37–39,15, 27; Fifth, 1, 12, 42, 182–83; Later Fifth, 76–77, 218; Post-Fifth, 12–13, 19, 185, 218; Sixth, 5, 107, 111, 115–16, 218, 224n.16
Generation X, 115–16, 133
German School, 2, 3, 16, 223n.3
Giannetti, Louis, 184
Gibbon, Edward, 9
Gimme Kudos (Qiuqiu ni, biaoyang wo), 47, 69
Go for Broke (Heng shu heng, 2001), 11, 166, 174–78

Good Morning, Beijing (Beijing, nizao), 23, 34–39, 169, 182–83
Gorky, Maxim, 229n.19
grand narrative, 1, 6, 12, 16, 28, 72, 74, 75, 149
Green Tea (Lü cha), 128, 130–33, 171
Guan Hu, 20, *106*, 111, 118–22
Guanzhong Swordsmen II (Guanzhong daoke xuji), 68
Guo Xiaolu, 211–12, 244n.2

Half Flame, Half Brine (Yiban shi haishui, Yiban shi huoyan), 78, 109
Han Xiaolei, 112
Happy Times (Xingfu shiguang), 74, *158*, 163–66
Haraszti, Miklós, 162
Havis, Richard James, 94
He Jianjun (aka Zhao Jisong), 111, 139–43, 167, 230n.34, 238n.12, 238n. 13
He Yong, 124
Heavy Gasps (Da chuanqi), 109, 113
Heidegger, Martin, 189–90
Hero (Yingxiong), 42
heterotopia, 19, 21–22
Hitchcock, Alfred, 152
Hollywood, 31, 32, 33, 42, 63, 68, 72, 83, 139, 161, 198, 217, 226
Horse Thief (Daoma zei), 42, 95, 185, 213, 234n.41
Hou Dejian, 191
Hu Bingliu, 38–39, 90
Hu Jun, 241n.41
Hu Xueyang, 72, 82–83, 120–21
Huang Jianxin, 20, *45*, 78, 94, 109, 113, 185, 217, 218
Huang Jianzhong, 185
Huang Shixian, 186
humanism, 3, 12, 15, 17, 58,
Huo Jianqi, 74, 76, 95–99, 218

I Have Graduated (Wo biye le), 175
I Love Beijing (Xiari nuan yangyang), 99, 101–4, 166, *211*, 234n.49
I Love You (Wo ai ni), 128–30
Imar Film Studio, 168, 240n.13, 243n.16
In Expectation (Wushan yunyu), 111, 200–202

In the Heat of the Sun (Yangguang canlan de rizi), 67, 115–16, 128, 207, 235n.16
In the Mood for Love (Hua yang nianhua), 43
independent filmmaking, 5, 11, 17, 175, 213, 240n.27, 241n.30
Italian Neorealism, 152, 160–61, 166–67, 168, 171, 214

Jaffee, Valerie, 213
Jia Hongsheng, 35, 154, 168–69, 229n.18, 240n.16
Jia Pingwa, 239n.31
Jia Zhangke, 20, 147, 156, 160, 167, 170, 171, 177, 184–85, 201, 203–10, 213
Jiang Wen, 67, 116, 125, 128, 130, 189
Jiang Wu, 199–200
Jiang Xiaozhen, 23, 24, 32–33, 218
Jin Yong, 125
Ju Xue, 127

Keep Cool (You hua haohao shuo), 110
Kieslowski, Krzysztof, 150
Kovatcheva, Sijka, 107
Kraicer, Shelly, 43
Kundera, Milan, 114
Kurosawa, Akira, 74, 229n.19
Kwan, Stanley, 33

Lady of the Camellias, The, 31
Lai, Linda Chiu-han, 21–22, 231n.1
Lao She, 196–97
Lao Tzu, 189
Last Emperor, The, 21, 99
Last Love (Zuihou de ai, zuichu de ai), 18
Leaving Las Vegas, 173
Leaving Me, Loving You (Dacheng xiaoshi), 18
Lee, Ang, 180
Lefebvre, Henri, 19
leftist filmmaking (production), 6, 24, 28, 31, 32, 44, 165
Lennon, John, 169
Les Bas-fonds, 229n.19
Letter from an Unknown Woman (Yige mosheng nüren de laixin), 136
Li Chunbo, 191
Li, H. C., 52

Li Liuyi, 145
Li Shaohong, 76, 89–95, 218, 233n.28
Li Xin, *134*, 135, 146–50, 185, 218
Li Yiming, 12–13, 110–11, 114–15
Li Yu, 178–82
Li Zehou, 215
Lianhua Studio, 41, 230n.31
Life Show (Shenghuo xiu), 74, 96, 98–99
lifestyles, 18, 97–98, 138–39
Lin Yutang, 64–65
Ling Zi, 145
Link, Perry, 224n.12
Liu Bingjian, 178–82
Liu Guangyu, 178
Liu, Rene, 33
Liu Xiaoqing, 145
Liu Xin, 134
liumang, 108–9, 110, 179
Loehr, Peter, 240n.13
Lou Ye, 150–56, 170–71, 177, 184–86
Love at First Sight (Yijian zhongqing), 17, 78, 80, 83–86
Lower Depths, The, 229n.19
Lu Chuan, 188–92
Lü Liping, 67
Lu, Sheldon, 17, 72
Lu, Tonglin, 12, 90
Lu Xuechang, 67, 166, 170, 218, 236n.18, 240n.25
Lu Xun, 52, 89
Lunar Eclipse (Yueshi), 182–87, 242n.46
Luo Mingyou, 230n.31

Ma Xiaoqing, 34
magical realism, 94
Maiden Work (Chunü zuo), 176
Making of Steel, The (Zhangda chengren), 67
Márquez, Gabriel Garcia, 89, 94
Marriage Certificate (Shei shuo wo bu zaihu), 47, 67–68
Masks (Jialian), 48
Masquerade in the City (Chengshi jiamian wuhui), 48
Masters of Mischief (Wanzhu), 109, 113
May Fourth (New Cultural Movement), 2, 6, 31, 72, 138, 86n.12,
McWorld, 132, 138–39, 165

Men, Men, Women, Women (Nan nan nü nü), 178–82
Meng Jinghui, 14
Mi Jiashan, 20, 109, 113
Mian Mian, 17, 227n.47
Minford, John, 108–9
Missing Gun, The (Xun qiang), 189–92
Mother (Mama), 171, 172–73
Mr. Wu: A Police Story (Shui bu zhao), 47, 62–64
Murakami, Haruki, 226n.40
My Father and I (Wo he baba), 17, 124–28
Myriads of Lights (Wan jia denghuo), 27

new documentary movement (xin jilu yundong), 175, 177
new-image movement, 5, 72
New Year's Gift (Ya sui qian), 26
Ni Zhen, 74, 199
Nietzsche, Friedrich, 136
Night Lodge (Yedian), 229n.19
Ning Dai, 230n.34
Ning Ying, 63, 76, 99–104, 166, 177, *211*, 218, 234n.46, 234n.49, 241n.29
Niu Zhenhua, 59, 62, 67
No One Cheers (Wuren hecai), 70, 70–71
Norwegian Wood, 226–27n.40
Not One Less (Yige dou buneng shao), 168

Old Well (Lao jing), 90
On the Beach (Haitan), 38–39
On the Beat (Minjing gushi), 63–64, 99–101
On the Hunting Grounds (Liechang zhasa), 42, 177, 234n.41
One Flew over the Cuckoo's Nest, 169
O'Neal, Eugene, 145
Orphan of Anyang, The (Anyang ying'er), 158–63, 165, 239n.7
Overload (chao zai) band, 118, 236n.20

Parish, William L., 7, 8
Parking Attendant in July, The (Kancheren de qiyue), 166
Pau, Peter, 123
Peng Xiaolian, 74, 76, 86–88, 89, 166, 218, 233n.26
Personals, The (Zhenghun qishi), 131

Pickowicz, Paul, 52
Pirated Copy (Manyan), 139–42, 157, 238n.12
pizi (hooligans and hooliganism), 17, 58, 107, 108–9, 110, 112–13, 126, 128, 132
Platform (Zhantai), 205–6
Postman (Youchai), 111, 140, 142–43, 167
Postmen in the Mountains (Na shan, na ren, na gou), 95–96, 97
Pulp Fiction, 141, 207, 208
Purple Butterfly (Zi hudie), 170

Q-version culture, 133
Questions for the Living (Yige sizhe dui shengzhe de fangwen), 185
Quitting (Zuotian), 11, 168–71

Raise the Red Lantern (Da hong denglong gaogao gua), 47–48
Red Beans (Xuanlian), 111, 140
Red Sorghum (Hong gaoliang), 90
Renoir, Jean, 229n.19
Rickshaw, 196–97
roots searching, 1, 6, 12, 18, 19, 21, 45, 47–48, 119, 121, 216, 217
Run, Lola, Run, 147–48, 149–50, 238n.19
rural migrants, 5, 8, 21, 192, 194, 195, 209

Samsara (Lunhui), 20, 46, 53–55, 57, 58, 66, 109, 113
Scenery (Fengjing), 140, 167, 238n.13
Sennett, Richard, 14–15
Shanghai Baby (Shanghai baobei), 16, 139
Shanghai Chronicle (Shanghai jishi), 87
Shanghai Panic (Women haipa), 17
Shanghai 24 Hours (Shanghai ershisi xiaoshi), 26
Shanghai Women (Jiazhuang mei ganjue), 74, 86, 88, 166
Shen Fu, 27
Shen Xiling, 24
Sheng Zhimin, 20, 198–99, 243n.15
Shi Runjiu, 166, 199–200, 243n.16
Shields, Stephanie, 80
Shower (Xizao), 168, 240n.13, 240n.25, 243n.16
Signal Left, Turn Right (Da zuodeng, xiang you zhuan), 47, 61–62

Silbergeld, Jerome, 180
Silver Snake Murder, The (Yinshe mousha an), 89
Simmel, Georg, 2
situation movie (zhuangtai dianying), 5, 72, 73, 74, 75, 76, 78, 104
Sliding Doors, 150
So Close to Paradise (Biandan, guniang), 198, 209, 243n.14
Something about Secret (Shuochu nide mimi), 47, 66–67
Song of China (Tian lun), 41
Sons (Erzi), 17, 171, 173–74
specific intellectuals, 6
Spengler, Oswald, 2–3, 8, 223n.6
Spicy Love Soup (Aiqing ma la tang), 168, 240n.13
Springtime in a Small Town (Xiaocheng zhi chun): by Tian Zhuangzhuang, 24, 39, 41–44; by Fei Mu, 24, 39–42, 70
Stay-Behind Wife, The (Liushou nüshi), 82–83
Stand Up, Don't Grovel (Zhan zhi le, bie pa xia), 47, 57–59, 65, 67
Stories from an Editorial Office (Bianjibu de gushi) 73
Street Angel (Malu tianshi), 24, 25, 34–36, 39, 228n.13
Suzhou River (Suzhou he), 150–56, 170, 184, 186, 217, 238n.26, 240n.16, 241n.31,
Sun Zhou, 11, 76, 168
Surveillance (Maifu), 47, 65–66

Tang Danian, 166, 195–96, 243n.13
Tang, Xiaobing, 10
Tangney, June Price, 136
Tao, 12–13, 75, 212
Tao Hong, 199–200
Teng Ruijun, 96, 97, 234n.44
Teng Wenji, 38–39
Thicke, Alan, 33
Three Women (Nüren de gushi), 86, 87–88, 233n.26
Tian Zhuangzhuang, 24, 39, 42–44, 94, 95, 177, 185, 230n.34
Tian'anmen Square, *1*, 5, 19–21, 54, 106, 117, 117, 119, 175

To the Northwest (Dao xibei qu), 27
Together (He ni zai yiqi), 42, 74
Tree in the House, A (Meishi tou zhe le), 65
Trouble Shooters (Wan zhu), 20
Two Hearts (Xin xin). 20, 198–99
Tykwer, Tom, 147, 238n.19

universal intellectuals, 6
Unknown Pleasures (Ren xiaoyao), 206–8
urbanism, 1–2, 7, 8, 9, 13, 17, 21–22, 30, 34, 35, 37, 213; in Fourth Generation filmmaking, 3, 37–39, 90, 192, 216–17; of German School, 2–3, 8, 16; in Huang Jianxin's films, 46, 47, 56, 62, 68; in the Later Fifth Generation films, 77, 85, 104, 217; of leftist filmmaking, 8, 26–27, 44
urbanization, 2–4, 12, 14–15, 21, 22, 90, 91–93, 101, 118, 121, 125, 189, 192, 196, 200, 209, 212, 216; anti-urban development, 7, 8, 25, 224n.20; developmental, 6, 7, 9, 21, 23, 39; utopian, 7, 11, 23, 26, 39

Vertigo, 152
videology, 132
Visit of the Dead to the Living, The (Yige sizhe dui shengzhe de fangwen), 48

Waiting for Godot, 189
Wallace, Clair, 107
Wang Anyi, 200
Wang Chao, 158–63
Wang, Eugene Yuejin, 55
Wang Guangli, 11, 166, 167, 174–78
Wang Hongwei, 205, 244n.26
Wang, Jing, 58, 126
Wang Quan'an, 34, 182–87, 229n.18, 242n.45
Wang Shuo, 57–58, 70, 73, 75–76, 78–79, 81, 108–9, 112–13, 115–16, 124–33, 235n.16, 236n.31
Wang Shuo fever (craze), 57–58, 78–79, 109, 128
Wang Xiaobo, 179, 180
Wang Xiaoshuai, 111, 165, 166–68, 196–98, 209, 213, 230n.34, 234n.46, 243n.13

Wang Yichuan, 112, 189–90
Wang Yu, 154
ways of life, 18, 97, 137–38
Weber, Max, 2
Wedding Banquet, 180
Weekend Lovers (Zhoumo qingren), 111, 114–15, 149, 152–56, 170, 186, 239n.31,
Weekend Plot (Miyu shiqi xiaoshi), 203
Wei Hui, 16, 139, 227n.41, 227n.47
We're Still Young (Women hai nianqing), 78
When Harry Met Sally, 80
Whyte, Martin King, 7, 8
Wildness, The (Yuanye), 1982 film, 145; Cao Yu's play, 144–46
Williams, Raymond, 10–11, 13, 38, 42, 215
Willis, Paul, 13
Wong Kar-wai, 43, 131, 150, 152, 154–56, 184
Wooden Man's Bride, The (Wu Kui), 48, 231n.4
World, The (Shijie), 20, 208–10
Wu Di, 111
Wu Tianming, 46, 90
Wu Wenguan, 175, 230n.34, 241n.30

X-Roads (Xin shizi jietou), 23–25, 27–34, 229n.15
Xia Gang, *1*, 17, 70, 70–71, 76–78, 78–86, 109, 166, *188*, 191, 192–94, 218, 232n.6
Xia Yan, 26
Xiao Wu, 204–5, 244n.25
xiaozi (petty-bourgeois), 15–18, 85–86, 130, 212, 214, 226–27n.40
Xie Fei, 39, 215
Xin Qiji, 103
Xu Fan, 127
Xu Jinglei, 17, 125–28, 136, 149

Yang, Edward, 189
Yang, Mayfair, 60
Yang Zaibao, 145
Ye Daying, 109, 113, 125, 128
Ye Weixin, 18
Yellow Earth (Huang tudi), 45, 213, 215
Yellow Goldfish (Huang jinyu), 111, 113
Yesterday's Wine (Yu wangshi ganbei), 78, 79
Yu Jin, 190
Yuan Muzhi, 24, 26–27

Zeng Nianping, 89, 233n.28
Zha, Jianying, 239n.31
Zhang Chu, 170
Zhang Jianya, 72
Zhang Kangkang, 130
Zhang Manyu (Maggie Cheung), 33
Zhang Ming, 111, 167, 200–203
Zhang Nuanxin, 11, 23, 34, 37, 39, 169, 183
Zhang Wei, 35
Zhang Xinxin, 158–63, 239n.1
Zhang Yang, 11, 135, 167–68, 168–71, 240n.13, 240n.15, 243n.16
Zhang Yimou, 42, 72, 74, 90, 110, *158*, 163–66, 168, 218
Zhang Yiwu, 71–73, 78, 112, 126, 185
Zhang Yuan, 11, 17, 107–9, 125, 128–33, 171–74, 177, 178–82, 185, 186, 196, 213, 230n.34, 241n.30, 243n.13
Zhang, Zhen, 5, 192, 242n.44
Zhang Ziyi, 135–36
Zhao Benshan, 164
Zhao Dan, 23–24, 227n.1
Zhao Tao, 209
Zhao, Vicky Wei, 130, 131, 135
Zheng Dongtian, 11, 215
Zhou Xiaowen, 76
Zhou Xun, 135–36
Zhu Lingyong, 95
Zhu Xi, 137
Zuo Ling, 229n.19
Zuo Shula, 111

Harry H. Kuoshu, also known as Haixin Xu, is an associate professor of Chinese and Asian studies at Furman University, where he teaches Chinese film, literature, culture, and language. His previous publications include *Lightness of Being in China: Adaptation and Discursive Figuration in Cinema and Theater* and *Celluloid China: Cinematic Encounters with Culture and Society*.